BRISTOL RECORD SOCIETY'S
PUBLICATIONS

General Editors: MADGE DRESSER
PETER FLEMING
ROGER LEECH

VOL. 53

THE PRE-REFORMATION RECORDS OF ALL SAINTS' CHURCH, BRISTOL

PART 2 : THE CHURCHWARDENS' ACCOUNTS

THE PRE-REFORMATION RECORDS OF ALL SAINTS' CHURCH, BRISTOL

THE CHURCHWARDENS' ACCOUNTS

EDITED

BY

CLIVE BURGESS

Published by
BRISTOL RECORD SOCIETY
2000

ISBN 0 901538 23 x

The Bristol Record Society acknowledges with thanks the continued support of Bristol City Council, the University of Bristol, the Bristol and West Building Society and the Society of Merchant Venturers. It is also pleased to welcome the support of the University of the West of England. It is grateful to the late Isobel Thornley's Bequest to the University of London for a grant towards the cost of this publication.

CONTENTS

PREFACE

This is the second volume of material culled from the archives of All Saints', Bristol; like the first, it has had a lengthy gestation and created its own history. It is chastening to recall how many people have played an essential part helping me to overcome awkward conditions and bring the work to completion; it is humbling, too, to admit my debt to the All Saints' archive itself, which, in my own often uncertain circumstances, has proved so constantly rewarding and so sustaining a pleasure on which to work. There are some debts, however, which must be specifically acknowledged. I am grateful to Dr Joseph Bettey for prompting this work with his initial enquiry whether I had materials that the Bristol Record Society might publish and for being prepared to countenance a more immoderate response than he probably anticipated. I am grateful, too, to Dr Peter Fleming for his enthusiasm and assistance in seeing the volume through the press. I offer heartfelt thanks to John Williams and all the staff in the Bristol Record Office for their unfailing efficiency, courtesy and affability; it has been my pleasure to work with them. Having never lived in Bristol, I have been obliged to rely on many friends for hospitality to enable me to undertake the extended stints of research on which this edition rests. Tony and Cathy Benjamin, Leonard Marsh, and Frances and Tony Bradshaw have borne the brunt at different times but, more recently, two friends in Cardiff, Mark Owen and Tony Carr, have been generous above and beyond the call of duty and I am deeply grateful to each of them, and also to other friends in Cardiff who have conspired to make trips away consistently enjoyable. It is a pleasure to thank the Leverhulme Trust for its generous support of the earlier stages of the research which went to produce this volume, and I must also mention the Research Fund of University College London for more recent help with travel expenses. Professor Caroline Barron and Miss Barbara Harvey have each made essential contributions to the lasting benefit of this editor and his work at different times and, once again, I acknowledge this with deep gratitude. Last, but by no means least, I thank my long-suffering parents, Kathleen and Frank Burgess, for their steadfast support and generosity, enabling me to keep both myself and a car on the road. Without them this work would not have been started, nor could it ever have been completed; I dedicate it to them.

INTRODUCTION

The parish of All Saints', Bristol, possesses a late medieval archive of remarkable range and depth which yields abundant information illustrative both of corporate practice and individual belief. Few English parishes can match it. This is the second volume in a series publishing the fifteenth- and early sixteenth-century materials which survive for All Saints'.[1] It prints the churchwardens' accounts (or proctors' accounts, to employ the term which contemporaries themselves used), presently kept in the Bristol Record Office [P/AS/ChW3]. These survive in a reasonably complete series from 1463–64, although two earlier survivals inaugurate the collection.[2] A terminal date of 1530 has been imposed to save this volume from becoming unwieldy, even though the series continues long after this. Fifty-two pre-1530 accounts are reproduced here in full; also included is one intriguing cognate document lodged with the collection,[3] and an appendix which lists the known pairs of All Saints' churchwardens in chronological order until 1530.[4] There is, therefore, a mass of raw data in this book. The reader can and will make of the material what he or she wishes: there are doubtless as many different 'agendas' as readers, as each seeks either to pursue research interests or to satisfy a passing curiosity. In this introduction I aim neither to give a conventional history of the parish (which would, ironically, be thin were I to rely on the accounts alone), nor

---

[1] The first was *The Pre-Reformation Records of All Saints', Bristol. Part I: The All Saints' Church Book*, ed. C. Burgess (Bristol Record Society, xlvi, 1995) [hereafter *A.S.C.B.*].

[2] From the 1440s, P/AS/ChW3 preserves a double sided sheet, which appears to be a substantial fragment of the 1446 account; it also preserves the account for 1449. Nothing survives for the 1450s, but thereafter we have accounts for 1463–69, 1472–76, 1477–82, 1485–86, 1487–90, 1491–92, 1494–95, 1496–1502, 1503–06, 1507–08, 1509–1516, 1517–1530. There are obviously gaps but, once the sustained series starts, none is particularly long. It should also be noted that one earlier account survives for the parish, for 1427–28, kept now in the Fox Mss. in the Bristol Record Office; this has already been transcribed and printed in *A.S.C.B.*, pp.139–41.

[3] An additional account was made for 1524–25; it was not compiled by the current churchwardens and, as will become clear, sheds invaluable light on parish procedures.

[4] Appended between the text and the index.

to discuss every detail of the entries (which, were it possible, would result in an introduction far longer than the text). Rather, my brief is to set the accounts in context: to discuss their appearance and consider their provenance, to assess their coverage of parish affairs, and to glean as much as possible about parish government, in this one location at least, before the Reformation.

Late medieval Bristol and the parish of All Saints'

Much smaller than London, Bristol, with some 10,000 inhabitants, trailed Norwich as the third largest town in late medieval England.[5] The period which generated the material contained in the present volume, *circa* 1450–1530, was not among the most successful in Bristol's commercial history: the loss of Bordeaux in the mid-fifteenth century had serious implications for trade in wine, and London's ever-tightening control of woollen cloth manufacture and export increasingly diverted economic activity and traffic to and through the metropolis. Bristol, nonetheless, had an economy of sufficient breadth and resilience to safeguard its commerce from too disastrous a contraction.[6] It sustained its pivotal importance in the economy of the south and west of England, remaining much the largest and most influential town on the Atlantic seaboard.

Possessed of proportionately fewer parishes than towns of more ancient provenance, Bristol numbered just over fifteen within or near its walls.[7] These differed substantially as to area and houselling population (ie, communicant numbers).[8] As a rule of thumb, parishes on the periphery of the town tended to be both bigger and more populous: to the north, St James's had, for instance, a houselling population of some 520; to the

---

[5]   London had a population of well over 50,000 in the later Middle Ages; the population of Norwich may have approached 15,000. Urban population estimates are always controversial, but this ranking has become established orthodoxy, see W.G. Hoskins, 'English Provincial Towns in the Early Sixteenth Century', *Transactions of the Royal Historical Society*, 5th series, x (1956), and D.M. Palliser, 'Urban Decay Revisited', *Towns and Townspeople in the Fifteenth Century*, ed. J.A.F. Thomson (Gloucester, 1988), pp.1–21.

[6]   E.M. Carus-Wilson, *Medieval Merchant Venturers* (London, 1954) is essential for the essay 'The Overseas Trade of Bristol in the Fifteenth Century'; a newer addition to the literature on Bristol's commerce is D.H. Sacks, *The Widening Gate: Bristol and the Atlantic Economy, 1450–1750* (California, 1991), cap 1.

[7]   London had slightly over 100 parishes within 'the square mile'; Norwich had in excess of 50. The total for Bristol depends on how many extra mural parishes are included; thus, J. Bettey, *Bristol Parish Churches during the Reformation*, Bristol Historical Association Pamphlet, xlv (1979), p.1, puts the total at 18.

[8]   The houselling population estimates are derived from the mid sixteenth-century Chantry Certificates, see 'Chantry Certificates, Gloucestershire', ed. J. Maclean, *Trans. Bristol and Gloucestershire Archaeological Society* [hereafter *T.B.G.A.S.*], viii (1883–84), 229–308; for excellent maps of Bristol, including a map of the parish boundaries, and a very useful general history of the town, see M.D. Lobel and E.M. Carus-Wilson, 'Bristol', *The Atlas of Historic Towns*, ii, ed. M.D. Lobel and W.H. Johns (London, 1975).

south, St Mary Redcliff and St Thomas Martyr each had a population said to number 600; extending along the quays of the Avon and the Frome, St Nicholas and St Stephen had 800 and 460 respectively. Parishes in the centre of the town were more constricted and each mustered many fewer parishioners: St Ewen's and St Werburgh's had respectively 56 and 160; St John the Baptist some 230 and Christ Church 330. With 180 houselling souls, All Saints' fits into the middle rank of the smaller, central parishes. At the heart of Bristol, with its church sited immediately to the south-west of the carfax where High Street, Wine Street, Broad Street and Corn Street meet, the parish of All Saints' extended south of Corn Street and to the west of High Street, including also a line of tenements to the east of the latter thoroughfare.[9] While it proves impossible to establish anything like a foundation date for the parish, the patronage of All Saints' had been acquired by the Augustinian Abbey of St Augustine's, Bristol, in the mid-twelfth century,[10] and successive abbots maintained their right of appointment to the living and acted as final arbiter in parish affairs. Neither abbot nor community played any very intrusive role in the life of the parish in the later Middle Ages.[11]

Compact, central and with relatively few communicant members, there is little in the history of All Saints', or, if one compares it with the likes of St Mary Redcliffe, its building, which is of note. Only two features merit particular attention. The first, briefly, is the presence of the Kalendars' Guild, relatively well known not least because of curiosity about its name and the tales which have entered Bristol's folklore.[12] It is hard to ascertain quite what the contribution of the group of secular clergy who comprised the fraternity's priests was to the life of All Saints', although it is to be noted that they lived in a house which physically jutted into the church at first-floor level in the north aisle.[13] At the very least, their existence ensured

---

[9] Much more detailed tenement maps of the relevant area, and a meticulous tenement history, are now available in R.H. Leech, *The Topography of Medieval and Early Modern Bristol, Part 1* (Bristol Record Society, xlviii, 1997) [hereafter *Topography*].

[10] *The Cartulary of St Augustine's Abbey, Bristol*, ed. D. Walker (Bristol and Gloucestershire Archaeological Society, x, 1998), 33; the charter of William Earl of Gloucester granting the advowson of All Saints', Bristol, to St Augustine's in free alms would seem to have been given in *c*.1150.

[11] *A.S.C.B.*, pp. 30–31, reveals how parishioners had established that the Abbot of St Augustine's, 'in return for tithes and various payments, has the responsibility for maintaining the chancel of All Saints' church'; one wonders whether parishioners would, in every circumstance, have welcomed overt intrusion by the Abbot. It should nevertheless be noted that the Abbot was a powerful advocate to whom they turned in emergencies – for instance, when they sought to prevent John Hawkes from acquiring Haddon's chantry endowment, *A.S.C.B.*, p. xvii.

[12] N. Orme, 'The Guild of Kalendars, Bristol', *T.B.G.A.S.*, xcvi (1978), 32–52 is essential corrective reading on the Kalendars.

[13] It should in addition be noted that the parish priest lived in a house similarly abutting the south aisle and that the Halleway's chantry priest was housed in a chamber in the churchyard.

a heavy clerical presence within the parish. As to the more personal relationships and influences fostered by numerous clergy in close proximity with parishioners, we can do little more than speculate; clearly, they sometimes were significant.[14] The second and, as far as this volume is concerned, much the most noteworthy aspect about All Saints', Bristol, is the survival of an exceptional quantity of pre-Reformation archival material. The Church Book and the churchwardens' accounts are now published,[15] but it should be noted that there are, in addition, chantry accounts and property deeds, as well as other miscellanea including parishioners' wills.[16] When most parishes, either urban or rural, have no surviving pre-Reformation records, quite why All Saints' has such a rare variety of materials defies convincing explanation. It seems simply to be a matter of good fortune. The churchwardens' accounts contain a wealth of lay-generated information reflective of parishioners' involvement in parish management. What emerges is an impression of competence: the pre-Reformation urban parish at 'high tide', as it were, with the laity making a well honed and essential contribution to the life of the parish. Given that, until recently, and despite its many achievements, the late medieval church at the local level was either ignored or habitually denigrated, the publication of rich material shedding light on this milieu and emphasising the significance of lay participation needs no special justification.[17]

There are, nevertheless, some points to be made to flag the broader significance of these accounts. First, when compared with the great majority of parishes in England, All Saints' (in common with other parishes in Bristol) was home to a disproportionate number of wealthy parishioners. There were men and women in the parish who had the means at their disposal to respond in generous measure to the teachings of late medieval Catholicism, their worldly success prompting, if anything, a particularly effusive provision.[18] Such parishioners furnish the historian with a valuable paradigm, highlighting the demands of late medieval religion and preserving (if now only in the documentation generated) the responses to it. Second, although parish life in Bristol was hardly 'typical', many who

---

[14] Prior Gyllard of the Kalendars worked closely with Richard Haddon in the mid fifteenth century, quite plausibly egging on the latter to striking generosity, see *A.S.C.B.*, p. xxx.

[15] See above, n.1.

[16] It is planned to publish the remaining pre-Reformation archive in a future Bristol Record Society volume.

[17] P. Heath, *The English Parish Clergy on the Eve of the Reformation* (London, 1969) predating the recent flurry of publications on local religion, is one study which should be mentioned as an exception to the general rule even though it concerns itself, of course, with the clergy rather than the laity.

[18] The investment in charity preceding the Reformation is eloquent testimony to the efficacy with which the Church instructed the wealthy as to their responsibilities; see also B.L. Manning, *The People's Faith in the Time of Wyclif* (2nd edn., Hassocks, 1975), cap 6 and M. Rubin, 'The Poor', *Fifteenth-Century Attitudes: Perceptions of Society in Late Medieval England*, ed. R. Horrox (Cambridge, 1994).

lived in the West of England – and beyond – would inevitably have travelled to and from the town and spent time in it. They may very well have sought to emulate what they saw or experienced there.[19] So, as a result of flamboyance, the endeavours of All Saints' and its ilk would have been influential, providing inspiration and pointing the way for many another parish, either in the countryside or in market towns. Third, a series of detailed churchwardens' accounts naturally reveals much about life within a parish, encompassing matters like building maintenance, liturgical elaboration and managing the endowment, disclosing whether and how these initiatives adapted over time. Equally the material paves the way to a better understanding of the more complex operations of faith on individuals and groups in a locality, shedding light on the corporate responses and procedures that had evolved at parish level, and on the interplay of individual and group, with each dependent on the other for mutual benefit. Parishes were prominent, not just in local communities, but in individuals' lives and priorities: in a period when a dearth of evidence forestalls close understanding of the great majority, churchwardens' accounts permit at least some appreciation of how men and women might cohere within a small community, and of how such a group managed itself to further its worldly and spiritual interests. The sum of these points is rendered the more significant, fourth, by dint of the quality and variety of the All Saints' archive. While any evidence affords insights, being able to set different strands one against the other significantly deepens understanding. The lessons derived from All Saints' may be measured against impressions from other parishes possessed of at least some comparable evidence and applied, albeit tentatively, more generally. Its relative modesty, in Bristol at least, may thus work to our advantage as it plausibly had more in common with a greater number of parishes overall than had, shall we say, St Mary Redcliffe. As the most voluminous of the materials surviving for All Saints' before the Reformation, the churchwardens' accounts are of prime importance in furthering an understanding of this parish and, by extension, others.

The documents

Where the great majority of England's parishes have no surviving pre-Reformation churchwardens' accounts, it is a measure of its archive that All Saints' has two sets, one copied in the Church Book (and already printed), and the other, printed in this volume, made up of a lengthy series of unbound booklets. The latter appear to be audited documents: some

---

[19] It is also true that parishioners would inevitably have travelled from Bristol to other towns and talked of what their own parish observed or had achieved; in so doing, they too may have sown seeds.

retain the traces of reckoning in their margins;[20] in many others the submitted arithmetic is corrected;[21] and, in more cases than not, the final sums are in a different hand,[22] as are memoranda (decided upon at the audit, presumably) appended to guide the future conduct of wardens and parishioners. In the following discussion I will, in the main, be concerned with the unbound accounts, but those surviving in the Church Book offer a number of useful comparisons. A brief summary of them proves a worthwhile preliminary.

The Church Book was for the most part compiled in the 1480s. It is a tome containing upward of 1100 pages, the majority of which are blank; the accounts are found towards its middle, between pages 437 and 596. Coverage starts in the first decade of the fifteenth century and extends, with some gaps, to 1481–82.[23] The accounts in the Church Book have been both tidied and abbreviated, offering a version of past affairs preserved in a formal archive itself compiled to commemorate the 'good works' of different benefactors – in this case, of the churchwardens whose labour, effectively summarised by the accounts, was essential for the well being of the parish.[24] The great majority of the accounts, down to the 1460s, are copied in the hand responsible for much of the material earlier in the Book. Those for the 1470s are written in a smaller, less attractive hand, and the last few, presented in a rushed and careless manner, may be in a different hand again. The earlier accounts are brief; those for the 1470s and 1480s fuller. If 'tidied', the accounts in the Church Book have their shortcomings, most obviously with dates: a number of them are adrift by a year or two simply because the scribe, converting from *Anno Domini* to regnal years, made errors.[25]

While it is possible that the scribes responsible for the version copied in

---

[20] Marginal dots, the product clearly of reckonings to check addition, are to be found in a number of the accounts, for instance for 1510–11, 1511–12 and 1518; but it should in fairness be pointed out that in some accounts totals have been left blank, for instance in that for 1504–5, which seems odd in an audited document. Sweeping generalisations are, as ever, hazardous.

[21] Emendations and additions to the accounts, presumably made as part of the audit process, are very common and may, for instance, easily be found in the sets of accounts surviving from 1505–06 to 1512–13.

[22] Whether these additions were written by the senior warden (the accounts having been written by a scribe) or by one of the auditors, is a question which at the present eludes an easy answer.

[23] Accounts are preserved in the All Saints' Church Book for the following years: ?1407–13, 1414– 15, 1421–23, 1427–31, 1434–35, ?1436–40, 1443–50, ?1452, ?1453–55, 1456–58, 1460–68 and 1472–82.

[24] The commemoration of benefactors, an imperative arising from the doctrine of Purgatory, was of prime importance in shaping the priorities and aspirations of contemporaries; for further discussion, see for instance my essay "A Fond Thing Vainly Invented': An Essay on Purgatory and Pious Motive in Later Medieval England', *Parish, Church and People. Local Studies in Lay Religion 1350–1750*, ed. S. Wright (London, 1988), pp.56–84.

[25] *A.S.C.B.*, pp.xxxiv–xxxv.

the Church Book could also have written some of the unbound accounts, to which we now turn, no certain matches can be made. A number of the earlier surviving unbound accounts, for the 1460s and 1470s, appear to be in the hand of one scribe, although interspersed by different hands. From the later 1470s, while one or two consecutive accounts may be in a uniform hand (eg those surviving for 1487–88 and 1488–89), the handwriting generally changes from one year to the next. The variety of watermarks would also confirm that the accounts were made year by year.[26] Diversity must, nevertheless, be set against broader uniformity. Unlike the survivals for some other parishes (where one encounters decidedly varied durations), each of the All Saints' accounts is for one year only, customarily starting and finishing at the feast of the Annunciation of Our Lady.[27] Each is contained in a booklet, the great majority of which are in sound condition, with ink still dark and writing easily legible.[28] All are of paper and have been formed by folding large sheets (typically 42cm by 30cm) in half (forming a booklet of four pages, 21cm broad and 30cm high) and sewing a number of these together to give a gathering of eight, twelve or sixteen pages. Some are still sewn together; others bear the traces.[29] A number preserve outer, or cover, pages bearing inscriptions such as 'The Church Book' and mentioning the name of the senior warden for that year;[30] but none has the coarse brown paper covers which still protect some of the earlier Halleway chantry accounts. Comparing chantry and parish accounts proves revealing: where the booklets comprising the former often contain a good number of blank pages, the latter have frequently had blank pages removed, and even unused half-pages cut away, although the accounts

---

[26] The variety of watermarks, when allied with the variety of handwriting, infallibly suggests that the unbound accounts were written at the date given rather than being copied up *en bloc*. The paper used in 1463–64 has a fine watermark of an ox; in the paper used between 1465 and 1478 the mark is of an ox head with a wand between the horns; in that for 1479–80, of a unicorn, but returning to an ox head with wand for the 1481–82 account; for 1485–86, the watermark is of a larger ox head, but in 1488–89 paper with a unicorn watermark is again used, although the next year's has a segmented circle. For much of the early sixteenth century the watermark is of a hand with outstretched fingers and a flower from the middle finger, although paper with the unicorn mark is used in 1504–05, and a segmented circle or catherine wheel mark appears in the early 1520s.

[27] March 25th, which date, it should be remembered, marked the start and finish of the calendar year for contemporaries.

[28] Ironically, the early accounts are generally in markedly better condition than those surviving for the 1530s and later. Some are flimsy or faded, but others are on stout paper and some have sooty outer pages which cast doubt on whether or not the accounts were always kept together in one pile.

[29] It is clear, either from needle holes at the fold of the document or, still more obviously, from surviving threads, that the booklets were once sewn; some, for example those for 1501–02, 1507–08, 1528–29 and 1529–30, still are.

[30] The accounts for 1494–95 and 1497–98, 1498–99, 1499–1500 have cover pages; that for 1502–03 has a cover page with signature (Thomas Davy's) and those for the years immediately following 1510–11 all have cover pages and senior wardens' signatures.

themselves appear complete.[31] Presumably sustained after the accounts were submitted, these excisions suggest that the churchwardens' parish accounts were accessible, ultimately becoming a source of spare paper; the chantry accounts were put away and forgotten. While the booklets comprising the churchwardens' accounts are of roughly uniform size, some are slightly taller or broader and some slightly shorter or narrower. Such variation, the survival of cover pages and that many booklets are still sewn, are factors which suggest that if the intention, ultimately, was to bind them together in a single volume (hence the title 'The Church Book' written on cover pages), this never occurred.[32]

Variations catch the eye, but, while some sets of the All Saints' accounts are neater than others, with attractive hand-writing or employing a ruled grid to ensure accurate tabulation,[33] the order of presentation is, on the whole, predictable.[34] There are, however, some developments which should be noted. The most obvious is that the accounts expanded steadily, those for the 1520s proving much longer than those for the 1470s.[35] The later accounts dealt with a substantially larger budget derived from a much increased endowment: this had to be maintained year by year, and extra property meant more anniversaries, all of which are itemised. It may also be noted that in the early accounts no distinction is made between property rents and rents of assize, all are lumped together.[36] In these accounts, moreover, 'void' is simply entered against an unoccupied property, or 'allowances' are listed for rents not paid.[37] Accounting techniques changed after 1485–86: rents and rents of assize are listed separately; at the same time, 'vacations, voids and abatements' are either entered at the foot of the 'income' section or, in the sixteenth century, directly after the rents and before customable revenues, and subtracted to disclose real income.[38] From

---

[31]   One or two of the accounts end abruptly (eg 1485–86) and one or two have pages which have at some stage or other been trimmed (eg 1494–95) meaning that the bottom half of some figures are lost; but, by comparison with some other series, their survival rate as complete documents is good.

[32]   The parish of St Andrew Hubbard in London, which also produced a series of separate booklets containing accounts, contrived to bind these together; from 1808 they have been in two volumes (which, of course, may have been a re-binding).

[33]   For example, accounts for 1492 and 1497–98.

[34]   Very broadly, rents come first, modified by 'vacations', but augmented by 'customable' revenues to yield total income. Expenditure, second, usually deals first with liturgical outlay and the costs of keeping anniversaries, then with repairs on the church building and on the properties comprising the endowment. Variation occurs, of course, with customable revenues occasionally heading the account, for instance; sometimes this was more radical, as in 1449 when expenditure precedes income.

[35]   The last one printed here, for 1530, had to have a separate folding tacked to the main booklet to contain all the material generated.

[36]   See below, note 63.

[37]   As in the case for 1468–69, reporting Jenkyn Sheparde's default on the rent assize in Marsh Street

[38]   Occasionally, as in the 1487–88 account, voids are placed in payments section.

the mid 1480s, then, and typical of many medieval accounts, income is presented in terms of potential totals, reckoned initially as if all properties were fully occupied. To compensate for the fact that this was a fiction, the 'voids and abatements' reveal which properties lay empty and itemise rents not received, if not for vacancy then because tenants either could not or would not pay.

One further development should be considered. Material in the early accounts is presented as if the accountants were in dialogue with parishioners: the wardens, as a pair, report in a reasonably informal manner to the community of which they are part. 'This, Sirs, is the money which we have allowed unto your tenants at the receiving of your rents and other casualties, the which you must abate of the receipts aforesaid', and 'Item against our Dedication day, we paid the organ maker for mending your organs from the church money besides that as was gathered' are entries that may characterise many others.[39] In the late fifteenth century the practice whereby one warden marked seniority by signing the cover of the accounts heralded a slow but significant change: John Batyn's signed his name on the cover of the 1494–95 accounts, for instance, and, subsequently, senior wardens signed both the cover and the top of the first inner page, apparently as a sign of validation. Later accounts might still refer to both wardens either owing or paying money to the parish, but senior wardens, like John Snygge in 1504–5 or John Dee in 1505–6, for instance, were singled out as the agents who, respectively, owed and delivered a particular sum of money to the church on the day of account, or personally received funds for the following year. By 1515, both churchwardens might still merit a joint reference, but it is significant that a codicil mentions that the next year's senior warden, Richard Wale, was to return the float that the parish had advanced 'at the next day of his accounts'. The next surviving account is for 1518, and by this time senior warden, Rawlyn Webbe, reported to the parish, if anything, in a more formal manner and had apparently assumed explicit responsibility for the year's finances. Similarly, in the accounts for 1519, when both John Hewes and John Mawnsell were wardens, Hewes signed his name on the outer cover, and in the accounts employed phrases such as 'Item paid to John Waxmaker for the church wax the whole year as it appears by his book and mine'. Having set out all that had been received and spent, and having computed the surplus for that year, Hewes is acquitted thus: 'The which sum the said accountant has delivered to the parishioners [on] the day of his accounts . . . so he is clearly discharged'. Rather more than half the surplus for the year was delivered 'to John Maunsell, senior proctor [for the following year . . . who was] to bring it in again at his account', which he duly did 'for his

---

[39] Respectively account for 1464–65, fo 2, and account for 1463–64, fo 2.

account'. The singular has replaced the plural; an authorial voice has replaced dialogue; the senior warden has assumed responsibility.

Comparisons

The run of unbound accounts begins in 1462–63; the All Saints' Church Book contains accounts down to 1481–82. Both series are now printed. The overlap is instructive: comparison of the two versions for the 1460s and 1470s discloses significant differences. Deliberation on these has a broad application paving the way to a more accurate appreciation of quite what we may, or may not, have at our disposal in the sets of churchwardens' accounts which survive for later medieval England generally.

The accounts included in the All Saints' Church Book are abbreviated versions of the unbound, audited accounts. Comparison of the two sets between 1464 and 1468, for instance, reveals how very much has been summarised or omitted from the Book.[40] It is, indeed, this process which often explains the volume's erroneous arithmetic: the scribe adhered to the original and full totals, but either omitted component material, leading to discrepancies, or re-ordered to such an extent that previous totals are blatantly misleading.[41] Even in the Book's version of the accounts for 1472 until 1482, written in a different hand (or hands) and providing a fuller version of affairs, detail has often been omitted, increasingly towards the end of the run when the scribe was either rushed or jaded.[42] Criticism of the scribes who compiled the Book is, of course, otiose. Were it not for their efforts, a very great deal would have been irretrievably lost. Not only would we have virtually nothing for the early and mid-fifteenth century, as we would have none of the pre-1460s material (save only the three early, unbound accounts for 1427–28, 1446 and 1449), but also gaps in the unbound series (eg 1476–77) could not be covered, the many later gaps in this series reinforcing this lesson. A more constructive course is to consider quite what the form of the accounts in the Church Book implies.

---

[40] These years see the first series of unbound accounts and the last of the main run in the Book written in the bold, rounded hand in which the volume was originally written.

[41] A good example is to be found in the Church Book's version of the accounts for the year 1466– 67: admittedly the receipts in the unbound accounts are somewhat erratic and the Book's version is much tidier, with receipts sorted first under sundries and then rents, but having reordered these items the scribe is unable to give totals for either category and both are left as blanks.

[42] While the Church Book version of the accounts for 1478–79 is reasonably full, the penultimate set (for 1480–81) summarises material concerning the liturgy and life of the parish, describing them simply as 'Payments by the said proctors on the church's behalf, of old custom and things necessary to be done, as appears for every thing in the quire of their accounts – 30s 6 ½d'; perversely, having summated these payments, the scribe then proceeds to give the costs of lights and the General Mind in more detail than usual.

Comparison of the two versions confirms, first, that the scribes who compiled the Book were fulfilling a commemorative brief. Although abbreviated, its version yields marginally more information about the churchwardens whose achievements are being celebrated. Impersonal references to wardens in the unbound accounts gain names in the Book: 'Item for a window in my pavement – 14d', in the unbound accounts for 1467 is rendered in the Book as 'Item for making 1 window in John Compton's pavement – 14d'. Wardens' trade affiliations are more frequently specified. Neither William Jenkins nor Thomas Philypps, for instance, were assigned any profession in the unbound accounts for 1466–67; the Book's version (said to be for 1465–66) reveals that the former was a painter and the latter a barber. Donors, too, are given names and due credit. So, to take one example, the vague 'Item received for a *forset* that was left in the house that was burned – 8s' in the unbound accounts for 1467–68, becomes 'Item for 1 *forset* that John Leynell gave to the church – 8s' in the Book.[43] It is also noticeable that the incumbent, very seldom mentioned in the unbound accounts, has more presence in the Book: in its account preambles, once the wardens for the year have been named, the accounts are consistently said to have been given 'before the vicar', who is himself named. This guarantees that the incumbent is named, year after year, as befits a book avowedly commemorating both parishioners and clergy – as well as reinforcing the impression that the proceedings for that year are being surveyed and summarised at a later date. It is, by contrast, only late in the run of the unbound accounts that the incumbents' presence at the audit is mentioned, and usually only in appended notes. It is, however, likely incumbents had always attended, if not presided over, the annual audit.[44]

Second, given that much of the material in the audited accounts was repetitious and that minutiae added little to the reputation of the churchwardens, it is understandable that the Church Book summarised entries concerned, for instance, with washing church cloths and clothes, or, to take another example, the small-scale recurrent expenses incurred at the General Mind.[45] Such endeavour is usually expressed in a single line, often without note of expenditure.[46] Similarly, information on candles purchased

---

43   The OED gives *forset* as an obsolete form for 'faucet', a tap or spigot; nevertheless the inventory of goods, made in 1464, for St Mary's Warwick (PRO, E/154/1/46) employs the word, as in '1 forcet of ivory harnessed with silver and with divers relics therein', to imply a small container

44   The vicar was not omitted in order to emphasise either the parishioners' independence or their achievement: it must be remembered that the unbound accounts essentially reflect procedures before the audit, whereas the Book's repeated reference to the audit emphasises the point that it was copied up later and therefore reflects the whole accounting process.

45   Discussed more fully below.

46   It is noticeable that, having summarised references to laundering items, the Book seldom enters an overall cost, presumably because scribes were not bothered to do the sums.

at different times during the year, or manufactured from recycled wax, given in detail in the unbound accounts, is frequently rendered by a single entry. Much is omitted from the Book because it is incidental detail. Information about ceremonial, and particularly functions taking place outside the church, is also discarded. So, the Book's account for 1468–69 omits the entry 'Item on St George's day paid to children for bearing up the best copes at the procession through the town', and adds the penny paid for this to the 3s spent on the dinner for the clergy on Corpus Christi day. Similarly, for 1466–67, the Book itemised the purchase of 3 pieces of freestone for 12d; the unbound accounts reveals that these were called procession stones 'set in the street for every man to know how far you ought to keep your procession way between parish and parish'. To us such material is of great significance; it was superfluous in the Book. Details, too, about the interior of the church are frequently given short shrift, even in the fuller accounts for the 1470s. The Book's version of the account for 1475–76, for instance, omits the 'coffer in the treasure house'; there is no description in 1477–7 to disclose that the seats being mended were 'next to the Kalendars' door in the nether end of the church'; also excised is the detail, given in 1478–79, concerning the battlement before the south door 'that the Dance of Pauls hangs upon'.[47] True to form, devotional details are often omitted, like the information describing Sir Thomas Furbore's Mass book in 1475–76 or, a propos of seats made in the Lady chapel in 1468–69, the fact that, strikingly, they were situated before a statue of Jesus.[48]

If regrettable, these excisions are understandable. The substance of the wardens' role could be conveyed without exhaustive detail. This leads to a third observation. While, occasionally, the reasons behind alterations are difficult to fathom – why, for instance, was it common practice to rearrange the order in which receipts were given in the Book, entering sundries first and taking rents second? – abbreviation could distort. Clergy in minor orders fared particularly badly. The following examples may stand for many. The unbound accounts for 1475–76 includes, 'Item paid to the suffragan that he was behind of his wages, paying 3s 4d', which made good the shortfall in the parish collection. The Book renders this, 'Item to the suffragan, 3s 4d', which, while strictly accurate, infallibly suggests that this is all that he received. So, too, in 1477–78, the Book omits to mention that the Corpus Christi dinner was 'for all the priests and clerks', and later gives no explanation that the payment of 3s 1d to the suffragan was simply arrears or, in the words of the unbound accounts, 'that he was behind in the payment of his year's wages'. The impression derived from the Church

---

[47] The latter would be a real loss if we only had the Book: references to the Dance of Pauls are frequent but cumulatively yield very little. The implication must be that it was a long hanging if it had to be 'looped' from a battlement.

[48] A detail which may help to explain why this chapel came to be designated not as a Lady chapel but as the chapel of Jesus by the end of the fifteenth century.

Book minimises, whether wittingly or not, the relatively enlightened treatment that the parish meted out to its lesser clergy.[49]

It is an undoubted irony, fourth, that abbreviation occasionally discloses extra information, which in turn raises questions about the precise relationship of the two texts. Fire damaged the two parish properties abutting the chancel in Corn Street at Whitsun in 1464–65. Funds to rebuild were needed and fast. The unbound accounts reveal that three pairs of parish worthies, Richard Haddon and William Rowley, William Boxe and Hugh Sadlare, and Thomas Golde and Thomas Taylore, responded with substantial contributions, amounting to £4 5s 4d. The Book tersely lays bare their donation: 'Item for ale selling – £4 5s 4d'.[50] It is salutary to note how ale selling, absent ordinarily from the All Saints' archive but a staple of parish fund-raising elsewhere, is camouflaged in the unbound accounts. If the Church Book's version of events is frequently so 'pared' as to be distorted, the unbound accounts may also obscure customs. Overall, the accounts in the Book afford just enough that is new to give rise to a suspicion that they were not simply redactions. That wardens' and donors' names might be inserted has already been indicated; others' names also emerge. The parish tenant Margery Manymoney, for instance, is named in the Book but referred to only as 'the schoolmistress' in the unbound accounts for 1467–68.[51] In the same year, the Book itemises a receipt of 6s 8d for Joan Phylypp's grave, the equivalent of an addition to that year's unbound accounts to the effect that 6s 6d [sic] had been received from Thomas Barbour for burying his wife. Given that warden Thomas Philypps was a barber it is plausible that Joan was his wife, but the change in name is intriguing. Further, the unbound accounts for 1479–80 mention that 8d had been paid 'for a hook of iron to bear up the wire at the cross altar'; in the Book this is rendered 'for a hook of iron to stay up the long iron at the cross altar that bears the cloth'. Later in this account, concluding a series of entries on aumbries in the choir and sealing and painting (referred to in the unbound accounts simply as sealing) the wall before the rood altar, the Book adds 'As necessary a thing as was this many year. Look well here to

---

[49] Charles Drew, in his introduction to the Lambeth Churchwardens' Accounts, attaches considerable weight to this point: 'A rate or collection which was entirely spent on the object for which it was provided was often omitted altogether from the general accounts. . . . Even more misleading is the practice by which, when a specific fund did not entirely cover the purpose for which it was intended, the churchwardens merely enter in their accounts the balance which they paid out of the common stock to make up the deficit. [It is very] often the case that the sum represented a balance and not the total sum expended'. He concludes, 'It is therefore unsafe to assume that churchwardens' accounts offer a complete picture of what would now be called expenses', *Lambeth Churchwardens' Accounts, 1504–1645 and Vestry Book 1610*, ed. C. Drew (Surrey Record Society, xviii and xx, 1941–50), xv- xvi. I return to consider this point in more detail below.

[50] Also discussed in more detail below.

[51] Which may imply that specification was important as there were subsequently other schoolmistresses.

those that come after'. And at the end of this account, the comment 'And so discharged every man pleased' is another interpolation.[52] Or again, comparison of the accounts for 1481–82, discloses numerous differences in the Book: it substitutes pews for seats; John Cock's house in the churchyard becomes the beerhouse; against the grain, where the unbound accounts mentioned that 2s 6d was paid 'for changing the sanctus bell and hanging it up and for a line', the Book devoted two lines to this, itemising the payment of 1d for the line separately; and where the unbound account refers to a payment of 23d 'for hanging up the cloth before the tabernacle of Our Lady which Mistress Chestre let make at the *Jhc* altar and for hoop and rings', the Book oddly omits reference to Alice Chestre and inserts 'for hanging up a painted cloth with 3 stories of Our Lady before the tabernacle at the Jesus altar and for the hoops of iron and rings'. The scribe may have relied on his own, or some one else's, memory; certainty is denied us. Exposure to the two sets of accounts poses more and more puzzles as to the precise nature of the relationship one with the other.

To have 'overlapping' sets of churchwardens' accounts is a luxury but, ironically, such abundance leads to the realisation that any given set of accounts may have had a provenance far more complex than ordinarily assumed. We are forced, in turn, to confront the question of quite what we do and, more probably, do not have in any surviving set of accounts. Given that, in the great majority of cases, only one set of accounts survives for any one parish, if we are lucky, the broader lesson of the All Saints' archive must be that surviving accounts, when tidied and bearing no obvious signs of audit, may very well fall far short of being the full record of the wardens' activities and concerns, and with abbreviation comes distortion.

The form and content of the accounts

In addition to a more ancient obligation to pay tithe, the pastoral reforms of the thirteenth century entrusted congregations with the responsibility for maintaining the material circumstances in which and with which incumbents should work for the cure of souls. Parishioners were to ensure that the church building (specifically nave and tower) was kept in good repair and that the equipment necessary for the fit administration of sacraments be both provided and maintained. Over time, the day-to-day management of these responsibilities devolved most evidently onto agents, churchwardens (usually referred to as proctors by contemporaries), who worked on behalf of the community. From the point of view of churchwardens and parishioners both, it was obviously prudent to compile accounts keeping track of what had been received from and spent in the

---

[52] An expansiveness which is at odds with the very short shrift given in the subsequent account to payments elsewhere described in full, and which surely does suggest that the Book's text was meant to be read and pondered on.

interests of the community. But they were also to be preserved as evidence of the standard of provision within a parish, so that bishop or archdeacon might inspect them on visitation.[53] Churchwardens were thus obliged to compile and keep accounts, but, in the long term, chance has proved the most potent factor determining whether or not any parish still has these records.

Churchwardens in All Saints' served in pairs. Any given pair served for a single year but, in the interests of continuity, wardens frequently served for a two-year stint, first as junior warden 'learning the ropes', and in the second year as senior warden with a new colleague his junior.[54] Over the years certain names reappear as individuals were selected, and agreed, to serve more than once.[55] At the end of each year, wardens evidently did submit a balance sheet of the income and expenditure to the parish worthies for audit. All Saints' has preserved no lists of auditors, but there are strong indications that parishioners who had previously been wardens would have officiated, assisted by the vicar, acting in the name of and for the good of the parish.[56] Once the accounts had been corrected, if necessary, and approved as accurate, the senior warden was quit; either his junior then replaced him or, sometimes, a new pair of wardens took office.

When considering the financial affairs of the All Saints' churchwardens – and I confine myself here to the unbound accounts – a budget summary proves a useful starting point. Although in any given year particular demands and developments might lead to sharp fluctuations in income or expenditure,[57] that said, the salient feature of these accounts is a steady increase in revenues. The wardens' income, as recorded at or towards the

---

[53] On the origins of the office of churchwarden, and the function both of wardens and their accounts, see C. Drew, *Early Parochial Organisation in England: The Origins of the Office of Churchwarden* (St Anthony's Hall Publications, vii, 1954); B. Kumin, *The Shaping of a Community. The Rise and Reformation of the English Parish, c 1400–1560* (Aldershot, 1996), cap. 2 and *passim*. On episcopal visitation, see for instance *Kentish Visitations of Archbishop William Wareham and his deputies, 1511– 1512*, ed. K.L. Wood-Legh (Kent Records, vol xxiv, 1984), D.M. Owen, *Church and Society in Medieval Lincolnshire* (Lincoln, 1971), pp.120–1 and R.N. Swanson, *Church and Society in Late Medieval England* (Oxford, 1989), pp.163–5, 256.

[54] No woman served as warden in All Saints'; although it was not unknown for women to serve in the office, it was rare (particularly in urban parishes).

[55] The procedure adopted at the election of wardens is unclear but information may be had in A.S.C.B., pp.2–3. A list of the wardens who served, some of them repeatedly, in All Saints' is to be found in the Appendix.

[56] This was certainly common form elsewhere, see C. Burgess, 'Shaping the Parish: St Mary at Hill, London, in the fifteenth century', *The Cloister and the World: Essays in Medieval History in Honour of Barbara Harvey*, ed. J. Blair and B. Golding (Oxford, 1996), pp.262–69 and *The Church Records of St Andrew Hubbard, Eastcheap, c1450–c1570*, ed. C. Burgess (London Record Society, xxxiv, 1999), pp.xxvii-xxx. All Saints' similarity to these regimes, and the importance also of the role played by the vicar, will become apparent in the following discussion.

[57] Comparison of the accounts for 1472–73 with those for the subsequent year, for example, reveal one year of high income and expenditure followed by another of reasonable income but markedly low expenditure.

end of each decade, rose as follows: in 1468–9, receipts were £9 18s 6d; in 1479–80, £12 13s 5½d; in 1489–90, £14 12s 4d; and at the end of the century, £15 14s 2d. Income continued to rise during the first decade of the sixteenth century, to stand at £17 6s 4d in 1509–10, but a number of parish properties were vacant during this period, significantly reducing proceeds. Investment, more successful letting and acquisitions increased revenue to £24 4s 5d in 1519 (from a notional total of £30). Property purchase in the mid 1520s and buoyant receipts from customable sources yielded a total in 1529 of £36 14s 4d (again after deductions of more than £5 for vacancies).

Income was made up of two elements, customable revenues and rents. A variety of regular sources constituted the first of these, the most reliable of which were collections, levied particularly at Easter, and charges made for pews and for burials ('pit and knell'). These were sporadically augmented, often significantly, by testamentary and other bequests, by special 'gatherings' (for instance, for new organs) and by sales and fines.[58] All told, customable revenues provided useful income which increased with time. Three points must be made, however, each of which applies only to the later accounts printed in the present collection, and which suggest that impressions of increase are to some extent inflated. Surpluses were reserved in the earlier accounts, only being made available in exceptional circumstances.[59] Form seems to have dictated that each set of wardens should be seen to manage from the year's receipts and return a profit.[60] Practice had changed by the 1520s, but even then, although senior wardens advanced sums to their successors, presumably to provide a float, instructions were issued that advances had to be repaid in full. Successive accounts reveal that they were. Whether such practice really was new, or merely specifically accounted for, is impossible to determine, but advances and repayments inflated the parish budget. Second, the Jesus Gild began to pay its host parish a healthy annual subscription which, while probably an innovation in accounting procedure rather than practice, inflated recorded income.[61] And third, late in the 1520s, it is noticeable that the accounts

---

58 A collection for the organs augmented parish income in 1472–73; likewise the bequests from Palmer and Darkyng in 1479–80 and that by Thomas Dale on behalf of his father in 1515. In 1522 and 1525–26 William Eireworth and John Whoper respectively paid £6 13s 4d and 26s 8d 'for the fine of his house'; quite what this was is not clear, but the sums involved were appreciable.

59 As in 1464–65, when the parish was obliged to repair fire damage to its Corn Street properties.

60 This was possibly actuated by the desire to show as clearly as possible quite what each set of wardens achieved to benefit the parish; it must be doubtful whether it accurately reflected practice as common sense would dictate that cash should be available to cover unexpected eventualities.

61 It is clear from *A.S.C.B.*, pp.136–7 that the Jesus Gild was extant and keeping accounts by 1480, apparently with the purpose of maintaining the 'service of Jesus'. The first receipt from the proctors of Jesus, of 10s 1d, is itemised in the accounts for 1509–10; the sums received rise rapidly thereafter, exceeding £3 in 1520, but fell away to £1 or so in the late 1520s and to 10s in 1530.

enter fuller collections and payments to the lower clergy, which while again inflating totals, certainly reflects a change in accounting as clerks and suffragans had long been in the parish but must previously have been paid from other budgets.[62]

Much the greater part of parish income (over three-quarters of the total in the earlier accounts, and over two-thirds in those later) derived from property revenues, separately categorised from 1485 as 'rent of assize' and property rents.[63] The former remained static, worth slightly over 25s during the period for which they were separately itemised. This at least was their theoretical value; in practice, the parish was able to gather in a diminishing proportion.[64] Decrease here was more than compensated by a steady accumulation of property. The parish had a reasonable portfolio to start with: the Green Lattice in High Street, devised by Alice Hailes in the late thirteenth century, remained its most lucrative asset yielding a rent of some £5 per annum;[65] two properties in Corn Street, adjacent to each other and abutting the church, yielded rents of £1 and 1 mark.[66] If all these were let, the annual rent of half a mark from the Halleways' endowment (for the chantry priest's chamber in the churchyard), brought the total neatly to £7. But the parish did well in the later fifteenth and early sixteenth century acquiring property devised by wealthy parishioners: from the Fylours in 1485, the Chestres in 1486, the Baker *alias* Spicers in 1509, and the Herveys in 1515.[67] Each ostensibly sought an anniversary in perpetuity, explaining the proliferation of these services in the accounts; but they were, in fact, a relatively superficial aspect of benefactors' arrangements, simply guaranteeing commemoration. The underlying intention of each was to

[62] Discussed more fully below.

[63] A rent of assize was a fixed rent due from a property or to secure a right of way. In All Saints', many of these resembled quit rents, small amounts paid annually by the freeholder or copyholder to the landlord, in this case the parish, in lieu of services which might otherwise be required; these were in practice often a fixed charge imposed on a property to be paid to a religious institution to benefit the soul of a previous owner. In the All Saints' rent portfolio these seem to have been some of the earliest acquisitions and usually involved sums of only a few shillings annually.

[64] Despite the apparent unwillingness of a number of 'tenants' to pay these rents, the All Saints' accounts steadfastly enter them as income only to have to abate the sums subsequently, illustrating parish tenacity (or pig-headedness) where rental income was concerned. Even though, in point of fact, rents in St Peter's parish and Marsh Street had long been lost, they are resolutely entered. The clearest example of the process occurred when, after problems a decade or more before, in 1518 the master of Tailors' suspended payments for a property in Baldwin Street of 12s annually, which meant that Newbury's obit had to be suspended; a total of years that the Tailors' had defaulted on their duties was entered in subsequent accounts.

[65] *Topography*, p.80: High Street west, property 41.

[66] *Topography*, p.67: Corn Street south, property 58.

[67] Some, at least, of these acquisitions can be precisely located: Fylour's devise, *Topography*, p., 80: High Street west, properties 39–40; the Chestres' devise, *ibid.*, pp.46–7: Broad Street east, properties 54–5; the Baker *alias* Spicers' devise, *ibid.*, pp. 153–4, Small Street, west, property 6. It is not yet clear where the Baker *alias* Spicer's devise in Wynch (Wine) Street was, nor where the Herveys' devise was.

enrich the parish, as the steady increase of income discloses.[68] The wardens' note concerning Hervey's devise in the codicil of the 1515 account leaves us in no doubt as to parish priorities: 'Also this year Master Humfrey Hervey's executors gave us the house in the High Street that John Repe grocer now holds, yearly rent 40s'; subsequent accounts disclose that the anniversary celebrated for Hervy and his wife, Anne, accounted for just 7s 11d of this income. The most important single acquisition, however, was different: in 1524–25, the parish acquired property in both the High Street and the Pithay from the estate of John Hawkes of St Leonard's parish. This bold and expensive decision (costing in excess of £60) was doubtless prompted because All Saints' saw the property as rightfully its own: the tenements had earlier formed part, at least, of the endowment devised to support John Haddon's perpetual chantry, which his son, Richard, had alienated in c.1470, much to the chagrin of the parish.[69] The process of acquisition will be described below, but it may for the present stand to demonstrate the tenacity of parish memory, a determination to right perceived wrongs, and All Saints' fiscal buoyancy.

The rise in the wardens' expenditure was marked: in 1468–9, their annual outgoings were in the region of £6; this rose to £8 in 1479–80, stood at a little over £10 in 1489–90, and exceeded £12 at the end of the century. After relatively stable levels in the first decade or two of the sixteenth century, by 1529 expenditure had risen to almost £20 per annum. Most wardens nevertheless achieved a surplus in the region of £3 or £4 on a year's dealings in the later fifteenth century and, after the difficulties experienced in c.1510, of nearer £10 per annum in the second and third decades of the sixteenth century. This was sufficient to permit ambitious endeavour and acquisition.[70] Churchwardens may have included more in their accounts in the 1520s but it is to be noted that while expenditure increased threefold, income rose fourfold.

Where expenditure was concerned, wardens were obliged to follow a number of well worn paths; three stand out. First, property meant responsibilities. Not only did churchwardens have to maintain the tenements which comprised the parish endowment, they were also obliged

---

[68] The All Saints' anniversaries each cost considerably less than the income accruing from their respective endowments: just as Newbery's endowment yielded an income of 12s, for example, so his anniversary cost 6s 1d; similarly, the Baker *alias* Spicers' endowment yielded 56s 8d, and their anniversary cost 9s. For a more detailed discussion of anniversaries in late medieval Bristol, see C. Burgess, 'A Service for the Dead: the Form and Function of the Anniversary in Late Medieval Bristol', *T.B.G.A.S.*, cv (1987), pp.183–211.

[69] *A.S.C.B.*, p.xvii.

[70] It is particularly noteworthy how, in the 1520s, the parish ploughed funds into the maintenance of the endowment which supported the Halleways' chantry, an appreciable holding of property adding to the parish's influence in the town. It is to be remembered, more generally, that parish coffers may have been swelled by profits in addition to those itemised in the wardens' accounts, as investigated below.

to maintain the fabric of the church building and its furnishings and equipment. This meant the regular refurbishment of and repair to property like the Green Lattice and all the other properties which the parish had been given or was acquiring, to make good the ravages of time and the elements, to keep present tenants satisfied and to attract new ones when necessary. Buoyant rents and a healthy resulting parish income could only be guaranteed by constant effort. Proper upkeep of the church was hardly less demanding. It, too, required constant vigilance: repairing the church roof or mending the ceiling, rebuilding, replastering or repainting walls, reglazing windows and levelling or repairing floor slabs disturbed by structural alteration or interment; wardens were, moreover, obliged to refurbish equipment at this or that altar, to mend this pax or that candlestick, to repair pews and replace locks on doors and chests, invariably buying new keys for the same – and on and on. The twin obligations to keep both the endowment and the church fabric and internal fixtures and fittings in good repair explain why the accounts teem with payments to masons, carpenters, tilers, plumbers and labourers.[71]

Second, the devise of property, both before and during the time covered by these accounts, meant that wardens had to orchestrate the reciprocal intercessory services. These were important: neglect them and the properties were confiscate. Fulfilling obligations faithfully, so far as we may judge, churchwardens observed the different specifications which each benefactor stipulated.[72] At this point it may, for the sake of convenience, be mentioned that wardens exercised additional commemorative responsibility.[73] They were obliged to organise the General Mind. This was a two-part observance: 'the names of good doers and well willers' and what they had given the parish were 'to be showed and declared unto the parishioners on the Sunday before Ash Wednesday and at high Mass and yearly'; a communal anniversary was celebrated with exequies on the following Thursday, with Requiem Mass on the Friday. Despite a parish ordinance designed to rein in spending (stipulating that if costs exceeded 13s 4d, then the senior warden was to pay the excess from his own pocket, a ruling that was intermittently reiterated in the accounts), the Mind inexorably became more elaborate and costly.[74] By the early sixteenth century, with steady expenditure on cakes and ale, to say nothing

---

[71] So much so, that they could easily furnish a data-base for local wage rates and the costs of commodities in the building trade.

[72] It emerges clearly that each perpetual anniversary differed, at least in detail, from every other.

[73] Note that this was in addition to maintaining the Halleways' chantry and anniversary, which, although demanding, was never dealt with in the parish accounts. The Halleways' chantry, and the efforts devoted to its maintenance, will be dealt with in full in a subsequent volume.

[74] *A.S.C.B.*, p.3; the ruling was reiterated in 1503–04, fo 4, and in 1519, fo 4v, when the total allowed is increased to 14s.

of considerable quantities of wine, whatever its function as communal memorial, it was well established as one of the social high spots of the parish's year. It is entirely likely that contemporaries regarded the combination of commemoration and celebration as both natural and desirable; and, although almost all overspent, senior wardens were not apparently surcharged.[75]

Third, the wardens paid for, and presumably organised, other activities arising from their brief. They paid for cleaning the church and its equipment: for tidying the churchyard, for rakers to sweep out and carry away dust year after year, for the clerk's wife and other women to wash cloths and clothes, for unnamed workers to scour candlesticks 'against Easter' – and so on. They paid for the repair and, as necessary, the replacement of essential equipment. Vestments were regularly repaired and, on occasion, provided anew; similarly books were mended or rebound, and sometimes purchased; and liturgical equipment, like candlesticks, censers or cruets needed repair and, on occasion, to be replaced.[76] But this leads to murkier waters. Wardens certainly purchased new equipment: this much is itemised in their accounts. But parishioners also donated or bequeathed goods, as well as presumably organising acquisitions themselves on occasion. Although no hard and fast rule applies, such generosity frequently by-passed the wardens' accounts.[77] It is, therefore, impossible to determine the proportion of parish equipment that wardens acquired from the funds that they managed. This caveat prompts further deliberation.

Assessing the wardens' role

Familiarity with the All Saints' accounts easily leads to complacency: churchwardens were busy men and their accounts preserve ample to occupy commentators. But these records were kept so that at visitation the parish could prove that the basic requirements incumbent upon the laity were being faithfully discharged. No such imperative dictated either that a detailed record of the wardens' 'extra curricular' activities or that the achievements of others in the parish organising more ambitious provision be preserved. In the absence of parallel sources we lose perspective and

---

[75] While it was clearly suitable to commemorate benefactors early in the penitential season, it seems somewhat odd to have held one of the parish's main celebrations at this time; one wonders whether the festivities came to function as a delayed Shrove Tuesday.

[76] One can, for instance, find references to the purchase or repair of vestments in 1475–76, fo 3, 1494–95, fo 3, 1499–1500, fos 4 and 4v, and 1519, fo 3; and references to the purchase or repair of books in 1475–76, fo 3, 1524–25, fo 4v and 5, and 1527, fo 4.

[77] Benefactions were sometimes included but, a comparison of the benefaction list in the All Saints' Church Book (*A.S.C.B.*, pp.7–30) with the churchwardens' accounts discloses how much was not mentioned; the latter contain no direct reference to, for instance, either Alice Chestre or Maud Baker *alias* Spicer making her benefactions to the church.

assign churchwardens unmerited prominence. They were caretakers, essentially, who had also acquired status as agents to represent the parish in certain circumstances. It is doubtful whether they might exercise much initiative; when not fulfilling routine duties, they invariably acted either in conjunction with, or possibly on instructions from, the parish executive. So, while pursuits, like the defence of parish interests at law, for instance, prompted the wardens to make occasional payments, it should not be assumed that they alone were responsible for initiating and pursuing legal activity, nor that All Saints' had recourse to law only in the instances which emerge in the accounts.[78] The problem of how comprehensive an impression of parish activity is recorded in and conveyed by the wardens' accounts is, naturally, a question of moment.[79] A number of issues must be investigated to decide matters. Did wardens discharge duties in addition to those itemised in their accounts? How much else others were doing? Who was in overall charge of parish affairs?

Churchwardens, for a start, did more. As mentioned, the All Saints' accounts fail to itemise monies collected and paid to the lesser clergy, more commonly mentioning only top-up payments.[80] In point of fact, it transpires that the senior warden collected what was to be paid to the clerk and, sensibly, kept his own account. Simon Hancock, senior warden in 1529, refers to the sum of £3 6s 8d which he 'received of the parishioners towards the clerk's wages as it does appear in my roll'.[81] This roll, perhaps more a personal *aide memoire* than an official record, has not survived. It is nonetheless clear that churchwardens discharged responsibilities over and above canonical necessities and that their contribution is under-represented in what survives. Other serious shortcomings in the accounts' coverage are also evident. Just as payments to the lesser clergy were invariably 'more than was gathered in the parish', so, too, many other payments were made to supplement parishioners' otherwise unrecorded contributions and

---

[78] Court cases are, for instance, mentioned against Fylour in 1467–68, fos 2 and 2v and 1468–69, fo 3; against Haddon in 1473, fo 3v; against Canynges in 1474–75, fo 3; and against Peyntar in 1497–98, fo 5.

[79] Kumin, *The Shaping of a Community*, pp.100–02 admits that much was beyond the ambit of churchwardens' accounts but nevertheless uses them to analyse 'parish' life and provision relying on the delphic formula 'It is unlikely, however, that the surviving records present us with a completely deficient picture of communal activities.' R. Hutton, *The Rise and Fall of Merry England: The Ritual Year, 1400–1700* (Oxford, 1994), p. 49 also places the burden of proof on critics of showing 'why it is likely that a ceremony or celebration should have existed before a certain time either without incurring expense or without having that expense entered into the accounts.' Both authors proceed on the assumption that churchwardens presided over parish government, recording most, if not all, of what was going on.

[80] Other surviving accounts, for instance, those for St Andrew Hubbard, Eastcheap, London, obeyed other conventions where collections for and payments to clerks were concerned and, certainly from the 1480s onwards, tended to include these activities in their coverage.

[81] This could have been a new duty, although it seems unlikely; certainty on the point is ultimately impossible.

donations. In 1463–64, for instance, the wardens paid 12s to 'the organ maker for mending your organs from the church money besides that as was gathered'. In 1500, the wardens paid 2s 'for mending the white copes more than my lady's money comes to'. And towards the end of the run of accounts as printed in this volume, churchwardens repeatedly authorised payments for the annual audit dinner which, on scrutiny, transpire to have made up the difference between what was collected from the diners and what was spent on the meal. The proportion of the wardens' payments that were supplementary will elude accurate assessment, but the principle was well established and applied to many areas of parish life.[82] Parishioners might take many initiatives, as confirmed by the codicil to the 1475–76 account, which reveals that while Morgan Lewis owed 26s 8d to the parish, he had to be allowed 6s 8d for work that he had himself carried out on his rented property.

The question of how much others were doing should be pursued. Churchwardens were obviously obliged to provide lights in the church. They purchased oil, new candles and, once or twice a year, returned spent wax to the waxmaker to be reprocessed. But, while these duties occupied a prominent niche in the wardens' record, one wonders whether wardens provided for all that was needed to light the church during the year or whether they were simply responsible for candles at certain altars, and for lamps before particular shrines. If more lights were burnt, who provided them? One wonders, too, whether the wardens footed the whole bill for the maintenance of the church bells, as expenditure on baldrics, clappers and ropes, although recurrent, seems relatively slight.[83] Similarly, while wardens had responsibilities towards the parish liturgy, the proportion of the parish's ceremonial they footed is far from clear. Some aspects of the ritual year were in their charge. They ensured that the Dance of Pauls was displayed twice annually, at St James tide and All Saints' tide;[84] they paid for banners to be carried on Rogation Day and Whitsun, provided fronds on Palm Sunday, funded the vigil at the sepulchre between Good Friday and Easter, and supported aspects at least of the parish's contribution to the town's Corpus Christi procession, to specify some of their more prominent duties. But it is, for instance, conspicuous that payments for anything like an adequate celebration either at All Saints' tide or for the parish's Dedication day are a glaring absence from these accounts,[85] which paves

---

[82] Attention is again drawn to Charles Drew's admonition, mentioned above in note 49.
[83] This judgement, based mainly on comparison with the accounts of St Andrew Hubbard, Eastcheap, London, is admittedly impressionistic.
[84] *A.S.C.B.*, pp. xxv–xxvi.
[85] Patronal feast and dedication days differed, the latter, as the name suggests, being the annual celebration to mark the day of the consecration and dedication of the parish church; in 1536 the English Convocation regularised procedure ordering that the Feast of Dedication be kept on the first Sunday in October 'throughout the realm'.

the way to the realisation that, fabric and equipment apart, the wardens' accounts are more often occupied with extras rather than essentials.[86] Consider musical provision: the wardens might transact the purchase (as distinct from authorising the purchase) of new organs, pay for repairs to this instrument, buy music on occasion and pay for extra performers at significant times, but all are either special provisions or are the peripherals to smooth performance.[87] In summary, let it be noted that wardens provided for the wine which the singers drank on Palm Sunday; they did not pay for the singers. In common with practice in other parishes, wardens in All Saints' had selective responsibilities towards the liturgy. They were far from meeting the whole bill. The more one ponders the accounts, the more obvious it becomes that where liturgical practice had become increasingly sophisticated with time, the wardens' duties had not commensurately broadened; by the later fifteenth and early sixteenth century, others shouldered the responsibility for much of what was, by then, 'core' provision.

In the absence of documentation fully descriptive of the role that others played, headway may be made by considering a parish emergency. 'On Whitsun Monday at night' in 1464, fire damaged the two properties in Corn Street 'next to the chancel'. Vivid details emerge, at least in the unbound accounts: 'On Tuesday in the morning we paid [the sum of 8d] to 4 men for ridding away the timber that lay abroad in the street and for taking up our lead that lay among the rubble.' The Church Book's coverage of this event and its aftermath is, by contrast, thin, surprisingly so in a compilation meant to glorify the wardens' achievements. One would have assumed it was their finest hour; but careful consideration of the unbound accounts suggests that men other than Clement Wilteshire and Howell aPrysse, that year's wardens, took the leading role in the financial and practical efforts which hastened reconstruction. As mentioned earlier, three pairs, Richard Haddon and William Rowley, William Boxe and Hugh Sadlare, and Thomas Golde and Thomas Taylore, together raised the appreciable sum of £4 5s 4d – by ale-selling, if the Book (which mentions none by name) is to be believed. While it proves impossible at this juncture to identify Thomas Taylore, three of the others had already served as churchwardens, and William Rowley and Richard Haddon, who would respectively serve in 1466–67 and in 1468–69, were already eminent members of the parish, and

---

[86] Typified by the entry in the account for 1480–81, fo 2, 'Item paid to Bonnok's clerk for singing and playing upon our Dedication day and All Hallows' day, 12d': it is clear that the parish marked these services, but the wardens' duties concerning them did not extend beyond the provision of extras – in this case, an extra singer and music.

[87] Noteworthy musical provision, which may have been for special performance, becomes more plentiful in the later 1520s: five pricked *carell* books are mentioned in the account for 1524–5, fo 5; pricked songs are purchased, 1525–6, fo 3v; and various pricksong books, 1527, fo 4. Whether or not such provision was either new or really more profuse than previously is debatable.

even town, community.[88] William Boxe was mentioned, again, as present with the vicar when 29s 9d was 'received out of the church coffer', which, along with the sum of £1 taken from the coffers of the Halleways' chantry, was among the expedients which boosted ordinary income in that year.[89] Moreover, in an entry which has no equivalent in the Book, the unbound accounts mention that 'on Friday the 8th day of June, Richard Haddon and Thomas Carpenter and Nicholas Baker and others more went to Pensforde [just to the south of Bristol] to choose 20 oaks'. Baker had served as warden in 1459; Carpenter's expertise was obviously more germane to the matter in hand. If others took the initiative organising emergency fund-raising and expenditure, the two wardens, Wilteshire and aPrysse, managed the current account, as it were, taking the sums raised by ale-selling and those from the parish and the chantry coffers, to swell funds so that they might cover ordinary liabilities and extraordinary outgoings. But other funds could, of course, have been raised and spent. Two principles are clear. First, that parishioners other than current churchwardens took a leading role raising and spending funds in the rebuilding programme. This explains why the Book's version is so terse. The wardens discharged customary duties, but others took the initiative in an emergency. Second, those who took the lead had, for the most part, already served as churchwardens, implying that the successful discharge of this office, rather than being an end in itself, was a rung on the ladder *en route* to a position among the parish governors.[90]

The 'masters' of the parish

The Constitutions and Ordinances listed at the beginning of the Church Book confirm the existence of an elite. Men 'who were of the council' were to be fined more heavily than men 'who were not of the council' for failure to attend the day of accounts; three men, moreover, 'one of the worshipful and two of the mean of the parish,' were to assess each parishioner's contribution towards the clerk's stipend.[91] The elite, while bearing greater responsibility, were nevertheless obliged to act with the wider swathe of parishioners when overseeing the audit or when setting rates. These twin aspects of parish management may be considered in turn.

---

[88] As the appendix reveals, William Boxe had served in 1460, and would serve again in 1465; Hugh Sadlare served in 1462 and 1463; Thomas Gold had served in 1463. If 'Taylore' was simply a trade name, it may have camouflaged another prominent parishioner like Thomas John, warden with Thomas Gold in 1463.

[89] This sum was transferred from the chantry account to save the wardens from going into deficit on the 'parish' account; given that the surplus for the year in this account was 11s 11d, they obviously took enough to leave themselves with some room for manoeuvre.

[90] Very much the same picture as emerges from St Mary at Hill and St Andrew Hubbard; see above, note 56. Attention is again drawn to the appendix for those eligible to join the elite.

[91] *A.S.C.B.*, pp.2–3.

The elite, also known as 'the masters', kept the keys to parish coffers and, when necessary, disbursed sums to supplement the wardens' funds. So, in 1507–08, the churchwardens refer to the sum of £4 2s which they had received 'of the masters of the parish to bestow in repairs'; or in 1519–20, to the sum of £5 3s which was 'received of the masters of the parish at the last day of the account'.[92] Further, the unbound account for the year of the fire refers to the money which the Halleways' chantry 'owed unto the said church of All Hallows', the which church book that is called the ledger makes mention of the said sum', implying that the overall balances of the different strands of parish finance were recorded in a book, the ledger, about which we know nothing save that it was kept by the 'masters'.[93] There were, then, monies available in excess of the revenues dealt with in the wardens' accounts (explaining what happened to recurrent surpluses), and also accounts of broader coverage than those that the wardens kept. Quite plausibly there were sources of income in excess of those husbanded by the wardens. These are ideas to be pursued. If the 'masters', who were successful men of affairs in a mercantile community, were in charge of an accumulating surplus, then it is at the very least possible that they would have invested parish capital for a return. There are strong indications that they did. They apparently lent to individuals, no doubt at interest. This would explain the occasional references to loan repayments found in surviving accounts, and solve the puzzle that the wardens never themselves mention a decision to lend. So, while, as in 1487–88, the wardens might itemise receipts from Thomas Koke of money 'lent out of the church', references to loans are more frequently found in codicils, like that appended to the 1507–8 account, which notes a loan of £7 to Arnold Stewte, brewer, 'by the consent of the which parish'. The likelihood is that the 'masters' took these decisions, but that they were ratified by the wider parish; repayments, indeed, were often noted at the day of audit in the presence of a parishioners. But, whether or not the masters emerge as usurers, the decision to exploit capital could have been lucrative. The 'masters' may have speculated in other ways, too. At the conclusion of the account for 1517, the decision was taken to advance the year's surplus to Thomas Snygge and Thomas Pacy, previous wardens significantly, who were 'to bestow it on the reparations on All Hallows' conduit'.[94] The conduit would appear to have been a parish amenity, but it

---

[92] In the same account there is also reference to a payment of 8d 'for wine at the Boar's Head when the masters took possession' – of what is unclear.

[93] Note that *A.S.C.B.*, p.137 records a series of memoranda, apparently jotted down on 7 April 1491, listing totals in the various parish budgets – 'in the purse of Jesus', 'in the treasure coffer of the church' and 'in the chantry coffer'.

[94] Both Pacys and Snygges were eminent parish dynasties: the former served, presumably father and son, as wardens in 1505–6, 1512–13, 1523–24 and 1524–25; Snygges as wardens, again father and son in 1487, 1496–97, 1504–05 and 1514–15.

is difficult not to conceive of it as a parish asset which, like other property, demanded investment to sustain or augment its return.[95] The 'masters', then, may very well have speculated, exploiting surplus funds and property not devised to the parish, just as they seem to have been in charge of more *ad hoc*, but potentially lucrative receipts, like church ales. The income enjoyed by the parish was more varied and, in all probability, much more appreciable than the revenues managed by the churchwardens; a few of the extra areas of activity are only partially revealed, but clearly considerably more was afoot than depicted in the surviving accounts.

In this context, it is worth considering one more possibility. Senior wardens appear to have speculated with the parish funds at their disposal. Rawlyn Webbe, senior warden in 1517–18, having amassed a surplus of £10 18s 5½d, paid £8 18s 5½d 'to the parishioners at his day of his account in money' but was said to 'owe to the church of this account for old timber, 40s.' Given that he had, almost at the beginning of his account, itemised a receipt of 40s for old timber, it appears that he had kept either the cash or the timber for ventures of his own. A memorandum insists that 'the same John Hewes [senior warden in the following year] must bring in at his accounts 40s that he shall receive of Rawlyn Cooke *alias* Webbe', and, sure enough, in addition to £4 from the parish's funds that Webbe delivered to Hewes, the latter was also able to itemise 'Received of Rawlyn Webbe for church timber, 40s'. He returned what he had commandeered but was in effective possession of parish assets for the best part of two years. Similarly, John Baten, who was senior warden for 1511–12 and who died whilst in office, amassed a surplus of £3 4s 9d on that year's accounts. His widow, who, note, was responsible for squaring his affairs with the parish, was only able to find the 4s 9d and was obliged to give the parish 'a flat cup overgilt' as surety for the £3 outstanding; in the following account Master Baten, John Baten's heir presumably, gave the parish a whole cloth worth 4 marks (53s 4d), presumably towards settling the debt. It very much looks as if John Baten, as senior warden, was risking parish money, possibly in cloth transactions, and, dying unexpectedly, left his widow and executrix with insufficient to cover immediate liabilities. It appears either that senior wardens strove to profit from their tenure of office, which may have been reasonable in that it was an onerous task,[96] or that senior wardens were

---

[95] A number of parishioners (some certainly members of the elite) left bequests to the conduit in the early sixteenth century: Spicer the younger, Thomas Pernaunt, and David Cogan, *A.S.C.B.*, pp. 23, 24, 30; and testators, David Philippe, 1509 and Johanne Stevyns in the same year. Their bequests could have been purely charitable, bolstering a public amenity, but it is worth pursuing the possibility at least that the parish may have derived some income from this source.

[96] From 1524, the parish agreed to allow [ie pay] the senior warden 6s 8d 'at his account yearly . . . for gathering church and chantry rents, for making the book of accounts and for reward money to the tenants at the payment of their rents,' in recognition of the fact that a substantial property acquisition in that year considerably increased subsequent wardens' responsibilities.

expected to demonstrate acumen and integrity by returning more to the parish coffer than they had initially been entrusted with. If they could manage the latter, then their honesty and talents (in both the worldly and scriptural sense) would be beyond question, and their suitability as a 'master' beyond dispute. The point is speculative, in more ways than one, but the surviving materials at least suggest that this was a possibility, and, to labour the point, enterprise was more in the lifeblood of a mercantile community than suffering funds to fester in a chest.

If, as is certain, parish reserves were more extensive than the sums recorded in the wardens' accounts, and if, more tentatively, financial activity, by both 'masters' and wardens was conceivably much more varied and ambitious than we might initially assume, it becomes far easier to explain, not only the striking generosity shown by the parish to the Halleways' chantry endowment throughout the 1520s,[97] but also the apparent equanimity with which the parish embarked upon substantial property acquisition in 1524–25 – of which more below. The parish community could support a far more ambitious standard of observance and provision than would have been possible if dependent solely on churchwardens' income. It may finally be noted that the existence of an executive other than and superior to the wardens solves a number of puzzles, such as the disappearance of endowments which the parish had received. The property in Wine Street which the Baker *alias* Spicers had devised to the parish, which was never successfully let, disappeared from the wardens' accounts after 1514; it may well have sold, or was, more probably, hived off to another account and put to uses beyond the wardens' competence.

'Masters' exercised considerable discretion but, as suggested, it would be wrong to conceive of parish government as solely elitist. Those 'not of the council' were also obliged to attend the annual audit, an occasion also witnessing the formulation of parish policy and decisions; similarly, the 'mean' were to outnumber the 'masters' when setting the rates at which parishioners were to contribute towards the parish clerk, the assessment which probably pegged other contributions. While parish affairs were generally 'streamlined', with 'masters' and wardens in charge of or responsible for specific duties, parishioners had a part in crucial decisions, not least to minimise the opportunity for subsequent complaint or non-compliance. Joint actions and decisions are referred to in the accounts as having been made or taken by the *paryschyngs*, which (in a variety of spellings) seems to have been a term of art employed when describing a collaborative action or decision by the wider parish community,

---

[97] To be printed in the third and final volume of *The Pre-Reformation Records of All Saints'*.

presumably comprising all house-holders.[98] When the parish acted *en masse* to raise funds, as with the purchase of organs in 1472–73, the wardens noted: 'Item we received of the *paryschyngs*, and of other divers strangers, the sum of £9 17s 7d'. Moreover, the joint decisions or actions of 'the masters' and 'the meaner sort' were said to have been taken by the *paryschyngs*. At successive days of account there are references to sums paid to or advanced by the *paryschyngs*, as at the audit for 1514–15, when they authorised a number of transactions concerning the chantry budget and the parish account for that year, in addition to which the sum of 3s 4d was paid 'by the *paryschyngs* to the clerk for keeping Our Lady Mass', and the surplus of 23s 4d on the year's account was 'delivered by the said *paryschyngs*' to Richard Wale, the next year's senior warden. Executive decisions, if taken initially by the 'masters,' were, it is important to note, ultimately ratified and carried out in conjunction with the 'meaner sort', the broader swathe of *paryschyngs*, and some at least are recorded in codicils.

The acquisition of property in the High Street and the Pithay in 1524–25 was a transaction of clear moment for the parish which sheds welcome light on the operation of its government, even though one or two details as to the arrangements are obscure.[99] The property had once comprised part at least of Haddon's chantry endowment, lost to John Hawkes of St Leonard's parish in the early 1470s. The death of Hawkes' son, another John, without issue, and the fact that Hawkes senior's wife, Elizabeth, nee Hervey, was a member of an eminent All Saints' dynasty, triggered default instructions which were to the benefit of the parish at Elizabeth's death.[100] The inheritance was to be sold for the best possible price and the proceeds split between St Augustine's Abbey, and the parishes of St Leonard and All Saints': the monastery was to take half with the remainder divided between the two parishes.[101] In the event the property was valued at £90, and All Saints' decided to buy out the other two legatees, paying St Augustine's £45 and St Leonard's £22 10s, a total of £67 10s. Plate, either pledged to or apparently in the possession of the church, underwrote the transaction. So, on 31 May 1524, 'in the presence of the vicar and of the whole *paryshons*' all such plate as was in pledge to the church by Thomas Pacy and Jerome Grene was delivered to the vicar and to Thomas Pacy and David Lawrens,

---

[98]   Given that *paryschyngs* seems to have been a term with a precise meaning, denoting householders entitled to take part in deliberations (rather than all those who lived in the parish and worshipped in the local church, which modern usage tends to imply), I have taken care to keep the (slightly differing) original spellings in the printed text of the accounts to preserve distinctions to which contemporaries may have attached significance.

[99]   The High Street property can be identified, *Topography*, pp.74–5: High Street east, property 10.

[100]   Her mother had been married to John Chestre, Henry and Alice Chestre's son, before marrying into the Hervey family.

[101]   All Saints' Deeds, HS B7 (John Hawkes' will, given 1503); *The Great Red Book of Bristol, Text part iv*, ed. E.W. Veale (Bristol Record Society, xviii, 1953), pp.1–3.

who, using additional plate as collateral as well as recalling debts and raising further cash, 'promised to discharge the said church and *p[ar]issons* against the Abbot and Convent of St Augustine's of £45 and against the vicar and parishioners of St Leonard's of £22 10s for the sales of Master Hawkes' lands'.[102] The main players were members of the parish elite who had been, or were about to be, wardens: Thomas Pacy had been sub warden in both 1512–13 and 1522–23 and senior warden in 1523–24;[103] Jerome Grene had been sub warden in 1521–22, and senior warden in 1522–23; David Lawrens was to be sub and then senior warden in the years following 1525.[104] In effect, Pacy and Grene appear to have lent to the parish plate respectively worth £20 and £25; it also seems to have been the case that plate bequeathed to the church by Thomas Snygge, a 'master' of the parish, senior warden of the parish in 1496–97 and 1504–05, who may recently have died, was being used.[105] The vicar, Pacy and Lawrens 'promised to discharge the church', which presumably implied that they assumed responsibility for repaying the debt incurred. There is little sign in the accounts immediately following that the wardens were responsible for repayments – the one payment made (1527, fo 4) was specifically authorised by Master vicar and parishioners, which may imply that the masters shouldered this responsibility, quite possibly using surpluses on the current account or other sources of revenue. Moreover, Pacy and another of the elite, John Hewes, who had been sub and then senior warden in 1517–19, undertook to administer and repair the property during the first year of All Saints' possession, to maximise its rental value. This involved collecting rent and making extensive repairs on the property in the Pithay. It is of considerable significance that the accounts kept by Pacy and Hewes survive; they are printed in this volume (following the wardens' accounts for 1524–25) and prove beyond any doubt that 'masters' both acted for *and* kept financial records on behalf of the parish.[106]

[102] The vicar of All Saints' at the time was one John Flooke, who was also one of John Hawke's executors, *ibid.*

[103] Pacy had, as senior warden, entered 'Also I received in plate that laid in pledge to the church, £20' and stood surety for the same sum in the following year; he had perhaps exchanged plate for cash in the expectation of supporting the parish's effort in the following year; Grene may previously have done the same for £25 worth of plate.

[104] A codicil to the 1523–24 account mentions plate, once Thomas Snygge's and which had been in pledge to the church, actually being 'delivered' to warden Gervis 'to furnish money necessary to the church's use', bringing in £13 6s 8d. Plate was clearly a recognised substitute for cash.

[105] There is a marginal note in the parish benefaction list, *A.S.C.B.*, p.21, that one John Snygge (Thomas's father) had bequeathed £5 to the parish in 1490, which the parish had only received via Thomas Snygge in 1525, implying that the cash had been realised from the sale of plate which the parish seems to have received from the younger Snygge, and that the parish was treating this as a benefaction.

[106] It should be noted that a loan of £8 made to John a Wood and John Folke in a codicil to the 1523–24 account is in part repaid in the account kept by Pacy and Hewes for 1525, implying that the 'masters' lent parish money without reference to churchwardens.

The current wardens were conspicuous by their absence from these proceedings, although the sub warden for the year, Thomas Yong, was at least named a feoffee in the deed transferring ownership to All Saints'.[107] Senior warden John Gervis was not involved even to this extent. This may have been a result of his current tenancy of the single most substantial property in the purchase, situated in the High Street. More probably, while busy enough with the ordinary business of the parish, for which he was ultimately personally responsible, he kept his distance from a collective, and ultimately speculative, endeavour.[108] His formal status apparently precluded involvement. Significantly, his only contribution was a supplementary payment. The parish, having gathered in debts and benefited from loans and support from the elite, was still short by £2 3s 9d; Gervis advanced this sum from his account: 'Item paid to Master Pase [Pacy] to make up the full payment of the lands that we bought of Master Hervey's executors – 43s 9d'. The implications are instructive. The senior warden is set apart, his only contribution a top-up payment. The 'masters' took the initiative, having first been endorsed by the vicar and *paryschons*, and subsequently acting in league with the vicar. When extra material affords a fuller impression of parish procedures, we must conclude that categorising wardens as 'chief executives' is mistaken; while evidently fulfilling an essential service, by the early sixteenth century at least they stood somewhat apart.[109] As wardens they were responsible for maintaining parish stock, by investment and repair, or at law if necessary. Acquisition fell to others.

Documentation was created to serve particular needs and survived, essentially, by chance. If our conclusion is that the wardens' accounts shed, at best, only oblique light on other officers within the parish, and thus yield a decidedly restricted impression of parish affairs, this need occasion no surprise. But in attempting to establish both a more accurate perspective and a more inclusive impression, we ought finally to consider the role of the incumbent who, in recent discussion, has come, if not to the fore, at least into sharper relief. Were we to rely on churchwardens' accounts alone, we could be forgiven for concluding that the clergy played hardly any role in parish affairs at all. Other sources, and admittedly the increasingly detailed accounts which survive for the 1520s, reveal the folly of this position. The benefaction list in the Church Book reveals the contribution of an incumbent like Maurice Hardwick: not only was he a notably

---

[107] All Saints' Deeds, HS B8; see also *Great Red Book. Text part iv*, p.2 which lists the same men representing All Saints', clearly the parish elite.

[108] And this despite the fact that some churchwardens certainly seem to have speculated privately with parish funds.

[109] Attention is drawn to the 'pyramid' drawn by contemporaries to depict the parish of St Mary at Hill, London, in my essay 'Shaping the Parish' (above note 56): the wardens' position, very much to one side of the diagram and away from other parishioner, may have been more accurate than previously realised.

generous benefactor, he was also a facilitator, persuading Agnes Fylour to devise property, prompting the compilation of the Church Book and pioneering the future safe-keeping of parish muniments.[110] Equal information on other incumbents would doubtless force further reassessment. In the absence of such detail, the accounts surviving for the 1520s do at least permit a fuller impression of the vicar, John Flooke's, pivotal role in parish affairs; and it is worth stating that if this information is unprecedented, this almost certainly reflects a simple increase in detail rather than any departure in practice. So, just as the procedure which secured the properties in the High Street and Pithay in 1525 had to be transacted 'in the presence of the vicar and of the whole *paryschons*' so, too, in 1527, when a sum of 50s 6d was paid to Jerome Grene, it was 'by agreement of Master vicar and the parish'; and when David Lawrence brought the surplus of £13 16d on this account, it was 'to the church . . . in the presence of the vicar and *paryschons* . . . and so he [was] dismissed and clearly discharged'. But, by the same token, just as the vicar and two of the 'masters' might promise 'to discharge the church' in the transactions of 1525, so codicils to the later accounts invariably reveal that the vicar was present, and presumably involved, when the senior warden's returns were scrutinised at the audit. The vicar was, in practice, clearly one of the 'masters' of the parish. So, in 1521, when the senior warden reveals that he received the sum of 50s 'of Master vicar and of Master Pacy of that they gathered towards the new organs', it suggests once again that agents other than and superior to wardens habitually took the initiative in parish musical provision.[111] The vicar worked in league by turns with the *paryschons* and the masters, and specifically too with the churchwardens on occasion.[112] Other items, like 'Item paid to Master vicar in part payment, £5 13s 4d' found in the accounts for 1525–26, infallibly suggest that the vicar was more closely involved in the parish's financial affairs than would ordinarily be assumed, although quite what was being discharged here is unspecified. Examples could be multiplied, but it is abundantly apparent that the vicar was involved as an integral player in parish life, working with the elite, with the wardens and the generality, as necessary, scrutinising proceedings, priming initiatives and even, apparently, funding expenditure. The distinction we all too easily make between clergy and laity, which applies in sacramental spheres, need not – indeed, should not – be applied across the board. In matters of parish management, co-ordinating the efforts of the elite and orchestrating acceptance by the generality, to ensure prudent conduct and future harmony, the vicar's ability to bridge gaps, being able to

---

[110] *A.S.C.B.*, pp. 9–11.

[111] One wonders how significant the title 'Master vicar' was in these circumstances.

[112] Parish deeds frequently name vicar and wardens as parish representatives, or as those who actually held tenements; and it may be noted that in a codicil to the account for 1510–11, the vicar, proctors and whole parish sanctioned a rent increase.

stand both as an outsider and as an integral member of the parish community, was crucial.

Ultimately, parish government is revealed as strikingly sophisticated. Different agents might combine to shape initiatives, to scrutinise the activities of others and guarantee that the canonical minimum should be safely provided, come what may; but they were capable, too, of providing very much more. Documentary shortcomings may, at times, project different elements within the parish as acting more in isolation than was probably the case; but, ironically, when additional information is available the senior warden is the agent who emerges as most detached, perhaps – in part – the better to demonstrate what he might achieve on his own. The churchwardens' accounts which survive for All Saints' suggest a steady development of senior wardenship as a rite of passage, to be successfully and even profitably discharged preparatory for entry into the parish elite. The impressions of parish life which the wardens' accounts can afford, therefore, are limited. They open a door into a room but from this room other doors open and these, at best, are only ajar; this, nevertheless, is consistent with the impressions of often more luxuriant parish provision, be it in extravagant purchase or benefaction or services, encountered elsewhere in All Saints' archive.

Editorial technique

The aim of this volume is to make the early, unbound accounts of All Saints', Bristol [BRO, P/AS/ChW3], as accessible as possible, easy both to read and to understand. As stated earlier, the accounts survive in booklets and these are easily dated (commonly by *Anno Domini* rather than regnal years) either by information on the front cover or in the preamble. All are for one year and most display the years when they were started and finished; in one or two instances, however, only one date is given in the original and, if the series is patchy at that point, it may not be entirely clear whether this signifies an end or a beginning. While the accounts are in English, roman numerals are used both for sums of money and numbers more generally; I have substituted their arabic equivalents throughout. In the few instances, which grew more common in the 1520s, where arabic numerals were originally used, I have remarked on this with a note.[113] In accordance with the policy of the Bristol Record Series, the English in which the original accounts were written has been modernised with both vocabulary and syntax being adapted to ease intelligibility. I would emphasise, first, that I have tried not to 'steam-roller' the original lest the

---

[113] Starting in 1520, for instance, arabic numerals were used for the *anno domini* date on surviving cover pages and, more casually, in the arithmetic employed in margins checking the addition (as in the accounts for 1522–23).

end result is too bland; at least some of the 'flavour' of the original is, I hope, still present. Second, the printed text is not a calendar: nothing of substance has been omitted; the most that has been done is to simplify usage and avoid repetition – so, to cite a common 'for instance', 'for the washing of the cloths' has been rendered 'for washing the cloths'. It should also be noted that while I have modernised Christian names, I have left surnames as they are. The same individual, then, may appear with a name spelled differently, even in the same accounts. Punctuation has been introduced sparingly to aid intelligibility; I have tried to be consistent, however, so that in the frequently encountered payment 'for two (or more) days' work', where the word 'work' has been omitted, I have kept the apostrophe on 'days''. I have indicated folio-breaks (recto and verso) throughout and have kept a number of the details in the originals, such as the Holy monogram 'Jhs' or 'Jhu' with which some scribes headed their accounts.[114] While I am relieved to say that the accounts are for the most part written clearly and are a pleasure to read, some present problems and, inevitably, contain phrases or words which are either difficult or impossible to read. There are, therefore, a number of guesses in the following: where I am not entirely certain of a reading, I have inserted a question mark – so the reader should note that '?' indicates a hazard, the reading is plausible rather than definite. Where the letters can be transcribed but the reader's guess is as good as mine as to what the scribe meant, I have left the word in italics.[115] I have also used italics where, occasionally, the original text is quirky but yields a phrase of sufficient interest as it stands to be left unaltered. Also, as mentioned above, I have left the word for parishioners in its (slightly varying) original form because it seems plain that the word as used, meaning perhaps householder or parish decision-maker, had a somewhat different meaning from the present day 'parishioner' to which the reader should be alerted. Some words have defied all attempts at transliteration, and have had to be marked (using [unintelligible]), but these instances, thankfully, are few. Square brackets are used generally to indicate, as it were, 'stage directions': a different hand, crossings out, an interpolation, unintelligibility, different ink in the original, and so on. I have, however, been relatively sparing with these to save the text from clutter. The index deals primarily with names (selecting the most common form of the surname and giving alternatives) and places. Were I to list and

---

[114] The monogram is found on one of the earliest survivals, that for 1449, and appears to have become somewhat more common from the later 1480s. In some accounts, those for 1507–08 and 1522–3 for instance, the practice was somewhat more elaborate, with 'Jhu [and] Maria' heading the page, while that for 1521 has 'Jhus, Maria, Om Sanctos orabz nobis' at the top of the first page. It is of interest that this practice became, if anything, more elaborate with time, while admittedly remaining sporadic.

[115] The word 'skarry', 'skary' or 'scary' (obviously some kind of iron implement or attachment) has, as yet, defied safe interpretation and has been left in the original throughout.

index every detail concerning, for instance, wax or washing, then the apparatus would be overlong and cumbersome. Rather than attempting an exhaustive index, I have been selective and include only the main features which emerge concerning either parish procedures or the appearance of the interior and exterior of the church. Finally, the following comprises a deal of detailed, often repetitious, material; to admit that there is ample scope for omission and error is understatement. While I have made every effort to be both accurate and consistent, I am fully aware that there must be mistakes and irregularities. For these I can only ask to be forgiven.

April 2000.

[1446; Single sheet survives, damaged at margins]

[recto]
Be it in mind that these are the receipts the which William Warde and
Da[vy Soccett] proctors of the church of All Hallows', Bristol, by the
grace of God [word lost].

First we received at Good Friday and at Easter day – 19s 8d.
Item received for hire of the cross and the foot for Roger Wellyschote –
[sum lost]
Item received for hire of the cross and the foot for Parkhouse's wife –
[sum lost]
Sum – 26s ?8d.

Be it in mind that these are the rents that the said proctors have received.
First received of Janet Filour for Saint Mary quarter – 6s 8d.
Item received of the same for Midsummer quarter – 6s 8d.
Item received of the same for Michaelmas quarter – 6s 8d.
Item received of the same for Midwinter quarter – 6s 8d.

Item received of John Kore, scrivener, for Saint Mary quarter – 8s 4d.
Item received of the same for Midsummer quarter – 8s 4d.
Item received of the same for Michaelmas quarter – 8s 4d.
Item received of the same for Christmas quarter – 8s 4d.

Item received for the rent of Perse Hoper's house in Baldwin Street of the
master of the Tailor's craft of Bristol for Saint Mary quarter – 3s.
Item received of the same for Midsummer quarter – 3s.
Item received of the same for Michaelmas quarter – 3s.
Item received of the same for Christmas quarter – 3s.
Sum – 12s.

Item received of the priest of Saint Nicholas – 2s 6d.
Item received of Thomas Asch, baker, [for] his house in Lewins Mead –
12d.
Item received of the house in Marsh Street – 2s.
Item received of John Laynell, draper – 3s 4d.
Item received of William Warde's house – [scored: 13s 4d.] £5.
Item received of William Chester's house – 4s.
Item received of Canynges for the house in Saint Peter's street – 6d.
Sum of all the receipts is – £6 5s.

Sum total – £10 11s 8d.

[verso]
Be it in mind that these are the costs of the church which William Warde
and [Da]vy Soccett have paid, proctors of the church of All Hallows',
against Easter

In primis for washing of 5 altar cloths and 4 towels and 3 *kanvas* and 4
surplices and 1 alb against Easter – 10d.
Item carrying away rubble – 4d.
Item 3 pair candlesticks and 12 latten bowls and 6 tenyn [tin] bowls – 9d.
Item for bearing the cross at Saint George's day – 4d.
Item to the official of the church at Worcester – 20d.
Item for bearing the banners [at] the Rogations days – 5d.
Item for bearing 2 torches at Corpus Christi day – 1d.
Item for mending the great bell, to Wanstre – 20d.
Item for wax against Easter for the paschal and the *vautapure* and for the
light on the rood loft – 9s 5 ½d.
Item for washing cloths – 12d.
Item to the keeper of the sepulchre – 11d.
Item for mending the sacring bell at the high altar – 2d.
Item I paid to Joce, the man of law, the morrow after Saint Mark's day –
[sum lost].
Item I paid for Newbery's mind – [sum lost].
Item for silk to mend the vestment and *bysymys* – [sum lost].
Item we spent in *dryng* [?drink] when we received our rent of Janet Fyler
and Lawrence Temsett – 1 ½d.
Item we spent for hanging of the quire, 1 nail – 2d.
Item we paid for making the judas amid the rood loft and 2 tapers beneath
at All Hallows' tide – 2s 7d.
Item I paid to Joce, the man of law, the 7th day of December – 3s 4d.
Item I paid to Roger Abynd for 1 piece of timber that is in the belfry –
2s 4d.
Item [for] candles that burnt in the rood loft at Midwinter – 4d.
Item I paid for ale on Ash Wednesday – 11 ½d.
Item for bread and cakes – 4 ½d.
Item for the knell to the clerk – 10d.
Item for mending of 2 keys to Philip Sadler – 2d.
Item for mending vestments – 6d.
Sum – 42s 4d.

[1449; Account is on one sheet, folded to give four sides in a booklet, the last page of which is blank apart from the phrase 'God save the queen, amen' written in a later hand]

fo 1
Jhc
Memorandum that these are the parcels of money that Thomas De[ne] and John Laynell, proctors of the church of All Hallows', Bristol, have paid for the needs of the said church, first at Easter.

Item paid to Harry Davy for scouring candlesticks and bowls of tapers – 8d. [In different ink: ?11d.]
Item paid for 1 cord to hang the paschal taper – 2d.
Item paid to the raker for leading away the dust of the church – 4d.
Item paid for washing the vicar's surplice and the clerk's surplice – 4d. [Added in different ink: ½d.]
Item for keeping the sepulchre – 13d.
Item paid to the ?friary of Worcester of Easter money – 2s.
Item paid for washing 2 corporases – 1 ½d.
Item paid for washing 9 altar cloths and 7 ?towels, 2 albs and 2 amices – 8d.
Item paid for making 2 holes for the bolts of the church door – 1d. [Added in different ink: 7 ½d.]
Item paid for bearing banners [at] the Rogations days – 4d.
Item paid for 1 cloth of hair for the high altar – 11d.
Item paid for William Newbery's mind – 6s 1d.
Item paid for bearing the cross on Corpus Christi day – 4d.
Item paid for mending the lock of the treasure coffer – 3 ½d.
Item paid to Richard Waxmaker for 50 ½ lb of wax, at 5 ½d the pound [superscript, scored, in different ink: 17s 10d] sum – 23s 1d.
Item for making 70 ¾ lb of church wax – 2s 11d.
Item paid for making clean the gutters of the church – 2d.
Item paid for scouring the lamp in the rood chapel – 1d.
Item paid for hanging cloths in the church at Saint James's tide – 3d.
Item paid for ringing bells at the King's coming – 3d.
Item paid to Black, carpenter, for to see the bells – 2d.
Item paid for 1 cruet for the high altar – 3 ½d.
Item paid for taking off and setting on the lock of the little vestry – 1d.
Item paid for washing 2 albs and 2 amices – 3d.
Item paid for the basin for the tapers before Our Lady – 23s 4d.
Item paid for 1 cord to hang the said basin – 3d.
Item paid for 2 ¾ lb of wax – 15d.
Item paid for making 7 ¼ lb of the church wax for the basin – 3d.
Item paid for besoms for the church – 1d.

Item paid for ?5 [ms. holed] girdles for vestments – 2d.
Item paid for 4 lb of candles for the high altar and the rood loft [on] All
Hallows' day – 4d.[superscript, different ink: 6d.]
Item paid for making 8 lb of church wax at All Hallows' tide – 4d.

fo 1v
Jhc
Item paid for scouring the candlesticks and bowls for tapers – 8d.
Item paid for washing the vicar's surplice, 2 rochets and 5 altar cloths –
8d.
Item paid for nails and for hanging cloths in the church and taking down at
All Hallows' tide – 5d.
Item paid for mending the new coffer before Our Lady's altar – 2d.
Item paid for 2 lb of candles for the rood loft on Christmas day – 2d.
Item paid for scouring the new basin with tapers – 4d.
Item paid for the General Mind on Ash Wednesday for the good doers – 3s
9d.
Item paid for 7 quarts of lamp oil – 2s.
Item paid to Richard Haddon – £4 6s 8d.
Sum – £8 1s 9 ½d.

fo 2
Jhc
Memorandum that these are the parcels that John Laynell and Thomas
Dene proctors of the church of All Hallows' in Bristol have received first
on Good Friday and Easter day – 18s 11d.
Item received of Sir ?Walter Saloman for the hire of the black cloth – 4d.
Item received for Richard Ysgar's pit in the church – 6s 8d.
Item received of John Ysgar that Richard Ysgar gave to the church work –
12d.
Item received of Hugh Sadler for his seat and his wife's – 16d.
Item received of ?Katherine that was Sharp's servant for her seat – 8d.
Item received of Janet Halloway for William Wytney's pit – 6s 8d.
Item received of ?Kenet Chandler for his seat and his wife's – 16d.
Item received of William Hosier of the brotherhood for his wife's seat –
8d.
Item received of Janet that was the wife of Richard Ysgar for her seat –
6d.
Item received of Martyne the wife of William Ysgar for her seat – 12d.
Item received Thomas Taylur for his seat and his wife's – 16d.
Item received of Janet Mors for her seat – 4d.
Sum – 40s 9d.

Item received for rent of John Forster for the new house – £ [ms. holed].

Item received of Sir Davy for rent of Robert Walshe's house – 2s 6d.
Item received of Robert Core for rent – 33s 4d.
Item received of the master of the Tailors craft for rent of the house in Baldwin Street – 12s.
Item received of William Chestre for rent of his house – 4s.
Item received of Nicholas Stock for rent of the house in Marsh Street – 2s.
Item received of Thomas Laker for rent of the house in Lewins Mead – 12d.
Item received of Thomas Fyler for rent of his house – 26s 8d.
Item received of John Laynell for rent of 1 *preve* – 3s 4d.
Sum – £9 4s 10d.

Sum total – £11 5s 7d.

[1463–64; right edge damaged on fo 1]

fo 1
The accounts of Thomas John and Thomas Golde, proctors of the church of All Hallows', Bristol, from the 22nd day of March in the third year of the reign of King Edward IV unto the 20th day of March in the year next ensuing, that is to say containing 1 whole year.

These have been the receipts of your rents

In primis of Richard Haddon for 1 tenement called the Green Lattice – £5.
Item of the chantry of Everard Frenche for the place that Robert Coke dwelt in – 2s 6d.
Item of Thomas Poyntmaker for Christmas quarter of 1 tenement in Corn Street next to the church – 4s. Our Lady Day's quarter, Midsummer quarter and Michaelmas quarter of the same tenement – void.
Item of John Leynell for 1 tenement next to the said place, by year – 23s 4d.
Item the place that William Chestre dwelt, in rent assize – void.
Item of Thomas Asche, baker, for rent assize, by year – 12[d.]
Item of the master of the Tailors for rent assize, by year of the place that John Alberton dwells in Baldwin Street – 12[s.]
Item of William Canynges rent assize of the place that the stainer dwells in in Saint Peter's parish, by year – 6d.
Item the place that Nicholas Stoke held in Marsh Street rent assize, by year – void.
Item of Thomas Halleway's chantry by year – 6s 8d.
Sum – £7 10s.

fo 1v

The receipts of Easter
Item received on Good Friday at the cross – 3s 9d.
Item received on Easter day on the pax – 8s 7d.
Sum – 12s 4d.

These have been the receipts of seats and of other casualties as shown
Item received of Howell aPrysse for changing his and his wife's seats –
8d.
Item received of William Bennett for his seat – 7d.
Item received of Thomas Abyngton for a seat to his wife – 8d.
Item received of John Lemsstyr, cook, for a seat to him and to his wife –
16d.
Item received of Isabel Skey for her seat – 6d.
Item received of Thomas Golde for a seat – 4d.
Item received of John Compton for his wife's burial – 6s 8d.
Item received for William Fylar's burial – 6s 8d.
Item received for Marjory Spicer's burial – 6s 8d.
Item received of Harry Chestre for the great candlestick – 4d.
Item received of Janet Roberts for an iron brooch – 3s.
Sum – 27s 4d.

Sum total the receipts – £9 9s 8d.

fo 2

These have been the payments which Thomas John and Thomas Golde
proctors of the church of All Hallows' have paid for the said church

In primis paid for washing 3 albs, 8 altar cloths, 2 surplices and 2 towels
against Easter – 12d.
Item paid for keeping the sepulchre – 8d.
Item paid for fire and for ale to the keepers – 1d.
Item paid to the raker for carrying away the church dust for the whole
year – 8d.
Item paid to the mother church of Worcester – 12d.
Item paid for holding William Newbery's mind – 6s.
Item paid to the suffragan for bearing the banners in Whitsun week and for
bearing the cross on Corpus Christi day – 8d.
Item paid for the dinner for the priests on Corpus Christi day – 2s 6d.
Item paid for scouring the candlesticks and bowls against Easter – 16d.
Item paid for hanging up the Dance of Pauls and for taking down thereof
and for folding up thereof again at St James's tide and at All Hallows' tide
– 8d.

Item against the bishop's coming when he gave orders here, we paid for washing 2 surplices and a *rachett* [?rochet] and a towel – 4d.

Item [at] the same time we paid for making the oil fat and for gilding thereof – 4s 4d.

Item against our Dedication day we paid the organ maker for mending your organs from the church money besides that as was gathered – 12s.

Item paid for a new lamp which hangs before the rood altar – 1d.

Item paid for 2 lb of tallow candles which burned in the rood loft at Christmas – 3d.

Item paid for a cord for the Lent cloth that hung before the high altar – ½d.

fo 2v.

Item paid for besoms to *streke* the church with – 1d.

Item paid to John Schoppe for 2 gallons of lamp oil which burns in the lamp before the rood altar – 2s.

Item paid for paper to write our accounts upon – ½d.

Item paid to Richard Haddon for the place called the Green Lattice – £4 6s 8d.

Item paid to the suffragan – 15d.

Item at the receiving of the basin which Isabel Tempyll gave to the church, we paid for a quart of wine which we gave on to Jay, and to the Prior of Bath man to be well willing unto us – 2d.

Sum – £6 1s 10d.

These have been the costs of your lights that burn before the Rood and in the church beneath

Item paid to John Mayowe, waxmaker, for making your square light and for making your round lights against Easter, that is to say we paid for making 65 lb of your own wax – 2s 8 ½d.

Item paid to John waxmaker for 11 ½ lb of his own wax to part-form the aforesaid square light and round – 4s 9 ½d.

Item paid to the same John for making 1 paschal taper of his own wax, weighing in clean wax, ?without the tree, 18 ½ lb, thereof wasted 1 ½ lb. The making and the waste came to – 23d.

Item paid for making a font taper made of 4 lb of your own wax – 2d.

fo 3

Item paid for 1 lb of new wax that was made in 4 quarttrons which stand upon the angels about the sepulchre – 5d.

Item paid to John Mayowe for making your round light against All Hallows' tide, that is to say for making 22 ½ lb of your own wax – 11d.

Item paid for 3 ½ lb of new wax to part-form the same light – 17 ½d.

Sum le wax – 12s 4 ½d.

These have been the costs for holding the General Mind
Item paid for loaf bread, cakes and buns with other spices that went
thereto – 2s 1d.
Item paid for ale – 16d.
Item paid for wine – 2s 4d.
Item paid to 5 priests and to the clerk – 18d.
Item paid for ringing the bells – 16d.
Sum – 8s 7d.

These have been costs done in reparations that belong to the church
In primis paid to Harry Plommer for soldering 6 *skarys* in the church
gutters in Easter week – 12d.
Item paid to the same Plommer for 8 lb of solder – 2s.
Item in the week of Ss Simon and Jude we paid to Robert Tiler and to his
man for tiling for 2 ½ days', that is to say Monday and Tuesday and
Wednesday half day, taking a day 6 ½d, that came to – 2s 8d, upon the
church and upon the steeple.

fo 3v.
Item paid to a labourer as for 2 ½ days' to serve the tilers and make their
mortar – 10d.
Item paid to Thomas Hall for 4 quarters of lime – 10d.
Item paid for a load of sand – 1d.
Item paid to a locker for making new wards and a new key for the lock
that stands upon the church door on the south side of the church – 12d.
Item paid for a board of elm to mend Thomas Tailor's mother's seat and
Janet Golde's seat – 3d.
Item paid for nails – ½d.
Item paid for mending Katherine Leynell's seat – 1d.
Item paid to Thomas Clerk for keeping our papers all this year and for
making this account – 12d.
Item paid to the glazier for mending your glass windows – 2s 4d.
Sum – 12s 1 ½d.

Sum total the payments – £7 14s 11d.

So accounted to be accounted and allowed to be allowed the said proctors,
all things clearly paid, at this present day of accounts they bring in clearly
to the *parysshons* – 34s 9d, and so they go clearly and freely out of their
offices.

[1464–65]

fo 1

The account of Clement Wilteshire and Howell aPrysse, proctors of the church of All Hallows', Bristol, from 20 March 4 Edward IV unto the 26 March in the year next ensuing, and so containing 1 whole year and 6 days.

These have been the receipts of your rents
In primis of Richard Haddon for 1 tenement called the Green Lattice – £5.
Item of the chantry of Everard Frenche for the place which Robert Coke dwelt in – 2s 6d.
Item of Thomas Poyntmakare for Our Lady Day quarter and for Midsummer quarter – 8s. Michaelmas and Christmas quarters of the same place – void.
Item of John Leynell for Our Lady Day quarter of the tenement next to the said place – 5s 10d. Midsummer, Michaelmas and Christmas quarters of the same place – void.
Item of Thomas Phillipps, barber, for rent assize for 2 $\frac{1}{2}$ years of the same place that he dwells in – 10s.
Item of John Sybly, baker, for rent assize of the same place that he dwells in – 12d.
Item of the master of the Tailors for rent assize by year of the place which John Alberton dwells in in Baldwin Street – 12s.
Item of William Canynges for rent assize of the place in which the stainer dwells in in St Peter's parish – 6d.
Item the place that sometime Nicholas Stok held in Marsh Street rent assize the whole year – void.
Item of Halleway's chantry by year – 6s 8d.
Sum – £7 6s 6d.

fo 1v

Receipts at Easter
In primis received of Good Friday at the Cross – 4s 1d.
Item received on Easter eve and on Easter day at the pax – 8s 6 $\frac{1}{2}$d
Sum – 12s 7 $\frac{1}{2}$d.

These have been the receipts of your seat money and of other casualties as shown
In primis received of Thomas Abynton for his seat – 8d.
Item received of Janet Barbur for her seat – 6d.
Item received of Janet Bennett for her seat – 6d.
Item received of Davy Ostelar for his wife's seat – 8d.
Item received of the said Davy for his own seat – 12d.

Item received of Nicholas Bakare, spicer, to the building of your place next to the church – 20d.
Item received of John Compton for a ?harness girdle – 5s.
Item received out of the church coffer in the presence of the vicar and William Boxe – 29s 9d.
Item received of Hugh Sadelar for James's pit – 5s.
Item received of William Lewis and for Clement's maid's pit – 6s 8d.
Item received of Alison Knyghte for her husband's pit – 6s 8d.
Item received of Hugh Hardwareman for Antony's pit – 6s 8d.
Item received of Nicholas Wyseby, butcher, for the best cross – 8d.
Item received of Watkyn Norton for the cross foot – 4d.
Item received of Thomas Cotton, tiler, for the timber that was burned of the place next to the chancel – 6s 8d.
Sum – £3 12s 3d.

fo 2
Other Casualties as shown
Item received of Richard Haddon and William Rowley – 31s 2d.
Item received of William Boxe and Hugh Sadlare – 40s 6d.
Item received of Thomas Golde and Thomas Taylore – 13s 8d.
Sum – £4 5s 4d.

Item be it had in mind that Clement Wilteshire and Howell aPryse, proctors of All Hallows', have received of the chantry of Thomas Halleway in part payment of the sum of money which the said chantry owes unto the said church of All Hallows', the which church book that is called the ledger makes mention of the said sum the which you must now abate thereof at this account, that is to say – 20s.
Sum – 20s.

Sum total the receipts – £16 16s 8 ½d.

Item, Sirs, this is the money the which we have allowed unto your tenants at the receiving of your rent and other casualties the which you must abate of the receipts aforesaid – 11d.
Sum – 11d.

fo 2v
These have been the payments which Clement Wilteshire and Howell aPryse, the proctors of the church of All Hallows', that they have paid as for the said church
In primis paid to Alison Monke for washing 2 surplices, a rochet, an alb, 5 altar cloths and 2 towels against Easter – 7 ½d.
Item paid to 2 men for keeping the sepulchre 2 nights – 8d.

Item paid for fire and for ale for those 2 keepers – 2d.

Item paid to the raker for carrying church dust away for the whole year – 8d.

Item paid for scouring all your candlesticks and bowls against Easter – 16d.

Item paid to the mother church at Worcester – 12d.

Item on Palm Sunday at the Passion paid for a quart of osey to the priests – 3d.

Item paid to the suffragan for bearing the banners in Rogation week and in Whitsun week – 4d.

Item paid to the suffragan for bearing the cross on Corpus Christi day – 4d.

Item paid for holding William Newbery's mind – 6s 1d.

Item paid for hanging up the Dance of Pauls and for taking down thereof and for folding up thereof at St James's tide and All Hallows' tide – 8d.

Item paid for holding the dinner on Corpus Christi day for the vicar and all his priests and clerks – 3s 6d.

Item paid to Alison Monke for washing 2 surplices and a rochet against All Hallows' tide – 5d.

Item paid for 2 lb of tallow candles which burned in the rood loft on Christmas day in the morning – 3d.

Item paid to the suffragan that he was behind in his year's wages – 2s 2d.

Item for a new rope to the salve bell – 5d.

Sum of this side – 18s 10 $\frac{1}{2}$d.

fo 3

Item paid to Richard Haddon for the place called the Green Lattice – £4 6s 8d.

Item paid to John Shoppe for 3 gallons of lamp oil which burned in the lamp before the rood altar – 3s.

Item paid for mending the lock and key of the rood loft door – 2d.

Item paid for a new hinge for the enterclose door before Our Lady and for the nails that went thereto and for setting on – 6d.

Item paid for nails to mend the *berys* with in the churchyard – $\frac{1}{2}$d.

Item paid for besoms to *streke* the church with – 1d.

Item to John Bedwelly for hanging up the fore bell – 3d.

Item paid to William Canynge, carpenter, for the new trussing of the said fore bell and for the iron gear that went thereto and for the making a new wheel to the same bell of his own sense – 5s 3d.

Item paid for paper to write this account on of all this year – 1d.

Item paid for keeping our paper all this year and for making this account – 20d.

Sum – £4 17s 8 $\frac{1}{2}$d.

These have been the costs of your lights burning before the rood and in the church beneath

In primis paid to John Mayowe, waxmaker, for making your square light and your round light against Easter, for making 51 lb of your own wax – 2s 1 ½d.

Item paid to the said John for 34 lb of his own wax to part-form your foresaid square light and round light and your font taper – 14s 2d.

Item to John Meyowe for 1 paschal weighing in clean wax 19 lb, thereof wasted 1 ½ lb. The making and the waste come to – 2s 1d.

fo 3v

Item paid to John waxmaker for making your round lights against All Hallows' tide, that is for 19 ½ lb of your own wax – 9 ½d.

Item paid to the said John for 6 ½ lb of new wax of his own to part-form the said round light – 3s 3d.

Sum le wax – 22s 5d.

These have been the costs of holding the General Mind

Item for loaf bread, cakes and buns with the other spices that went thereto – 2s 5 ½d.

Item paid for ale – 13d.

Item paid for red wine, 3 gallons and 1 pottle – 18d.

Item paid for 4 gallons of osey – 3s.

Item paid to 4 priests and to the clerk – 16d.

Item paid for ringing the bells – 16d.

Sum – 10s 8 ½d.

Memorandum that these have been the costs and payments which we have paid for the two places of yours in Corn Street next to the chancel

In primis on Whitsun Monday at night, when the event of the fire fell, we paid to Richard Haddon for wine that the men drank which laboured about the fire – 22d.

Item paid to Amice Andrew and to Janet Howell for ale and beer which men drank that laboured about the fire – 4d.

fo 4

Item on Tuesday in the morning we paid to 4 men for the *rydynge* [?ridding] away the timber that lay abroad in the street and for taking up our lead that lay among the rubble – 8d.

Item paid to 3 labourers for cleaning the said places and for bearing the rubble out into the street – 8d.

Item paid to a haulier for hauling the rubble away that lay in the street before the *meyre* shop – 2s 4d.

Item on Friday the 8th day of June, Richard Haddon and Thomas

Carpenter and Nicholas Baker and others more went to Pensforde to chose 20 oaks, wherefore we paid to Thomas Carpenter for his labour – 6d.

Item the same day and time, paid for wine and ale – 13d.

Item upon Monday the morning next upon Midsummer's day, Thomas Carpenter and we rode to Pensford to mark out the timber, the which costs come to – 17 $\frac{1}{2}$d.

Item paid for riding to Pensford to make Cok bring home the timber – 4d.

Item paid to a haulier for hauling 9 pieces of timber from Temple Gate unto All Hallows' church – 18d.

Item paid to Robert Tiler for tiling the east side of the cope of the roof and for all manner of stuff that went thereto of the place next to John Leynell, the which he late held – 2s.

Item for 950 laths – 4s 7d.

Item paid to Ball carpenter and to Steven carpenter in part payment of £6 for building your place – £4.

Item paid to a mason for taking down the chimney and for breaking the wall and the wall *platts* – 8d.

Item paid to Ball, laying the first piece of timber of the house – 1d.

Item paid to a labourer for ridding away with the stones and the rubble, and for bearing out thereof – 3d.

Sum of this side – £4 18s 3 $\frac{1}{2}$d.

fo 4v.

Item paid to Thomas Phillipps for 6 welsh boards for the gutters – 6d.

Item paid to a smith for making 2 crampets of iron for the gutters and for the nails that went thereto – 6d.

Item paid to a man of the forest for 4000 lath nails – 4s 2d.

Item paid to Thomas Weskote for 12 *borddyns* of moyse – 12d.

Item paid to Harry Plomer on the Backe for casting 5 $\frac{1}{2}$ cwt and 14 lb of your own lead for the gutters – 7s 6d.

Item paid to the same Harry Plomer for 2 lb of solder – 6d.

Item paid to the same Harry Plomer for soldering 1 *skare* – 2d.

Item paid to Roger Plomer for casting 1 cloth of your own lead weighing 1 $\frac{3}{4}$ cwt and 14lb for the said gutters – 2s 6d.

Item paid to a haulier for hauling the same lead to the plumber's and home again – 2 $\frac{1}{2}$d.

Item paid to Robert Dasschel for 5000 tile stones at 6s the thousand, which comes to – 30s.

Item paid to 1 mason for breaking down the walls and for laying the gutter – 3d.

Item paid to Kyddale for 6 loads of sand – 6d.

Item paid to Thomas Cotton, tiler, for 5000 tile pins – 12 $\frac{1}{2}$d.

Item paid to Thomas Phillipps for hatch nails and tack nails for the said tiler – 3d.

Item to Clement Wilteshire for 3 dozen and 2 crests – 19d.
Item paid to Mors Thomas, Hall's man, for 9 quarters of lime – 22 ½d.
Item paid to William Mason on Redcliffe Hill for making the 2 chimneys and the *pynyon* wall a baste [?behind] and for setting in a new window in the same wall, taking for his hand task work – 5s.

fo 5
Item paid to Thomas Cotton, tiler, for tiling your foresaid 2 places, task work taking for his handiwork – 17s 8d.
Item on Thursday in the second week of Lent paid to Rawlyn, tiler, for making clean these 2 places and the gutters about and for bearing out all the rubble – 8d.
Sum – £3 15s 10 ½d.

Sum total the payments – £16 4s 9 ½d.

So accounted to be accounted and allowed to be allowed the said proctors, all things clearly paid at this present day of their accounts, they bring in clearly on to the *parysschons* – 11s 11d, and so they have gone clearly and freely out of their offices.

[1465–66]

fo 1
The accounts of William Box and John Schopp, proctors of the church of All Hallows', Bristol, from 26 March 5 Edward IV until 27 March in the year next following, so containing a whole year.

These have been the receipts of your rents
In primis of Richard Haddon for 1 tenement called the Green Lattice – £5.
Item of the chantry of Everard [Frensch] for the place that John Barnfeld dwells in – 2s 6d.
Item of Thomas Denne for Michaelmas quarter and for Christmas quarter – 10s. Our Lady Day quarter and Midsummer quarter the same place – void.
Item of John Denne for Christmas quarter – 3s 4d. Our Lady Day quarter, Midsummer quarter and Michaelmas quarter standing void.
Item of Thomas Phillipps, barber, rent assize for the whole year – 4s.
Item of the master of Tailors rent assize for the whole year of the place that John Alberton dwells in in Baldwin Street – 12s.
Item of William Canynges rent assize for the whole year of the place that the stainer dwells in in St Peter's parish – 6d.

Item of John Syble, baker, rent assize of the same place that he dwells in in Lewins Mead for the whole year – 12d.

Item the place that sometime Nicholas Stok dwelt in in Marsh Street, the whole year – void

Item of the chantry of Thomas Halleway for the whole year – 6s 8d.

Sum – £7.

fo 1v

These have been the receipts of Easter and of other casualties as shown

In primis received on Sheer Thursday and on Good Friday and on Easter eve and on Easter day on the pax – 14s 2d.

Item when we came in first we received of the church's money the which Howell aPryse and Clement Wilteshire brought in at their account making – 11s 11d.

Item received of John Nancoddan for the soul of his wife to be prayed for – 3s 4d.

Item received of Master Thomas Reyns for his mother's pit – 6s 8d.

Item received of the harpmaker for his seat and his wife's seat – 8d.

Item received of Isabel of the almshouse for her seat – 4d.

Item received of Thomas Denne for his seat and his wife's [seat] – 12d.

Item received of Katherine Hardware for her seat – 4d.

Item received of John Myllan for 1 seat for him and his wife – 8d.

Item received of John Aleyn for 1 seat for him and his wife – 12d.

Item received of Isabel Payne for her seat – 4d.

Item received of the chantry of Thomas Halleway in part payment of the sum of money which the said chantry owed unto the said church of All Hallows' – £4 4s 5 $\frac{1}{2}$d.

Sum – £6 4s 10 $\frac{1}{2}$d.

Sum total receipts – £13 4s 10 $\frac{1}{2}$d.

Item, Sirs, this is the money which we have allowed unto your tenants at the receiving of your rents and other casualties, the which you must abate of the receipts aforesaid, that is to say – 11d.

Sum – 11d.

fo 2

These have been the payments which William Box and John Schopp, the proctors of the church of All Hallows', have paid for the said church

In primis paid to Janet Colman for washing 2 albs, 2 surplices, 1 rochet, 7 altar cloths and 2 towels against Easter – 10d.

Item paid to 2 men for keeping the sepulchre 2 nights – 8d.

Item paid for fire and for ale for the 2 keepers – 2d.

Item paid for scouring your candlesticks and bowls against Easter – 16d.

Item paid to the mother church – 12d.

Item paid to the raker for carrying away the church dust for a whole year – 8d.

Item paid to the suffragan for bearing banners in Rogation week – 4d.

Item paid to the suffragan for bearing the cross on Corpus Christi day – 4d.

Item paid for holding the dinners on Corpus Christi day for the vicar and for all his priests and clerks – 3s 6d.

Item paid for holding William Newbery's mind – 6s 1d.

Item paid for hanging up the Dance of Pauls and for taking down thereof and for folding up thereof at St James's tide and at All Hallows' tide – 8d.

Item paid to Janet Colman for washing 2 surplices and 1 rochet against All Hallows' tide – 4 $\frac{1}{2}$d.

Item paid for 2 lb of tallow candles which burned in the rood loft on Christmas day in the morning – 2d.

Item paid for besoms to *streke* the church with and for a pannier to bear out the dust in – 2d.

fo 2v

Item paid to John Schoppe for 2 gallons and 1 quart of lamp oil which burned in the lamps before the rood altar – 2s 3d.

Item paid to Richard Haddon for the place called the Green Lattice – £4 6s 8d.

Item paid for paper to write our account on – 1d.

Item paid for making this account – 20d.

Item paid to the suffragan that he was behind of his year's wages – 2s 8d.

Sum – £5 9s 7 $\frac{1}{2}$d.

Item sirs, these have been the costs of your lights which burn before the rood and in the church beneath

Item paid to John Mayowe, waxmaker, for making your square light and your round light against Easter, that is to say for making 65 $\frac{3}{4}$ lb of your own wax – 2s 8 $\frac{1}{2}$d.

Item paid to the said waxmaker for 17 lb of his own wax to part-form your foresaid square light and round and your font taper – 9s 2 $\frac{1}{2}$d.

Item paid to John waxmaker for 1 paschal taper weighing in clean wax 21 lb, thereof wasted in making 1 $\frac{1}{2}$ lb. The making and waste come to – 2s 4d.

fo 3

Item paid to John waxmaker for making your round light against All Hallows' tide, that is to say for making 16 lb of your own wax – 8d.

Item paid to the said waxmaker for 10 lb of new wax to part-form the said round light – 5s.

Item paid to the said waxmaker for making a 2 lb taper – 1d.
Sum – 20s.

Item sirs, these have been the costs of holding the General Mind
Item paid for loaf bread, cakes and buns with other spices that went
thereto – 21 $\frac{1}{2}$d.
Item paid for 15 gallons of ale, with the bearing – 16d.
Item paid for 2 gallons and 1 pottle of red wine – 20d.
Item paid for 2 gallons and a pottle of osey – 20d.
Item paid for 5 priests and the clerk – 18d.
Item paid for ringing the bells – 16d.
Sum – 9s 3 $\frac{1}{2}$d.

fo 3v
These are the costs and payments of repairs done in your 2 places in Corn
Street next to the chancel
In primis on Saturday in Easter week to Thomas Carpenter for 2 planks of
elm the which the *bulke* is made of *a forstrett* [?ie facing the street] – 16d.
Item on the same Saturday paid to the same Thomas Carpenter for timber
to the said *bulke* – 5d.
Item paid for calf foot nail to the said *bulke* – 1 $\frac{1}{2}$d.
Item paid to a haulier for hauling the said planks and timber from St
James's to the said place in Corn Street – 1d.
Item paid to Thomas Carpenter for the handiwork of a man of his working
1 $\frac{1}{2}$ days to make the said *bulke* – 9d.
Item paid to John Plasterer on Saturday 11th May for making the water
table by the steeple side and the gutter, taking for his plaster and
handiwork – 17d.
Item paid for nails to the said gutter – 1d.
Item on the foresaid Saturday paid to 2 labourers for cleaning out the
gutter and for closing it up again – 4d.
Item for lime stones for the same gutter – $\frac{1}{2}$d.
Item paid to 1 carpenter for turning the stairs in the kitchen, taking for 4 $\frac{1}{2}$
days' work at 6 $\frac{1}{2}$d a day – 2s 5d.
Item paid for boards to make the stairs with – 6d.
Item paid for calf foot nail, for board nail and hache nail – 7d.
Item paid for 1 labourer for 6 days' labour at 4d the day – 2s.
Item paid to 1 mason for 2 $\frac{1}{2}$ days' – 16d.
Item paid for 2 quarters of lime – 5d.
Item paid for salt to the chimney – 2d.
Sum – 12s.

fo 4

Item paid to 1 mason for flooring and paving the kitchen, taking for 4 ½ days' – 2s 5d.

Item paid to 1 mason for 1 ½ days' work – 9d.

Item paid to 1 labourer for 3 ½ days' – 15 ½d.

Item paid to Harry Mors sawyer for 1 plank for 1 ?bench – 6d.

Item paid to Kydall for 6 loads of clay and 2 loads of sand – 14d.

Item paid to William Went haulier for hauling away rubble out of Thomas a Denne's house – 8d.

Item paid to 1 labourer for 1 day's labour – 4d.

Item paid for board nail, hatch nail and tack nail – 6d.

Item paid for 1 lattice – 6d.

Item paid for boards for the windows – 4d.

Item paid for 1 rope for the stair – 2d.

Item paid to William Went for hauling 7 pieces of timber from Temple Gate to the carpenter – 14d.

Item paid to Steven Carpenter and William Ball the which they were behind paying their bargain as for 2 places next to the chancel – 40s.

Item paid to Steven Carpenter for making 1 *partsom* and 1 stair in to the Cok loft taking for his handiwork and for the stuff that went thereto – 4s.

Item paid for 6 foot of freestone for the chimneys – 9d.

Item paid for 1 wagon load of paving stones – 22d.

Item paid for boards to John a Dene's house – 5s 5d.

Item paid to Harry Sawyer for planks, *bacys*, timber and *stapps* – 8s 2d.

Item paid for calf foot nail, board nail, hatch nail and tack nail – 2s 4d.

fo 4v

Item paid for 28 lb of iron gear, that is to say for twists, hooks and spikes at 1 ¼d the pound, sum – 2s 11d.

Item paid to 2 carpenters for their handiwork of 12 days in John a Dene's house – 13s.

Item paid for 12 days' work for 1 man of theirs – 2s.

Item paid to 1 labourer for bearing out rubble into the street – 6d.

Item paid to William Went for hauling away the same rubble – 8d.

Item paid to John Plasterer for plastering both places, task work, taking there for – 20s.

Sum – £5 11s 4 ½d.

Sum total the payments – £13 3s 2 ½d.

So accounted to be accounted and allowed to be allowed the said proctors all things clearly paid at this present day of their accounts they bring in clearly to the *parysschons* – 20d. And so they have gone clearly and freely out of their offices.

[1466–67]

fo 1

The accounts of William Jenkins and Thomas Phyllyps, proctors of the church of All Hallows', Bristol, from the 27th day of March in the 6th year of the reign of King Edward IV unto the 28th day of March in the year next ensuing, so containing a whole year.

These have been the receipts of your rents
In primis of John Compton for a tenement called the Green Lattice – £5 6s 8d.
Item of the chantry of Everard Frensche for the place that John Barnfelde dwells in – 2s 6d.
Item of Thomas Denne for the whole year – 20s.
Item of Margery Mony received for 11 weeks of the Michaelmas quarter and for Christmas quarter – 6s 4d. Our Lady Day quarter and Midsummer quarter and 1 fortnight of Michaelmas quarter – void.
Item of Thomas Phyllypps rent assize for whole year – 4s.
Item of the master of Tailors for rent assize for the whole year of the place which John Alberton dwells in in Baldwin Street – 12s.
Item of William Canynges rent assize for the whole year of the place that the stainer dwells in in St Peter's parish – 6d.
Item of John Syble, baker, rent assize of the same that he dwells in in Lewins Mead for the whole year – 12d.
Item the place that sometime Nicholas Stok dwelt in in Marsh Street, the whole year standing void and nought paid.
Item of the chantry of Thomas Halleway for the whole year – 6s 8d.
Sum – £7 19s 8d.

fo 1v

These have been the receipts of Easter and of other casualties as shown
In primis received on Sheer Thursday, on Easter eve and on Easter day on the pax – 12s 3 ½d.
Item we received of Katherine Hardware for the *warthrop*, that is to say for Michaelmas quarter and for Christmas quarter – 20d.
Item received of Margery Mony for her seat – 7d.
Item received of Janet Roberd for her seat – 8d.
Item received of Janet Bennet for the best cross – 4d.
Item received of Henry Chestre for the great candlestick to St Werburgh's – 4d.
Item received of the vicar of All Hallows' for Alison Knight's burial – 6s 8d.
Item received of Janet Howell for her husband's burial – 6s 8d.
Item received for a basin that we sold, the which Isabell Tempyll gave to

the church – 4s.

Sum – 33s 2 ½d.

Sum total of receipts – £9 12s 10 ½d.

Also Sirs, this is the money which we have allowed unto your tenants at the receipt of your rents and other casualties, the which you must abate of the receipts aforesaid – 19d.

Sum – 19d.

fo 2

These have been the payments which we the foresaid proctors have paid as for the said church of All Hallows' in this foresaid year.

In primis paid to Anneys Monk for washing the surplices and altar cloths against Easter and All Hallows' tide – 8d.

Item paid to 2 men for keeping the sepulchre 2 nights – 8d.

Item paid for fire and for ale to the 2 keepers of the sepulchre – 2d.

Item paid for scouring your candlesticks and bowls against Easter – 16d.

Item paid to the mother church at Worcester – 12d.

Item paid to the raker for hauling away church dust for all the year – 8d.

Item paid to the suffragan for bearing the banners in Rogation week – 4d.

Item paid to the suffragan for bearing the cross on Corpus Christi day – 4d.

Item paid for holding the dinners on Corpus Christi day for the vicar and for all his priests and clerks – 2s 2 ½d.

Item paid for holding William Newbery's mind – 6s 1d.

Item paid for 2 lb of tallow candles which burned in the rood loft on Christmas day in the morning – 2d.

Item paid for besoms and for pack thread at All Hallows' tide – 1d.

Item paid to the suffragan that he was behind in his year's wages – 3s.

Item paid for mending the vestments – 8d.

[Scored: Item paid for 2 new torches – 10s 2d.]

[Scored: Item paid for changing a torch – 2d.]

Item paid for mending the best cross – 11d.

Item paid for a new lock to the church door with a new key – 4s.

Item paid for a ring to the same church door – 16d.

Item paid for mending the glass windows in the church – 6s 8d.

Item paid for hauling rubble out of the churchyard – 3d.

Item paid for the mending in Thomas Denne's seat – 2d.

fo 2v

Item paid for mending the fire pan – 3d.

Item paid for mending the paring iron of the church – 2d.

Item paid for a new lock which lies upon your treasure coffer in the treasure house – 7d.

Item paid for wine which was drunk in the rood loft on Palm Sunday – 2d.

Item paid for 1 pottle of wine at Haddon's when Mawsell did oversee the church evidence – 4d.

Item paid for parchment for the rent roll – 1d.

Item paid for cleaning the church gutters – 2d.

Item paid for 3 pieces of freestone, the which are called *pressescion* [procession] stones, which are set in the street for every man to know how far you ought to keep your *pressescion* way between parish and parish – 12d.

Item paid for 1 $\frac{1}{4}$ gallons of lamp oil which burns in the lamp before the rood altar – 15d.

Item paid to Steven Hiswife that was your suffragan that he was behind in payment of his wages for this year – 18d.

Item paid for writing these accounts – 14d.

Sum – 37s 4 $\frac{1}{2}$d.

fo 3

Item, Sirs, these have been the costs of your lights which burn before the rood and in the church beneath

In primis paid to John Mayowe, waxmaker, for making your square light and round light against Easter, that is to say for making 54 lb of your own wax – 2s 3d.

Item paid to the aforesaid John waxmaker for 22 $\frac{1}{2}$ lb of his own wax to part-form your foresaid square light and round light and your font taper – 11s 3d.

Item paid to the said waxmaker for your paschal taper weighing 21 $\frac{1}{2}$ lb in clean wax, of which 1 $\frac{1}{2}$ lb is waste. The making and the waste come to – 2s 5d.

Item paid to John waxmaker for making your round light against All Hallows' tide, that is to say for making 22 lb of your own wax – 11d.

Item paid to John waxmaker for 2 new torches weighing 43 lb – 10s 9d.

Item paid for the change of a broken torch – 2d.

Item paid for an old end of 1 torch weighing 4 $\frac{3}{4}$ lb the which Sir John of London sings withal – 12d.

Sum – 28s 9d.

fo 3v

These have been the costs for holding the General Mind

In primis paid for loaf bread, cakes and buns with other spices that went thereto – 2s 2d.

Item paid for 1 dozen of ale, with the bearing – 13d.

Item paid for 2 gallons and 1 pottle of red wine – 20d.

Item paid for 2 gallons of white wine, osey – 18d.

Item paid to five priests and to the clerk – 18d.
Item paid for the ringing – 16d.
Sum – 9s 3d.

Item, Sirs, these have been the costs and payments of reparations done upon your Beer house and upon your churchyard gates
In primis paid for boards and legs for the door and the windows – 22d.
Item paid to a smith for making twists and hooks that belong thereto – 12d.
Item paid for a lock to the door – 4d.
Item paid for the workmanship of the said door and windows – 18d.
Item paid for the 2 new gates for your churchyard, that is to say for boards, timber, nails and twists and for the workman hand of the said gates – 4s 7d.
Item paid for casting the lead for the said gates and for the lead that lies in the holy water stone at the church door and for lead nails – 4s 4d.
Item paid for mending the pipe in the churchyard by the church wall, paid for a cramp of iron and for solder and workman hand – 7d.

fo 4
Item paid for the spikes of iron and for 2 cramps of iron, which are set on the churchyard gates and upon the churchyard walls – 17d.
Item paid for 1 piece of freestone that is set upon the churchyard wall – 7d.
Item paid for lime and sand for the churchyard walls and to mend faults about the church – 12d.
Item paid to a mason for 3 days' work – 19 ½d.
Item paid for a new lock for one of the churchyard gates – 4d.
Item paid for nails and for lime stones – 2d.
Sum – 19s 3 ½d.

Also these have been the reparations done in Thomas a Denne's house next to the church in Corn Street
Item paid for timber and boards and for 1 new door and for a stair and for nails and twists for the said door and for the hand work thereof – 7s 6d.
Item paid to a plasterer for mending divers faults in the said place – 4d.
Item paid for a new lattice to the same house – 10d.
Item paid for a new lock – 4d.
Item paid for a bolt of iron to a door in the said house – 3d.
Item paid to Harry Plomer for lead which was laid in Thomas Denne's house, payment for which was behind last year, that is to say – 5s.
Sum – 14s 3d.

fo 4v

Also these have been the reparations done in the silk woman's house next to Thomas Denne

Item paid for 2 planks for a bench – 8d.

Item paid for boards – 8d.

Item paid for nails – 5d.

Item paid for a board for a window – 1d.

Item paid for a lattice to a window in the hall – 8d.

Item paid to a carpenter for 2 days' work – 11d.

Item paid to a woman to clean the house – 1d.

Item paid for 3 new locks – 12d.

Item paid for a board to a *wardrop* – 2d.

Item paid for a ladder and a water board – 5d.

Item paid for the mending of a lock to the ?over door – 2d.

Item paid for tile stones to tile the pentys [lean-to] with *a forestreet* – 3s 8d.

Item paid for *evys* board – 7d.

Item paid for nails – 1d.

Item paid for lime and sand – 3 $\frac{1}{2}$d.

Item paid for tile pins – 1 $\frac{1}{2}$d.

Item paid for closing up between Thomas Denne's house and the said place – 8d.

Item paid for 1 lattice for the chamber window – 7d.

Item paid for mending the lock upon the cellar door – 3d.

Item paid for nails for a little *partson* in the shop – 3d.

Sum – 11s 9d.

fo 5

Also these have been the costs of reparations done in John Compton's place called the Green Lattice

Item paid for a load of paving stones to pave the parlour with – 2s 2d.

Item paid to a mason for 2 days' work – 13d.

Item paid for 2 quarters of lime – 5d.

Item paid for 2 loads of sand – 2d.

Item paid to a labourer – 4 $\frac{1}{2}$d.

Sum – 4s 2 $\frac{1}{2}$d.

Sum total the payments £6 6s 5 $\frac{1}{2}$d.

So accounted to be accounted and allowed to be allowed, the said proctors all things clearly paid at this present day of their accounts, they bring in clearly unto the *parysschons* – £3 6s 5d. And so they go clearly and freely out of their offices.

[1467–68]

fo 1

The accounts of William Rowley and John Compton, proctors for the church of All Hallows', from the 20th day of March in the 7th year of the reign of King Edward IV unto the 27th day of March next ensuing, so containing a whole year.

These are the receipts of your rents and the receipts of Easter and of other casualties

In primis we received on Palm Sunday, Good Friday and Easter day – 15s 10d.

Item for rent of a tenement that John Compton dwells in – £5 6s 8d.

Item for a year's rent for a seat of Katherine Hardware woman – 3s 4d.

Item for a year's rent of the school mistress – 13s 4d.

Item for three quarters' rent of Thomas a Dene – 15s.

Item received of Giles Hardware man and his wife for a seat – 16d.

Item of the master of the Tailors – 12s.

Item of Thomas Walshe's wife – 8d.

Item of Walter Trevet and his wife for their seats – 2s.

Item of Thomas Nores for a seat – 8d.

Item of Richard Aleyn and for his wife – 16d.

Item received of Halleway's chantry – 6s 8d.

Item of Sir Mylis of the chantry of Everard Frensche for John Barnefeld's baste door – 2s 6d.

Item of Thomas Barbor, otherwise called Thomas Phillips, for rent of assize – 4s.

Item William Canynges for rent of assize of the place that the stainer dwells in in St Peter's parish – 6d.

fo 1v

Item of John Sible, baker, rent assize of the same house that he dwells in in Lewins Mead, for the whole year – 12d.

Item the place that some time Nicholas Stock dwelt in in Marsh Street, the whole year stands void and not paid.

Item received for a *forset* that was left in the house that was burned – 8s.

Sum amount of the receipts of the church amounts to – £9 14s 10d.

These are the payments following that we the aforesaid proctors have paid the year before written

In primis for wine on Palm Sunday – 2 ½d.

Item for keeping the sepulchre – 8d.

Item for John Brown's labour to scour the candlesticks – 12d.

Item to the mother church – 12d.

Item for washing the altar cloths – 12d.

Item for John Brown's service for 1 quarter – 20d.

Item for besoms and a pannier to bear out dust – 2 ½d.

Item for carrying the dust to the raker – 8d.

Item for holding Newbery's mind, the 10th of May – 6s.

Item to the waxmaker for making old wax – 15s 3d.

Item for making the round tapers and renewing of them – 4s 4d.

Item for bearing the cross [at] Rogation tide and the Corpus day Christi [sic] – 8d.

fo 2

Item for a breakfast to the vicar and to the priests on Corpus day Christi – 2s 6d.

Item for making of a *partesome* in the school mistress's house in the shop – 2s 1 ½d.

Item for a window in my pavement – 14d.

Item for 2 little bells and for hanging them – 3s.

Item for washing 2 surplices – 4d.

Item for hanging and taking down the Dance of Pauls – 8d.

Item for proving and sealing Agnes Fyler's testament – 10s.

Item for a proctor in the *ppnall* law – 20d.

Item for entering a plaint against Thomas Fyler – 8d.

Item for costs of the court of *pypowdrs* – 4s 2d.

Item for entering the declaration – 12d.

Item for a supper to Mawnsell and Harry Weston – 10d.

Item in wine at 3 times to Mawnsell and Harry Weston – 12d.

Item to Harry Weston to be of our counsel – 3s 4d.

Item to Mawnsell to be of our counsel – 8s 4d.

Item for withdrawing and continuing of the court against Thomas Fyler – 6d.

Item for entering and sealing Agnes Fyler's testament to the mayor, town clerk and sergeants – 11s.

Item for besoms and pack-thread – 1d.

Item for mending a lock to the church door – 2d.

Item for soldering a gutter between Thomas Chestre and the house that John Compton dwells in – 5 ½d.

Item for making a chimney and a seat in the tenement that John Compton dwells in – 28s 3d.

Item for 9 ½ ells of Holland cloth for a surplice, at 8d the ell – 6s 4d.

Item for making of the surplice – 2s.

fo 2v
Item for washing the surplice – 2d.
Item for breaking a gutter in the pavement that Compton holds – 7d.
Item for mending the window in *Jhc is yelde* [?Jesus Guild] – 6d.
Item for 5 ells of cloth for an alb and an amice to Agnes Fyler's vestment
– 3s 6d.
Item for making the alb and the amice – 8d.
Item for washing the alb and setting on the *parell* – 2d.
Item to *core* for writing the indenture between the church and Thomas
Fyler – 8s 4d.
Item for paper and writing of this reckoning – 12d.
Sum of the costs before written amounts to – £6 17s 2d.

The allowance that we have allowed towards the tenants of the church
amounts to – 9d.
Item for 1 quart of lamp oil to the church – 3d.
Sum – 12d.

fo 3
The costs of the General Mind for all the good doers amounts to in all –
13s 8d.

Sum total of all the costs in general that belong to the church amounts to –
£7 11s 10d.
Rests clear to the church – 43s.

These are the debts that are owing to the church
Item Thomas a Denne for a quarter part of the last year – 5s.

Item received of Davy Hosteler for his wife's seat – 12d.
Rests to the church – 44s.

Item received of Thomas Barbor for burying his wife – 6s 6d.
Rests to the church – 50s 6d.

[1468–69]

fo 1
The accounts of Martin Symonson and John Barnfelde, proctors of the
church of All Hallows', from the 27th day of March in the 8th year of the
reign of King Edward the IV unto the 27th day of March in the year next
following, so containing a whole year.

These have been the receipts of your livelode

In primis of John Compton for 1 tenement called the Green Lattice –
£5 6s 8d.

Item of the chantry of Everard Frenche for the place that John Barnfeld
dwells in – 2s 6d.

Item of Thomas Denne per annum – 20s.

Item of Marjory Money, the silk woman, per annum – 13s 4d.

Item of Katherine Hardware for 1 *wartheroppe* per annum – 3s 4d.

Item of Thomas Phillipps, barber, rent assize for the place that he dwells
in, per annum – 4s.

Item of John Syble, baker, in Lewins Mead rent assize for the place that he
dwells in, per annum – 12d.

Item of the master of the Tailors rent assize for the place that John
Alberton dwells in in Baldwin Street, per annum – 12s.

Item of William Canynges rent assize for the place in St Peter's parish, the
which John Stainer dwells in – 6d.

Item of John Sheparde the elder rent assize for the place in Marsh Street,
the which sometime Nicholas Stock dwelt in, per annum – 2s.

Item of the chantry of Thomas Halleway, per annum – 6s 8d.

Sum total of this rental – £8 12s.

fo 1v

These have been the receipts of Easter and of other casualties, as shown
after

In primis received at Easter on the pax – 8s 10d.

Item received of John Pynner for his seats – 2s 8d.

Item received of John Chestre for his seats – 16d.

Item received of Alison Chestre for her husband's burial – 6s 8d.

Item received for Margaret Abyngton's burial – 6s 8d.

Item received of an hardwareman for his standing under the church wall –
4d.

Sum – 26s 6d.

Sum total receipts – £9 18s 6d.

Allowance

Also this is the money the which of courtesy is rewarded unto your tenants
at the receiving of your rents and of other casualties, the which you must
abate of your receipts afore said, that is to say – 20d.

Allowance

Item you must abate for the place in Marsh Street the which Jenkyn
Sheparde withholds from you the rent assize – 2s.

fo 2

Also these have been the payments which we the said proctors have paid for the church of All Hallows' in this foresaid year

Item against Easter paid for washing 2 surplices, a rochet, 7 altar cloths, 3 ing towels – 8d.

Item paid to 2 men for keeping the sepulchre 2 nights – 8d.

Item paid for bread, ale and fire for the said keepers – 4d.

Item paid for scouring your candlesticks and bowls against Easter – 16d.

Item paid for 1 quart of osey for the singers in the rood loft on Palm Sunday at the Passion – 2 ½d.

Item paid to the mother church of Worcester – 12d.

Item on St George's day paid to children for the bearing up the best copes at the procession through the town – 1d.

Item on Tuesday the 10th day of May paid for the holding of William Newbery's mind – 6s 1d.

Item paid for bearing the banners in Whitsun week – 4d.

Item paid for bearing the best cross on Corpus Christi day at the procession about the town – 4d.

Item paid for holding the dinner on Corpus Christi day, to the vicar and to all the priests and clerks – 3s.

Item paid for hallowing the vestment the which Agnes Fyler gave to the church – 2d.

Item paid to the suffragan that he was behind to paying of his year's wages – 2s 4d.

fo 2v

Item paid for hanging up the Dance of Pauls against St James's tide and against All Hallows' tide – 8d.

Item paid for 2 lb of tallow candles which burnt in the rood loft on Christmas Day in the morning – 2 ½d.

Item paid for washing 2 surplices and a ?rochet against Candlemas – 5d.

Item paid for besoms to *streke* the church with – 1d.

Item paid to the raker for carrying away the church dust for all the year – 8d.

Item paid for mending the middle lock that stands on the iron coffer in the treasure house – 2d.

Item paid for mending the seats *a lowe* in the church by the Kalendars' door – 2d.

Item paid for the parchment to make your rent roll – 1d.

Item paid for 3 boards for mending the little *bere* [?bier] – 3d.

Item paid for nails for mending the said *bere* – 1d.

Item paid for making the said *bere* – 2d.

Item post for the churchyard gate and for 1 piece of lead and for making and setting thereof and for lime that went to the wall – 14d.

Item on Tuesday in Whitsun week paid to Roger Kemes for seeing Fyler's evidence and for giving his counsel – 20d.

fo 3

Item on Wednesday the 19th day of October paid for a breakfast to Roger Kemes at the Green Lattice, for copying Fyler's testament and for seeing the deeds of Skadspyll – 17d.
Item paid for keeping our paper all this year and for making these accounts – 20d.
Sum – 25s 5d.

Also these have been the costs of your lights which burn before the rood and in the church beneath
In primis paid to John Mayowe, waxmaker, for making your square light and round light against Easter, that is to say for making 58 lb of your own wax – 2s 5d.
Item paid to the said waxmaker for 13 lb of his own wax to part-form your foresaid square and round light with your font taper – 7s 8d.
Item paid to John Mayowe for your paschal taper weighing in clean wax 17 $\frac{1}{4}$ lb, thereof wasted 2 $\frac{1}{4}$ lb. The making and the waste comes to – 2s 6 $\frac{1}{2}$d.

fo 3v

Item paid to John waxmaker for making your round light against All Hallows' tide, for 16 lb of your own wax, making – 8d.
Item paid to John waxmaker for 6 lb of new wax to part-form the said 11 tapers, after 2 lb every piece – 3s 6d.
Sum of your lights – 16s 8 $\frac{1}{2}$d.

Also these have been the costs for holding your General Mind on Ash Wednesday
In primis paid for loaf bread, cakes and buns with spices that went thereto – 2s 8d.
Item for ale – 18d.
Item paid for 4 gallons of sweet wine – 2s 8d.
Item paid for 3 pottles of red wine – 12d.
Item paid to 7 priests and to the clerk – 2s.
Item paid for ringing the bells – 16d.
Sum – 11s 2d.

Also these have been the costs of reparations done in Thomas Denne's house in the said year
In primis paid to a workman for the ceiling of the chamber, as for 3 days' work, taking for the day 6 $\frac{1}{2}$d, sum – 19 $\frac{1}{2}$d.

fo 4

Item paid for 200 laths for the said ceiling – 8d.

Item paid for lath nails – 9d.

Item paid for 3 quarters of lime – 7 ½d.

Item paid for hair – 1d.

Sum – 3s 9d.

Also these have been the costs of the gutter in the High Street going along by John Pynner's cellar

In primis paid to 1 mason for 5 days' work, taking for the day 6 ½d, sum – 2s 8 ½d.

Item paid to 1 labourer for 1 ½ days' work – 6 ½d.

Item paid for 3 quarters of lime – 7 ½d.

Item paid for 1 load of sand – 1d.

Item paid for 2 *fattys* [?vats] full of rubble to *hawns* [?enhance] the ground with – 2d.

Item paid for pendant stones for the bottom of the gutter and for *kevyrs* [?covers] – 10d.

Item paid for cleaning the ground and for hauling away rubble – 3d.

Sum – 5s 2d.

fo 4v

Also these have been the costs of reparations done in the place next to Thomas Denne, which Margery Money the silk woman dwells in

Item paid for 5 boards of elm for the flooring of the kitchen in the said place – 11 ½d.

Item paid for board nail – 1 ½d.

Item paid for 2 loads of clay for the said kitchen floor – 4d.

Item paid for 2 quarters of lime – 5d.

Item paid for 2 paving stones for paving the said floor – 4d.

Item paid to a mason for 1 ½ days' work, taking for the day 6 ½d – 9 ½d.

Sum – 2s 11 ½d.

Also these have been the costs and payments as for the stuff and the handiwork of your new seats in Our Lady's chapel *afore Ihc* [before the image of Jesus]

In primis paid for timber and boards – 13s 8 ½d.

Item on Saturday the 8th day of October paid to John Hyll, carpenter, for 6 days' work in the said week, taking for the day 6 ½, sum – 3s 3d.

fo 5

Item on the said Saturday paid to the said carpenter for 3 days' work by a man of his in the said week, taking for the day 2d, sum – 6d.

Item on Saturday the 15th day of October paid to John Hyll Carpenter for 5 days' work in the same week, taking for the day 6 ½d, sum – 2s 8 ½d.
Item paid to his man for the said 5 days' work – 10d.
Item on Saturday the 22nd of October paid to John Hyll carpenter for 5 days' work in the same week – 2s 8 ½d.
Item paid to his man for the said 5 days' work – 10d.
Item on Saturday the 22nd day of October paid to John Gryffythe, carpenter, for his handiwork of the said 5 days' work in the week of Saint Luke – 2s 8 ½d.
Item in the same foresaid week paid for 4 pieces of timber – 4d.
Item paid for 1 piece of timber – 6d.
Item paid for 1 other piece of timber – 8d.
Item paid for tallow candles to give light to the carpenters to work by on evenings and at mornings – 1d.
Item paid for glue – ½d.
Item on Saturday the 29th day of October paid to John Hyll, carpenter, for 4 ½ days' work in the same week – 2s 5d.

fo 5v
Item on the said Saturday paid to John Hyll, carpenter, for the said 4 ½ days' work of his man in the said week – 9d.
Item on Saturday the 29th day of October paid to John Gryffythe, carpenter, for the said 4 ½ days' work in the foresaid week – 2s 5d.
Item on Saturday the 5th day of November paid to John Hyll, carpenter, for 3 days' work in the same week – 18d.
Item on the said Saturday paid to John Hyll, carpenter, for the said 3 days' work of his man in the said week – 6d.
Item on Saturday the 5th day of November paid to John Gryffythe, carpenter, for the said 3 days' work in the foresaid week – 16d.
Item paid for 4 short pieces of timber – 4d.
Item on Saturday the 12th day of November paid to John Hyll, carpenter, for 6 days' work in the same week – 3s.
Item on the said Saturday paid to John Hyll for the said 6 days' work of his man in the said week – 12d.
Item on the said Saturday the 12th day of November paid to John Gryffythe, the carpenter, for 6 days' work in the said week – 2s 9d.
Item on Monday the 14th day of November paid for 1 piece of timber – 4d.
Item on Saturday the 19th day of November paid to John Hyll, carpenter, for 6 days' work in the same week – 3s.

fo 6
Item on the said Saturday paid to John Hyll, carpenter, for the said 6 days' work of his man – 12d.

Item on Saturday the 19th day of November paid to John Gryffythe, carpenter, for 6 days' work in the same week – 2s 9d.

Item on the said Saturday paid for 1 board of oak – 4d.

Item paid for hinges and for 2 locks and for *tynde* nails – 2s 11d.

Item paid for board nail and hatch nail – 3 ½d.

Item paid for tallow candles to give light to the carpenters on evenings and mornings – 1d.

Item paid for 3 clamps of iron which bind the seats to the church wall – 3d.

Item paid to 1 mason for the making of the *stap* before Ihc – 2d.

Sum – 56s.

Sum total the receipts – £9 18s 6d.

Sum total the costs and payments – £6 4s 10d.

Rests clear to the church and parishioners – £3 13s 8d.

So accounted to be accounted and allowed to be allowed the said proctors all things clearly paid at this present day of their accounts, they bring in clearly unto the *parysschons* – £3 13s 8d, and so they [have] gone clearly and freely out of their offices.

fo 6v
These are the debts that are owing
Thomas Denne owes for Christmas quarter – 5s.

[1472–1473]

fo 1
The Church Book anno 12 R Edwardi IV
Clement Wilteshire and John Chestre proctors

fo 1v
The accounts of Clement Wilteshire and John Chestre, proctors of the church of All Hallows', from the feast of the Annunciation of Our Lady in the 12th year of the reign of King Edward IV unto the said feast in the year next following after, so containing a whole year.

These have been the receipts of your rents that follow
Item Morgan Lewis, per annum – £5 6s 8d.
Item the chantry of Everard Frensche for John Barnfeld's baste door and for his water gutter – 2s 6d.

Item Thomas Denne, per annum – 20s.

Item Margery Manymoney, silkwoman, per annum – 13s 4d.

Item Katherine Hardware, per annum – 3s 4d.

Item Thomas Phillips, barber, rent assize for his place – 4s.

Item John Syble, baker, in Lewins Mead rent assize for his, per annum – 12d.

Item the master of the Tailors rent assize for the place that John Albyrton dwells in in Baldwin Street, per annum – 12s.

Item John Canynges rent assize for the place in Saint Peter's parish that John Steynour dwelt in, per annum – 6d.

Item John Scheperde the elder rent assize for the place in Marsh Street that some time Nicholas Stocke held, per annum – 2s.

Item the chantry of Thomas Halleway for the house in the churchyard, per annum – 6s 8d.

Sum total of this rental – £8 12s

[In different ink and hand: Item received of William Payntor for the beer house – 2s.
Sum – 2s.]

fo 2

Also these have been the receipts of Easter and other casualties, as follows

In primis on Sheer Thursday, on Easter eve and on Easter day, received on the pax – 17s 10d.

Item received of James Hardwareman for a seat – 8d.

Item received of the widow of Gloucester for a seat – 16d.

Item received of Anneys Palmer for a seat – 8d.

Item received of William Bowde for a seat – 12d.

Item received of John Martylment for a seat – 16d.

Sum – 22s 10d.

Item you shall understand that we received for your old organs – 53s 4d.

Item received of the *parysschyng*, and of other divers strangers, the sum of – £9 17s 7d.

Sum – £12 10s 11d.

Sum total of all the whole receipts – £22 7s 9d.

Allowance

Also we ask allowance for the place in Marsh Street, the which some time Nicholas Stocke held, the which John Sheparde withholds now from us wrongfully, sum – 2s.

Item we ask allowance for a rent assize for the place in St Peter's parish, the which Sir William Canynges wrongfully withholds from us, sum – 6d.

Sum – 2s 6d.

Allowance

Also these have been certain payments the which the said proctors have
paid for the said church in the said year, as rehearsed after
In primis on Palm Sunday paid for 1 pottle of osey for the priests and
clerks that sang the passion in the rood loft – 6d.
Item against Easter and All Hallows' tide paid for washing the church
surplices and altar cloths – 11d.
Item paid for keeping the sepulchre and the light for the night's watching –
8d.
Item paid for bread and ale and coals for the said keepers – 2d.

fo 2v

Item paid for scouring your candlesticks and bowls against Easter – 16d.
Item paid for cleaning the churchyard lane – 1d.
Item paid to the raker for carrying away the church dust – 8d.
Item paid to the suffragan that he was behind of his wages – 22d.
Item paid for hallowing 3 altar cloths – 4d.
Item paid to Isabel Wyn for marking 2 of the best altar cloths and the best
houselling towel with silk, the which my Mistress Chestre gave in – 4d.
Item paid for scouring the basin in the quire before the high altar – 8d.
Item paid for 1 rope that the said basin hangs withal – 4d.
Item paid 1 lamp for the same basin – 1d.
Item paid for hanging up the Dance of Pauls twice a year and for rolling
[it] up again – 8d.
Item paid for mending your best suit of vestments – 11d.
Item paid to the mother church of Worcester – 12d.
Item paid for 2 lb of tallow candles for the rood loft on Christmas day in
the morning – 2 ½d.
Item paid for 1 new key to the little vestry door at the rood altar end – 2d.
Item paid for bearing the banners in Rogation week – 4d.
Item paid for bearing the best cross on Corpus Christi day – 4d.
Item paid for dinner to the priests and to the clerks on Corpus Christi day
after the procession – 3s.
Item paid to the king's collectors for the church rents – 10s 4d.
Item paid for holding William Newbery's mind – 6s.
Item paid for 1 new rope to the salve bell – 5d.
Item paid for besoms to *streke* the church with – 1d.
Item paid for making the rent roll – 1d.
Sum – 31s 5 ½d.

fo 3

Also these have been the costs of your lights that burn before the rood and beneath in the church, as rehearsed after

Item at Easter paid to John Mayowe, waxmaker, for making 53 lb of your own wax that was of your square lights and your round lights – 2s 2 ½d.

Item paid to the said waxmaker for 22 lb of new wax to part-form your square lights and round lights and your font taper, at 10d the pound, sum – 18s 4d.

Item paid to John waxmaker for making the paschal taper of his own wax and for the waste – 2s 6d.

Item paid for making your round lights against All Hallows' tide and for new wax to part form the said lights, sum – 2s 8 ½d.

Item paid for 2 new torches for the high altar weighing 42 lb, at 3d the pound, sum – 10s 6d.

Sum the costs of your lights – 36s 3d.

These have been the costs for holding your General Mind on Ash Wednesday

Item paid for loaf bread, cakes and spices that went thereto – 3s 2d.

Item paid for 1 dozen ale – 12d.

Item paid for baking the foresaid cakes – 2d.

Item paid for red wine and sweet wine – 4s 4d.

Item paid to 6 priests and to the clerk – 22d.

Item paid for ringing the bells – 16d.

Sum the costs of the General Mind – 11s 10d.

fo 3v

Also these have been the costs done in repairs in the steeple, that is to say in trussing the bells and in mending the baldrics and in latticing the steeple windows, as is rehearsed after, *y wryte ev[er]y parssell*

In primis paid for 1 stock which is set upon the great bell – 2s 6d.

Item paid for hauling the said stock to the church – 1d.

Item paid for 2 new spindles of iron for the great bell – 16d.

Item paid for iron work to hang the great bell and the second bell with – 16d.

Item paid for mending the 2 baldrics of the 2 bells – 6d.

Item paid for the *hawkys* of the 2 bells – 4d.

Item paid for the 6 bundles of laths for the steeple windows – 2s.

Item paid for 500 tack nails for the said windows – 15d.

Item paid for 4 penny boards for the said windows – 4d.

Item paid to John Dawe, carpenter, and to his man, for hanging the said 2 bells and for closing in the steeple windows – 8s 6d.

Sum – 18s 2d.

Also these have been the costs of making your churchyard gates

In primis paid for 1 piece of timber to make the posts for the said gates –

2s.

Item paid for hauling the said piece of timber – 1d.

Item paid for 7 boards of oak for the said doors – 2s 2d.

Item paid for 2 quarters of lime and 1 load of sand – 5d.

Item paid to a mason for setting the 4 posts of the gates – 8d.

Item paid for the 2 pairs of iron hinges and 2 iron bolts for the said gates – 22d.

Item paid to Richard Rede, smith, for the iron work of the said gates – 16d.

Item paid for 100 door nails and 50 hatch nails – 8 ½d.

fo 4

Item paid to Richard Carpenter for making the 2 gates – 2s 2d.

Item paid to John Wythypoll for ?60 lb of lead – 3s 4d.

Sum of the costs of the churchyard gates – 14s 8 ½d.

Allowance

Item this is the money which of courtesy is rewarded unto your tenants when paying their rents, sum – 13d.

Item paid for making and writing this account – 20d.

Sum – 2s 9d.

Allowance

Also these have been the costs of your rood loft and the enterclose beneath, the which closes in the quire, as is rehearsed after

In primis paid to John Hill, carpenter, for making the rood loft that the organs stand upon, and for the enterclose underneath, taking for his timber and his *handework taskework*, sum – 53s 4d.

Item paid for 4 pairs of hinges that the quire doors hang with – 14d.

Item paid for board nail and lath nail for flooring the rood loft and for the *selyng* [ceiling] underneath – 6d.

Item paid for the iron work that the *dex* [desk] in the rood loft stands upon for the singers – 8d.

Sum the rood loft and the enterclose – 55s 8d.

fo 4v

Also these have been the costs of the new organs that stand in the rood loft

In primis paid to Thomas Wotton, organmaker, for your new organs – £13 6s 8d.

Item paid for the hire of the house that the said organs was made in – 5s.

Item paid to Watkyn Plomer for 120 lb of lead, which is the *peys* of the organs – 10s.

Sum cost of the said organs – £14 20d.

Sum total of all the whole expenses with the organs – £22 15s.
Rest clear to the proctors – 7s 3d.

[1473–74]

fo 1
The Church Book Anno 13 R Edwardi IV
Clement Wilteshire and John Chestre

fo 1v
The accounts of Clement Wilteshire and John Chestre, proctors of the
church of All Hallows', from the feast of the Annunciation of Our Lady in
the 13th year of the reign of King Edward IV unto the said feast in the
year next following after, so containing a whole year

These have been the receipts of your rents belonging to the church, as
follows
Item Morgan Lewys, per annum – £5 6s 8d.
Item the chantry of Everard Frensche for John Barnefelde's baste door and
for his water gutter – 2s 6d.
Item Thomas Denne, per annum – 20s.
Item Margery Money, per annum – 13s 4d.
Item Katherine Hardware, per annum – 3s 4d.
Item Thomas Phyllippes, per annum – 4s.
Item John Syble, baker, in Lewins Mead, rent assize for the place that
John Alberton dwells in in Baldwin Street, per annum – 12s.
Item John Canynges, rent assize, for the place in St Peter's parish that
John Stenore dwelt in, per annum – 6d.
Item John Scheparde the elder, rent assize, for the place in Marsh Street
that sometime Nicholas Stok held, per annum – 2s.
Item the chantry of Thomas Halleway for the house in the churchyard, per
annum – 6s 8d.
Sum total of this rental – £8 12s.

[In different ink and hand: Item received of William Payntore for the Beer
house – 2s.
Sum – 2s.]

fo 2
Also these have been the receipts of Easter and of other casualties, as
follows
In primis on Sheer Thursday, on Easter eve and on Easter day, received on

the pax – 16s 8d.
Item received of Matthew Cotyngton for his seat – 8d.
Item receievd of Robert Kachmay for a seat – 4d.
Sum – 17s 8d.

Sum total of all the whole receipts – £9 11s 8d.

Allowance
Also we ask allowance for the place in Marsh Street the which sometime
Nicholas Stok held, the which John Scheparde withholds from us, sum –
2s.
Also we ask allowance of a rent assize for the place in St Peter's parish
which Sir William Canynges wrongfully withholds from us, sum – 6d.
Sum – 2s 6d.

Allowance
Also these have been certain payments that the said proctors have paid for
the said church in the said year, as is rehearsed after
In primis on Palm Sunday paid for 1 pottle of osey for the priests and
clerks that sang the passion in the rood loft – 5d.

fo 2v
Item against Easter paid to Alison Monke for washing the church surplices
and altar cloths – 8d.
Item paid for keeping the sepulchre and the lights, as for 2 nights – 8d.
Item paid for bread and ale and coals for the said keepers – 2d.
Item paid for cleaning the churchyard – 1d.
Item paid for scouring your candlesticks and bowls against Easter – 16d.
Item paid to the raker for carrying away the church dust – 8d.
Item paid to the suffragan the which was behind with his wages – 2s.
Item paid for hanging up the Dance of Pauls twice a year, and for rolling
[it] up again – 8d.
Item paid to the mother church of Worcester – 12d.
Item paid for 2 lb of tallow candles for the rood loft on Christmas day in
the morning – 3d.
Item paid for bearing your banners in Rogation week – 4d.
Item paid for bearing your best cross on Corpus Christi day – 4d.
Item paid for the dinner to the priests and to the clerk on Corpus Christi
day after the procession – 3s.
Item paid for holding William Newbery's mind – 6s.
Item paid for a new rope for the salve bell – 4d.
Item paid for besoms to *streke* the church with – 1d.
Item paid for making the rent roll – 1d.
Item paid for paper to write the accounts in of both the books – 1d.

Item paid for writing these accounts – 12d.
Item paid to Alison Monke for washing the surplices and the altar cloths
against All Hallows' tide – 6d.
Item paid to 1 plumber for mending the church gutters – 12d.
Item paid for wood to the plumber – 1d.
Item paid to Robert Steynor for mending the glass windows – 3s 4d.
Item paid to Richard Reybalde for a board which closes in the corbels over
the choir – 16d.
Item paid for 1 deed for the hardwareman house – 8d.
Item paid to John Tavyrner 1 quit rent for the house that Matthew
Cotyngton dwells in – 11s 3d.
Item paid for mending the organs – 4d.
Sum – 37s 8d.

fo 3
Allowance
Also these have been the costs of your lights which burn before the rood
and beneath in the church, as is rehearsed after
In primis at the feast of Easter paid to John Mayowe, waxmaker, for
making 58 lb of your old wax that was of your square lights and round –
2s 5d.
Item paid to the said waxmaker for 17 $\frac{1}{2}$ lb of new wax to part-form your
square light and your round light and your font taper, at 7d the pound, sum
– 10s 2 $\frac{1}{2}$d.
Item paid to John waxmaker for making 1 paschal taper of his own wax,
and for the waste thereof – 2s 7d.
Item paid for making your round light against All Hallows' tide, as for
making 26 lb of your own wax – 13d.
Sum the costs of your wax – 16s 3 $\frac{1}{2}$d.

Allowance
These have been the costs as for the holding of your General Mind on Ash
Wednesday
In primis paid for loaf bread and cakes and spices that went thereto, and to
the baker for baking – 3s 3 $\frac{1}{2}$d.
Item paid for ale – 16d.
Item paid for 2 gallons of red wine – 16d.
Item paid for 1 pottle of osey – 8d.
Item paid to 5 priests and to the clerk – 18d.
Item paid for ringing the bells – 16d.
Item paid to the suffragan – 1d.
Sum costs of the General Mind – 9s 6 $\frac{1}{2}$d.

fo 3v

Allowance

This is the money which of courtesy is rewarded unto your tenants at the paying of their rents – 12d.

Sum – 12d.

Allowance

Item, Sirs, you shall understand that these are the costs of the pleas between Richard Haddon and the church as it is rehearsed after

In primis paid to John Bagote for the search of the mortifications above at London – 10s.

Item paid for 1 gallon of wine for Master William Fawxe and for Roger Kemes – 8d.

Item paid to a man to ride with John Chestre to speak with Sutton that was Abbot of Saint Austins – 6s 8d.

Item paid for horse hire – 2s.

Item paid for the proctors' costs for riding to the vicar of Chewe to speak to him, he for to be a counsel with us – 4d.

Item paid to Roger Kemes, he for to be a counsel with us – 10s.

Item paid for the vicar of Chewe his dinner and Roger Kemes' dinner – 16d.

Item on St Margaret's eve paid to the vicar of Chewe, he for to be a counsel with us and for his labour – 6s 8d.

Item on St Margaret's eve paid for the vicar of Chewe's dinner and for his expenses – 2s.

Item paid for 4 men's dinners, the Parson of St Peter's, the vicar of Chewe, Roger Kemes and Thomas Norton, the which were *?dayors* between us and Haddon the which *?doryde* 3 days, sum – 4s 4d.

Item paid for the vicar of Chewe as for his costs 3 days – 20d.

Sum – 45s 8d.

fo 4

Sum total of all the whole costs and payments – £5 12s 8d.

Rests clear to the church – £3 19s.

[1474–75]

fo 1
The Church Book of anno 14 R Edwardi IV
Hugo Foster and Thomas Baker Spicer proctors

fo 1v
The accounts of Hugo Foster and Thomas Baker Spicer proctors of the church of All Hallows' from the feast of the Annunciation of Our Lady in the 14th year of the reign of King Edward IV unto the said feast in the year next following after, so containing a whole year

These are the receipts of the church rents that follow
Item Morgan Lewys, per annum – £5 6s 8d.
Item the chantry of Everard Frensche for John Barnfeld's baste door and for his water gutter – 2s 6d.
Item Thomas Deenne, per annum – 20s.
Item Margery Mone, silk woman, per annum – 13s 4d.
Item Katherine Hardware for a *warthropp*, per annum – 3s 4d.
Item Thomas Phyllyppes, barber, rent assize for his place, per annum – 4s.
Item John Syble, baker, in Lewins Mead, rent assize for his place, per annum – 12d.
Item the master of the Tailors, rent assize for the place that John Alberton dwells in in Baldwin Street, per annum – 12s.
Item Cannynges rent assize for the place in St Peter's parish that sometime John Stenore dwelt in, per annum – 6d.
Item John Schepwarde the elder rent assize for the pace in Marsh Street, the which sometime Nicholas Stok held, per annum – 2s.
Item the chantry of Thomas Halleway, for the house in the churchyard, per annum – 6s 8d.
Sum total of this rental – £8 12s.

fo 2
Also these are the receipts of Easter and of other casualties that follow
In primis on Good Friday, on Easter eve and on Easter day, received on the pax – 10s 2d.
Item received for John Leynell's pit – 6s 8d.
Item received of Maud Atkyns for her seat – 6d.
Item received of Hugo Foster for his daughter's seat – 6d.
Item received of John Tailor for his seat – [scored: 8d.]
Item received of William Wodynton for the foot of the cross – 2d.
Item received of John Jenkins for his seat – 8d.
Item received of Isabell Skey for the best cross – 4d.
Item received of Nicholas Baker, ?jailer, for his daughter's seat – 6d.

Item received of Richard Mede for the foot of the best cross – 4d.
Item received of William Jenkyns for the beer house in the churchyard –
2s.
Item received of John Baten for 1 seat – 6d.
Sum – 22s 4d.
Sum total the rents and casualties – £9 14s 4d.

Allowance
Also we ask allowance of a rent assize for the place in Saint Peter's parish
which stands void – 6d.
Item we ask allowance of a rent assize for the ground in Marsh Street, the
which *some* Nicholas Stok held the which John Shipward the elder
withholds from us – 2s.
Sum – 2s 6d.

Allowance
Also these are certain payments that the proctors have paid for the church
in this year, as is after rehearsed
In primis paid for washing of albs and surplices and towels – 19d.
Item paid for mending an alb – 2d.
Item paid for mending the bocys [?box] of the best mass book – 2d.

fo 2v
Item paid to the raker for bearing away the church dust – 8d.
Item paid for a new lock for the treasure house door and 2 new staples to
receive the 2 shuttles – 2s 2d.
Item paid to the mother church of Worcester – 12d.
Item paid for holding William Newbery's mind – 6s.
Item paid for bearing banners in Rogation week – 4d.
Item paid for dinners to the priests and clerks on Corpus Christi day, after
the procession – 5s 8d.
Item paid for bearing the best cross on Corpus Christi day – 4d.
Item paid for a surplice without sleeves for the clerk – 2s 4d.
Item paid for 2 little hand towels for the high altar – 4d.
Item paid for scouring the basin before Our Lady – 20d.
Item paid for making the paring iron – 4d.
Item paid for tallow candles for the rood loft at Christmas – 1 ½d.
Item paid for 1 new key for 1 of the *mystyrs afore ihc* – 2d.
Item paid for tucking girdles for the vestments – 2s.
Item paid for 1 new rope for the salve bell – 5d.
Item paid for mending a seat underneath the Kalendars, beneath in the
church – 2d.
Item paid for mending the ?hope afore Our Lady *pytte* [?of Pity] – 4d.
Item paid for 1 pannier to bear away the church dust – 2d.

Item paid to a mason for mending the wall over the little vestry – 8d.
Item paid to 1 plumber for soldering 3 *skarys* over the little vestry – 6d.
Item paid for wood to heat his irons – 1d.
Item paid to a clerk for seeing the evidence that belongs to John Pynner's house – 4d.
Item paid for paper to write your parcels in – ½d.
Item paid for besoms to *streke* the church with – 1d.
Item paid for mending the glass windows in the church – 3s 4d.
Item paid for mending the monstrance at the high altar – 2d.

fo 3
Item paid to the Recorder and to Roger Kemes, they to be our defenders against Cannyngs for John Pynner's place – 4s 8d.
Item paid for making the rent roll – 1d.
Item paid for hanging up the Dance of Pauls – 8d.
Item paid for scouring all your candlesticks and bowls – 16d.
Sum – 36s 3d.

Allowance
Also these are the costs of your lights burning before the rood and beneath in the church, as is rehearsed after

In primis paid to John Mayowe, waxmaker, for making your square light and round and for the increase of new wax to part-form the said light against Easter – 16s 11d.
Item paid for making your round light and for the increase of new wax that went to the said light against All Hallows' tide – 4s 10d.
Item paid to John Mayowe, waxmaker, for 2 new torches weighing 50 lb, at 3d the pound, sum – 12s 6d.
Sum – 34s 3d.

Allowance
These are the costs for holding your General Mind
In primis paid for cakes, loaf bread and spices that went thereto – 4s 7d.
Item paid for osey and red wine – 4s 6d.
Item paid for ale – 16d.

fo 3v
Item paid for baking the foresaid cakes – 2d.
Item paid to 7 priests – 22d.
Item paid to the clerk for his bells and for his dirige – 18d.
Sum costs of the General Mind – 13s 11d.

Allowance

Also these are the costs of repairs done in your steeple gutters and upon the church [scored: and ?in the little vestry]

In primis paid for soldering 3 ½ *skarys* in the steeple gutters – 7d.

Item paid for soldering 1 ½ *skarys* in the gutter between the church rent and the chancel – 3d.

Item paid for coals and wood for the plumber's irons – 1d.

Item paid for cleaning the little pavement by the little vestry and for hauling away the rubble – 3d.

Item paid to 2 tilers for 1 day's work *wyrchynge* upon the church those 2, taking for the day's work – 11d.

Item paid for 100 cornish tiles – 5d.

Item paid for 1 cloth of lead weighing half a hundredweight and 16 ½ lb [72 ½ lb], the which is laid to keep out *dryfte of reyne* over Our Lady's altar on high upon the Kalendars' roof – 5s 1 ½d.

Item paid to a mason for 1 ½ days' to lay the said lead into the steeple wall, a part thereof – 8d.

Item paid for a quarter of lime – 2d.

Item paid for hauling away the rubble – 1 ½d.

Sum – 8s 7d.

Allowance

Item this is the money which of courtesy is rewarded to your tenants at the paying of their rents, sum – 12d.

Item paid for making and writing these accounts – 20d.

fo 4

Item paid to Thomas Clerk who was behind in his wages when he was suffragan – 3s 4d.

Item paid for mending of the *bere* in the churchyard – 4d.

Sum – 6s 4d.

Sum the costs and payments – £5 22d.

Rests clear to the church – £4 12 6d.

[1475–76]

fo 1

The Church Book of All Hallows'

Thomas Abyngton and Thomas Phyllypps proctors

Anno 15 R Edwardi IV

fo 1v

The accounts of Thomas Abyngton and Thomas Phyllyps, barber, proctors of the church of All Hallows' from the feast of the Annunciation of Our Lady in the 15th year of the reign of King Edward IV unto the said feast in the year next following, so containing a whole year.

These are the receipts of your rents that follow
Item Morgan Lewys, per annum – £5 6s 8d.
Item the chantry of Everard Frensche, per annum – 2s 6d.
Item Thomas Denne, per annum – 20s.
Item Margery Mony, for Our Lady quarter and for Midsummer quarter – 6s 8d.
Item Amy Howell for Michaelmas quarter and for Christmas quarter of the foresaid place – 8s.
Item Katherine Hardware for 1 *wartheroppe*, per annum – 3s 4d.
Item Thomas Phillipps, barber, rent assize for his place, per annum – 4s.
Item John Syble, baker, rent assize for his place in Lewins Mead, per annum – 12d.
Item the master of the Tailors, rent assize for the place that John Albyrton dwells in in Baldwin Street, per annum – 12s.
Item the place in St Peter's parish, the which sometime John Stenore dwelt in, per annum rent assize – 6d.
Item John Schepwarde the elder, rent assize for a place in Marsh Street, the which sometime Nicholas Stok held, per annum – 2s.
Item the chantry of Thomas Halleway, for the chamber that the chantry priest dwells in in the churchyard, per annum – 6s 8d.
Sum total of this rent for the year – £8 13s 4d.

fo 2

These are the receipts of Easter and other casualties as follows
In primis on Sheer Thursday, on Easter eve and on Easter day, received on the pax – 8s.
Item received for Richard Walshe, cook, the which he bequeathed to the church work – 20d.
Item received for Jennett Baker's burial – 6s 8d.
Item received for Margery Money's burial – 6s 8d.
Item received for Alison Chestyr, cook, her burial – 6s 8d.
Item received of John Jenkins for his seat and his wife's – 16d.
Item received of Thomas Cogan for his seat and his wife's – 2s.
Item received of Richard Arondell for his seat and his wife's – 16d.
Item received of William Chestyr for his seat – 6d.
Item received of Thomas Parnell for a seat and for his wife's – 8d.
Item received of John Byrley for a seat for him and another seat for his wife – 12d.

Item received of Robert Cachemay for his wife's seat – 8d.
Item received of Thomas Dyare, barber, for his wife's seat – 8d.
Item received of William Payntor for the hire of the beer house – 2s.
Sum the casualties – 39s 10d.

Also you shall understand that we received, the which we found in the
coffer in the treasure house – 53s 4d.
Item we have made sale of your old organs, the which we have received
for the said organs – 53s 4d.
Sum – £5 6s 8d.
Sum total – £15 19s 10d.

Allowance
Also you shall understand that we have paid unto Robert Bonnoke a mark
in clear money of the foresaid organs money, which money Robert
Bonnok paid unto the proctors of All Hallows' church, Clement Wilteshire
and John Chestre being proctors, in part payment of the said organs. We
could have no deliverance of our organs til the time that Bonnok was paid,
the which we ask allowance for – 13s 4d.
Sum – 13s 4d.

fo 2v
Allowance
Be it known to you that these are certain tenements which have been void,
unoccupied in this foresaid year, as is after rehearsed
In primis the Green Lattice, 3 quarters void, sum – £4.
Item the place in Marsh Street which some time Nicholas Stok held, which
John Shipward the elder withholds from us wrongfully – 2s.
Item we ask allowance of a rent assize for the place in St Peter's parish
that John Steynore dwelt in, the which Canynges wrongfully withholds
from us – 6d.
Sum – £4 2s 6d.

Allowance
Also these are certain payments which the said proctors have paid for the
said church in this foresaid year, as after rehearsed
In primis on Palm Sunday, paid for wine for the priests and clerks which
sang the passion in the rood loft – 3d.
Item at Easter paid to Alison Monke for washing 2 surplices and 1 rochet
and 9 altar cloths and 4 towels – 12d.
Item paid for watching the sepulchre and the lights that burn about, for 2
nights – 8d.
Item paid for bread and ale and coals – 2d.
Item paid to the raker for carrying away the church dust – 8d.

Item paid for scouring all the candlesticks and bowls in the church that belong to the parish – 16d.

Item paid to the suffragan which he was behind of his wages, paying – 3s 4d.

Item paid for holding William Newbery's mind – 6s.

Item paid for bearing your banners in Rogation week – 4d.

Item paid for burnishing the church jewels, that is to say the best cross and the monstrance upon the high altar, the cowpe [bowl] and the censers, with all other jewels, sum – 5s 4d.

Sum this side – 20s 1d.

fo 3

Item paid to Our Lady of Worcester – 16d.

Item paid for holding the dinner on Corpus Christi day [for] all the priests and the clerks in the church – 4s 4d.

Item paid for bearing the best cross on Corpus Christi day – 4d.

Item paid to a book binder for binding the epistle book and for a new covering for the same book – 20d.

Item paid for a new cover for the little psalter book and for the *helynge* [?mending] thereof – 16d.

Item paid to John Grant writer in Horstreet for 2 quires of parchment and for the writing thereof, and for the flourishing and the turning of the letters, the which is called a sequence and is set in the old mass book that Sir Thomas Furbore sings on, sum – 4s.

Item paid to the same said writer, for writing of 2 new parchment leaves, and for the flourishing and turning of the letters, the which is set in the said little old mass book – 6d.

Item paid for the covering of the said book, and for new clasps to the said mass book – 4d.

Item paid to a vestment maker for making a new vestment of green for the high altar that was the *sudekyns tonekyll* of the green suit – 3s 4d.

Item paid for canvas for the said vestment – 6d.

Item paid for buckram for the said vestment – 4d.

Item paid for ribbon for the said vestment – 7d.

Item against All Hallows' tide, paid for washing 2 surplices and 1 rochet – 5d.

Item paid for hanging up the Dance of Pauls twice a year – 8d.

Item paid for making 1 new battlement in the quire against All Hallows' tide, to hang *bedes* upon – 8d.

Item paid for spike nail and *rak hokys* for the said battlement – 2d.

Item paid for besoms to *streke* the church with – 1d.

Item paid for 1 pannier to bear out the church dust – 1d.

Item paid for 2 lb of tallow candles for the rood loft at Christmas – 2d.

Item paid for pins at All Hallows' tide – ½d.

Item paid for washing 2 surplices and 1 rochet against Christmas – 5d.
Sum this side – 21s 3 ½d.

fo 3v
Item paid for washing the second suit of vestments and for washing the alb
and amice that Sir Thomas Furbore sings with – 7d.
Item paid for washing 5 albs and 3 hand towels – 9d.
Item paid to Horn for the deed of Margery Money's place that Amy
Howell dwells in, for we should not else have had it out of his hands, sum
– 6s 8d.
Item paid for wine unto him to please him with – 8d.
Item paid for a gallon of wine to the recorder because he brought us and
delivered us 2 deeds from Thomas Phyler of London, the which deeds are
of the place on the High Street, sum – 8d.
Item paid for parchment to write your rent roll upon and for the writing
thereof – 1 ½d.
Item at divers times of courtesy rewarded to your tenants at the paying of
their rent – 6d.
Item paid for the making and writing of these accounts – 20d.
Item paid for a lock and a chain to make fast the church ladders with – 8d.
Sum – 12s 3 ½d.
Sum the payments – 52s 8d.

Allowance
Also these are the costs of the church lights, as rehearsed after
In primis at Easter paid to John Mayowe, waxmaker, for making 47 ¾ lb of
your own wax – 2s.
Item paid to John waxmaker for 28 lb of new wax to part-form your
square lights and your round lights and your font tapers, at 6 ½d the pound,
sum – 15s 2d.
Item paid to John Mayowe for making your paschal taper of his own wax,
weighing 17 ¾ lb in clean wax, price the making and the waste – 2s 7d.
Item against All Hallows' tide paid to John Mayowe for making 18 ½ lb of
your own wax for your round lights – 9d.
Item paid to John Mayowe for 7 ½ lb of new wax to part-form the said
lights, that is to say 13 tapers, every taper 2 lb, sum – 4s ½d.
Sum the wax – 24s 6 ½d.

fo 4
These are the costs for holding your General Mind on Ash Wednesday

Allowance
Item paid for loaf bread, cakes and spices that went thereto – 3s.
Item paid for 1 dozen ale and the bearing – 13d.

Item paid for wine – 5s 8d.
Item paid to 7 priests – 23d.
Item paid to the clerk for ringing the bells – 16d.
Sum the costs of the General Mind – 13s.

Allowance
Also these are the costs for paving your churchyard pavement
In primis paid for 5 wagon loads of paving stones – 13s 4d.
Item paid to a mason for 3 days' work, taking 5 $\frac{1}{2}$d for the day, sum –
16 $\frac{1}{2}$d.
Item paid to a labourer for 3 days' labour, taking 3 $\frac{1}{2}$d for the day, sum –
10 $\frac{1}{2}$d.
Item in the week next before Candlemas, paid to 1 mason for a whole
week's work, taking 5 $\frac{1}{2}$d for the day, sum – 2s 9d.
Item paid to a labourer for 4 $\frac{1}{2}$ days', taking 3 $\frac{1}{2}$d for the day, sum –
15 $\frac{1}{2}$d.
Item paid to 2 masons for a whole week's work, taking a man for the day
6 $\frac{1}{2}$d, sum – 6s 6d.
Item paid to a labourer for a whole week's labour, taking for the day
4 $\frac{1}{2}$d, sum – 2s 3d.
Item paid to 2 masons for a whole week's work, taking for the day 6 $\frac{1}{2}$d a
man, sum – 6s 6d.
Item paid to a labourer for a whole week's work, taking for the day 4 $\frac{1}{2}$d,
sum – 2s 3d.
Item paid to 2 masons for a whole week's work, taking a man for the day
6 $\frac{1}{2}$d, sum – 6s 6d.
Item paid to a labourer for 1 whole week's work, taking for the day 4 $\frac{1}{2}$d,
sum – 2s 3d.

fo 4v
Item paid for 2 paving stones – 16d.
Item paid for hauling the said stones – 1d.
Item paid for hauling 2 draughts of rubble – 2d.
Item paid to 2 masons for 2 days' labour taking a man for the day 5 $\frac{1}{2}$d,
sum – 2s 2d.
Item paid to a labourer for the foresaid 2 days' labour, taking for the day
4 $\frac{1}{2}$d, sum – 9d.
Item paid for sand – 18d.
Item paid for 6 $\frac{1}{2}$ weys of lime – 6s 6d.
Sum costs of the churchyard – 58s 4 $\frac{1}{2}$d.

Allowance
Also these are the costs of repairs done in the Green Lattice, the place that
Thomas Cogan dwells in in the High Street

In primis paid for 1 load of paving stones – 2s 8d.
Item paid for 100 feet of oaken boards for flooring the kitchen – 2s 10d.
Item paid for 4 boards of oak – 4d.
Item paid for hauling all the foresaid boards – 1d.
Item paid for 6 loads of clay – 12d.
Item paid for 4 loads of sand – 4d.

fo 5
Item paid for 1 piece of timber which lies in the flooring of the kitchen –
3d.
Item paid to a carpenter for 2 days' work, taking for the day 5 $\frac{1}{2}$d, sum –
11d.
Item paid for nails for the flooring of the said kitchen – 8d.
Item paid to a mason for 5 days' handiwork, taking for the day 5 $\frac{1}{2}$d, sum –
2s 3 $\frac{1}{2}$d.
Item paid to a mason for 3 days' handiwork, taking for the day 5 $\frac{1}{2}$d, sum –
16 $\frac{1}{2}$d.
Item paid to a labourer for 8 days' labour to serve the said masons, taking
for the day 3 $\frac{1}{2}$d, sum – 2s 4d.
Item paid for 5 quarters of lime – 10d.
Item paid for 3 $\frac{1}{2}$ lb of tallow candles for the workmen, the which caused
them to *wyrch* [work], both even tide and morning tide – 3 $\frac{1}{2}$d.
Item paid for hauling away 5 draughts of rubble – 5d.
Item paid to 2 labourers for making a gutter clean in the foresaid place –
7d.
Item paid for 1 board for the said warthrop in the kitchen – 2d.
Item paid for mending a lock, and for a new key, the which stands upon
the counter door – 3d.
Item paid for a new key for the myster at the stair head – 2d.
Item paid for a new lock and a key to the *spence* door in the baste hall –
4d.
Item paid for a new lock and a key for the baste door that goes into the
pavement – 5d.
Item paid for mending the wall between the Green Lattice and Alison
Chestre's house – 3d.

fo 5v
Item paid to the *langabyll* [land-gavel] for the said place called the Green
Lattice – 4d.
Sum costs of the Green Lattice – 19s 1 $\frac{1}{2}$d.

Allowance
Also these are the costs done upon the pentys [lean-to] of the house in
Corn Street, *Euens the mayre schopp*, in which Amy Howell dwells

In primis paid for boards of oak – 16d.
Item paid for a piece of timber for rafters for the said pentys – 2d.
Item paid for 3 hinges of iron for the said pentys – 8d.
Item paid for nails to the said pentys – 3d.
Item paid to a carpenter for 1 day's work upon the said pentys, taking for the day – 6 ½d.
Sum – 2s 11 ½d.

Sum total the whole receipts with the money that was received out of the coffer – £15 19s 10d.

Allowance
Sum total the vacations, payments and costs in repairs – £13 6s 6d.

Rest clear to the *paryschynge* – 53s 4d.

Of the which 53s 4d there is in certain pledges – 36s 8d.
And in ready money – 16s 8d.
Sum – 53s 4d.

fo 6 [This side is written in a different hand]
Of this 36s 8d, after that the foresaid Thomas Abyndon and Thomas Barbour had made their foresaid account, [they gave] in the foresaid 16s 8d in money and showed the pledges and debtors of the 36s 8d. Of this 36s 8d, Morgan Lews owed 26s 8d, of which he was allowed for certain costs done by him on the Green Lattice, that is to note the lattice of the sign, a lattice at the stair head, a lattice at the little parlour window and other small things [the sum of] 6s 8d, so he owed clearly 20s, the which he has promised to pay in haste within 5 days following. This account was made the 2nd day of April.

Also 10s that rests of the 36s 8d afore written is of Thomas a Dene's duty of debt of rent for the which is pledged a standing *myster* with 2 doors and a white *jakke* and a lattice – 10s.

[1477–78]

fo 1
The Church Book of All Hallows'
Davy Vaghan and Pers Grenfelde being proctors
Anno 17 R Edwardi IV

fo 1v

The accounts of Davy Vaghan and Pers Grenfelde, proctors of the church of All Hallows', the said accounts made clearly for a whole year, from the feast of the Annunciation of Our Lady in the 17th year of the reign of King Edward IV, unto the said feast in the year next following, so containing a whole year

These are the receipts of your rents that follow
Item Thomas Cogan, per annum – £4 13s 4d.
Item the chantry of Everarde Frensche, for John Barnfeld's baste door and for a water gutter, per annum – 2s 6d.
Item Thomas Went, tailor, per annum – 20s.
Item Amy Howell, per annum – 16s.
Item Katherine Hardware, per annum – 3s 4d.
Item Thomas Phillipps, barber, rent assize for the place that he dwells in, per annum – 4s.
Item John Syble, baker, rent assize for the place that he late dwelt in in Lewins Mead – 12d.
Item the master of the Tailors, rent assize for the place that John Alberton dwells in in Baldwin Street – 12s.
Item the place in St Peter's parish, the which sometime John Steynore dwelt in, rent assize per annum – 6d.
Item John Scheparde, rent assize, for the place in Marsh Street that sometime Nicholas Stok held, per annum – 2s.
Item the chantry of Thomas Halleway, for the chamber the which the chantry priest dwells in in the churchyard, per annum – 6s 8d.
Sum total of this rental – £8 16d.

fo 2

These are the receipts of Easter and other casualties, as after rehearsed
In primis on Good Friday, on Easter eve and on Easter day, received on the pax – 11s 11d.
Item received of Thomas Box for a seat – 10d.
Item received of Herry Dale for his wife's burial – 6s 8d.
Item received of Richard Androwe for his wife's burial – 5s.
Item received of Katherine Leynell for the burial stone – 5s.
Item received of Christiane Myllance for the change of her seat – 4d.
Item received of John Syble, baker, for a lattice, the which stood in the place called the Green Lattice in the High Street – 8s.
Item received of William Payntor for the beer house – 2s.
Sum the casualties – 39s 9d.
Sum total the whole receipts – £10 13d.

Allowances

Be it known to you that there are certain tenements which have lain void in this said year, as after rehearsed

In primis the place in Marsh Street the which sometime Nicholas Stok held, the which John Schepwarde withholds – 2s.

Item a rent assize for the place in St Peter's parish the which stands void – 6d.

Sum – 2s 6d.

fo 2v

Allowance

Also these are certain payments that the said proctors have paid for the church in this said year, as after rehearsed

In primis paid for wine on Palm Sunday for the singers that sang the passion in the rood loft – 3 ¼d.

Item paid for washing of the church clothes against Easter – 8d.

Item paid for keeping the sepulchre and the lights that burn about, to 2 men for 2 nights – 8d.

Item paid for bread, ale and coals – 3d.

Item paid for scouring the church candlesticks and bowls – 16d.

Item paid to the raker for carrying away the church dust – 8d.

Item paid for making the churchyard clean – 1d.

Item paid to Our Lady of Worcester – 8d.

Item paid for a new rent roll – 1d.

Item paid for holding William Newbery's year's mind – 6s.

Item paid for bearing your banners in Rogation week – 3d.

Item paid for mending your best cross – 12d.

Item paid for holding the dinner on Corpus Christi day for all the priests and clerks – 6s 5d.

Item paid bearing the best cross on Corpus Christi day – 4d.

Item paid to the suffragan that he was behind in payment of his year's wages – 3s 1d.

Item paid for 9 ells of holland cloth for a new surplice for the vicar – 6s.

Item paid for making the said surplice – 2s.

Item against All Hallows' tide, paid for washing the church clothes – 9d.

Item paid for *rak hokys*, nails and pins for the hanging of the church at All Hallows' tide – 3d.

Item paid for besoms to *streke* the church with – 1d.

Sum – 30s 10d.

fo 3

Item paid for making the churchyard clean at divers times – 3d.

Item paid for a stone which closes in [encloses] the cellar door in the churchyard pavement – 10d.

Item paid for 2 cramps of iron that bind the stone to the wall – 2d.

Item paid to a workman for making fast the said stone to the wall – 2d.

Item paid for hanging up the Dance of Pauls twice a year and folding up again – 8d.

Item paid for mending the seats next to the Kalendars door in the nether end of the church – 8d.

Item paid for mending the pissing gutter – 4d.

Item paid for washing 2 surplices and a rochet against Christmas – 5d.

Item paid for 2 lb of tallow candles for the rood loft at Christmas – 2d.

Item paid for the *snoffe* that the candle sticks in afore the rood in the rood loft – 1d.

Item paid for bringing in Matthew Cotyngton before the mayor – 2d.

Item paid for 2 new twists and for a new key for the little coffer in the vestry that the vestments and the chalice lie in – 6d.

Item paid for a new key for the little vestry door at the rood altar end – 2d.

Item paid for a new key for the door of the little myster underneath the rood altar end – 2d.

Item paid for a new key to the myster door and for mending the lock at Our Lady altar end – 3d.

Item paid for a breakfast to the priests of the church for keeping Our Lady Mass by note in Lent – 2s 1d.

Sum this side – 7s 1d.

fo 3v

Allowance

Also these are the costs of your church lights, as after rehearsed

Item at Easter paid to John Mayowe, waxmaker, for making 56 lb of your own wax and for 14 $\frac{3}{4}$ lb of new wax to part-form your square lights and your round lights – 9s 2 $\frac{1}{2}$d.

Item paid for the waste and making your paschal taper – 2s $\frac{1}{2}$d.

Item paid for making and renewing your round lights against All Hallows' tide – 6s 5 $\frac{1}{2}$d.

Item paid for 2 round torches weighing 42 lb – 10s 6d.

Sum costs of your lights – 28s 2 $\frac{1}{2}$d.

Allowance

These are the costs for holding your General Mind

Item paid for bread, ale and wine – 8s 6 $\frac{1}{2}$d.

Item paid to 7 priests – 22d.

Item paid for ringing the bells – 16d.

Sum costs of the General Mind – 11s 8 $\frac{1}{2}$d.

Allowance

These are the costs of the scaffold that was set in the rood aisle

In primis paid for 16 poles of timber for the scaffold – 5s 4d.
Item paid for 5 pieces of timber for the said scaffold – 2s 11d.
Item paid for the hire of a dozen boards – 12d.
Item paid for 5 *bewdley schydys of wud* for the trestles' feet – 1d.
Item paid for hauling the timber and boards – 9d.
Item paid for board nails – 1d.
Item paid for making the scaffold – 3s.

fo 4
Item paid to Thomas Cogan for 14 semes of welsh boards for sealing the roof in the rood aisle – 14s.
Item paid to John Sneg for 4 semes of welsh boards for the said seal – 4s.
Item paid to Thomas Spicer for 300 lath nails – 4 ½d.
Item paid to John Hyll, carver, for the handiwork in sealing the aforesaid roof – 26s 8d.
Item paid for taking down the scaffold – 16d.
Item paid for bread and ale to the men that took down the scaffold – 3d.
Item paid for hauling home the scaffold board again – 2d.
Item paid for hauling the scaffold timber from the church to the store house – 4d.
Sum costs of the scaffold and the sealing – £3 1 ½d.

Allowance
These are the costs of the frontels that Thomas Cogan let make for the Ihc [Jesus] altar and before the high altar
In primis paid for 2 ells of canvas – 8d.
Item paid for a quarter of an ell of flemish – 2d.
Item paid for 2 ells of green ribbon – 12d.
Item paid for 1 yard of red buckram – 8d.
Item paid for 8 yards of fringe – 23d.
Item paid for the stuff and the making of a jhu [Jhesu] – 6d.

fo 4v
Item for the stuff and making of 10 stars – 4s 2d.
Item for making 3 frontels – 2s.
Item for making 2 corporas cases – 10d.
Item for 1 ell of flemish cloth the which is sewed onto the frontel – 10d.
Sum costs of the frontels – 12s 9d.

Allowance
These are the costs of repairs done in Thomas Went's house in Corn Street
In primis paid for timber and boards for the kitchen floor – 2s 8d.
Item paid for paving stones for the kitchen floor – 19d.
Item paid for stones – 10d.

Item paid for 3 loads of clay – 6d.
Item paid for 3 quarters of lime – 6d.
Item paid for board nail – 1 ½d.
Item paid for 1 board – 1d.
Item paid to 2 masons for 3 days' work, taking a man for the day 6 ½d,
sum – 3s 3d.
Item paid to a mason for 1 day's work – 6 ½d.
Item paid to a labourer for 3 days' work – 13d.
Item paid for candles – ½d.
Item paid for a new key – 2d.
Sum – 11s 4 ½d.

fo 5
Allowance
These are the costs done at Thomas Cogan's and in Corn Street
Item paid to a mason for mending Thomas Cogan's gutter and for mending
Thomas Wente's chimney, and for mending a wall in Amy's house –
6 ½d.
Item paid for a new lock and a key for the shop door in Amy's house – 5d.
Item paid for a piece of timber to make a post for Thomas Cogan's door –
6d.
Item paid for 2 planks for his bulk – 10d.
Item paid for 3 pairs of hinges for the said bulk at Thomas Cogan's – 8d.
Item paid for nails – 2d.
Item paid for a rail which binds the post to the door at Thomas Cogan's –
2d.
Item paid for a piece of timber for a *groundsell* for the foresaid post at
Thomas Cogan's door – 1d.
Item paid to a carpenter for his handiwork – 12d.
Item paid for a load of tile stones – 20d.
Item paid to 2 tilers for 3 ½ days' handiwork, taking for the day 5 ½d, sum
– 3s 2 ½d.
Sum – 9s 3d.

Item more paid for writing and making this account – 20d.

fo 5v
Item this is the money which of courtesy is rewarded to your tenants at the
paying of their rents – 16d.
Item paid to the old suffragan that which was the bedeman by the
commandment of the good men of the parish – 20d.
Sum – 4s 8d.

Sum total the vacations, costs, payments and repairs – £8 18s 6d.

Rests clear to the church – 22s 7d.
The which said money paid and quit.

[1478–79]

fo 1
The Church Book of All Hallows'
Davy Vaghan and Pers Grenfelde being proctors
Anno 18 R Edwardi IV

fo 1v
The accounts of Davy Vaghan and Pers Grenfelde, proctors of the church
of All Hallows', the said accounts made clearly for a whole year, that is to
say from the feast of the Annunciation of Our Lady in the 18th year of the
reign of King Edward IV to the said feast in the year next following, so
containing a whole year

These are the receipts of your rents that follow
Item Thomas Cogan, per annum – £4 13s 4d.
Item the chantry of Everarde Frensche for John Barnfeld's baste door and
for a water gutter, per annum – 2s 6d.
Item Thomas Went, tailor, per annum – 20s.
Item Amy Howell, per annum – 16s.
Item John Bowde and Paul Hardwareman, per annum – 3s 4d.
Item Thomas Phillyppes, barber, rent assize, per annum – 4s.
Item Richard Erle, rent assize, for the place in Lewins Mead that John
Syble late dwelt in, per annum – 12d.
Item the master of the Tailors, rent assize for the place that John Alberton
dwells in in Baldwin Street, per annum – 12s.
Item the place in St Peter's parish the which some time John Steynore
dwelt in, per annum – 6d.
Item John Schepwarde, rent assize for the place in Marsh Street, the which
some time Nicholas Stok held, per annum – 2s.
Item the chantry of Thomas Halleway, for the chamber which the chantry
priest dwells in in the churchyard, per annum – 6s 8d.
Sum total of this rental – £8 16d.

fo 2
The receipts of Easter and other casualties, as after rehearsed
In primis of Good Friday, on Easter eve and on Easter day, received on the
pax – 10s 6d.
Item received of John Sneg for his daughter's burial – 5s.
Item received of John Cokks for his seat – 8d.

Item received for a gown and 1 kirtle of the bequest of Thomas Cogan's maid – 8s, abate 8d that the upholsterer had for the sale.
Item received of Poll's wife for her seat – 8d.
Item received of Crystianne Myllan for changing her seat – 6d.
Item received of Richard Went for his seat and for his wife's seat – 8d.
Sum the casualties – 26s
[Different hand: Sum total the receipts – £9 7s 4d.]

Allowance
Also there are certain tenements which have stood void in this said year as after rehearsed
In primis the place in Marsh Street which Nicholas Stok sometime held, which John Schepward withholds – 2s.
Item a rent assize of the place in Lewins Mead of Richard Erle, and because it lies in decay the said Richard will not pay – 12d.
Item a rent assize for the place in St Peter's parish which stands void – 6d.
Sum the vacations – 3s 6d.

fo 2v
Allowance
Also these are certain payments which the proctors have paid for the said church in this said year
In primis paid on Palm Sunday for a quart of wine for the singers of the Passion in the rood loft – 2d.
Item paid for washing of the church clothes at Easter – 12d.
Item paid for keeping the sepulchre for 2 nights – 8d.
Item paid for bread, ale and fire for the keepers of the sepulchre – 2d.
Item paid for the loan of a raw cloth for Palm Sunday – 1d.
Item paid for the scouring of your candlesticks and bowls of the church – 16d.
Item paid for scouring the basins that hang in the church – 2s 8d.
Item paid to a mason for mending the wall behind the great door in the church by the long coffer – 8d.
Item paid to the suffragan that he was behind of his wages – 4s 1d.
Item paid for 1 new rope that the basin hangs with before Our Lady – 4d.
Item paid a new rope [for] the basin that hangs before the rood altar – 3d.
Item paid for a new line to pull up the cloth which hangs before the rood on Palm Sunday – 3d.
Sum this side – 11s 8d.

fo 3
Item paid to the raker for carrying away the church dust – 8d.
Item paid for bearing your banners in Rogation week – 4d.
Item paid to Our Lady of Worcester – 8d.

Item paid for holding William Newbery's mind – 6s.

Item paid for a dinner on Corpus Christi day for the vicar and all the priests and clerks of the church – 8s 6d.

Item paid for bearing the best cross on Corpus Christi day – 4d.

Item paid for a coffer with 3 floors for the church books – 7s.

Item paid for a pair of new trestles for the hearse board – 10d.

Item paid for making and setting up the battlement before the south door in the church that the Dance of Pauls hangs upon – 14d.

Item paid for mending the lych bell – 6d.

Item paid for washing the church cloths against Whit Sunday – 4d.

Item paid for washing Sir Thomas Furbor's alb and his amice and for setting one of the orfreys – 3d.

Item paid for mending the checker board that you bear the church cake upon – 2d.

Item paid for besoms to *streke* the church with – 1 $\frac{1}{2}$d.

Item paid for paper to write this account upon – $\frac{1}{2}$d.

Item paid for 1 pot to fill the holy stock withal – $\frac{1}{2}$d.

Sum this side – 26s 11 $\frac{1}{2}$d.

fo 3v

Item paid for washing 2 surplices and a rochet – 5d.

Item paid for 1 new rope for the salve bell – 6d.

Item at All Hallows' tide paid for nails and pins for hanging cloths in the church – 2d.

Item paid for hanging *bedes* in the church, and taking down and folding up – 4d.

Item paid for 2 lb of tallow candles for the rood loft at Christmas – 2d.

Item paid for washing the church cloths at Christmas – 10d.

Item paid to the singer of Saint Austins for mending your organs – 20d.

Item paid for hanging the Dance of Pauls and taking down twice a year – 8d.

Item paid for cleaning a gutter in Thomas Cogan's house – 12d.

Item paid for mending the pavement at Thomas Cogan's door – 2 $\frac{1}{2}$d.

Item paid for 1 new rent roll – 1 $\frac{1}{2}$d.

Item of courtesy rewarded to your tenants at the paying of their rents – 16d.

Item paid for writing and making this account – 20d.

Item paid for mending the baldric of the great bell – 6d.

Sum this side – 9s 7d.

fo 4

Allowance

These are the costs of the church lights, as after rehearsed

In primis at Easter paid to John Mayowe, waxmaker, for making 45 $\frac{3}{4}$ lb of your own wax – 22 $\frac{1}{2}$d.

Item paid to John Mayowe for 28 $\frac{1}{2}$ lb of new wax to part-form your square lights and your round lights – 14s 3d.

Item paid to John Mayowe, waxmaker, for making your paschal taper of his own wax, weighing in clean wax 19 $\frac{1}{2}$ lb, making and waste come to – 2s 5d.

Item at All Hallows' tide paid to John Mayowe for making your round lights [from] 15 lb of your own wax – 7 $\frac{1}{2}$d.

Item paid for 11 lb of new wax to part-form the said round lights, that is to say for 13 tapers, every taper 2 lb apiece, sum – 5s 6d.

Item paid to John Mayowe, waxmaker, for the overplus of the torches that Matthew Cotyngton brought in, which torches weighed more than his duty was to bring in, sum – 19 $\frac{1}{2}$d.

Sum costs of your wax – 26s 3 $\frac{1}{2}$d.

fo 4v

Allowance

These are the costs of your General Mind on Ash Wednesday

In primis paid for loaf bread, cakes and spices that went thereto, and to the baker for baking thereof – 5s 7d.

Item paid for a dozen ale and for the bearing – 13d.

Item paid for 7 gallons of wine – 4s 10d.

Item paid to 7 priests for the dirige and the mass – 22d.

Item paid to the clerk for ringing the bells – 12d.

Sum the General Mind – 14s 4d.

Allowance

Also these are the costs of the gutter that lies in the entry in the house next to the Green Lattice which belongs to the chantry of Walter Frampton at St John the Baptist's church

In primis paid for 4 loads of paving stones – 6s 8d.

Item paid for 20 loads of clay, every load 1 $\frac{1}{2}$d – 2s 6d.

Item paid for 22 bushels of lime stones – 3s 8d.

Item paid for a wey of lime – 12d.

Item paid for 18 loads of sand – 15d.

Item paid for 12 lb of tallow candles – 12d.

Item paid for 6 bushels of lime stones – 12d.

fo 5

Item paid for 6 loads of clay – 9d.

Item paid for pack thread for the masons' lines – $\frac{1}{2}$d.

Item paid to 2 masons for 12 days' work, taking a man for the day 5 $\frac{1}{2}$d, sum – 11s.

Item paid to 2 labourers for 12 days' work, taking a man for the day

3 ½d, sum – 7s.
Sum of the gutter – 35s 10 ½d.

These are the costs done at the rood altar that follow
In primis paid to a smith for the iron work that the cloth hangs [on] before
the altar, that is to say 43 lb at 1 ½d the pound – 5s 4 ½d.
Item paid to 1 mason for setting the irons in the wall – 3d.
Item paid for 42 rings that the cloth hangs upon – 10d.
Item paid for 4 staples of iron that the riddels hang on at the altar ends –
2d.
Sum – 6s 7 ½d.

fo 5v
Item paid to the suffragan that is now in part payment of his year's wages
the which you must take up so much of his wages again on Palm Sunday –
2d.
Sum – 2d.

Sum total of vacations, costs and payments – £6 15s.
Rest to the church – 52s 4d. [Different hand: Received and quit.]

fo 6
Item, sirs, you shall receive for 1 pan and 1 lattice that was pledged of
Thomas Denne *in partty of the more sowme* [as part of a larger sum] – 4s.
[Different hand: Received and quit.]

[1479–80]

fo 1
The accounts of John Snyge and Thomas Box proctors of the church of All
Hallows', the said accounts made clearly for a whole year, that is to say
from the feast of the Annunciation of Our Lady in the 19th year of the
reign of King Edward IV to the said feast in the year next following, so to
containing a whole year

These are the receipts of our rents that follow
Item Thomas Cogan, per annum – £4 13s 4d.
Item the chantry of Everarde Frensche for John Branfeld's baste door and
for a water gutter, per annum – 2s 6d.
Item Thomas Went, tailor, per annum – 20s.
Item Amy Howell, per annum – 16s.
Item John Bowde and Paul Hardermon, per annum – 3s 4d.
Item Thomas Phelips, barber, rent assize, per annum – 4s.

Item Richard Erle, rent assize for a place in Lewins Mead that John Syble late dwelt in, per annum – 12d.

Item the master of the Tailors, rent assize for the pace that John Alberton dwells in in Baldwin Street, per annum – 12s.

Item received of Thomas Canynges for rent assize of a place in St Peter's parish which John Steynore dwelt in, per annum – 6d.

Item John Schipward rent assize for the place in Marsh Street which Nicholas Stok held – 2s.

Item the chantry of Thomas Halleway for the chamber which the chantry priest dwells in in the churchyard – 6s 8d.

Sum the rent amounts – £8 16d.

fo 1v

The receipts of Easter and other casualties, as rehearsed hereafter

In primis on Sheer Thursday, Good Friday and Easter eve and on Easter day on the pax – 12s 1 ½d.

Item received for the suffragan of the parish [as] part of his wages – 3s 6d.

Item received of Thomas Parnell for the hire of the cross for Sir William Wele's burial – 8d.

Item received of Davy Ostelar for his wife's grave – 6s 8d.

Item received of Clement Wilteshire for T Wyell's grave – 6s 8d.

Item received of Gylame Delafowntt for a broad stone – 10d.

Item received of Bett of Gellos End for a seat – 8d.

Item received of Hugh Cork for his seat and his wife's – 12d.

Item received of William Palmer of London of his bequest – 40s.

Item received of Robert Darkyng of London of his bequest – 20s.

Sum the vacations – £4 12s ½d.

Sum total the rents and other receipts – £12 13s 5 ½d.

These are the rents that have stood void this year

A place in Marsh Street that John Shipward withholds, that is to say rent assize of a place in Marsh Street sometime called Scalpyll Street wherein Nicholas Stoke dwelt – 2s.

fo 2

Also these are certain payments which the said proctors have paid for the church [in] the said year

In primis paid on Palm Sunday for wine into the rood loft to the singers of the passion – 4 ½d.

Item paid for washing the church clothes against Easter and Whit Sunday – 17d.

Item paid for keeping the sepulchre for 2 nights – 8d.

Item paid for bread, ale and coals – 2 ½d.

Item paid for mending the sepulchre – 1d.

Item paid for scouring our candlesticks and bowls of the church – 16d.

Item paid for scouring the basins and lamps that hang in the church – 2s 4d.

Item paid to the suffragan for his year's wages – 6s 8d.

Item paid to the raker for carrying the church dust – 8d.

Item paid for bearing our banners in Rogation week – 4d.

Item paid for an alb and 2 amices the which had 5 $\frac{1}{4}$ ells of cloth at 6d the ell, amounts to – 2s 5d.

Item paid for an amice more to the high altar – 5d.

Item paid for 2 ells of cloth to make new banners for the church – 2s 1d.

Item paid to Our Lady of Worcester – 8d.

Item paid for the priests' dinner for to sing Our Lady Mass in the Lent – 3s.

Item paid to a *schipstar* for making an alb and 3 amices – 8d.

Item paid for a dinner on Corpus Christi day for the vicar and all the priests and clerks of the church – 6s 8d.

Item paid for holding William Newbery's mind – 6s.

Item paid to a smith for mending the church door key – 3d.

Item paid for parchment for the rent roll – 1d.

Item paid to a *schipstar* for making sheets to cover our best copes in the *Tryall* – 4d.

Item paid for paper – 1d.

Sum this side amounts – 36s 9d.

fo 2v

Item paid to the clerk for hanging up the Dance of Pauls and taking down 2 times a year – 16d.

Item paid to the clerk for washing 17 pairs of albs and amices and for setting 1 of the orfreys and for washing 3 altar cloths and 3 towels – 2s 4d.

Item paid for washing 3 surplices and a rochet – 7d.

Item paid for *rachokys* and nails and pins to hang up the *bedes* at All Hallows' tide – 2 $\frac{1}{2}$d.

Item paid for a *Tampyn* to the *vante* and for a water pot to the church – 1d.

Item paid for besoms at 2 times to *streke* the church – 1d.

Item paid for nails to mend the choir door – 1d.

Item paid for a key to the box that the evidence lies in – 3d.

Item paid for small nails – $\frac{1}{2}$d.

Item paid for cleaning and hauling rubble out of the steeple – 12d.

Item paid for 2 cruets *chanegyng* [chaining] to the high altar – 4d.

Item paid for a lamp before the high altar – 1d.

Item paid for a plank in the choir at the high altar – 3d.

Item paid for 11 feet of battlement – 11d.

Item paid for mending 12 pins of iron. To new set them and for plates of tin – 12d.

Item paid for a new fire pan to the church – 2d.

Item paid a carpenter for his labour to the church – 4d.

Item paid for nails – $\frac{1}{2}$d.

[Scored: Item paid for rent assize of John Syble's house – 2s.]

Item paid to the player of organs from Christmas to Candlemas – 10d.

Item paid for sconces against Christmas for the choir – 3 $\frac{1}{2}$d.

Item paid for washing the vicar's surplices and the clerk's – 3s

Item paid for lime to the church – 1d.

Item paid for making and writing this account – 20d.

Item paid in rewarding our tenants at their payments – 16d.

Item paid for a dinner to receive the money of the bequest of William Hardyng and Robert Darkyng – 3s 4d.

Sum this side amounts clear – 16s 11d.

fo 3

These are the costs of the church lights as rehearsed by the items following

In primis paid at Easter to John Mayowe, waxmaker, for making 53 $\frac{1}{4}$ lb of our own wax – 2s 2 $\frac{1}{2}$d.

Item paid to John Mayowe for 24 lb of new wax to part-form our square lights and our round lights – 12s 3d.

Item paid for tapers of 1 lb for the sepulchre – 6d.

Item paid to John Mayowe for making our paschal taper of his own wax weighing, tree and all, 28 $\frac{3}{4}$ lb, the making and the waste coming to – 2s 9d.

Item paid at All Hallows' tide to John Mayowe for making our round light [from] 16 lb of our own wax – 8d.

Item paid him for 10 lb of new wax to part-form the said round lights, that is 13 tapers, each of them 2 lb apiece – 5s.

Sum the costs of our wax amounts – 23s 4 $\frac{1}{2}$d.

These are the costs of our General Mind on Ash Wednesday

In primis paid for loaf bread, cakes and spices that went thereto and to the baker – 4s 5d.

Item paid for a dozen ale and the bearing – 18d.

Item paid for wine – 4s 6d.

Item paid for 7 priests for the dirige and the mass – 22d.

Item paid to the clerk for ringing of the bells – 12d.

Sum the costs of the General Mind amounts – 13s 3d.

fo 3v

These are the costs of repairs done upon the church and the church rents

In primis paid to a carpenter for a day's labour to mend the bell house that the salve bell hangs in – 6d.

Item paid for spike nails to the same bell house – 1d.

Item paid for a load of tile stones to the church and to the church rents with the hauling – 20d.

Item paid to John Schyre, tiler, for 3 days' labour upon the church – 18d.

Item paid to Robert Megs for 21 lb of solder and for mending 8 *skarys* upon the steeple and the gutters of the church – 6s.

Item paid for wood to the plumber – 2d.

Item paid John Schyre for 1 ½ days' work upon Richard Went's house and Amy Howell's house – 8 ½d.

Item paid for boards to mend the said 2 houses – 7 ½d.

Item paid for mending a lock to Amy Howell's cellar door – 2d.

Item paid for a key to Amy Howell's door above – 3d.

Item paid for mending a lock and making a key to the great coffer in the rood loft – 4d.

Item paid to Robert Megs for mending Thomas Cogan's gutter – 10d.

Item paid for cleaning a gutter in Thomas Cogan's house – 12d.

Item paid for mending and soldering the church gutter – 5d.

Item paid for a hook of iron to bear up the wire at the cross altar – 8d.

Sum this side amounts clear – 14s 11d.

fo 4

These are the costs of the almerys [aumbries] in the choir before All Hallows and for sealing the arch and sealing the wall before the rood altar, as follows

Item paid for boards and timber that went to the arch and almerys of the choir and boards that went to the wall of the rood altar – 16s 4 ½d.

Item paid to the carver, mason and *sawyng* and all hands of the same, the sum amounts – 29s 7d.

Item the locks and twists and rings to the same with nails that went to all the work – 9s 4d.

Sum this side – 55s 3 ½d.

Sum total of allowances amounts – £8 2s 6d.

So rest we owe to the church – £4 10s 11 ½d.

Item delivered and paid at the making of our accounts – £4 10s 11 ½d.

So this is quit and paid.

[1480–81]

fo 1

These are the accounts of John Jenkyns and Thomas Pernaunt proctors of the church of All Hallows', Bristol, clearly made for a whole year that is to say from the feast of the Annunciation of Our Lady in the 20th year of the reign of King Edward IV unto the said feast next following

These are the receipts of our rents for the whole year
In primis the Green Lattice that Thomas Cogan dwelt in – £4 13s 4d.
Item of the chantry house of Everarde Frensche for a baste door and a gutter – 2s 6d.
Item of Paul Hardwareman – 3s 4d.
Item of Richard Went, tailor – 20s.
Item of Amy Howell – 16s.
Item of Thomas Phylyppes, barber, rent assize – 4s.
Item of the chantry of Thomas Halleway for the chamber house that the chantry priest dwells in – 6s 8d.
Item of Richard Erle's house in Lewins Mead that John Sybly dwells in, rent assize – 12d.
Item of the master of the Tailors for the house that John Albyrton dwelt in in Baldwin Street, rent assize per annum – 12s.
Item of a house in St Peter's parish that John Steynor dwelt in, rent assize – 6d.
Item of a place of John Schypward in Marsh Street otherwise called Skadpyll Street, rent assize – 2s.
Sum – £8 16d

fo 1v
In primis of Sheer Thursday, Good Friday, Easter eve and Easter day – 13s 3 ½d.
Item received of Master Recorder that Mistress Rowley be prayed for – a torch.
Item received of Thomas Cogan for midsummer quarter – 13s 4d.
Item received of Thomas Adene for his ?jacke in part payment – 8s.
Item received of John Cox for the house in the churchyard 3 quarters – 15d.
Item received of David Vaghan for rent assize of Erle's house in Lewins Mead that was unpaid in David's year – 12d.
Item received of the said David for his son's grave – 5s.
Item of Joan Goolde for the bequest of her husband – 12d.
Item of Thomas Skinner for 2 seats, 1 for him and another for his wife – 16d.
Item of Garret Corveser for a seat – 7d.
Item of Rafe Bysschope for a seat – 7d.
Item of Alison Hyckys ?under Jenett Howell for a seat – 4d.
Sum – 45s 8 ½d.
Sum total the receipts – £10 13s 6 ½d.

These are the vacations of this year
In primis the Green Lattice 3 quarters – £3 10s.
Item of the house in St Peter's parish, rent assize – 6d.
Item in Marsh Street rent assize that John Schypward withholds – 2s.
Sum – £3 12s 6d.

Receipts for brass that we have sold of the church
In primis a pan that Isabel Key gave to the church that weighed 20 lb at 2d
the pound – 3s 4d.
Item a pot of brass that weighed 12 lb – 2s.
Item a pan that weighed 7 lb – 14d.
Sum – 6s 6d.

fo 2
These are certain payments which the said proctors have paid for the said
church the said year, as it follows
In primis for 2 boards to stop a hole in the tower – 1 ½d.
Item scouring the candlesticks and bowls with the *hongells* for lamps –
3s 4d.
Item for washing surplices, altar cloths, towels and albs against Easter,
Whitsun tide and other times of the year – 2s 3d.
Item paid to the clerk to watch the sepulchre – 8d.
Item paid for bread, ale and coals – 2d.
Item paid to the mother church – 8d.
Item paid to the clerk for the suffragan's wages – 20d.
Item paid to the raker – 8d.
Item paid for besoms and a pannier and pins for altars – 2 ½d.
Item for a dinner for keeping Our Lady Mass – 2s 2d.
Item for Newbery's mind – 6s.
Item for bearing banners in Rogation week – 4d.
Item for bearing the cross on Corpus Christi day – 4d.
Item for a dinner to the vicar and priests that day – 5s 6d.
Item for mending vestments – 6d.
Item to John Baten for soldering and gilding the clasps of the best cope
and for a plate of latten *wtynforth* – 17d.
Item for the change of a new *tynnell* – 2s 3d.
Item paid for a cord to hang the paschal taper by – 4d.
Item paid to Bonnok's clerk for singing and playing on our Dedication day
and All Hallows' day – 12d.
Item for making a new foot to the trestle to be borne on Candlemas day –
2d.
Item for 2 lb candles on Christmas day – 2d.
Item for a pulley to draw the cloth at the rood altar *of and fro at all times
that nedyth* – 1d.

Item paid to a carpenter to dress it – 1d.
Item paid for cleaning of the glass windows in the north aisle of ihc
[Jesus] – 2d.
Item paid for a rent roll – 2 ½d.
Item paid for paper – 1d.
Sum – 30s 6 ½d.

fo 2v

Item paid to John Hyll the carver for sealing the wall in the north aisle of
the church by the image of Jesus – 3s 4d.
Item paid for boards to seal it, to John Snygge – 3s 8d.
Item for 3 stakes – 4d.
Item for nails – 2d.
Item paid for painting of the said sealing and repairing the glass windows
of the church – 4s 8d.
Item paid to the carver for making a case in timber work for the rope of
the salve bell by Our Lady of Pity – 20d.
Item for 2 oaken boards to it – 6d.
Item for nails – 3d.
Item for tallow to anoint the case – 1d.
Item for clamps of iron to the said case – 10d.
Item paid to the carver for making a new front, otherwise called a reredos,
with 3 houses for St Thomas' altar – 43s 4d.
Item paid for hanging up and taking down of the Dance of Pauls to the
clerk – 16d.
Item for a paring iron – 5d.
Item allowance in receiving rent – 8d.
Item for making and writing this account – 12d.
Sum – £3 2s 3d.

fo 3

Repairs in divers places
In primis for mending of the gutter in the churchyard – 7d.
Item to a labourer – 2d.
Item for mending the style in the churchyard – 3d.
Item for lime to all together – 4d.
Item for mending a gutter in the Green Lattice going through the pavement
– 14d.
Item for lime – 2d.
Item for soldering a *skare* in a gutter of the said house and for solder – 3d.
Item for cleaning the said house – 2d.
Item for cleaning a gutter in Amy Howell's house and Richard Went
tailor's house – 14d.
Item for a new lattice in Richard Went's house and nails – 16 ½d.

Item for boards, twists and nails and for the carpenter's labour in Amy Howell's house – 13d.
Sum – 6s 8 ½d.

These are the costs of the church lights
In primis paid for square light and round light to John Mayowe, waxmaker, against Easter – 11s 8d.
Item for the paschal and font tapers – 4s 1d.
Item for 2 new standards of 4 lb in the choir – 2s.
Item for the change of 2 standards at Christmas – 5d.
Item for the change of the round light at All Hallows' tide – 3s 11 ½d.
Item for a new torch – 4s.
Sum – 26s 1 ½d.

fo 3v
These are the costs of the General Mind
In primis for bread, cakes and all other stuff belonging thereto – 4s ½d.
Item for wine – 4s 2d.
Item for ale – 21d.
Item to 6 priests – 18d.
Item to the clerk for ringing – 14d.
Sum – 12s 7 ½d.

Sum total of allowances of all manner costs – £10 10s 9d.

The sum remaining clear to All Saints for this year – 2s 9 ½d.

Memorandum the 19th day of April, that is to say the day of these accounts, John Jenkins and Thomas Pernaunt before the vicar and the parish paid the foresaid money remaining, that is to say – 2s 9 ½d, and so were clear discharged of their office and of this account.

[1481–82]

fo 1
These are the accounts of Clement Wilteshire and Thomas Pernaunt proctors of the church of All Hallows' of Bristol, clearly made for a whole year, that is to say from the feast of the Annunciation of Our Lady in the 21st year of the reign of King Edward IV unto the said feast next following

These are the receipts of our rents of the whole year
In primis the Green Lattice that Thomas Cogan dwelt in – £4 13s 4d.

Item of the chantry house of Everarde Frensche for a baste door in the churchyard and a gutter – 2s 6d.

Item of Paul Hardwareman – 3s 4d.

Item of Richard Went, tailor – 20s.

Item of Amy Howell – 16s.

Item of Thomas Phylypps, barber, rent assize – 4s.

Item of the chantry of Thomas Halleway for the chamber house that the chantry priest dwells in – 6s 8d.

Item of Richard Erle's house in Lewins Mead that John Sybly dwelt in, rent assize – 12d.

Item of the master of the Tailors for the house that John Albyrton dwelt in in Baldwin Street, rent assize per annum – 12s.

Item of a house in St Peter's parish that John Steynar dwelt in, rent assize – 6d.

Item of a place of John Schypward in Marsh Street other wise called Skadpyll Street, rent assize – 2s.

Sum – £8 16d.

fo 1v

These are the receipts of Easter and other casualties as follows

In primis received of the parish for the suffragan's wages upon Palm Sunday – 2s 7d.

Item received on Sheer Thursday, Good Friday, Easter eve and Easter day – 12s 4d.

Item received of George Baderand for his seat and his wife's – 12d.

Item received of Richard Kendell for his seat and his wife's – 12d.

Item received of William Fryth, tailor, for his seat and his wife's – 2s.

Item received of Thomas Snygge for his seat – 12d.

Item received of John Cokkys for the house in the churchyard – 20d.

Sum – 21s 7d.

[Different hand: Sum total receipts – £9 2s 11d.]

fo 2

These are the vacations of the year

In primis the Green Lattice a whole year – £4 13s 4d.

Item a place of John Shipward in Marsh Street which Nicholas Stocke dwelt in, rent assize for a whole year – 2s.

Sum – £4 15s 4d.

These are certain payments which the proctors have paid for the church the said year, as follows

In primis paid on Palm Sunday for a pottle of wine to the priest that sang in the rood loft – 6d.

Item for 100 pins to the church – 1d.

Item paid for the priests' dinner for singing Our Lady Mass in Lent – 2s 8d.

Item paid to Ellyn Foroke for scouring the candlesticks and the bowls and the hangings of the lamps of the church – 14d.

Item for oil and scouring stones to the said candlesticks – 2d.

Item paid to the raker for his year's wages – 8d.

Item paid to the clerk for watching the sepulchre – 8d.

Item paid to the clerk for coals and ale – 2d.

Item paid for changing the sanctus bell and hanging it up and for a line – 2s 6d.

Item paid for Newbery's mind – 6s.

Sum – 14s 7d

fo 2v

Payments

Item paid for hanging up the cloth before the tabernacle of Our Lady which Mistress Chestre let made at Jhc [Jesus] altar and for the hoop and rings – 23d.

Item paid for making a lock in Amy Howell's house – 4d.

Item paid for bearing banners in Rogation week – 4d.

Item paid to the clerk of St James for his earnest – 1d.

Item paid to Thomas Clarke for binding a *porteose* [breviary] – 3s 4d.

Item paid for mending the best chasuble – 2d.

Item paid on Corpus Christi day for the priests' dinner – 5s 3d.

Item paid to the suffragan for bearing the cross on Corpus Christi day – 4d.

Item paid for a latten cross at St James' tide – 5s.

Item paid for hanging of the Dance of Pauls at 2 times – 16d.

Item paid for mending the new cross which Mistress Chestre gave us – 8d.

Item paid to the suffragan for 3 quarters of his wage at 10s the year – 7s 6d.

Item paid for cloth and the making the clerk's surplice – 6s 3d.

Item paid for mending a glass window in the Green Lattice – 6d.

Item paid to a mason for 2 days' labour in the said Green Lattice for mending a *foren* in the baste house – 13d.

Sum – 34s 1d.

fo 3

Payments

Item paid to a labourer in the said Green Lattice for 2 days' at 4 $\frac{1}{2}$d the day – 11d.[sic]

Item paid for 3 bushels of limestones to the said work – 6d.

Item paid for laths and nails to the said work – 4d.

Item paid for washing surplices, altarcloths, towels and albs against Easter,
Whitsun tide and other times of the year – 2s.
Item paid for making a stone to *hele* [?mend] the holy-water stock – 2d.
Item paid for mending the second suit – 20d.
Sum – 5s 7d.

These are the costs of the church light
In primis paid to John Mayowe, waxmaker, for square light and round
light against Easter – 12s 10d.
Item for the paschal and the font taper – 3s 2d.
Item for 2 new standards of 4 lb in the choir – 2s 4d.
Item for changing 2 standards against Christmas – 12d.
Item for change of round light at All Hallows' tide – 5s 5d.
Sum – 24s 9d.

fo 3v
These are the costs of the General Mind
In primis paid for bread and cakes and all other stuff belonging thereto –
4s 6d.
Item paid for wine – 4s 10d.
Item for ale – 2s 3d.
Item for 7 priests – 21d.
Item paid to the clerk for ringing – 14d.
Sum – 14s 6d.

Item paid to Thomas Clarke of the church money which was lacking that
we could not get in the parish – 16d.
Sum – 16d.

Sum total allowance of all manner of costs – £9 10s 2d.
So rest that the church owes the said proctors of this account – 7s 3d.

[On the end page of the booklet in which this account is written, after
three blank pages, is an inscription which reads The Church Book of
Alhallon. Clement Wylscherr and Thomas Pernaunt]

[1485–86]

fo 1
[Top right-hand corner of folio is torn. The heading is in Latin]
Anno dm 1485
Thomas Skynner

Rental of the church of All Hallows' in the town of Bristol from the feast
of the Nativity 1485 until the same feast in the year following, Thomas
Skynner and John Batyn proctors

The High Street
In primis received of John Snygge by the year – 4 marks 12[s.]
Item received of William Frith by the year – £3 10s.
Item John Tanke by the year – 20s.
Item Thomas Went by the year – 16s.
Item the chantry priest of Thomas Halleway by the year – 6s 8d.
Item for a shop that John Cokkys holds in the churchyard – 20d.
Item of William Meredith for the first quarter – 10s.
[Different hand: Sum – £9 9s 8d.]

Rents assize by the year
Item received of John Branfeld for his bast house – 2s 6d.
Item of Richard Erle by the year – 12d.
Item John Carlene by the year – 4s.
Item the master of the Tailors by the year – 12s.
Item for a tenement in St Peter's parish that late John Steynar held – 6d.
Item for a tenement of John Shepward in Marsh Street – 2s.
Item for a tenement that Povley hardwareman [holds], by year – 3s 4d.
[Different hand: Sum – 25s 4d.
Sum – £10 15s.]

Vacations
Item John Shipward void – 2s.
Item the tenement in St Peter's parish void – 6d.

fo 1v
[Top left-hand corner torn]
?Receipts of Good Friday and Easter day
[Folio torn] Good Friday and Easter day – 15s.
Sum – 15s.

Receipts for burying in the church
Item of Thomas Spicer for his wife's grave – 6s 8d.
Item of the *dene* for Traharyn Davy and his wife's grave – 13s 4d.
[Scored: Item for Mistress Chestre's grave.]

Receipts for seats in the church
Item of Richard Stevyn's and his wife's seats – 2s.
Item William Brown for his seat and his wife – 2s.
Item of Hew Foster for a seat – 10[?d.]

Receipts of bequests
Item of William Freyth's bequest – 3s 4d.
Item of Jenett Golle's bequest – 12d.
Item for 2 torches to Halleway's mind – 12d.
Sum total – 45s 4d.

Sum total receipts the vacations allowed – £12 17s 10d.

fo 2
The payments for the church by the said proctors
Item for a quart of *malmesence* [malmsey] on Palm Sunday, the priests – 4d.
Item for scouring *scarys* – 1d.
Item for scouring of the standards and the bowls and the candlesticks against Easter – 3d.
Item for the raker for hauling of the church dust – 8d.
Item for watching the sepulchre to the clerk and the suffragan on bread, ale and coals – 12d.
Item for a staple and a pin to the sepulchre – 1d.
Item for making the church rent roll – 3d.
Item for mending the lock on the treasure house door – 3d.
Item for a purse to set the church money in – 1d.
Item for a dinner to the priests for Our Lady Mass in lent – 4s.
Item for bearing the banners in Rogation week – 4d.
Item for a dinner to the priests on Corpus Christi day – 8s 2d.
Item to the clerk for hanging the Dance of Pauls – 16d.
Item paid to the suffragan to make his wages fully with the money that we gathered on Palm Sunday – 5s 1d.
Item for rent assize to Christ Church and Saint John's for the house on Broad Street that William Meredith dwells in – 20s.
Item for setting up the judas in the rood loft to the ?carver – 10d.
Item for dressing of the ?ironwork thereto – 8d.
Item for nails thereto – 1d.
Item for a piece of wire thereto – 3d.
Item for a cord and a *peys* [weight] to hang the *bow* [?bowl] afore the rood – 2d.

fo 2v
Item for pulling down of the cock and the cross off the steeple – 16d.
Item for a mason to point the steeple for 7 days – 3s 1d.
Item for lime thereto, 3 quarters – 6d.
Item for a labourer to serve the mason – 3d.
Item for making a case for the trestle – 8d.

Item for dressing a gutter in Tank's house – 8d.

Item paid for 2 penny boards to mend a pentys [lean-to] in William Frith's house and ?man-hire and nails – 6d.

Item for the mother church of Worcester – 8d.

Item allowance to tenants when [they] pay rent – 12d.

Item for making of the church book – 12d.

Item for a rope to the little mass bell that rings the first mass – 6d.

Item to Thomas Pernaunt for 7 gallons of oil for the lamp – 7s.

Item for washing of the church cloths to the launderer – 16d.

Sum – £3 2s 6d.

fo 3

These are the costs of wax and the making thereof

Item in primis for 30 lb of wax for the paschal and font tapers to Thomas Spicer for Easter – 30s.

Item for making the same, to the waxmaker – 15d.

Item for Our Lady light and 8 tapers in the church for 8 lb of wax at 8d the pound – 5s 4d.

Item for making the same light – 12d.

Item for making 2 tapers upon the standards in the high choir [recte: altar?], for 1 ½ lb wax and for the making – 12d.

Item for 13 lb of wax to the rood light at 9d the pound – 9s 9d.

Item for the making – 13d.

Sum – 49s 5d.

fo 3v

Here follows the costs of William Newbery's mind

In primis paid to the vicar for his wax and dirige – 16d.

Item for 5 priests for their dirige – 20d.

Item paid to the clerk for his dirige and bells – 10d.

Item paid to the bedeman – 4d.

Item paid for bread to poor people – 2s.

Sum – 6s 2d.

The costs of Thomas Fyler and Agnes his wife at their year's mind

In primis to the vicar for wax and dirige – 12d.

Item paid for 8 priests for dirige and mass – 2s 8d.

Item paid to the clerk for bells and dirige – 14d.

Item paid to the vicar to oversee this to be done for the bede roll – 12d.

Item paid to the bedeman – 2d.

Item paid to the poor people in bread – 5s.

Item paid to the 2 proctors for their diligent labour – 12d.

Sum total – 12s.

fo 4

The costs of the General Mind

Item paid for 2 bushels of wheaten meal – 16d.

Item paid for an ounce of saffron – 10d.

Item paid for a pottle of osey to the cakes – 6d.

Item paid for salt and *barm* – 1d.

Item paid for a pint of oil to the cakes – 2d.

Item paid for baking the cakes – 6d.

Item paid for 2 dozen double ale – 2s 11d.

Item paid for divers wines Roscolom, claret and osey – 4s 2d.

Item paid to the vicar for his dirige – 4d.

Item paid to the priests for dirige – 15d.

Item paid to the clerk for the bells and dirige – 14d.

Item paid for offering to mass – 1d.

Sum total – 14s 4d.

The costs of Harry Chestre's mind and Alice Chester his wife

Item to the vicar for his light and dirige – 12d.

Item for 6 priests – 2s.

Item to the clerk for the bells and dirige – 12d.

Item to the bell man – 4d.

Item for offering at mass – 1d.

Item for bread to poor people – 2s 8d.

Sum – 7s 1d.

[Account ends abruptly]

[1487–1488]

fo 1

1487

fo 2

Jhs

[Heading in Latin] Rental of the church of All Saints', Bristol, from the feast of the Nativity 1487 to the same feast in the year next following and [scored: John Batyn and Thomas Snygge] Thomas Snygge and Richard Stevyns proctors for the same year

The High Street

In primis John Snygg by the year – £3 6s 4d.

Item Sacare, draper, by the year – £3 10s.

Item John Tank by the year – 20s.

Item Thomas Went by the year – 16s.

Item Sir John Penyston by the year – 6s 8d.
Item Thomas Koke by the year – £4.
Item John Cokes for a shop by the year – 20d.
Sum – £13 12d.

The rent assize by the year
In primis John Branfeld for his baste door – 2s 6d.
Item Richard Erle by the year – 12d.
Item John Carlen by the year – 4s.
Item the master of the Tailors by the year – 12s.
Item John Steynard for a tenement in St Peter's parish – 6d.
Item John Schepard for a tenement in Marsh Street – 2s.
Item Paul Hardyrman by the year – 3s 4d.
Sum – 25s 4d.
Amount – £14 6s 4d.

The receipts of money lent out of the church
Item received of Thomas Koke for the *dewte* [debt] of William Meredith, in part payment of £10 – £3.
Item received of Thomas Koke in part payment of obligation of £7 – 20s.
Sum – £4.
Amount the whole receipts and the debts to our accounts – £18 6s 4d.

fo 2v
The receipts on Good Friday and Easter day and the receipts of their casualties
In primis received on Good Friday and Easter day – 15s 10d.
Item received for waste of 2 torches at Halleway's mind – 12d.
Item received for waste of 4 torches at Nicholas Ket's burying – 12d.
Item received for Clement Wilteshire for his wife's pit – 6s 8d.
Sum – 24s 6d.

Amount the whole charge of the proctors the year afore rehearsed – £19 10s 10d.
Vacations
In primis John Shepard decay – 2s.
Item there as John Tanck dwelt, decayed – 15s.
Sum – 17s.

The payments of the church of All Hallows by the proctors
In primis paid rent assize to the master of St John's – 6s 8d.
Item paid rent assize to Christ Church – 13s 4d.
Item paid for repairing the glazed windows – 4s.
Item paid for 8 ells of normandy cloth for a surplice to the clerk at 6d – 4s.

Item paid for making the same surplice – 16d.
Item paid for making the church lock – 12d.
Item paid for a pottle of wine of Palm Sunday – 5d.
Item paid the raker of his year – 8d.
Item paid for watching the sepulchre – 12d.
Item paid for bread and ale the same time – 4d.
Item paid for scouring the church ?gear – 20d.
Item paid for hanging the sacring bell – 2d.
Item paid for bearing the banners – 4d.
Item paid for a dinner to the priests in Lent – 3s.
Item paid for a dinner on Corpus Christi day – 6s.
Item paid for bearing the cross – 2d.
Sum – 44s 1d.

Rest to our charge – £16 9s 9d.

fo 3
The costs belonging to the church
Item paid to the suffragan for his wages – 6s.
Item paid to the new suffragan – 5d.
Item for besoms at 2 times – 1d.
Item for workmanship of the 2 *pellers in ?fresco* [?pillars in fresco] – 20d.
Item for washing the church cloths – 2s.
Item for pins at 2 times – 1d.
Item for a quart pot to set oil in – 10d.
Item for hanging the Dance of Pauls – 16d.
Item for a key to the store house door – 2d.
Item for hauling rubble – 1d.
Item for plating the 2 ?staffs – 11s.
Item for repairing a gutter in Sir John Penystone's house – 6d.
Item for a *noblygacyon* [an obligation] upon Thomas Koke – 2d.
Item paid to Our Lady church in Worcester – 8d.
Item paid for making the rent roll – 3d.
Item for 2 cords for the altar – 6d.
Item for 4 ells of cloth for a rochet – 2s 2d.
Item for making the same rochet – 12d.
Item for boards to the churchyard door – 15d.
Item for 100 board nail – 2 $\frac{1}{2}$d.
Item for a lock to the same door – 4d.
Item for changing the lead upon the door – 4 $\frac{1}{2}$d.
Item for lead nails to the same door – 1d.
Item for 4 spikes and a twist to the same door – 5d.
Item for a carpenter to the same work – 9d.
Item for pence to the tenantry – 12d.

Sum – 28s 4d.

Rest to our charge – £15 17d.

fo 3v
The costs of the wax at Easter and All Hallows' tide
In primis at Easter 18 ¼ lb of wax at 8d the pound – 12s 3d.
Item for making 32 lb of wax besides – 16d.
Item for 24 ¾ lb of wax against All Hallows' tide at 8d the pound –
16s 6d.
Item for making 38 lb of wax besides – 19d.
Item for changing 2 standards before the high altar – 10d.
Sum – 32s 6d.

The costs of William Newbery's mind
In primis paid to the vicar for his wax and dirige – 16d.
Item 5 priests for their dirige – 20d.
Item the clerk for his dirige and bells – 10d.
Item paid for bread for poor people – 2s.
Item paid to the bedeman – 4d.
Sum – 6s 2d.

The costs of the dirige of Thomas Fylour and Agnes his wife
In primis paid to the vicar for his wax and dirige – 12d.
Item 8 priests for their dirige and wax – 2s 8d.
Item to the clerk for his bells and dirige – 14d.
Item the vicar to see that this be done and for the bede roll – 12d.
Item the bedeman for his labour – 2d.
Item bread to poor people – 5s.
Item the proctors for their labour – 12d.
Sum – 12s.

The costs of the dirige of Harry Chestre and Alice his wife
In primis paid the vicar for wax and his dirige – 12d.
Item 6 priests for the dirige and mass – 2s.
Item the clerk for his bells and dirige – 12d.
Item bedeman for his labour – 4d.
Item offering at mass – 1d.
Item in bread to poor people – 2s 8d.
Sum – 7s 1d.

Rest to our charge – £12 3s 8d.

fo 4

The costs of the General Mind

In primis 2 bushels of flour – 2s 6d.

Item 1 ¼ oz saffron – 14d.

Item in cloves and *massys* [mace] – 2d.

Item in *barme* – 1d.

Item for bread to poor people – 6d.

Item for baking the cake – 8d.

Item for a pottle of wine ?to the cake – 5d.

Item for a pound of *suker* [?sugar] to the cake – 4d.

Item for oil to the cake – 2d.

Item for 2 dozen ale – 3s.

Item for spices to the same ale – 6d.

Item for 2 gallons Roscolye – 16d.

Item for a quart of claret wine to the mayor – 2d.

Item for a gallon Roscolye – 8d.

Item for 4 gallons and a penny pot of osey – 3s 5d.

Item for 4 gallons of claret wine – 2s 8d.

Item to the vicar for his dirige – 4d.

Item to 5 priests for their dirige – 15d.

Item to the clerk for his dirige and bells – 14d.

Item for offering at mass – 1d.

Sum – 20s 7d.

The repairs done in Tancke's house

In primis 4 keys – 8d.

Item for a ?mason 3 days' – 19d.

Item for laths – 1d.

Item for 2 quarts of lime – 5d.

Sum – 2s 9d.

Rest to our charge £11 4d.

fo 4v

The reparation of Thomas Koke's house

In primis 600 boards at 2s 2d the 100 – 13s.

Item 1500 boards at 2s 4d the 100 – 35s.

Item 600 boards at 2s 8d the 100 – 16s.

Item for mending of all the gutters – 4s 6d.

Item for pieces of timber to cover the well – 21d.

Item for a base to the stair – 6d.

Item for 8 steps to the same – 21d.

Item for 2 stair blades – 8d.

Item for 2 planks to the same – 6d.

Item for 2100 board nails at 5d the hundred – 8s 9d.
Item for 200 hatch nails – 8d.
Item for spikes to the same – 2 ½d.
Item for hauling the boards at divers times – 14d.
Item for 200 tack nails – 6d.
Item for 2 carpenters' wages for a fortnight – 15s 2d.
Item for 6 poles to *juste* – 3s.
Item for a *corbell*, 2d, and a *polte of hier*, 5d – 7d.
Item for a labourer 6 days' – 2s
Item for 5 ?studs at 2d the piece – 10d.
Item for calf nail – 2d.
Item for making a *chevre* – 6s 8d.
Item for 6 lb solder to the gutters – 18d.
Item for a plank to a step – 10d.
Item for a *partson* 4 studs – 5d.
Item for ?hair and lime – 1d.
Item for 3 poles – 12d.
Item for passing the *fawt* and mending the stair – 10s.
Item day ?half to a carpenter – 8d.
Sum – £6 7s 8 ½d.

Amount the costs and charges – £14 18s 2d.

Rest to our charge in debts – £4 12s 8d.

Paid for performing the ?scolle [?school] – 10s 1d.
Item of Hugh Sadeler – 12d.
[Scored: Item received of Sakare, draper, for rest of rent – 10s.]
Rest – £4 3s 7d

fo 4
Item paid for ?oil to Thomas Pernaunt – 8s.

Rest to our charge in debts – 4 [unfinished].

[1488–89]

fo 1
Jhs
[Heading in Latin] Rental of the church of All Saints' in the town of Bristol from the feast of Christmas 1488 until the same feast in the year following, Richard Stevyns and Thomas Pernaunt proctors for the same year

The High Street
In primis John Snygg by the year – £3 6s 8d.
Item Marjory Husschear by the year – £4.
Item John Bowde by the year – 20s.
Item Thomas Wentt by the year – 16s.
Item Sir John Peyntor by the year – 6s 8d.
Item Thomas Coke by the year – £4.
Item John Cocks for a ?shop by the year – 20d.
Sum – £13 11s.

The rent assize by the year
In primis John Branfeld for his basedoor – 2s 6d.
Item Richard Erle by the year – 12d.
Item John Carlen by the year – 4s.
Item the master of the Tailors by the year – 12s.
Item John Steynard for a tenement in St Peter's parish – 6d.
Item John Schepard for a tenement in Marsh Street – 12s.
Item Poulle Hardman by the year – 3s 4d.
Sum – 25s 4d.

Amount – £14 16s 4d.

fo 1v
The receipts on Good Friday and Easter day and the receipts of other casualties
In primis received on Good Friday and Easter Day and Palm Sunday – 16s.
Item received for a piece of timber – 4d.
Item received of Master Schreve for Richard Andrew's grave – 6s 8d.
Item received of William Bowyer for his and his wife's seat – 12d.
Item received of Thomas Langley's wife for her seat – 6d.
Item received for wasting 2 torches at Halleway's mind – 12d.
Item received of Watkyn Master, Schreve's cook, for the house at the cross for 7 weeks – 2s 8d.
Item received of Thomas Coke in part payment of the obligation – 20s.
Sum – 47s 10d.

Amount the receipts and the amount of our account – £17 4s 2d.

Vacations
In primis John Scheparde decay – 2s.
Item there as John Tancke dwelt, decay – 20s.
Item the Green Lattice decay a quarter – 20s.
Sum the vacations – 42s.

fo 2
Payments rent assize
In primis paid for rent assize for the Master of St John's – 6s 8d.
Item paid for rent assize to Christ Church – 13s 4d.
Item paid to the town chamber for *longabull* [land-gavel] – 2s 4 ½d.
Sum – 22s 4 ½d.

The payments of the church of All Hallows' by the proctors
Item paid on Palm Sunday for wine to the priests and the clerks – 4d.
Item paid to the suffragan for his year's wage – 8s.
Item paid to the raker for hauling away the dust of the church – 8d.
Item paid for scouring the candlesticks and the bowls of the church – 6d.
Item paid for scouring the great basin before Our Lady – 2s.
Item paid for oil and scouring stone – 1d.
Item paid for watching the sepulchre – 8d.
Item paid to the clerk for ale and coals – 4d.
Sum – 12s 7d.

fo 2v
Payments of the church
Item paid for a fire pan to set fire to the church – 4d.
Item paid for besoms – 1d.
Item paid for the lenten dinner to the priests – 3s 4d.
Item paid for setting on 10 pairs of vestments to the *ffygerys* [?vicar's]
mother – 10d.
Item paid to the waxmaker for wax against Easter – 21s 4d.
Item paid for bearing the banners in Rogation week – 4d.
Item paid to the clerk for hanging up the Dance of Pauls against Saint
James tide – 8d.
Item paid for mending the ladders – 2d.
Item paid to the waxmaker for wax against All Hallows' tide – 25s 7d.
Item paid for washing the church cloths – 2s 8d.
Item paid to the clerk for hanging up the Dance of Pauls against All
Hallows' tide – 8d.
Item paid for 2 *spryngellys* [?sprinklers] for the church – 2s 8d.
Item paid for a hinge to the enterclose door – 4d.
Item paid for tack nails – ½d.
Item paid for 2 pins to set on the 2 cross[es] upon before the high altar –
2d.
Sum – 59s 2 ½d.

fo 3
Payments on Corpus Christi day
Item paid to the vicar – 8d.

Item paid to the 4 priests – 16d.
Item paid to the clerk – 4d.
Item paid for bearing the cross – 4d.
Item paid for a pottle of wine for the priests in the march – 4d.
Item paid for mending the *tynnell* of the church – 1 ½d.
Item paid for pins and *rachokys* – 1d.
Item paid for a gallon and a pottle of wine to the bishop's officers – 12d.
Item paid for making the church book – 12d.
Item for allowance to the tenants – 12d.
Sum – 6s 2 ½d.

Costs of William Newbery's mind
In primis paid to the vicar for his wax and dirige – 16d.
Item paid to 5 priests for their dirige – 20d.
Item paid to the clerk for his dirige and bells – 10d.
Item paid for bread for poor people – 2s.
Item to the bedeman – 4d.
Sum – 6s 2d.

fo 3v
The costs of Thomas Fylour and Agnes his wife their dirige
In primis paid to the vicar for his wax and dirige – 12d.
Item paid to 8 priests for their dirige and mass – 2s 8d.
Item paid to the clerk for his bells and dirige – 14d.
Item paid to the vicar to see that this be done and for the bede roll – 12d.
Item paid to the bedeman for his labour – 2d.
Item paid for bread to the poor people – 5s.
Item to the proctors for their labour – 12d.
Sum – 12s.

The costs of Harry Chester and Alice his wife their dirige
In primis paid to the vicar for wax and his dirige – 12d.
Item paid to 6 priests for their dirige and mass – 2s.
Item paid to the clerk for his bells and dirige – 12d.
Item paid to the bedeman for his labour – 4d.
Item for offering – 1d.
Item paid for bread for poor people – 2s 8d.
Sum – 7s 1d.

fo 4
The costs of the General Mind
Item paid for 2 ½ bushels of flour – 2s 6d.
Item paid for a dozen of white cake – 12d.
Item paid for saffron to the same cake – 12d.

Item paid for baking the cake – 8d.
Item paid for a pottle of wine to the same cake – 4d.
Item paid for oil to the same cake – 2d.
Item paid for 3 dozen ale – 4s 6d.
Item paid for 3 pottles of wine – 12d.
Item paid to the vicar for his dirige – 4d.
Item paid to the 4 priests – 12d.
Item paid to the clerk for his bells – 14d.
Item for offering – 1d.
Sum – 13s 9d.

fo 4v
The reparation of Thomas Coke's house
In primis paid for a lead pipe and casting solder to the said pipe – 9s 4d.
Item paid for 200 board nails to the same house – 10d.
Item paid for clay to make 2 floors in the same house – 2s.
Item paid for hay and labour to the same floor – 18d.
Item paid for 200 board nails to the same house – 10d.
Item paid for 150 boards – 3s 6d.
Item paid for a base to a stair – 4d.
Item paid 23 feet of stairs steps – 23d.
Item paid for 2 stairs' blades – 10d.
Item paid for 2 carpenters' hire for ?11 days' labour in the said house –
5s 6d.
Item paid for calf-foot nail – 2d.
Item paid for 3 boards – 8d.
Item paid for a piece of timber for a *garnar* – 6d.
Item paid for 2 boards – 12d.
Item paid for nails – 1 $\frac{1}{2}$d.
Item paid for making of the same *garnar* – 16d.
Item paid for 3 studs – 1 $\frac{1}{2}$d.
Item paid for a plank that the stair blades are nailed to – 2d.
Sum – 29s 10d.

fo 5
The reparation in John Tanke's house
Item paid for cleaning a gutter in John Tanke's house – 16d.
Item paid to the plumber for mending a gutter in the Kalendars, and solder
to the same work – 8d.
Item paid for ridding a gutter in the church yard – 1d.
Sum – 2s 1d.

fo 5v

The Reparation in the Green Lattice

In primis paid for a piece of timber to bear up the kitchen in the Green Lattice – 6d.

Item paid for hauling of the same piece of timber from the quay – 1d.

Item paid for 2 lanterns to lay under the windows in the baste house in the Green Lattice – 8d.

Item paid to William Were for 175 oaken boards to lay under the paving in the kitchen – 2s.

Item paid for a plank to make *dobyng* – 4d.

Item paid for 3 studs – 3d.

Item paid to Hampton the carpenter for 3 days' labour in the Green Lattice – 19 $\frac{1}{2}$d.

Item paid for nails to the same house – 4d.

Item paid for 3 paving stones to pave the kitchen in the Green Lattice – 10d.

Item paid for stones to pitch the hearth in the kitchen of the Green Lattice – 6d.

Item paid to the lime burner for 6 quarters of lime to the same house – 12d.

Item paid to Kedell for clay to the same house – 5d.

Item paid to Cornell the mason for 14 days' labour in the same house – 7s 10 $\frac{1}{2}$d.

Sum – 16s 6d.

fo 6

The reparations in the Green Lattice

Item paid to a labourer ?3 $\frac{1}{2}$ days' labour in the Green Lattice – 18d.

Item paid for hauling the dust out of the Green Lattice – 1d.

Item paid for mending a *skare* in the gutter of the Green Lattice – 5d.

Item paid for cleaning a gutter in the Green Lattice – 4d.

Sum – 2s 4d.

Amount the costs and charges – £11 12s 1 $\frac{1}{2}$d.

So rest to our charge in debt – £5 12s 1 $\frac{1}{2}$d.

Received the day of account – £5 12s 1 $\frac{1}{2}$d.

Received of Hugh Saddeler – 12d.

Sum total of the rest – £5 13s 1 $\frac{1}{2}$d.

[1489–90]

[Front cover cut from booklet]
fo 1
Jhs
[Heading in Latin] The rental of All Saints' in the town of Bristol from the feast of Christmas 1489 until the same feast in the year following, Thomas Pernaunt and Paul James proctors for the same year

The High Street
In primis John Snygg by the year – £3 6s 8d.
Item Morgan Usscher by the year – £4.
Item John Bowde by the year – 16s.
Item Thomas Went by the year – 16s.
Item Sir John Penyston by the year – 6s 8d.
Item Thomas Coke by the year – £4.
Item John Coks for a shop by the year – 20d.
Sum – £13 7s.

The rent assize by the year
In primis John Branfeld for his bastedoor – 2s 6d.
Item John Carlen by the year – 4s.
Item the master of the Tailors by the year – 12s.
Item Paul Harddeman by the year – 3s 4d.
Item Master Crofftys for a house in St Peter's parish – 6d.
Item Richard Erle by the year – 12d.
Item John Schepard by the year – 2s.
Sum – 25s 4d.

Amount – £14 12s 4d.
Amount the whole receipts and the debts to our accounts – £14 12s 4d.

fo 1v
The receipts on Good Friday and Easter eve and Easter day and the receipts of our casualties
In primis received on Good Friday and Easter eve and Easter day – 17s.
Item received of John Asche for his seat – 6d.
Item received for waste of 2 torches at Halleway's mind – 12d.
Item received of Thomas Coke – 20s.
Sum – 38s 6d.
Amount the whole charges of the proctors the year afore rehearsed – £16 10s 10d.

Vacations
In primis John Chepard decay – 2s.
Item Richard Erle decay – 12d.
Item John Bowde a quarter decay – 4s.
Sum – 7s.

The payments of the church of All Hallows' by the proctors
In primis paid for rent assize to the Master of St John's – 6s 8d.
Item paid for a rent assize to Christ Church – 13s 4d.
Item paid on Palm Sunday for wine to the priests – 4d.
Item paid to the suffragan for his year's wage – 8s.
Item paid for besoms for the church – 1d.
Item paid for the priests' lenten dinner – 4s.
Item paid for scouring the candlesticks and the bowls of the church – 10d.
Item paid for oil and scouring-stone to the same – 2d.
Item paid to Our Lady of Worcester for the church – 16d.
Item paid to the raker for hauling away the rubble of the church – 8d.
Item paid to the *colectowrs* [collectors] for the church rents – 25s 10 $\frac{1}{2}$d.
Item paid for the rent roll – 2d.
Sum – £3 18 $\frac{1}{2}$d.

fo 2
The payments of the church by the proctors
In primis paid to the clerk for watching the sepulchre – 12d.
Item paid to William Clarke of St Nicholas' for mending the organs – 20d.
Item paid to Richard Stevyns for the rest of the money of Sacry's house –
2s 6d.
Item paid for a rope for the sanctus bell – 6d.
Item paid for mending the lead – 1d.
Item paid for mending the church ?lock – 5d.
Item paid for mending the copes – 6d.
Item paid for mending the clapper of the bells – 8d.
Item paid for baldrics for the bells – 12d.
Item paid for lines to draw the altars – 2d.
Item paid for a ?loop – 1d.
Item paid to William Cachemay, goldsmith, for setting the precious stones
on Jesus' foot – 3s 5d.
Item paid to the clerk for hanging up the Dance of Pauls – 16d.
Item paid for pins to hang up cloths – $\frac{1}{2}$d.
Item paid for 2 irons at the high altar – 4d.
Item paid for wire to make fast the tapers in the rood loft – 4d.
Item paid for a baldric for the sacring bell – 4d.
Item paid for washing of the church cloths – 2s.
Item paid for pence to the tenants – 12d.

Item paid for making the church book – 12d.
Item paid to the suffragan for bearing the banner in Rogation week – 4d.
Sum – 18s 8 ½d.

fo 2v
The payments on Corpus Christi day
In primis paid to the vicar – 8d.
Item paid to 4 priests – 16d.
Item paid to the clerk – 4d.
Item paid for bearing the cross – 4d.
Item paid for a pottle of wine in the march to the priests of Corpus Christi day – 4d.
Sum – 3s.

The costs of wax at Easter and All Hallows' tide in the church
In primis paid for wax against Easter – 17s.
Item paid for 2 torches, weighing 47 lb at 3d the lb – 11s 9d.
Item paid for making the square lights and the round lights against All Hallows' tide – 22s 6d.
Item paid for 2 torches, weighing 39 lb at 3d the lb – 9s 9d.
Sum – £3 12d.

The costs of Thomas Fyler and Agnes his wife's dirige
In primis paid to the vicar for [scored: his dirige] and his wax – 12d.
Item paid to 8 priests for dirige and their mass – 2s 8d.
Item paid to the clerk for his dirige and his bells – 14d.
Item paid to the vicar to see that this be done and for the bede roll – 12d.
Item paid to the bedeman for his labour – 2d.
Item paid for bread to the poor people – 5s.
Item paid to the proctors for their labour – 12d.
Sum – 12s.

fo 3
The costs of William Newbery's mind
In primis paid to the vicar for his wax and dirige – 16d.
Item paid to 5 priests for their dirige – 20d.
Item paid to the clerk for his dirige and his bells – 10d.
Item paid for bread to poor people – 2s.
Item paid to the bedeman – 2d.
Sum – 6s.

The costs of Harry Chester and Alice his wife their dirige
In primis paid to the vicar for his dirige and his wax – 12d.
Item paid to 6 priests for their dirige and mass – 2s.

Item paid to the clerk for his dirige and his bells – 12d.
Item paid to the bedeman for his labour – 4d.
Item our offering at Mass – 1d.
Item paid for bread to poor people – 2s 8d.
Sum – 7s 1d.

fo 3v
The costs of the General Mind
In primis paid for flour to make the cake – 2s 3d.
Item paid for saffron – 12d.
Item paid for cloves to the cake – 2d.
Item paid for wine – 2s 1d.
Item paid for ?sugar – 4d.
Item paid for baking the cake – 8d.
Item paid for oil to the cake – 2d.
Item paid for 3 dozen ale – 4s.
Item paid to the vicar for his dirige – 4d.
Item paid to 4 priests – 12d.
Item for our offering – 1d.
Item paid to the clerk – 14d.
Sum – 13s 3d.

The repairs of Thomas Cook's house
Item paid to William Wythchurch for lathing and healing the *parteson*
[?partition] in Thomas Coke's house – 10d.
Item paid for 500 lath nails – 6d.
Item paid for 150 laths – 9d.
Item paid for hair – 1d.
Item paid for 6 quarters lime – 12d.
Item paid to the *chamborlens* for paving his baste door – 15d.
Sum – 4s 5d.

fo 4
The repairs of John Bowd's house
Item paid for boards – 8d.
Item paid for nails – 2d.
Item paid for boards – 6d.
Item paid for 2 days' labour to a carpenter – 11d.
Item paid to a labourer for cleaning the same house – 2d.
Item paid for a load of clay – 2d.
Item paid for a load of sand – 1d.
Item paid to a mason for 2 days' labour in John Bowd's kitchen – 10d.
Item paid to a labourer for 1 $\frac{1}{2}$ day's labour – 5d.
Item paid for a quarter of lime – 2d.

Item paid for setting up a stone in the Green Lattice upon a chimney – 3d.
Sum – 4s 4d.

The repairs of Thomas Went's house
Item paid for a piece of timber to the kitchen floor – 10d.
Item paid for hauling the same piece of timber – 1d.
Item paid for 36 feet of boards – 10d.
Item paid for nails – 2d.
Item paid to a carpenter for 2 days' labour – 13d.
Item paid to John Fawlonde, mason, for 2 days' labour – 13d.
Item paid to a labourer – 4d.
Item for 2 quarters lime – 4d.
Item paid for 2 loads of clay – 4d.
Item paid for 2 stones to the same house – 2d.
Item paid for hauling of 2 ?vats of rubble – 2d.
Sum – 5s 4d.

fo 4v
Repairs in the Churchyard
Item paid to a mason for to make up the wall in the churchyard, for 2 $\frac{1}{2}$ days' labour – 16d.
Item paid to a labourer for 2 $\frac{1}{2}$ days' labour – 11 $\frac{1}{2}$d.
Item paid for lime to the same wall – 8d.
Item for sand to the same work – 2d.
Item paid for hauling stones from Thomas Cook's house to the same work – 3d.
Item paid for a sack of lime – 1d.
Item paid for pikes to the said wall – 14d.
Item paid for making of *stole* and 2 *gymoss* and 2 feet to the said *stole* in the rood loft – 7d.
Item paid for nails – $\frac{1}{2}$d.
Item paid for a mason to set in the spikes – 9d.
Item paid for wood to the said work – 2d.
Item paid to a labourer for 1 day's labour – 6d.
Sum – 6s 8d.

Sum the payments by the year – £10 11s 3d.
Rest all [words illegible] – £6 7d.

[Different hand: Item of Hewe Sadeler – 12d.]

[1492 – presumably 1491–92, but not specified]

fo 1
1492
Jhu

This book is of accounts made by Thomas Spicer [and] John Stayner
prokatourres [proctors] of the church of All Hallows' for the year of our
lord 1492.

fo 2
Here follows the rental of the livelode of All Hallows' church of Bristol,
the year of our lord 1492.

In the High Street
John Snygg by the year – £3 6s 8d.
Humphrey Holt by the year – £4.
John Bowde by the year – 16s.
Thomas Went by the year – 16s.
Sir John Pennyston by the year – 6s 8d.
Thomas Kokys, brewer, by the year – £4.
John Kokys for the beer house – 20d.
Sum – £13 7s.

Received of Thomas Kokys, brewer, for money lent of the church – 20s.
Sum – 20s.

The rents of assize belonging to All Hallows' church
John Branfyld for his baste door – 2s 6d.
John Carleon by the year – 4s.
Master of the Tailors by the year – 12s.
Paul James by the year for a *wardrop* – 3s 4d.
Master Browne for a house in St Peter's parish – 6d.
Richard Erle for a house in *Lyen his mede* [Lewins Mead] that Robert
Recard now holds by the year – 12d.
John Schepard for a house in Marsh street by the year – 2s.
Sum – 25s 4d.

Amount this side – £15 12s 4d.

fo 2v
These are the casualties received on Palm Sunday, Sheer Thursday, Good
Friday, Easter eve and Easter day.

Item received on Palm Sunday – 2s 6d.
Item received on Good Friday – 2s 10d.
Item received on Easter day – 7s 4d.
Sum – 12s 8d.

Here follow the receipts of [the] casualties of the church
Item received of Pers Grynfeld for Janet Howell's grave – 6s 8d.
Item received of William Adamys for the foot of the cross – 12d.
Item received of John Snygg for Hugh Flemyng's grave – 6s 8d.
Item received of Mistress Wyllsche[re] for her husband's grave – 6s 8d.
Item received of Maud Spicer for her husband's grave – 6s 8d.
Sum – 27s 8d.

Amount the whole receipts – £17 12s 8d.

Payments of rent assize
Paid to the Master of St John's for the year – 6s 8d.
Paid to the proctors of Christ Church for the year – 13s 4d.
Sum – 20s.

Here follow the costs done of the church
Paid of Palm Sunday for wine to the readers of the Passion – 4d.
Paid for besoms – ½d.
Paid for scouring the candlesticks – 12d.
Paid to the raker for hauling – 8d.
Paid to 2 men for watching the sepulchre – 12d.
Paid for coals at that time – 3d.
Paid for bread and ale – 2d.
Paid to Our Lady Church of Worcester – 8d.
Paid to the suffragan for his wages – 8s.
Sum – 12s 1 ½d.

Amount the payments on this side – 32s 1 ½d.

fo 3
The costs of the church light against Easter
Item paid to John Raynold for making of the light – 3s 4d.
Item paid to John for 27 lb 6 oz of wax at 7d, sum – 15s 11d.
Sum – 19s 3d.

Paid for a dinner to the priests for keeping Our Lord's Mass in Lent – 4s.
Sum – 4s.

The costs done on Corpus Christi day
Item paid to Master ?Den for his labour – 8d.
Item paid to 5 priests for their labour – 20d.
Item paid to the clerk for his labour – 4d.
Item paid to the suffragan for his labour – 4d.
Sum – 3s.

Item paid to John Raynold waxmaker for 6 torches weighing 118 lb at 3d
the pound – 29s 6d.
Sum 29s 6d.

The costs done upon the Green Lattice
Item paid to the town clerk for making a release – 3s 4d.
Item paid for wine at that time – 4d.
Item paid to Davy Carpenter for 3 days' – 16d.
Item paid for removing the setts – 2d.
Item paid for 5 studs to make [illegible] to the ?pentys – 6d.
Item paid for 1 ¼ hundredweight and 8lb of cast lead at 6s the
hundredweight – 7s 10d.
Item paid for 2 quarters of lime – 4d.
Item paid for cleaning the gutters – 1d.
Item paid for a *crampett* of ?iron for the pipe in the pavement – 4d.
Item paid for 4 *crampetts* for the gutter *a forstrett* – 14d.
Item paid to the man ?Parnaunt for boards and nails – 2s 8d.
Item paid to Davy Carpenter for work necessary at the same house – 11d.
Item paid for a pair of twists and 2 hooks – 11d.
Sum – 19s 9d.

Amount – £3 15s 9d.

fo 3v
Costs done upon the church and *dewts* [debts] for the same
Item paid to John Clerk for setting up and taking down the Dance of Pauls
– 16d.
Item paid to the suffragan for bearing the banners in Rogation week – 4d.
Item paid at 2 times for washing the church stuff – 18d.
Item paid for 10 ?bars of ?iron weighing 1 hundredweight and 17 lb at
1 ¼ the pound – 13s 5 ¼d.
Item paid for 7 stones and 6 lb wire at 3s the stone, sum – 22s 3d.
Item paid for small wire to bind this, 9 lb at 4d – 3s.
Item paid for John Kecks for his labour upon the ?basins – 2s 10d.
Item paid for setting and taking out of the 10 ?bars – 2s 9d.
Item paid for 6 ells of worsted at 3s 10d, sum – 23s.
Item paid for a yard and a half of buckram – 9d.

Item paid for canvas – 18 ½d.
Item for making the same – 8s.
Item paid for wine to the suffragan of Wells – 6d.
Item paid for carriage of the stuff ?there – 2d.
Item paid for mending a clapper – 1d.
Item paid for mending a baldric – 4d.
Item paid for quarter *mallmysser* [?malmsey] at taking feoffment of the church lands – 3d.
Item paid for 10 ells of *Brewolls* at 11d the ell – 9s 2d.
Item paid for making the same surplice – 3s 4d.
Item paid for 3 loads of tile stones with the ?capping – 4s 4 ½d.
Item paid for 350 lath nails – 3 ½d.
Item paid to a tiler for 4 days' work – 22d.
Item paid to a mason for 3 ½ days' work at 6 ½d – 22 ½d.
Item paid to John Sulle for mending the glass windows – 10s.
Item paid for land-gavel for this year – 2s 3d.
Sum this side – £5 15s 2d.

fo 4
The costs done in John Bowde and Thomas Went's houses
Item paid for 2 loads of stones – 2s 10d.
Item paid for 1 ½ loads of ?Row free stone – 3s 9d.
Item paid for hauling from Redcliffe – 4d.
Item paid for 3 loads of sand – 3d.
Item paid for 16 days' to Cornyll mason at 6 ½d – 8s 6d.
Item paid for 13 days' to a labourer at 4 ½d – 5s ½d.
Item paid for 16 quarters of lime – 2s 8d.
Sum – 23s 6 ½d.

The costs of William Newbery's mind
Item paid to Master Den for his wax and dirige – 16d.
Item paid to 5 priests for their dirige – 20d.
Item paid to the clerk – 10d.
Item paid for bread for poor people – 2s.
Item paid to the bellman – 2d.
Sum – 6s.

The costs of Thomas Fyler's mind
Item paid to Master Den for wax and dirige – 2s.
Item paid to 8 priests for their dirige – 2s 8d.
Item paid to the clerk for the bells and dirige – 14d.
Item paid to the bellman – 2d.
Item paid for bread for poor people – 5s.
Item paid for the proctors' labour – 12d.

Sum – 12s.

The costs of Harry Chester's mind
Item paid to the vicar for his wax and dirige – 12d.
Item paid to 6 priests – 2s.
Item paid to the clerk – 12d.
Item paid to the bellman – 4d.
Item paid for bread for poor people – 2s 8d.
Item offering – 1d.
Sum – 7s 1d.

Amount this side – 48s 7½d.

fo 4v
The costs of the General Mind
Item paid for 2 bushels flour – 17d.
Item 2 dozen double ale – 3s 2d.
Item [an] ounce saffron – 12d.
Item quarter oil – 4d.
Item 3 quarters ?osey – 6d.
Item baking the cakes – 8d.
Item Master Dene – 4d.
Item 5 priests – 15d.
Item the clerk – 14d.
Item offering – 1d.
Item wine at dirige – 20d.
Sum – 11s 7d.

Vacations of the rent of All Hallows' church
Item John Shepard for a house in Marystreet – 2s.
Sum – 2s.

Item for making this book – 12d.
Item for allowance given in pence to the tenants – 8d.
Item to Richard Locker for locks in Thomas ?Pernaunt's house – 18d.
Sum – 3s 2d.

Sum this side – 16s 9d.

fo 5
Memorandum that Master Spicer gave unto All Hallows' church to be
prayed for a *gooddede* the year of our lord 1492 – 40s.
Item Janet Saddler for her husband's grave – 6s 8d.
Item Maud Spicer gave to the church 2 torches weighing the both 20 lb
which cost – 5s.

Sum – 5s.

Sum of all the rents of the church of All Hallows' and of the profits that
have grown this year in *grassis* and bequests as it appears in the beginning
of this book – £19 19s 4d.

Sum total of all vacations and reparations and of customary charges done
by Thomas Spicer and John Stayner as it appears in parcels afore written –
£14 8s 5d.
Sum – £14 8s 5d.

Rest clear of the church money in Thomas Spicer's hand – £5 10s 11d.

[The rest of the accounts appears to be an addition in different ink]
Received of Mistress Wilsche[re] as her husband's bequest – 13s 4d.
Received of Mistress Saddler for her shege [seat?] – 6d.

Vertiz ffoleon
Turn the tother side

fo 5v
Paid to John Kokys for a reward of the windows – 6d.
Paid to John Raynold at All Hallows' tide to the change of 13 tapers and 7
lb of wax at 7d the pound – 4s 1d.
Paid to John Raynold for making 26 lb of wax – 13d.
Paid for making the 2 standards of 5 lb – 2d.

Rest in Thomas Spicer's hand – £5 12s 2d.
Memorandum received of Thomas Spicer for his clear accounts –
£5 12s 2d.

Memorandum that the 15 day of April Ao [14]93 that Janet Saddler came
to the church of All Hallows' and gave [unintelligible] for the *parrischons*
to the proctors, for that time being John Stayner and Richard Sutton, a
mazer weighing 11 $\frac{1}{4}$ oz and a flat pece of silver weighing 8 oz. She to
have it during her life and then after to remain unto the church.
In the bottom of the pece marked O and [en]graved the church of All
Hallows in the bottom.
Memorandum where Janet Saddler should have paid for her husband's
grave and for her ?duties [illegible] 13s 4d the whole *parrs* [parish] gave it
her by the reason of her gift.

[1494–1495]

fo 1
Pro ecclie Omni Sanctorum
Anno dm 1494
John Baten

Rental of the church of All Hallows', Bristol, from the feast of the Nativity
in the year of Our Lord 1494 unto the same feast in the year following, at
the time when John Esterfeld was mayor of the said town, Matthew Jubbs
sheriff and William Essteby and John Rowland bailiffs, John Baten and
Thomas Davy churchwardens of the said church.

Rents assize by the year
Of John Brandfeld for his *bake* door and a gutter – 2s 6d.
Of Richard Erle for rent assize in Lewinsmede – 12d.
Of John Carlyon for Master Peynter's house – 4s.
Of the master of the Tailors – 12s.
Of Master Croffts for rent assize in St Peter's parish – 6d.
Of John Shepard for a house in Marsh Street – 2s.
Of Paul James for a rent assize – 3s 4d.
Sum – 25s 4d.

In the High Street
Of John Snygg by the year – £3 6s 8d.
Of Thomas Pernaunt by the year – £4.
Of John Stradelyng by the year – 16s.
Of Thomas Went by the year – 16s.
Of Halleway's priest by the year – 6s 8d.
Of John Cokkys by the year – 20d.
Sum – £9 7s

Broad Street
Of Thomas Coke brewer by the year – £4

Sum – £14 12s 4d.

fo 1v
Receipts at Palm Sunday
Item received on Palm Sunday for the suffragan – 2s 9d.
Item at Sheer Thursday – 10 $\frac{1}{2}$d.
Item at Good Friday – 2s 9d.
Item at Easter eve – 18 $\frac{1}{2}$d.
Item on Easter day – 8s 4d.

Sum – 16s 3d.

Received of bequests and for graves in the church
Item for Master John Snygg's grave – 6s 8d.
Item of John Forbore – 3s 4d.
Item of Sir Richard *Kenchanon* of Saint Davids bequest to All Hallows' –
20d.
Item for 2 torches for Halleway's mind – 12d.
Sum – 12s 8d.
The vacations of this year [blank]

Amount rents, casualties and bequests – £16 15d.

fo 2
Payments for the church of All Hallows' for this year
Item to the suffragan for his year's wages – 8s.
Item for a baldric for the morrow mass bell – 3d.
Item for a cord to the paschal – 3d.
Item for scouring the bowls and 2 lamps – 16d.
Item to the raker for hauling the church dust – 8d.
Item for watching the sepulchre – 12d.
Item for a sack of coals – 2d.
Item for cleaning a gutter in Thomas Went's house – 13d.
Item for sand and hauling a ?ton – 3d.
Item for paving – 5d.
Item for parchment for the rent roll – 1d.
Item for the mother church of Worcester – 8d.
Item for a quart of wine on Palm Sunday – 2 $\frac{1}{2}$d.
Item for mending the collar of the clerk's surplice – 8d.
Item for a dinner to the priests for Our Lady Mass in Lent – 3s 4d.
Item for a new *jemeve* [hinge] for the great organs and 6 pins of iron and
setting on – 10d.
Item for dressing a baldric to the great bell – 14d.
Item for the hanging up the Dance of Powlys – 16d.
Item for a dozen *tannytt* skins for the eagle and the 4 ?standards – 19d.
Item for making the 5 *borssys* – 8d.
Item for a cross staff – 2d.
Sum – 24s 1 $\frac{1}{2}$d.

The costs of Corpus Christi day
Item to the vicar – 8d.
Item for 6 priests – 2s.
Item for the clerk – 4d.
Item to the suffragan for bearing the cross – 4d.

Item for bearing the banners in Rogation week – 4d.
Item for cleaning the charnel house – 18d.
Item for besoms – 1d.
Item for washing the church cloths – 2s 8d.
Item for pins – 1d.
Item paid for a cellar for our store house – 6s 8d.
Sum – 14s 8d.

Amount – 38s 9 $\frac{1}{2}$d.[Bottom half of figues lost because page has been trimmed.]

fo 2v

Payments of wax against Easter
Item for 30 $\frac{1}{4}$ lb of wax at 7d the pound – 17s 7 $\frac{1}{2}$d.
Item for making [it] up – 3s 4d.
Sum – 20s 11 $\frac{1}{2}$d

Payments of wax for All Hallows' tide
Item for 12 lb of wax against All Hallows' day at 7d the lb – 7s.
Item for making the *Royne* light – 12d.
Sum – 8s.

Repairs of Stradelyn's house and Thomas Went's house
Item for half a seme of cardiff boards – 5d.
Item for *leggys* for a window – 2d.
Item for making the same window – 4d.
Item for nails to the same window – 2d.
Item for 2 loads of paving stones – 2s 8d.
Item for hauling them from St Peter's cross – 4d.
Item for 1 load of tile stones – 16d.
Item for hauling them – 2d.
Item for 2 masons a whole week at 6 $\frac{1}{2}$d a day – 6s 6d.
Item for a labourer for 3 $\frac{1}{2}$ days' at 4 $\frac{1}{2}$d a day – 15 $\frac{1}{2}$d.
Item for 4 quarters of lime – 8d.
Item for lath nails, hair and candles – 2d.
Item for a piece of timber – 2d.
Item for a mason for 4 days' at 6 $\frac{1}{2}$d a day – 2s 1d.
Item for a labourer for 2 days' – 8d.
Item for 17 lb of ?iron for bars for a window at 1 $\frac{1}{2}$d the pound – 20d.[sic]
Item for 2 loads of sand – 2d.
Item for hauling 4 loads of rubble – 4d.
Item for hauling a load of stone from Thomas Coke's house – 1d.
Item for 2 masons a whole week at 6 $\frac{1}{2}$d a day – 6s 6d.

Item for 2 loads of sand – 2d.
Item for 2 wey and 2 quarters of lime – 2s 4d.
Sum – 28s 5d

fo 3
Item for a labourer a whole week – 2s.
Item for candles and a ?wire – 1d.
Item for a ?newys board at 4d the seme – 2d.
Item for 100 laths – 4d.
Item for a mason to parget chimney in his ?chamber and a sack of lime –
3 ½d.
Sum – 2s 10 ½d.

Repairs upon the church vestments
Item for 2 pieces of ribbon – 6d.
Item for 12 yards of fringe at 1 ½d the yard – 18d.
Item for a yard of tuke – 8d.
Item for 5 ells of lockram at 4 ½d the ell – 22 ½d.
Item for thread – 3d.
Item for 1 ⅝ yards of black say – 3s 3d.
Item for 3 pipes of copper gold – 9d.
Item for 2 skeins of *twyne* silk – 4d.
Item for the making of 2 albs and amices – 4d.
Item for ⅝ ell of lockram – 2d.
Item for a yard and the nail of buckram – 7d.
Item for half a yard of red cyprus of *borgens* – 7d.
Item for strings for amices – 1d.
Item for a searing candle – 1d.
Item for silk – 4d.
Item for 5 yards of blue satin of cyprus for the *borys* at 14d the yard –
5s 10d.
Item for blue thread – 1d.
Item for green buckram – 2d.
Item for a yard of black buckram – 3d.
Item for *bred* to *skoyr* the *borys* – 1d.
Item for dressing a frontel with stars – 14d.
Item for 5 weeks and 2 days' wages and table at 2s 8d the week – 14s 3d.
Sum – 33s 2d.
Amount – 36s ½d.

fo 3v
Repairs upon the steeple
For a carpenter to mend the frame of the great bell – 14d.
Item for 15 lb of iron for the frame of the bells at 1 ¼d the pound – 8d.

Item for load of tile stones – 16d.
Item for hauling of them from St Peter's cross – 2d.
Item for nails – 1d.
Item for 2 tilers a whole week at 5 $\frac{1}{2}$d a day – 5s 6d.
Item for a thousand tile pins – 3d.
Item for a quarter of lime – 2d.
Sum – 10s 2d.

Repairs of Thomas Parnell's pentys [lean-to]
Item for 2 pieces of timber to John Parnell – 5s 6d.
Item for sawing of them to rafters – 16d.
Item for 300 foot of elm board at 21d the hundred – 5s 3d.
Item for a thousand laths for the store house – 4s 4d.
Item for hauling them from the key – 1d.
Item for a thousand cornish tiles – 2s 6d.
Item for hauling them from Flannyngam's house – 4d.
Item for a carpenter and his man – 2s 7d.
Item for casting of $\frac{3}{8}$s of lead – 4 $\frac{1}{2}$d.
Item for 3 studs – 18d.
Item for 21 feet of *eves* board – 7d.
Item for great spikes – 3d.
Item for 8 sacks of lime – 8d.
Item for 2 loads of tile stones – 2s 8d.
Item for hauling them from St Peter's cross – 4d.
Item for 2 thousand tile pins – 6d.
Item for a tiler and a labourer – 3s 6d.
Item for bearing tile stones and boards to the store house – 1d.
Item for 500 lath nails – 6d.
Item for calf-foot nails – 4d.
Item for board nail – 4 $\frac{1}{2}$d.
Item for 50 hatch nails – 2d.
Item for crests – 4 $\frac{1}{2}$d.
Item for hauling the timber from the marsh gate – 7d.
Sum – 34s 8 $\frac{1}{2}$d.
Amount – 44s 10 $\frac{1}{2}$d.

fo 4
Repairs on Thomas Coykkes house
Item for 50 laths – 6d.
Item for 500 lath nails – 6d.
Item for 19 foot of gutter case at a 1 $\frac{1}{2}$d the foot – 2s 5d.
Item for 100 lath nails – 6d.
Item for 11 studs and rafters – 2s.
Item more for 3 studs – 6d.

Item for 4 crampetts of iron weighing 11 lb at 1 $\frac{1}{4}$d the pound – 13 $\frac{1}{2}$d.
Item for a load of tile stones – 16d.
Item for hauling them from St Peter's cross – 2d.
Item for 2 tilers for 4 $\frac{1}{2}$ days' at 5 $\frac{1}{2}$d the day – 4s 1 $\frac{1}{2}$d.
Item for a load of tile stones – 16d.
Item for hauling of them from St Peter's cross – 2d.
Item for 2 tilers for 4 $\frac{1}{2}$ days' – 4s 1 $\frac{1}{2}$d.
Item for half a hundred[weight] of new lead and casting a hundred[weight]
and 3 quarters of old lead – 4s 9d.
Item for tack nail – 1d.
Item for 500 lath nail – 6d.
Item for 7 crests – 3d.
Item for a load of tile – 16d.
Item for hauling them – 2d.
Item for 2 tilers for 4 days' at 5 $\frac{1}{2}$d the day – 3s 8d.
Item for another load of tile stones – 16d.
Item for hauling them from St Peter's Cross – 2d.
Item for quarter wey of lime – 3d.
Item for 2 tilers for 4 days' at 5 $\frac{1}{2}$d the day – 3s 8d.
Item for 3000 tile pins – 9d.
Item for a load of tile stones – 16d.
Item for hauling them from St Peter's Cross – 2d.
Item for 2 tilers for 6 days' at 5 $\frac{1}{2}$d the day – 5s 6d.
Item for 2 loads of tile stones – 2s 8d.
Item for hauling them from St Peter's Cross – 4d.
Sum – 45s 5 $\frac{1}{2}$d.

fo 4v
Item for 1000 lath nails – 2s.
Item for board nails and hatch nails – 2d.
Item for rent assize to Christ Church – 13s 4d.
Item paid to the Master of St John's for rent assize – 6s 8d.
Item paid for the making of this book – 12d.
Item for allowance to the tenants – 12d.
Sum – 24s 2d.

The costs of William Newbery's mind
Item paid to the vicar for his wax and dirige – 16d.
Item paid to 5 priests for their dirige – 20d.
Item paid to the clerk for his dirige and bells – 10d.
Item for bread for poor people – 2s.
Item to the bedeman – 4d.
Sum – 6s 2d.

The costs of Thomas Fyler and his wife's dirige
Item paid to the vicar for his wax and dirige – 12d.
Item paid to 8 priests – 2s 8d.
Item paid to the clerk for his dirige and bells – 14d.
Item paid to the vicar to see that this to be done and for the bede roll every Sunday – 12d.
Item paid to the bedeman – 2d.
Item paid for bread for poor people – 5s.
Item paid to the 2 proctors for their labour – 12d.
Sum – 12s.
Amount – 42s 4d.

fo 5
The costs of Harry Chester's mind and Alice his wife for their dirige and mass
Item in primis to the vicar for his wax and his dirige – 12d.
Item for 6 priests for dirige and mass – 2s.
Item paid to the clerk for bells and his dirige – 12d.
Item paid to the bedeman – 4d.
Item paid for offering – 1d.
Item paid for bread to poor people – 2s 8d.
Sum – 7s 1d.

The costs of the General Mind
Item paid for 2 bushels of meal – 16d.
Item paid for bread to poor people – 6d.
Item paid for an ounce of saffron – 14d.
Item paid for baking the cakes – 8d.
Item paid for oil and sugar – 4d.
Item paid for a pottle of wine to the same cakes – 5d.
Item paid for 2 dozen and 4 gallons of ale – 3s 4d.
Item paid to the vicar – 4d.
Item paid to 7 priests – 21d.
Item paid to the clerk – 14d.
Item for offering – 1d.
Sum – 13s 4d.

Amount – 20s 5d.
Amount the charges and receipts of the church – £16 15d.
Amount the costs and repairs – £14 4s 11 $\frac{1}{2}$d.
The [ar]rearage to be paid from the proctors for this year – 36s 3 $\frac{1}{2}$d
Item received of Janet Saddeler – 6d.
[Sum –] 36s 9 $\frac{1}{2}$d

[1496–97]

fo 1
The Church Book

fo 2
Jhs

Memorandum here after follows the book of the rental of the church of All Hallows' in the town of Bristol and also pertaining in the same book the allowances, costs and expenses and customable charges done from the feast of Candlemas in the year of our lord 1496 unto the same feast next following, that is to say the year of our lord 1497, by Thomas Snygg and Paul James for that year proctors, and in the same year Harry Dayle being mayor.

Rent assize by the year
Item Paul James by the year – 3s 4d.
Item John Carlen by the year – 4s.
Item John Banfeld by the year – 2s 6d.
Item Richard Erle by the year – 12d.
Item the master of the Tailors by the year – 12s.
Item Master Crowme by the year – 6d.
Item John Sheppard by the year – 2s.
Sum – 25s 4d.

In the High Street by the year
Item Alice Snygge by the year – £3 6s 8d.
Item Thomas Pernaunt by the year – £4.
Item Richard Taylor by the year – 16s.
Item Thomas Went by the year – 16s.
Item Sir William Whode by the year – 6s 8d.
Item John Cokkys by the year – 20d.
Sum – £9 7s.

In Broad Street by the year
Item Thomas Kokys by the year – £4.

Amount the whole rent of the church – £14 12s 4d.

fo 2v
Jhs
The receipts of customable duties belonging to the church
Item received on Palm Sunday – 2s 9d.

Item received on Sheer Thursday – 10d.
Item received on Good Friday – 2s 10d.
Item received on Easter eve and Easter day – 8s 4d.
Sum – 14s 9d.

The seat money
Item William Whip ?mercer for a seat – 16d.
Item John Straddlyng – 8d.
Item John Lord – 12d.
Item Richard Taylor – 12d.
Item John Hasche – 6d.
Item Jenet Sakare – 8d.
Item William Rawlyns, mariner – 12d.
Item John Parnant – 12d.
Item John Browne – 2s
Sum – 9s 2d.

The casualties and bequests of this year
Item of John a Morgan for his ?burial – 6s 8d.
Item of the bequest of Thomas Abynton – 40s.
Sum – 46s 8d.

Amount rents, customable duties, casualties and bequests – ?£18 3s 5d.

The vacations of this year
[Scored: Item John Shepard for a house in Mersh Street – 2s.
Item John Cokkes ½ a year – 10d.
Sum – 2s 10d.]

The rent assize for this year
Item paid to the Master of St John's for Cokes house – 6s 8d.
Item paid to the proctors of Christ Church for the same house – 13s 4d.
Sum – 20s.
Amount the costs of this side – 20s.

fo 3
Jhs
The costs of William Newbery's mind
Item paid to Master Den for his wax and dirige – 16d.
Item paid to 5 priests for the dirige – 20d.
Item paid to the clerk for his dirige and bells – 10d.
Item paid for bread for poor people – 2s.
Item paid the bedeman – 4d.
Sum – 6s 2d.

The costs of Thomas Fyler and Agnes his wife of their mind
Item paid to the vicar for wax and dirige – 12d.
Item paid to 8 priests for their mass and dirige – 2s 8d.
Item paid the clerk for his dirige and bells – 14d.
Item paid to the vicar for his oversight and bede roll – 12d.
Item paid the bedeman – 2d.
Item paid for bread to poor people – 5s.
Item paid to the proctors for their labour – 12d.
Sum – 12s.

The costs done at the mind of Harry Chester and Alice his wife
Item paid the vicar for wax and his dirige – 12d.
Item paid to 6 priests for the dirige and mass – 2s.
Item paid to the clerk for his bells and dirige – 12d.
Item paid to the bedeman – 4d.
Item paid to the proctors for the offering – 1d.
Item paid for bread to poor people – 2s 8d.
Sum – 7s 1d.

The costs done at the General Mind
Item paid for 2 bushels [of] flour and a peck – 2s 6d.
Item paid for 1 ounce saffron – 16d.
Item paid for dinner wines – 2s 6d.
Item paid for oil, sugar and *barme* and bread – 13d.
Item for 2 $\frac{1}{2}$ dozen of ale – 3s 6d.
Item paid to Master Den and 5 priests – 19d
Item paid ?John clerk for his dirige and bells – 14d.
Sum – 13s 4d.

Amount costs of this side – 38s 7d.

fo 3v
Jhs
The customable costs of the church of All Hallows'
Item paid to the suffragan for his year's wages – 8s.
Item paid for scouring the candlesticks and other *abyllyments*
[habiliments] – 2s.
Item paid for wine to read the Passion – 4d.
Item paid for coals – 2d.
Item paid for watching the sepulchre – 12d.
Item paid for the dinner for keeping Our Lady Mass – 4s.
Item for the overplus of the ?supper of the day of reckoning – 20d.
Item for besoms – 1d.

Item paid to our lady church of Worcester – 8d.

Item for bearing the banners [in] the Rogation week – 4d.

Item paid the suffragan for bearing of the cross at Corpus Christi – 4d.

[Margin: Corpus Christi day (referring to the next few entries)].

Item paid the clerk for his labour – 4d.

Item paid 5 priests for their labour – 20d.

Item paid Master Dene for his labour – 8d.

Item paid for wine to the *marsse* [?marsh] – 4d.

Item paid for 48 ½ lb of wax at Easter at 7d the pound – 28s 4 ½d.

Item paid the clerk for hanging the Dance of Pauls – 16d.

Item paid the waxmaker for ?20 ½ lb of wax against All Hallows' tide – 6s 8 ½d.

Item paid for making this book – 12d.

Item paid for *langgabyll* [land-gavel] of T. Pernaunt's house – 11d.

Item for allowance of the tenants – 12d.

Item paid the raker for his labour – 8d.

Item paid for washing the church clothes – 2s 8d.

Item paid for making the church light – 3s 4d.

Sum – £3 7s 6d.

The costs ?uncertain done in the church of All Hallows for this present year

Item for *rechooks* – ½d.

Item for making clean the treasure house – 1d.

Item for mending a lock and making a key to the same – 8d.

Item paid for 2 long studs for the *Be* – 21d.

Item paid for 4 long studs – 3s 6d.

Item paid for nails – 2d.

Item for 2 boards to the *Be*

Item for 5 ½ days' to Davy Carpenter – 2s 11d.

Item for ?*hide* work to the *Be* – 22d.

Sum – 11s 7 ½d.

Amount – £3 19s 1 ½d.

fo 4

Jhs

Item for making of the treasure house and mending [superscript: key] of the church – 4d.

Item for 2 labourers to have out the 2 ?torn stones – 4d.

Item for hauling the ?piece of timber under All Hallows' foot – 1d.

Item for making a key to the charnel house – 3d.

Item for 3 ells *helle* to mend the *habis* – 18d.

Item for mending the church *habys* – 8d.

Item to Sir John ?Dyer for Christmas quarter – 2s 6d.
Item for a board to the shrine – 4d.
Item for a *wensket* [wainscott] board to the shrine – 18d.
Item paid Davy for his ?hand – 10s.
Item paid for hanging of the little bell – 2s 7d.
Sum – 20s.

Repairs done in Master Snygg's and Thomas Pernaunt's houses for this year
Item for lime to mend the chimney – 9d.
Item for 3 loads of sand – 3d.
Item for paving stone – 3d.
Item paid to a mason for 4 days' – 2s.
Item paid for a load of stones with the carriage – 18d.
Item for a free stone for the chimney – 5d.
Item for mending a gutter between Master Snygge's and T. Pernaunt's for a quarter of lead – 18d.
Item paid for 4 $\frac{1}{2}$ lb solder – 13 $\frac{1}{2}$d.
Item paid for soldering of 3 *skarys* – 5d.
Item paid for casting of half a hundredweight of lead – 6d.
Item paid the tiler for 2 days' for his wages – 13d.
Item for 2 crests – 1 $\frac{1}{2}$d.
Item a carpenter, 2 days' – 13d.
Item for timber to underset the *Kessters* – 18d.
Item for paving stones to his porch – 7d.
Item for hauling of rubble – 1d.
Sum – 13s 9 $\frac{1}{2}$d.
Amount – 33s 2 $\frac{1}{2}$d.

fo 4v
Jhs
Item paid for hauling of stones – 2d.
Item to a mason for paving T. Pernaunt's porch – 17d.
Item paid for ?lime to T. Pernaunt – 7d.
Item to Davy Carpenter for a day in [words unintelligible] ?parlour – 5 $\frac{1}{2}$d.
Item 50 boards – 14d.
Item for nails – 7 $\frac{1}{2}$d.
Sum – 4s 5d.

Repairs done in Edmond's house and [word illegible] costs
Item paid for 2 studs for a cupboard – 4d.
Item paid for timber – 3d.
Item paid for nails – 4d.

Item paid to the king for the church land – 17s 8d.
Item paid for a carpenter with labourer – 10d.
Item paid for 2 keys – 4d.
Item paid for 2 lb solder to Thomas Coke's house – 6d.
Item paid for mending a lock – 2d.
Item paid for 3 quarters [of an] ell and a quarter ell for the shrine – 5d.
Item 3 quarters lockeram – 8d.
Sum – 21s 6d.

Amount – 25s 11d.

[The writing on the remainder of the side is much inferior]
Item received for a ?knowledge of Pers Grenefeld for a stone [phrase illegible] – 12d.
Rests [clear] – £7 19s 9 ½d.

Item received of John Books for this half year – 10d.
Rest – £8 7 ½d.

Item received of John Saddeler – 6d.
Rest upon this account to the church – £8 6s 4d.
[Other illegible additions]

Rest – £7 20s 8d.[sic]

fo 5
Jhs
The costs of the pews of the church
Item received of Master Dene and Sir John Baten and Thomas Pernaunt for the name of all the parish for the pew money – £6 13s 4d.
Sum – £6 13s 4d.

Item paid for boards as it appears in parcels – 12s 9 ½d
Item paid for timber as it appears – 22s 11d.
Item paid for sawing the timber – 10s.
Item paid for 22 pairs of hinges – 11s.
Item paid for nails – 4s 2 ½d.
Item paid for hauling the timber – 7d.
Item paid for lime – 2d.
Item paid for taking up the old pews – 6d.
Item paid for drink, money – 2 ½d.
Item paid for clearing the ?store house – 5d.
Item paid for the carvers' hand work – £3 13s 4d.
[Illegible line]

Sum – £6 16s 1d.

[1497–98]

fo 1
Anno domini 1498

The church book
Watkyn Coke

fo 2
Here after follows the rental of the church of All Hallows' in the town of
Bristol and also contains in the same book the allowances, costs and
expenses and customable charges done from the feast of Candlemas in the
year of our lord God 1498 by Watkyn Coke and Thomas Pernaunt proctors
of the said church for that year, and in the year [when] Nicholas Brown
[was] mayor of the same town and Phillip Green sheriff.

The rents assize by the year
Item Paul James by the year – 3s 4d.
Item John Carlyon by the year – 4s.
Item John Branfyld by the year – 2s 6d.
Item Richard Erle by the year – 12d.
Item the master of the Tailors by the year – 12s.
Item Master Crowmar by the year – 6d.
Item John Sheppward by the year – 2s.
Sum – 25s 4d.

In the High Street by the year
Item Alice Snygge by the year – £3 6s 8d.
Item Thomas Pernaunt by the year – £4.
Item Richard Tailor by the year – 16s.
Item Thomas Went by the year – 13s 4d.
Item Sir William Woodde for his chamber by the year – 6s 8d.
Item John Cokkys by the year – 20d.
Sum – £9 4s 4d.

In Broad Street
Item Thomas Coke by the year – £4.

Sum the whole rents of the church amount – £14 9s 8d.

fo 2v
The receipts of the customable duties belonging to the church
In primis received on Palm Sunday – 2s 6d.
Item received on Sheer Thursday – 13d.
Item received on Good Friday – 2s 6d.
Item received on Easter eve – 15d.
Item received on Easter day – 5s 8d.
Sum – 13s.

The seat money
Item received of William Walsall for his seat and his wife's seat – 20d.
Item received of Davy Thomas's wife – 6d.
Item received of Lewis John – 20d.
Item received of Edmond the Sargant – 4d.
Item received of Edmond Newton for his seat and his wife's – 20d.
Sum the seat money – 5s 10d.

Sum total of all the rents and the receipts with casualties – £15 8s 6d.

Vacations following
John Cokkes for the whole year – 20d.

Rest due to the church – £15 6s 10d.

[At foot, small writing: Sum allowance of vacations – 20d.]

fo 3
Costs follow of the rent assize
In primis paid to the Master of St John's for Thomas Coke's house – 6s 8d.
Item paid to the proctors of Christ Church for the same house – 13s 4d.
Sum – 20s.

The costs of William Newbery's mind
Item paid to Master vicar for his wax and diriges – 16d.
Item paid to 5 priests for diriges and mass – 20d.
Item paid to the clerk for his dirige and his bells – 10d.
Item paid for bread to poor people – 2s.
Item paid to the bellman – 4d.
Sum – 6s 2d.

The costs of Thomas Fyler and Agnes his wife for their obit
In primis to Master vicar for wax and diriges – 12d.
Item paid to 8 priests for their diriges and mass – 2s 8d.
Item paid to the clerk for his dirige and the bells – 14d.

Item paid to the vicar for his oversight and for the bede roll – 12d.
Item paid to the bellman – 2d.
Item paid to the baker for bread for poor people – 5s.
Item paid to the proctors for their labour – 12d.
Sum – 12s.

[At foot, small writing: Sum this side of allowance – 38s 2d.]

fo 3v
The costs of the obit of Harry Chestre and Alice his wife
In primis paid to Master vicar for wax and his dirige – 12d.
Item paid to 6 priests for their diriges and mass – 2s.
Item paid to the clerk for his bells and dirige – 12d.
Item paid to the bellman – 4d.
Item paid to the proctors for their offering – 1d.
Item paid for bread for poor people – 2s 8d.
Sum – 7s 1d.

The costs done on the obit for all good doers
In primis paid for 2 bushels and half a peck of meal – 20d.
Item for 1 ounce of English saffron – 16d.
Item for divers wines – 2s 4d.
Item for sugar and oil and *barme* for bread wine and baking – 18d.
Item for 2 dozen of double ale – 4s.
Item to Master Dene and to 5 priests – 19d.
Item to the proctors for their offering – 1d.
Item to Richard Clarke for his dirige and the bells – 14d.
Sum – 13s 8d.

[At foot, small writing: Sum this side, allowance – 22s 9d.]

fo 4
Here after follow the customable costs of the church of All Hallows'
In primis paid to 2 friars for bearing the shrine – 4d.
Item for thread – 1d.
Item paid for Catys at the last day of account – 2s 8d.
Item paid for *snofulling* the cypress for the shrine – 1d.
Item paid to the vicar on Corpus Christi day – 8d.
Item paid to 5 priests on Corpus Christi day – 20d.
Item paid to Richard Clarke – 4d.
Item paid to the suffragan for bearing the cross – 4d.
Item paid for wine into the Marsh – 4d.
Item paid to 2 friars for bearing the shrine – 12d.
Item paid to 2 children to bear the copes – 1d.

Item paid to the suffragan for cleaning the store house – 4d.
Item paid for wine on Palm Sunday – 4d.
Item paid for besoms and coals – 3d.
Item paid for a key to the churchyard door – 2d.
Item paid for a rope to the mass bell – 5d.
Item paid for a breakfast for Master Arthur – 2s.
Item paid to the clerk for hanging up the Dance of Pauls – 16d.
Item paid for a ward to a key for the clerk – 1d.
Item paid for wax at Easter and against our Dedication day to John Waxmaker – 30s 3 $\frac{3}{4}$d.
Item paid for watching the sepulchre – 12d.
Item paid for washing the church's ornaments – 2s.
Item paid to the suffragan for his year's wages – 20s.
Item paid to Sir Thomas Meryfyld for making 4 quires of the story of Jhc [Jesus] and for setting in – 6s 8d.
Item paid for mending the copes – 1 $\frac{1}{2}$d.
Item paid for mending 3 towels of old altar cloths – 3d.
Item paid for making a new foot to the trestle – 3d.
Item paid for cleaning the treasure house – 1d.
Item paid for making this book – 12d.
Sum this side – £3 14s 2 $\frac{1}{4}$d.

fo 4v
Costs of repairs to Thomas Went's house
Item paid for boards for the repairs on Thomas Went's house – 16d.
Item paid for nails – 2d.
Item paid to a carpenter for his labour – 6d.
Item paid for boards – 9d.
Item for nails – 1d.
Item paid for a lattice and a man's hire – 17d.
Item paid to the plumber for 3 $\frac{1}{2}$ lb of solder – 7d.
Item for soldering 2 *skarys* – 3d.
Sum – 5s 1d.

Item paid for a lattice to John Tanner's house – 8d.
Item more to Thomas Went's house for a piece of lead – 5d.
Item for soldering the said piece – 4d.
Item paid to a tiler for 3 days' – 19 $\frac{1}{2}$d.
Item for a labourer for 3 days' – 12d.
Item for tile pins – 2d.
Item for half a load of stones – 8d.
Item for making a new window and for nails – 5 $\frac{1}{2}$d.
Sum – 5s 4d.

Item paid to a plumber for Mistress Snygge's house – 5d.
Item paid to a tiler for his labour – 8d.
Item paid for lime – 2d.
Item paid for a quarter of lime to the Green Lattice – 4d.
Sum – 19d.

Item paid to Paul James for the vacation of Edmond Sargant's house –
12d.
Item more to the said Paul for John Cokkys – 5d.
Sum – 17d.

Sum this side allowance – 13s 5d.

fo 5
Item paid to John Collys for making the *entrement* against Thomas
Peyntar – 3s 4d.
Item paid to Sir John Hawley for his seal – 12d.
Item paid for wine and ale at the agreement with Thomas Peyntar – 10d.
Item paid for the allowance to the tenants – 10d.
Sum – 6s.

Repairs done in Thomas Coke's house
Item paid for 700 feet of board at 2s 4d the hundred – 16s 4d.
Item paid to the carpenter for his labour – 3s 4d.
Item for 2 pieces of timber – 20d.
Item paid for nails and mending a lock to the back door – 2 ½d.
Item for nails – 2s 8d.
Sum this side – 30s 2 ½d.

Amount all the costs afore written – £8 16s 8d.
Rest clear of money – £6 10s 2 ½d.

Paid for a piece of *lampardewke* to Thomas Snygge – 3s 4d.
Rest to the church – £6 6s 9d

[Different hand: Received of Wattekyne Coykke of this *boyke* [?book] in
money – £6 6s 9d.

[Written on back cover: Watken Coke's book]

[1498–1499]

fo 1
[Entry scored: To be had in remembrance that William Abyngton owes for the bequest of his mother's testament – 20s.]

fo 2
Here follows the rental of the church of All Hallows' in the town of Bristol and also contains in the same book the allowances, costs and expenses and customable charges done from the feast of Candlemas in the year of our lord God 1498 unto the same feast next after following, that is to say the year of our lord God 1499, by Paul James and Watkyn Coke proctors of the said church for that year, and in the year [when] Master Phillip Ryngston [was] Mayor of the same town and John Jay sheriff.

Rents assize by the year
Item Paul James by the year – 3s 4d.
Item John Carlyon by the year – 4s.
Item John Branfyld by the year – 2s 6d.
Item Richard Erle by the year – 12d.
Item the master of the Tailors by the year – 12s.
Item Master Crowmar by the year – 5d.
Item John Shepphard by the year – 2s.
Sum – 25s 4d.

In the High Street by the year
Item Alice Snygge by the year – £3 6s 8d.
Item Thomas Pernaunt by the year – £4.
Item Richard Tailor by the year – 16s.
Item Thomas Went by the year – 13s 4d.
Item Sir William Woode by the year for his chamber – 6s 8d.
Item John Cokkys by the year – 20d.
Sum – £9 4s 4d.

In Broad Street by year
Item Thomas Coke by the year – £4.

Sum the whole rents of the church, amount – £14 9s 8d.

fo 2v
The receipts of the customable duties belonging to the church
Item received on Palm Sunday – 3s 1d.
Item received on Sheer Thursday – 15d.
Item received on Good Friday – 3s 1d.

Item received on Easter eve – 18 $\frac{1}{2}$d.
Item received on Easter day – 7s $\frac{1}{2}$d.
Sum – 16s.

The seat money
Item William Abynton and his wife for their seats – 16d.
Item Edmond the sergeant for his seat – 4d.
Item Joan Sadler for her seat – 6d.
Item Phillip Welshe for his seat – 6d.
Sum – 2s 8d.

The casualties of this year
Item for William Baker's grave – 6s 8d.
Item for Joan Abynton's grave – 6s 8d.
Item *lawnd* that was bought for the shrine which was sold for – 14d.
Item received for the hire of 2 torches at Halleway's mind – 12d.
Item received of William Abyngton for the bequest of his mother – 20s.
Sum – 35s 6d.

The vacations of the year
Item John Cokkys for 3 quarters vacant – 15d.
Item Edmond the sergeant's house for 1 quarter and a half
thereof I should receive 12d – 5s.
Sum – 6s 3d.

Sum total of all the receipts of this present year, amount, the vacations
abated and the rent assize – £16 17s 7d.

fo 3
Costs follow of the rents assize
In primis paid to the Master of Saint John's for Thomas Coke's house –
6s 8d.
Item paid to the proctors of Christ Church for the same house – 13s 4d.
Sum – 20s.

The costs of William Newbery's mind
Item paid to Master vicar for his wax and diriges – 16d.
Item paid to 5 priests for their diriges and mass – 20d.
Item paid to the clerk for his dirige and for the bells – 10d.
Item paid for bread to poor people – 2s.
Item paid to the bedeman – 4d.
Sum – 6s 2d.

The costs of Thomas Fyler and Agnes his wife of their mind
In primis to Master vicar for his wax and dirige – 12d.
Item paid to 8 priests for their dirige and mass – 2s 8d.
Item paid to the clerk for his dirige and for the bells – 14d.
Item paid to the vicar for his oversight and for the bede roll – 12d.
Item paid to the bedeman – 2d.
Item paid for bread to the poor people – 5s.
Item paid to the proctors for their labour – 12d.
Sum – 12s.

The costs of Harry Chestre and Alice his wife of their mind
In primis paid to Master vicar for wax and dirige – 12d.
Item paid to 5 priests for their diriges and mass – 2s.
Item paid to the clerk for his bells and dirige – 12d.
Item paid to the bellman – 4d.
Item to the proctors for their offering – 1d.
Item paid for bread to poor people – 2s 8d.
Sum – 7s 1d.

Sum this side – 45s 3d.

fo 3v
The costs done at the General Mind
Item paid for 2 bushels and a peck of flour – 2s 6d.
Item for 1 ounce of English saffron – 16d.
Item for divers wines – 2s 6d.
Item for oil, sugar and *barme* and bread – 13d.
Item for 2 dozen and half of ale – 3s 3d.
Item paid to Master Dene and to 5 priests – 19d.
Item to Richard Clarke for his dirige and his bells – 14d.
Sum – 13s 1d.

The customable costs of the church of All Hallows'
In primis paid to the suffragan for his year's wages – 8s.
Item paid for wine *whylle the passyon was areding* – 4d.
Item paid for scouring the church stuff – 2s.
Item paid for coals – 2d.
Item for watching the sepulchre – 12d.
Item for the dinner for keeping of Our Lady Mass – 4s.
Item for the overplus of the supper on the day of account – 2s 6d.
Item paid for besoms and pins – 2d.
Item paid to Our Lady church of Worcester – 8d.
Item for bearing the banners in Rogation week – 4d.
Item to the suffragan for bearing the cross on Corpus Christi day – 4d.

Item paid to the clerk for his day's labour – 4d.

Item paid to 5 priests for their labour on Corpus Christi day – 20d.

Item paid to Master vicar for his labour – 8d.

Item for wine into the Marsh – 4d.

Item paid for wax at Easter for 42 lb at 7d the pound – 24s 6d.

Item paid to the clerk for hanging the Dance of Pauls – 16d.

Item paid to the waxmaker for repairing tapers against our Dedication day, for 10 $\frac{1}{2}$ lb at 7d the pound – 6s 1d.

Item paid for making this book – 12d.

Item paid to the raker for his labour – 8d.

Item for washing the church cloths – 2s 8d.

Item for bearing the sacrament on Corpus Christi day – 8d.

Item for making the church light – 3s 4d.

Item for the allowance to the tenants – 12d.

Item for 2 torches weighing 67 lb at 2 $\frac{3}{4}$d the pound – 15s 4 $\frac{1}{2}$d.

Sum – £3 19s $\frac{1}{2}$d.

Sum this side – £4 12s 1 $\frac{1}{2}$d.

fo 4

Costs done in the church this present year

Item paid for 3 lb of wire – 12d.

Item for drawing and holing and hooks – 5d.

Item for 2 boards in the rood loft – 8d.

Item paid for nails – $\frac{1}{2}$d.

Item paid to Sir John Dyar for 3 quarters' wages – 7s 6d.

Item paid for a pulley and a cord – 2d.

Item for 1 lamp and a ?stopell to the ?font and for a line – 2 $\frac{1}{2}$d.

Item for 4 ounces of curtain rings – 2d.

Item paid to John Sulby for dressing the shrine – 7s.

Item paid for making the canopy for the shrine and for the stuff that belongs thereto – 3s 1d.

Sum – 20s 3d.

Item paid for *lavnde* [?lavender] – 19d.

Item paid for mending the church gutter – 6d.

Item paid for writing the composition of the calendar – 5s.

Item paid to John Moresse – 5s.

Item paid to the town clerk for an old rest [sic] that was owing – 3s 4d.

Item paid for 40 welsh boards and for hauling – 3s 5d.

Item paid for mending the great candlestick – 2s 8d.

Item for mending the key of the church door – 5d.

Item paid for 2 *gogysse* for the great bell – 4s 8d.

Item to a carpenter for his labour – 19d.

Item for 4 lb solder in the church gutter and for his labour – 15d.

Item for a key for the churchyard and for nails – 2 $\frac{1}{2}$d.
Item for mending the common gutter – 3s.
Item for mending 2 keys and the locks in the vestry – 5d.
Item paid for the store house – 6s 8d.
Sum this amount – 39s 8 $\frac{1}{2}$d.

Sum this side, amount – 59s 11 $\frac{1}{2}$d.

fo 4v
Repairs done in Thomas Pernaunt's house
In primis for 4 sacks of lime for the kitchen – 4d.
Item paid for 1 load of clay – 2d.
Item for a man's labour for 1 day – 6 $\frac{1}{2}$d.
Item for a labourer for a day and a half – 6d.
Sum – 18 $\frac{1}{2}$d.

Repairs done in Thomas Koke's house
Item paid for ridding and covering the gutter from the well – 12d.
Item paid for 3 lb of solder spent upon the gutter between the house aforesaid and the hall – 9d.
Item paid for calf-foot nails that were spent upon the stairs up into the hall – 2d.
Sum – 23d.

[In different ink and scored: Item received of William Abynton for his mother's bequest – 20s.]

Sum this side, amount – 3s 5 $\frac{1}{2}$d.

Amount the costs of the present year – £10 6 $\frac{1}{2}$d.

So rest that the proctors owe to the church for this present year – £6 17s $\frac{1}{2}$d.

[1499–1500]

fo 1
The church book

fo 2
[At head, in different ink: Anno domini 1500 Thomas Pernaunt]

Here after follows the rental of the church of All Hallows' in the town of

Bristol and also contains in the same book the allowances, costs and expenses and customable charges done from the feast of Candlemas in the year of our lord God 1500 [sic] by Thomas Pernaunt and Rawlyn Coke, for that year proctors of the said church, and in the year [when] Richard Vaghan [was] mayor of the same town, [and] Hugh Ellyat and John Baten sheriffs.

The rents assize by the year
Item Paul James by the year – 3s 4d.
Item John Carlyon by the year – 4s.
Item John Branfyld by the year – 2s 6d.
Item Richard Erle by the year – 12d.
Item The master of the Tailors by the year – 12s.
Item Master Crowmar by the year – 6d.
Item John Shypward by the year – 2s.
Sum – 25s 4d.

In the High Street
Item Alice Snygge by the year – £3 6s 8d.
Item Thomas Pernaunt by the year – £4.
Item John Tavarnar by the year – 16s.
Item Thomas Went by the year – 13s 4d.
Item Sir William Woode for his chamber by the year – 6s 8d.
Item John Cokkys by the year – 20d.
Sum – £9 4s 4d.

In Broad Street
Item Thomas Coke by the year – £4.

Sum of the whole rents of the church, amount – £14 9s 8d.

fo 2v
The receipts of the customable duties belonging to the church
In primis received on Palm Sunday – 2s 10d.
Item on Sheer Thursday – 18d.
Item on Good Friday – 2s 8d.
Item on Easter eve – 2s.
Item on Easter day – 6s 2d.
Item received of William Wallsall for John Peyntar of Tewkesbury – 10s.
Sum – 25s 2d.

Received of Michael the tanner for his seat and his wife's seat – 12d.

Sum total – £15 15s 10d.

Vacations
John Cokkys house the whole year – 20d.

Rest due to the church – £15 14s 2d.
[At foot of page, scored entries under heading of 'Costs following' which are given properly at the head of fo 3]

fo 3
Costs following
In primis paid to the Master of Saint John's for Thomas Coke's house for rent assize – 6s 8d.
Item paid to the proctors of Christ Church for the same house – 13s 4d.
Sum – 20s.

The costs of William Newbery's mind
Item paid to Master vicar for his wax and dirige – 16d.
Item paid to 5 priests for dirige and mass – 20d.
Item paid to the clerk for his dirige and his bells – 10d.
Item paid for bread to poor people – 2s.
Item paid to the bellman – 4d.
Sum – 6s 2d.

The costs of Thomas Fyler's mind and Agnes his wife
Item to Master vicar for wax and his dirige – 12d.
Item to 8 priests for their dirige and mass – 2s 8d.
Item to the clerk for his dirige and his bells – 14d.
Item paid to the vicar for his oversight and for the bede roll – 12d.
Item paid to the bellman – 2d.
Item paid to the baker for bread for poor people – 5s.
Item paid to the proctors for their labour – 12d.
Sum – 12s.

Sum this side – 38s 2d.

fo 3v
The costs of the obit of Harry Chestre and Alice his wife
In primis paid to Master vicar for wax and his dirige – 12d.
Item paid to 6 priests for their dirige and mass – 2s.
Item paid to the clerk for the bell and his dirige – 12d.
Item paid to the bellman – 4d.
Item to the proctors for their offering – 1d.
Item paid for bread for poor people – 2s 8d.
Sum – 7s 1d.

The costs done on the obit for all the good doers

In primis for 2 bushels and a half of meal – 3s 1 $\frac{1}{2}$d.

Item paid to 6 priests and the vicar – 22d.

Item paid to the clerk for the bells and his dirige – 14d.

Item for wine, oil, bread and for baking the cakes – 16d.

Item for 1 $\frac{1}{4}$ oz of English saffron – 12 $\frac{1}{2}$d.

Item for divers wines – 4s 6 $\frac{1}{2}$d.

Item for 2 dozen of ale – 4s.

Item for the proctors' offering – 1d.

Sum – 17s 1 $\frac{1}{2}$d.

Sum this side – 24s 2 $\frac{1}{2}$d.

fo 4

Here after follow the costs customable of the church of All Hallows'

In primis paid for wine on Palm Sunday to the priest and clerks – 4d.

Item for besoms and coals – 3d.

Item for scouring of the church stuff – 2s.

Item paid to the raker for his year's wages – 8d.

Item paid for watching the sepulchre – 12d.

Item paid to Our Lady church of Worcester – 8d.

Item paid for the supper on the day of account – 2s 8d.

Item paid for mending the blue copes and the black vestments – 5d.

Item paid for mending the white copes *more than my lady ys money comyth to* and for mending the 2 tunicles – 2s.

Item paid to John Collys for making a letter to Master Chancellor – 4d.

Item paid for making the rent roll – 4d.

Item paid for making 2 stoles and mending a blue vestment – 14d.

Item for an amice and making the black vestments – 4d.

Item paid to the suffragan for bearing the banners in Rogation week – 4d.

Item paid to 2 friars for bearing the sacrament upon Corpus Christi day – 8d.

Item to Master vicar on Corpus Christi day – 8d.

Item to 7 priests – 2s 4d.

Item paid to the clerk – 4d.

Item paid to the suffragan for bearing the cross – 4d.

Item paid to 2 young men for bearing the 2 white tunicles – 2d.

Item paid for wine into the Marsh – 4d.

Item for a rope to hang the lamp before the altar, weighing 5 $\frac{1}{4}$ lb at 1 $\frac{1}{4}$d the pound – 6 $\frac{1}{2}$d.

Item for 3 ells of lockram to make the clerk a surplice – 18d.

Item for making the said surplice – 8d.

Item for mending the old surplice – 2d.

Item paid for hanging up the Dance of Pauls at St James' tide – 16d.

Sum this side – 21s 6 $\frac{1}{2}$d.

fo 4v

Item for mending the clerk's surplice – 1d.

Item for washing the church gear – 2s 4d.

Item paid to master Sheryff for mending a candlestick – 2s 6d.

Item paid to a carpenter for setting up and making the battlements in the chancel, for 2 days' labour – 12d.

Item for *recke* hooks – $\frac{1}{2}$d.

Item for lime stones – 1d.

Item for 3 lb red lead to paint the said battlements – 6d.

Item for nails to nail fast the battlements – 2d.

Item paid to Nicholas suffragan for waiting on the carpenter and painting the battlements – 4d.

Item for curtain rings – 2d.

Item for renewing wax against All Hallows' day – 7s.

Item for 2 torches *peysyng* 44 lb – 11s.

Item for making the church stuff – 3s 4d.

Item for mending the lock off the *tryangle* – 1d.

Item paid for wax to John waxmaker – 19s 5 $\frac{1}{2}$d.

Item paid for a mat to lie before the high altar – 21d.

Item paid for 2 lb of candles that burnt on Christmas day in the morning – 2d.

Item paid for a Lenten dinner to the priests – 4s 8d.

Item paid to the suffragan for his whole year's wages – 20s.

Item for a gallon of wine to master Chancellor – 8d.

[Scored: Item paid for washing the church and chantry gear – 2s.]

Item paid to the clerk for [what was] lacking of his wages – 2s 2d.

Item paid to the clerk for [what was] lacking of his wages at midsummer quarter at his departing – 2s 1d.

Item for a gallon of claret wine to master Chancellor – 8d.

Sum this side – [erasures] ?£4 4d.

fo 5

Item paid for 3 $\frac{3}{4}$ yards of white fustian to the Lenten vestments – 22 $\frac{1}{2}$d.

Item for $\frac{3}{4}$ of an ell of *sulltwyche* – 3d.

Item for 1 yard of red cyprus satin – 8d.

Item for 3 $\frac{1}{2}$ yards of crest cloth at 3d – 10 $\frac{1}{2}$d.

Item for 1 ell of canvas – 4d.

Item for 4 $\frac{1}{4}$ ells of *bryssell* at 6d – 2s 1 $\frac{1}{2}$d.

Item for the making – 20d.

Item for 2 $\frac{1}{2}$ pieces of ribbon for the vestments – 2 $\frac{1}{2}$d.

Item for hallowing the said vestment – 10d.

Item paid to John Sulby for staining the altar cloths and the curtains to the same for Lent – 26s 8d.

Item paid to Thomas Snygge for the cloth that belonged to the said altar cloths and curtains – 17s 9d.

Item paid unto William Whyte's wife for dressing the altar cloths and the curtains – 3s.

Item for searing candles to the said work – 1d.

Item for curtain rings to the cloths and curtains – 12d.

Item for 2 irons to hang the cloths on – 10d.

Item for hauling rubble out of the chancel – 6d.

Item for allowance to the tenants – 8d.

[Two repetitions erased]

Sum – 59s 4d.

fo 5v

Repairs following

In primis paid for half a load of stones for the church – 8d.

Item for 1 quarter of lime – 2d.

Item for 1 $\frac{3}{4}$ lb of solder and the handwork to the plumber – 8d.

Item for 2 days' to a tiler for his labour – 12d.

Sum – 2s 6d.

Item more to a carpenter for mending the *sege dorys* [?seat doors] within the church within the entreclose – 6d.

Item for nails – 1 $\frac{1}{2}$d.

Item for 2 studs – 4 $\frac{1}{2}$d.

Item for nails – 1d.

Sum – 13 $\frac{1}{2}$d.

The repairs done on Thomas Coke's house

Item for a load of stones and the hauling – 18d.

Item paid to the tiler for 2 $\frac{1}{2}$ days' labour – 15d.

Item for tile pins – 2d.

Item for 4 quarters of lime – 8d.

Item for a labourer for 2 days' – 9d.

Item for taking down a *pentys* [lean-to] in Thomas Coke's house – 5d.

Sum – 4s 9d.

Sum this side – 8s 4d.

fo 6

Repairs done in Thomas Pernaunt's house

In primis paid to a mason for making a *wardroppe* and carrying it out of the shop [and] into the chamber – 3s 4d.

Item paid to a carpenter for 2 days' labour – 12d.

Item for lead and casting the lead to the wardrope – 2s 6d.
Item for 5 lb of solder – 12 ½d.
Item for soldering 3 *skarys* – 6d.
Item for 6 studs – 12d.
Item for nails – 4d.
Item paid to a tiler – 4d.
Item for 3 quarters of lime – 6d.
Item paid for tile stones – 8d.
Item paid for 2 boards to make the chamber door – 12d.
Item for 2 twists – 4d.
Item for half a hundred of board nail and tent nail – 3d.
Item paid to a carpenter for his labour – 6d.
Item for a lock and a key and a latch – 10d.
Item for mending 5 *skarys* and 2 lb solder – 10d.
Item for mending a gutter – 4d.
Item for making this book – 12d.
Sum – 16s 3 ½d.

Sum the costs of this book – £12 8s 1d.

Rest £3 5s 1 ½d.

[1500–1]

fo 1
Here after follows the rental of the church of All Hallows' in the town of
Bristol and also containing in the same book the allowances, costs and
expenses and customable charges done from the feast of Candlemas in the
year of Our Lord God 1500 unto the feast of Candlemas next following,
that is to say in the year of Our Lord God 1501, by Rawlyn Coke and
Thomas Dave barber proctors of the said church for that year, and in the
year [when] George Mimoys [was] Mayor of the same town, Thomas
Pernaunt and Thomas Snygge being sheriffs.

The rent assize by the year
Item Paul James by the year – 3s 4d.
John Carlyon by the year – 4s.
John Branfylde by the year – 2s 6d.
Richard Erle by the *erthe* – 12d.
The master of the Tailors by the year – 12s.
Master Crowmar by the year – 6d.
John Shipward by the year – 2s.
Sum – 25s 4d.

In the High Street
Alice Snygge by the year – £3 6s 8d.
Thomas Pernaunt by the year – £4.
John Tannar by the year – 16s.
Thomas Went by the year – 13s 4d.
Sir William Woode for his chamber – 6s 8d.
John Cokkys by the year – 20d.
Thomas Coke in Broad Street by the year – £4.
Sum – £13 4s 4d.

Sum the whole rent of the church – £14 9s 8d.

fo 1v
The receipts of customable duties belonging to the church
In primis received on Palm Sunday – 2s 8d.
Item received on Sheer Thursday – 12d.
Item received on Good Friday – 2s 10d.
Item received on Easter eve and Easter day – 7s 11 ½d.
Item received of young Watkyn Coke for his seat and for his wife's – 12d.
Item received for wax at Saint Roche's mass – 5d.
Item received for a Welshman's grave – 7s.
Item received for Gyllett's grave in the churchyard – 2s.
Item received of Thomas Gyllett for his pew – 8d.
Item received of the parish for the clerk's wages – 5s 4d.
Item received of Master ?Harvey's mind for the bells – 8d.
Item received for John Tavarnar for the bells – 12d.
Item received for Master John Chestre's mind – 8d.
Item received for Halleway's mind for the bells – 2s.
Sum – 35s 2 ½d.

[Different ink and hand: Sum the rents and the casualties for this year –
£16 4s 10 ½d.]

Vacations following
Item Master Crowmar for the whole year – 6d.
Item Master Shipward for the whole year – 2s.
Item John Coxe for the year – 20d.
Sum – 4s 2d.

Rest due to the church – £12 10s 3 ½d. [sic]

[Different ink and hand: Rest due to the church the vacations abated –
£16 8 ½d.]

fo 2
Costs following
In primis paid to the Master of Saint John's for Thomas Coke's house for
rent assize – 6s 8d.
Item paid to the proctors of Christ Church for the same house – 13s 4d.
Sum – 20s.

Costs of William Newbery's mind
In primis paid to the vicar for his costs of wax and dirige – 16d.
Item paid to 5 priests for dirige and mass – 20d.
Item paid to the clerk for his dirige and his bells – 10d.
Item paid for bread to poor people – 2s.
Item paid to the bellman – 4d.
Item for offering – 1d.
Sum – 6s 2d.

Costs of Thomas Fylour's mind and Agnes his wife.
In primis paid to Master vicar for his wax and dirige – 12d.
Item to 8 priests for dirige and mass – 2s 8d.
Item to the clerk for his dirige [erased: and his bells] – 14d.
Item paid to the vicar for his oversight and for the bede roll – 12d.
Item paid to the bellman – 2d.
Item paid to the baker for bread for the poor people – 5s.
Item paid to the proctors for their labour – 12d.
Sum – 12s.

Sum this side – 38s 2d.

fo 2v
Costs of the obit of Harry Chestyr and Alice his wife
In primis paid to Master vicar for wax and his dirige – 12d.
Item paid to 6 priests for their dirige and mass – 2s.
Item paid to the clerk for his dirige and the bells – 12d.
Item paid to the bellman – 4d.
Item to the proctors for the offering – 1d.
Item more for bread to the poor people – 2s 8d.
Sum – 7s 1d.

Costs done over the obit for all the good doers
In primis paid for 2 ½ bushels of wheat at 16d the bushel – 3s 4d.
Item paid for grinding it – 2d.
Item paid for 2 dozens of ale – 4s.
Item paid to the vicar and to 4 priests – 16d.
Item paid to the clerk for the bells and his dirige – 14d.

Item paid for wine, oil, bread and for baking the cakes – 20d.
Item paid for 1 ¼ ounces of English saffron – 12 ½d.
Item paid for divers wines – 4s 11d.
Item paid for sugar and for white salt and straw – 5 ½d.
Item paid for the proctors' offering – 1d.
Sum – 18s 2d.
Sum this side – 25s 3d.

fo 3
Hereafter follow the customable costs of the church of All Hallows'
In primis paid for making the rent roll and for paper – 6d.
Item paid for making a window over the ceiling of the chancel – 2s.
Item paid for scouring the candlesticks against Easter – 2s.
Item paid for 1 pottle of wine to the clerks on Palm Sunday – 5d.
Item paid for watching the sepulchre – 12d.
Item paid for nails and for coals – 2 ½d.
Item paid to the raker for his year's wages – 8d.
Item paid to the mother church of Worcester – 8d.
Item paid at the day of account for a supper for the *paryshonys* – 2s 6d.
Item paid for wine when the communication was with Master Twenewe
about Thomas Coke's house – 4d.
Item paid to the suffragan for bearing the banner in Rogation week – 4d.
Item paid for 1 lock and a key to the *monestarye* – 5d.
Item paid for making the choir door – 20d.
Item paid for besoms – 2d.
Item paid for stopping the holes in the chancel – 17d.
Item paid for lime – 4d.
Item paid to the vicar on Corpus Christi day – 8d.
Item to the Prior of the Kalendars – 8d.
Item to 3 priests – 12d.
Item to the clerk – 4d.
Item to the sexton for bearing the cross – 4d.
Item paid to 2 friars for bearing the shrine – 8d.
Item paid to 3 lads – 4d.
Item paid for a pottle of wine – 4d.
Item paid to the clerk for hanging up the Dance of Pauls at Saint James'
tide – 8d.
Item paid for wax to John Waxmaker – 36s 7d.
Item paid for ringing the bells for Halleway's mind – 12d.
Sum this side – 57s 2 ½d.

fo 3v

Costs

Item paid for rivetting an image of St Michael on the best cross – 12d.

Item for mending a surplice and for *racke hokys* – 1 ½d.

Item paid to the clerk for hanging up the Dance of Pauls – 8d.

Item paid for washing the church stuff – 2s 4d.

Item paid to a plumber for mending 5 *skarys* over the church – 12d.

Item paid for a key to the charnel door – 2d.

Item paid to Richard clerk for 6 weeks – 3s 4d.

Item paid for mending 2 surplices – 4d.

Item paid Nicholas suffragan for his year's wages – 20s.

Item paid to the singers of [the] Jesus Mass for half a year – 20s.

Item paid for earnest of the holy water stock – 12d.

Item paid for candles – 3d.

Item paid to Thomas Grene for the making the iron before Our Lady – 20d.

Item paid to Hugh Mason for his labour – 9d.

Item paid to the clerk for his wages – 5s.

Item paid for ringing John Chestyr – 4d.

[Scored: Item paid for ringing of Clement Wilteshire – 4d.]

Item paid for ringing of Master Halleway – 4d.

Item paid for ringing of John Tavarnar – 4d.

[The following entries (to the foot of the page) are bracketed with the note in the right margin: The cost of the lower enterclose – 53s 4d.]

Item paid for timber for the enterclose – 11s 5d.

Item paid to the carpenter for his labour – 6s 8d.

Item paid for boards – 3s 4d.

Item paid more to the carpenter – 6s 8d.

Item paid more to the carpenter – 6s 8d.

Item paid more to the carpenter for his labour – 5s.

Item that I paid the earnest to the carpenter – 1d.

Item paid more to the carpenter for his labour – 5s 2d.

Item paid more to the carpenter for his labour 8s 4d.

Sum – £5 11s 11 ½d.

fo 4

Repairs done in Thomas Pernaunt's house

In primis paid to the plumber for soldering a *skare* and for solder – 5d.

Item paid more to the plumber for mending the gutters and for solder and his handiwork – 15d.

Item paid to Hugh Mason for his handiwork for making a chimney in the kitchen – 14s.

Item paid for sand – 10d.

Item paid for 2 stones and the hauling – 11d.

Item paid for a carpenter for 2 days' labour – 12d.
Item paid for 1 load of paving stones and the hauling – 17d.
Item paid for nails – 4d.
Item paid to a tiler for 1 day's labour – 6d.
Item paid to a labourer for 3 days' – 12d.
Item paid for 2 studs and for 2 semes of boards – 17d.
Item paid for lime – 6s 10d.
Item paid for hauling away the rubble – 14d.
Item for a key to the back door – 2d.
Item for mending of lead pipe of and for solder – 10d.
Item for sealing the porch – 10d.
Item for laths – 21d.
Item for lime – 4d.
Sum – 35s.

fo 4v
Repairs done in Thomas Went's house
Item paid for the breaking a *gowte* between John Tavarnar and Thomas
Went – 8d.
Item paid to a labourer for mending Thomas Went's house and John
Smith's house – 12d.
Item paid for mending of a window – 3d.
Sum – 23d.

Repairs done in Master Snygge's house
Item paid for mending a floor – 2d.
Item paid for sealing the buttress, for lime and laths and nails and
workmanship – 10d.
Item paid for mending the ladder in the belfry – 1d.
Sum – 13d.

Item for making this book – 12d.
Item for allowance to the tenants – 5d.

Sum – 4s 5d.

[The remainder in a different hand]
Sum the costs and repairs – £13 12s.
Rest in *dewyth* [due] to the church – 48s 8 ½d.

Which money is received at the day of account – 48s 8 ½d.

[1501–1502]

fo 1
Anno domini 1501
Thomas Davy barber
The church book of All Hallows'

fo 2
Here follows the rental of the church of All Hallows of Bristol and also in
the same book is contained the allowance, costs, expenses with
customable charges done from the feast of Candlemas 1501 unto the same
feast next following in the year of Our Lord God 1502, Thomas Davy
barber and John Lord proctors of the said church for that year, and then
being mayor Hugh Jones brewer, John ?Golas and John Cabull sheriffs.

Rent assize by year
In primis Paul James – 3s 4d.
Item of John Carlyon – 4s.
Item of Rawlyn Coke – 2s 6d.
Item of the master of the Tailors – 12s.
Item of Master Crowmere – 6d.
Item of John Shipward – 2s.
Sum – 25s 4d.

In the High Street by the year
Alice Snygge – £3 6s 8d.
Item of Thomas Pernaunt – £4.
Item of John Taverner – 16s.
Item of Thomas Went – 13s 4d.
Item of Sir William Wood for his chamber – 6s 8d.
Item of John Cokkes – 20d.
Item of Thomas Cook – £4.
Sum – £13 4s 4d.

Sum total the whole rent of the church – £14 9s 8d.

fo 2v
Received of customable duties belonging to the church
In primis received on Palm Sunday – 2s 8d.
Item on Shere Thursday – 12d.
Item on Good Friday – 2s 10d.
Item on Easter eve and Easter day – 7s 11 $\frac{1}{2}$d.

Received for pews

In primis of Jenkin Die and his wife – 12d.
Item of Thomas Gillet's wife – 12d.
Item of John Bek cook – 12d.
Item of Hugh Bromwell – 12d.
Item of the new grocer next Hugh Elyote ?taverner – 12d.
Sum – 5s.

Sum total of the rents and casualties of this year – £15 9s 1 ½d.

Vacations following
In primis Master Cromere – 6d.
Item John Shipward – 2s.
Item Paul James – 3s 4d.
Item Cokkes – 20d.
Item John Taverner for [a] half year – 8s.
Item Thomas Cook – £4.
Sum of the vacations – £4 15s 6d.
And so rest to the church clear – £10 13s 7 ½d.

fo 3
Costs upon obits following

Thomas Fylour's mind
In primis to the vicar for his wax and dirige – 12d.
Item to 8 priests – 2s 8d.
Item to the clerk – 14d.
Item to the vicar for his oversight and bede roll – 12d.
Item to the bellman – 2d.
Item for bread to the poor people – 5s.
Item to the proctors for their labour – 12d.
Sum – 12s.

William Newbery's mind
In primis to the vicar for his wax and dirige – 16d.
Item to 5 priests – 20d.
Item to the clerk – 10d.
Item for bread to the poor people – 2s.
Item to the bellman – 2d.
Item for offering – 1d.
Sum – 6s 1d.

Harry Chestre's mind and Alice his wife
In primis to the vicar for his wax and dirige – 12d.
Item to 6 priests – 2s.

Item to the clerk – 12d.
Item to the bellman – 4d.
Item for offering – 1d.
Item for bread to the poor people – 2s 8d.
Sum – 7s 1d.

Sum total on this side – 25s 2d.

fo 3v
The obit of all good doers
In primis for 2 ½ bushels of wheat – 3s 4d.
Item for grinding the same – 2d.
Item for 2 dozen of ale – 4s.
Item to the vicar and 4 priests – 16d.
Item to the clerk – 14d.
Item for wine and oil to the cakes and baking – 20d.
Item for 1 ¼ ounces of English saffron – 12 ½d.
Item for divers wines – 4s 11d.
Item for sugar, white salt and straw – 5 ½d.
Item for offering – 1d.
Sum – 18s 2d.

Costs and repairs of the church
In primis for making the rental – 6d.
Item for a pulley to hang the paschal – 2d.
Item for an iron to hang the paschal – 1d.
Item for a pottle of wine on Palm Sunday – 6d.
Item for besoms – 1d.
Item for scouring the church stuff – 2s.
Item for hooks to the sepulchre – 1d.
Item for coals – 1 ½d.
Item for a key to the church door – 4d.
Item for watching the sepulchre – 12d.
Item for a pottle of wine when the bargain was made to gild the rood – 4d.
Item for a pottle of wine to the vicar of St Leonard to move Master Hawke – 4d.
Item to Comyn Raker for the whole year – 8d.
Item to the same raker for 3 loads of rubble – 3d.
Sum – 6s 5 ½d.
Sum total on this side – 24s 12 ½d [sic].

fo 4
Item for 8 quarters of lime to the enterclose – 16d.
Item to the paver for paving the enterclose – 2s 3d.

Item to a labourer for 4 ½ days' – 18d.
Item for 4 boards to mend the seat – 4d.
Item to the paver for a day – 6d.
Item for a board to the enterclose – 1d.
Item for the holy water stone – 6s 8d.
Item for hauling of the same stone – 2d.
Item to the plumber for lead and solder for the same stone – 2s.
Item lent to the carpenter that made the enterclose – 3s 4d.
Item paid to the smith for locks, hinges and iron bars to the enterclose –
8s 10d.
Item for nails – 10 ½d.
Item for candles – 3d.
Item for mending a surplice – 1d.
Item for mending 2 copes – 4s.
Item for mending a vestment – 12d.
Item for bearing banners in Rogation week – 4d.
Item paid for 2 torches of 34 lb – 7s 10d.
Item for setting up the branch before Our Lady – 8d.
Item for a key to the steeple door – 2d.
Item for ringing for the Queen – 8d.
Item for a fire pan – 4d.
Item for 2 hinges to hold the torches – 2d.
Item for mending Master Pernaunt's seat – 4d.
Item for a load of tile stones for the church – 16d.
Item for hauling the same – 2d.
Item for a seme of boards – 8d.
Item for lath nail and hatch nail – 4d.
Sum – 46s 2 ½d.

fo 4v
Item to a tiler for 4 days' – 2s 2d.
Item to his man the same space – 16d.
Item for 100 laths – 6d.
Item for cleaning the gutter and hauling away the rubble – 2d.
Item for a board – 1 ½d.
Item for hanging the Dance of Pauls – 16d.
Item for washing the church stuff – 2s 4d.
Item for a supper at the day of reckoning – 2s 8d.
Item to Nicholas the suffragan for the year – 20s.
Item to Richard singer – 4s 5d.
Item to William clerk for Christmas quarter – 3s 7d.
Sum – 38s 7 ½d.

To John Waxmaker for wax

In primis he received 13 square tapers weighing 77 lb and he delivered 13 weighing 93 lb at 7d the pound – 9s 4d.

Item he received the paschal weighing 31 lb and he delivered the same weighing 33 $\frac{1}{2}$ lb – 17 $\frac{1}{2}$d.

Item he received 3 $\frac{1}{2}$ lb of wax and delivered a taper of 4 lb – 3 $\frac{1}{2}$d.

Item 4 tapers for the sepulchre of 1 lb – 7d.

Item for the change of 2 old torches – 9d.

Item he received 18 lb of wax and delivered 15 tapers weighing 31 lb, rest 13 lb – 7s 7d.

Item he received 19 $\frac{1}{2}$ lb wax and delivered 15 tapers [weighing] 31 lb, rest 11 $\frac{1}{2}$ lb – 6s 8 $\frac{1}{2}$d.

Item for making the church wax – 3s 4d.

Sum – 30s $\frac{1}{2}$d.

Sum total on this side – £3 8s 8d.

fo 5

Costs on Corpus Christ day

In primis to the vicar – 8d.

Item to the prior of Kalendars – 8d.

Item to Sir John Dyar – 4d.

Item to my lady Spicer's priest – 4d.

Item to Sir Thomas Furber – 4d.

Item to 2 friars – 8d.

Item to the suffragan for bearing the cross – 4d.

Item to 4 men to bear copes – 8d.

Item to 6 children to bear candlesticks and censers – 4d.

Item for a pottle of wine – 4d.

Item to Richard Clarke – 4d.

Item to the mother church of Worcester – 8d.

Item paid costs of court and resting of Thomas Cook's *pykkard* – 10d.

Sum – 6s 6d.

Repairs on Went's house

In primis for mending a gutter – 12d.

Item for 2 sacks of lime – 2d.

Item for a board – 1d.

Item to a carpenter for his labour – 2d.

Item for making 2 doors in M. Snygge's solar – 18d.

Sum – 2s 11d.

Repairs on Newton's house

In primis for boards – 16d.

Item for half a hundred laths – 3d.
Item for nails – 6 ½d.
Item to a carpenter a day – 6 ½d.
Item for haspes and hinges – 3d.
Item for a clamp of iron – 1d.
Sum – 3s 1d.

Sum total on this side – 12s 6d.

fo 5v
Repairs on Master Pernaunt's house
In primis paid to a tiler – 2d.
Item for a sack of lime – 1d.
Item for a crest – ½d.
Item for allowance to the tenants – 5d.
Item for making this book – 12d.
Sum – 20 ½d.

Item for a dinner to the priests for Our Lady Mass in Lent – 4s 3d.

Sum total of all costs and repairs, amount – £8 18s 10d [sum altered].

So rest clear that the proctors owe to the church – 39s 2d [sum altered].

So rest clear to the church – 34s 11d.

[1503–1504]

fo 1
[In dark ink: Ao dm 1503   John Lord]
Here follows the rental of the church of All Hallows of Bristol with
allowance, repairs, costs and expenses with customable charges done from
the feast of the Annunciation of Our Lady in the year of Our Lord God
1503 unto the same feast next following in the year of Our Lord God
1504, John Lord and Richard Sutton for that year proctors of the said
church, then being mayor Harry Dale, Robert Thorne and William Redford
sheriffs.

Rent assize by year
In primis of Paul James – 3s 4d.
Item of John Carlyon – 4s.
Item of Rawlyn Cook – 2s 6d.
Item of Richard Erle – 12d.

Item of the master of the Tailors – 12s.
Item of Master Croft – 6d.
Item of John Shipward – 2s.
Sum – 25s 4d.

In High Street by year
Alice Snygge – £3 6s 8d.
Item of Thomas Pernaunt – £4.
Item of Thomas Newton – 16s.
Item of Thomas Went – 13s 4d.
Item of William Wode for his chamber – 6s 8d.
Item of John Cokks – 20d.
Item of Thomas Cook – £4.
Sum – £13 4s 4d.

Sum total the rent of the church – £14 9s 8d.

fo 1v
The receipts of customable duties belonging to the church
In primis received on Palm Sunday – 2s 4d.
Item Sheer Thursday – 16d.
Item on Good Friday – 2s 7d.
Item on Easter eve and Easter day – 7s 5d.
Item of Mighell's wife for his grave – 6s 6d.
Item for Master Doctor Estmondes grave – 6s 8d.
Item of Master Monose for Thomas Cook's house – 7s 1d.
Item for a pew to Hugh Bromewell's wife – 12d.
Item for a pew to William Thomas and his wife – 12d.
Item for a pew to John Waxmaker and his wife – 12d.
Sum – 36s 11d.

Sum total the rents and casualties this year – £16 6s 7d.

Vacations following
In primis Master Croftis – 6d.
Item of John Shipward – 2s.
Item of Paul James' house – 3s 4d.
Item of Cokks – 20d.
Item a quarter void of Newton's house at Tolsey – 4s.
Item of Thomas Cook's house – £4.

Sum total vacations – £4 11s 6d.
And so rest clear to the church – £11 15s 1d.

fo 2

Costs upon obits following

Thomas Fylour's mind

In primis to the vicar for his wax to burn at dirige and at mass – 12d.
Item to 8 priests – 2s 8d.
Item to the clerk – 14d.
Item to the vicar for his oversight and the bede roll – 12d.
Item to the bellman – 2d.
Item for bread to the poor people – 5s.
Item to the proctors for their labour – 12d.
Sum – 12s.

William Newbery's mind

In primis to the vicar for his wax and dirige – 16d.
Item to 5 priests – 20d.
Item to the clerk – 10d.
Item for bread to the poor people 2s.
Item to the bellman – 2d.
Item for offering – 1d.
Sum – 6s 1d.

Harry Chestre's mind

Item to the vicar for wax to burn at dirige and mass – 12d.
Item to Master vicar and 5 priests – 2s.
Item to the clerk – 12d.
Item to the bellman – 4d.
Item for bread to the poor people – 2s 8d.
Item for offering – 1d.
Sum – 7s 1d.

fo 2v

Costs and payments of the church
In primis besoms – 1d.
Item paid for scouring the candlesticks and other gear against Easter – 2s.
Item for a sack of coals to the church – 2d.
Item for mending an old surplice – 1d.
Item paid for mending the best chasuble – 8d.
Item paid to the raker for the church – 8d.
Item for cloth and making the clerk's surplice – 5s 8d.
Item for watching the sepulchre – 12d.
Item for washing the clerk's surplice – 1d.
Item paid for a hook to the paschal – 1d.
Item for making the rental – 6d.

Item paid for supper on the day of reckoning – 2s 5d.

Item to the mother church of Worcester – 8d.

Item for 2 *tokkyng* girdles – 2d.

Item for bearing the banners in Rogation week – 4d.

Item for a pottle of wine at singing of the Passion – 5d.

Item for washing the church stuff – 2s 4d.

Item paid to the summoner [on] the day of the visitation – 4d.

Item paid to the summoner for summoning Hugh Grigge – 2d.

Item paid for mending the parish surplices and cloth – 3d.

Item for withdrawing the court at St James before the Chancellor – 4d.

Item paid to the clerk for his wage that could not be gathered of Our Lady quarter – 2s 1d.

Item of midsummer quarter that could not be gathered – 3d.

Item for an obligation between Fulby and the church – 3d.

Item paid to the suffragan – 20s.

Item for candle against Christmas – 3d.

Item for a lock to the ladder – 2d.

Item for cleansing the gutters after the snow – 1d.

Sum – 41s 6d.

fo 3

Repairs on Edmund Newton's house

In primis for 2 vats of *sopers* lime – 3d.

Item to a workman a day for mending floors and [the] hearths of his chimneys – 6d.

Item for nails – ½d.

Sum – 9 ½d.

Repairs in High Street Master Pernaunt's and Master Snygge's houses

In primis paid for 3 ½lb of solder – 10 ½d.

Item for 4 staves – 8d.

Item for ?soldering of a ?pipe – 2d.

Item for 2 loads of tile stones with the hauling – 3s.

Item more for a load of tile stones and hauling – 18d.

Item for a load of sand – 1d.

Item for 7 crests – 3d.

Item for laths – 2 ¼d.

Item for lath nail – 4d.

Item for 3 welsh boards – 4d.

Item for tile pins – 4d.

Item to 2 tilers for 9 days', 6d a day – 9s.

Item for hauling rubble – 1d.

Item for mending a chimney – 6d.

Item for a wey and 2 sacks of lime – 13d.

Sum – 18s 5d.

Sum total this side – 19s 2 ½d.

fo 3v
Repairs of the gates of the churchyard and others

Item paid for 3 oaken boards – 10d.
Item for nails – 7d.
Item to the carpenter for his labour – 6d.
Item for 7 lb of rosin for the same gates – 3d.
Item for mending of the doors of Agnes Walsall's pew and Paul's wife –
3d.
Item for a twist for the same door – 6d.
Item for a lock – 4d.
Item for spikes – 4d.
Item more for 1 pottle of lamp oil afore Jesus – 7d.
Item for small cord to hang the lamp by – 3d.
Item for *lev* to the cloths of the rood loft – 6d.
Item for a piece of broad *lere* containing 7 yards – 6d.
Item paid to Nicholas suffragan for setting up and taking down the Dance
of Pauls at Saint James' tide – 8d.
Item for the same at All Hallows' tide – 8d.
Item to the said suffragan for setting on 2 pieces of linen cloth for the
pillars of the rood loft – 1d.
Item for 3 quarters of a lb of curtain rings – 9d.
Item paid for irons to the rood loft – 9s.
Item more paid to the clerk for Christmas quarter – 4d.
Sum – 16s 11d.

fo 4
Costs upon Corpus Christi day
Item to 2 friars to bear the shrine – 8d.
Item to Sir Elys parish priest of St Nicholas – 4d.
Item to *powlis* priest – 4d.
Item to my lady Spicer's priest – 4d.
Item to Sir William Wood – 4d.
Item to the clerk – 4d.
Item to the suffragan – 4d.
Item for a pottle of wine – 4d.
Item to 4 young men for bearing the *tynecles* [tunicles] – 8d.
Item to the children for bearing the censers – 4d.
Item to *poulys* priest for bearing relics on relic Sunday – 2d.
Sum – 4s 2d.

The obit of all good doers
[Interpolation in different ink (matching entries at the end of the account):
Memorandum that it is determined [word indecipherable] that the chief
proctor shall not pass in his costs of the obit of good doers 13s 4d; if he
do, at his charge without any ?receipts]
Item for 2 ½ bushels of meal – 3s 1 ½d.
Item for 2 dozen of ale – 3s 4d.
Item to the vicar and 7 priests – 16d.
Item to the clerk – 14d.
Item for wine and oil to the cake baking – 21d.
Item for 1 ¼ ounces of saffron – 12 ½d.
Item for divers wines – 4s 11d.
Item for sugar, salt and straw – 4d.
Item for offering – 1d.
Sum – 17s 1d.

Sum total this side – 21s 3d.

fo 4v
To John Waxmaker
In primis we delivered the paschal weighing 31 lb and we received the
same weighing 32 lb, rest 1 lb – 7d.
Item delivered 13 square tapers weighing 70 lb and we received the same
tapers weighing 89 ½ lb, rest clear new wax 19 ½ lb – 11s 4 ½d.
Item delivered 15 tapers weighing 20 lb, received 15 tapers weighing 31 ½
lb, rest new wax 11 ½ lb – 6s 8 ½d.
Item for 4 tapers of 1 lb to the sepulchre – 7d.
Item more delivered 20 lb old wax and we received 15 tapers weighing 31
lb, rest new wax 11 lb – 6s 5d.
Item for 2 torches weighing 43 lb, price the pound 3d – 10s 9d.
Item for making the wax this year – 3s 4d.
Sum – 39s 9d.

For a dinner to the priests and clerks of Our Lady Mass
In primis for 2 pigs – 12d.
Item for 2 ribs of beef – 10d.
Item for 2 *costs* of mutton – 5d.
Item for bread – 6d.
Item for ale – 6d.
Item for wine – 12d.
Item for fire and spice – 3d.
Sum – 4s 6d.

Sum total this side – 44s 3d.

fo 5
Payments
Item for making this book – 12d.
Item for allowance to the tenants – 12d.
Item for paper – 2d.
Sum – 2s 2d.

Sum total of costs, repairs and payments – £8 10s 5 $\frac{1}{2}$d.

And so rests clear to the church – £3 4s 7 $\frac{1}{2}$d.

[Remainder of account is in different hand and ink (matching the interpolation on expenditure limits for the General Mind).]
Item received of Catherine ?Yenanys for her husband's bequest – 12d.
Rest clear £3 5s 7 $\frac{1}{2}$d.

[Scored and largely illegible entry follows concerning a payment of 25s $\frac{1}{2}$d from John Lord and Richard Sutton for Michael Bull's house. A final line reports that £4 11s 1d rested clear 'for his old account', which sum is scored and the sum of £3 5s 7 $\frac{1}{2}$d is written superscript.]

[1504–1505]

fo 1
[In dark ink: Ao dm 1504   Thomas Snygg]
Here follows the rental of the church of All Hallows' of Bistol with allowance, repairs, costs and expenses with customable charges done from the feast of the Annunciation of Our Lady in the year of Our Lord God 1504, Thomas Snygge and John Dee proctors of the said church for that year, unto the same feast next following in the year of Our Lord God 1505, then being mayor Master Davy Phylippe, William Gefferye and Edmond Penson sheriffs.

Rent assize by the year
In primis of Paul James – 3s 4d.
Item of John Carlyon – 4s.
Item of Rawlyn Cook – 2s 6d.
Item of Richard Erle – 12d.
Item of the master of the Tailors – 12s.
Item of Master Crofte – 6d.
Item of John Shipward – 2s.
Sum – 25s 4d.

In High Street by the year
Thomas Snygge – £3 6s 8d.
Item of Thomas Pernaunt – £4.
Item of Thomas Newton – 16s.
Item of Thomas Went – 13s 4d.
Item of Sir William Woode for his chamber – 6s 8d.
Item of John Cokks – 20d.
Item of Thomas Cook – £4.
Sum – £13 4s 4d.

Sum total the rent of the church – £14 9s 8d.

fo 1v
The receipts of customable duties belonging to the church
In primis received on Palm Sunday – 2s 4d.
Item Sheer Thursday – 16 $\frac{1}{2}$d.
Item on Good Friday – 2s 8d.
Item on Easter eve and Easter day – 7s 7d.
Item of Master Monose for Thomas Coke's house – 7s 1d.
Item of Thomas Pace for his 1 children – 3s 4d.
Item of Thomas Forbor for his grave – 6s 8d.
Item of Mistress Harvy for her grave – 6s 8d.
Item received of Richard Sutton for my reward which I gave to the church
– 3s 4d.
Item received of Master Maire for 2 pews – 3s 4d.
Item received of John Batten for his son's grave – 3s 4d.
Item received of Master Hotton for my lady's grave – 6s 8d.
Item of Alice Pynke for her grave – [blank]
Item of Pers Grenefeld for his grave – 8d.
Item of Thomas Pace for his pew – 12d.
Item of Robert Rogers for their pews – 16d.
Sum – 57s 4 $\frac{1}{2}$d.

Vacations following
In primis of Richard Erle – [blank]
Item of Master Croft's in St Peter's parish – [blank]
Item of John Shipward for a house in Marsh Street – 2s.
Item of the house that Paul James late held – 3s 4d.
Item of John Cokks – 20d.
Item of the house that Thomas Cook dwelt – £4.
Sum vacations – £4 7s.

And so rest clear to the church – £13 $\frac{1}{2}$d.

fo 2

Thomas Fylar's obit

In primis to the vicar for his wax to burn at dirige and mass – 12d.
Item to 8 priests – 2s 8d.
Item to the clerk – 14d.
Item to the vicar for his oversight and the bede roll – 12d.
Item to the bellman – 2d.
Item for bread to the poor people – 5s.
Item to the 2 proctors for their labour – 12d.
Sum – 12s.

William Newbery's obit

Item to the vicar for his wax and dirige – 16d.
Item to 5 priests – 20d.
Item to the clerk – 10d.
Item for bread to the poor people – 2s.
Item to the bellman – 2d.
Item for offering – 1d.
Sum – 6s 1d.

Harry Chestre's obit

Item to the vicar for his wax to burn at dirige and at mass – 12d.
Item to the vicar and 5 priests – 2s.
Item to the clerk – 12d.
Item to the bellman – 4d.
Item for bread to the poor people – 2s 8d.
Item for offering – 1d.
Sum – 7s 1d.

Sum total this side – 25s 2d.

fo 2v

Costs and payments customably

Item for besoms – 1d.
Item paid to the suffragan for his year's wages – 20s.
Item for coals – 2d.
Item for scouring the candlesticks – 2s.
Item for washing the church cloths – 2s 4d.
Item for watching the sepulchre – 12d.
Item to the raker for his year's wages – 8d.
Item for making the rent roll – 6d.
Item for the supper at the accounts – 18 $\frac{1}{2}$d.
Item paid [to] the proctors of Our Lady Worcester – 8d.
Item for bearing the banners – 4d.

Item for mending of a vestment of the church's – 12d.
Item for a pottle of wine on Palm Sunday – 4d.
Item for mending 2 candlesticks afore the rood altar – 6d.
Item for hanging up the Dance of Pauls – 16d.
Item paid John Sulby for that he was to pay off the rood loft – 4s 3d.
Item paid the king's collectors – 13s 9d.
Item paid for candles to set about the church on Christmas Day – 4d.
Sum – 50s 9 ½d.

Repairs done in the west end of the church
Item paid [to] a smith for 2 bars of iron to bind the beams – 9d.
Item for timber to the same – 6d.
Item for 2 men's labours 1 day – 13d.
Item for nails – 4 ½d.
Item for mending the morrow mass bell – 4d.
Sum – 3s ½d.

Amount this side – 53s 10s.

fo 3
Costs upon Corpus Christi day
Item paid to 2 friars to bear the shrine – 8d.
Item to Master vicar – 4d.
Item to *pollys* priest – 4d.
Item to 2 priests of the Kalendars – 8d.
Item to Sir Richard and Sir John my lady's priests – 8d.
Item to Sir William Woode – 4d.
Item to the clerk – 4d.
Item to the suffragan for bearing the cross – 4d.
Item a pottle [of] wine – 4d.
Item to the children for bearing the candlesticks – 3d.
Item for bearing up the copes – 3d.
Item to Sir Harry Byrd – 4d.
Sum – 4s 10d.

Costs of the obit for all good doers
Item to the vicar and 4 priests – 15d.
Item to the clerk – 14d.
Item for 2 bushels meal – 20d.
Item for an ounce of saffron – 16d.
Item for a quart of oil – 5d.
Item for a gallon of osey – 8d.
Item for *barme* – 4d.
Item for baking – 6d.

Item for 2 dozen ale – 3s 4d.
Item for divers wines – 4s 4d.
Item for bread to the poor people – 8d.
Item for offering – 1d.
Sum – 15s 9d.

Sum total this side – 20s 7d.

fo 3v
Here follow the parcels of wax delivered and received
Item delivered 13 square tapers weighing 68 lb. Received 13 square tapers weighing 92 lb. So new wax 24 lb at 6 $\frac{3}{4}$d. Sum – 13s 6d.
Item delivered 15 round tapers weighing 19 $\frac{3}{4}$ lb. Received 15 tapers weighing 31 lb. So new wax 11 $\frac{1}{4}$ lb at 6 $\frac{3}{4}$d.
Item delivered the paschal weighing 29 lb. Received the paschal weighing 32 $\frac{1}{4}$ lb. So new wax 3 $\frac{1}{4}$ lb at 6 $\frac{3}{4}$d.
Item delivered 4 lb wax. Received the font taper weighing 4 lb.
Item delivered 2 lb of wax. Received 4 tapers weighing 1 lb. So rest he oweth in wax 1 lb. Clear to him of this 3 parcels afore rehearsed 2 $\frac{1}{4}$ lb at 6 $\frac{3}{4}$d. Sum – 7s 6 $\frac{3}{4}$d.
Item paid for making all the wax – 3s 4d.
Item delivered 15 round tapers weighing 21 lb. Received 31 lb wax at 6 $\frac{1}{2}$d, sum – 5s 5d.
Sum – 29s 9 $\frac{1}{2}$d.

Repairs between Thomas Pernaunt and Thomas Snygge
In primis paid for a gutter case 16 $\frac{1}{2}$ feet long – 2s.
Item for hauling – 1d.
Item for a load of stone – 15d.
Item for hauling the same – 2d.
Item paid for 3 lb of solder for the church porch and a gutter between Thomas Pernaunt and Thomas Snygge – 8d.
Item paid for ?half a hundred weight and 17 lb of lead – 3s 4d.
Item for 8 lb of solder – 22d.
Item paid the plumber for his day's labour – 8d.
Item paid to a tiler for 2 days' labour – 13d.
Sum – 11s 1d.
Sum total this side – 40s 10d.

fo 4
Repairs in Thomas Snygge's house between Mistress Hawke and the church
Item paid for half a principal beam – 12d.
Item for half carriage of the same – 1 $\frac{1}{2}$d.

Item for half carriage of 6 poles to underset the house – 1d.
Item for half waste of timber – 6d.
Item paid for 8 $\frac{1}{4}$ lb of solder between Thomas Snygge and Thomas Pernaunt and also partible between the church and Mistress Hawke – 12d.
Item paid to 2 carpenters for the church part – 6 $\frac{1}{2}$d.
Item to 4 carpenters for half a day – 13d.
Item to 2 carpenters a day – 6 $\frac{1}{2}$d.
Item for laths – 1 $\frac{1}{2}$d.
Item for lath nails – 1 $\frac{1}{2}$d.
Item for lime and hair – 1 $\frac{1}{2}$d.
Item for a man's hire to make the same – 8d.
Item to a labourer for the business of all the foresaid work – 4d.
Item to a plumber for his labours in the foresaid work – 8d.
Item paid Hugh Carpenter for half a day's labour, he and his man – 6 $\frac{1}{2}$d.
Sum – 7s 5 $\frac{1}{2}$d.

Costs done to the church
Item for 4 lb of solder to the holy water stock and for mending the roof of the charnel house and for his labour – 18d.
Item for *lere* and making the curtains of Sir William's altar – 4d.
Item paid Nicholas for pins against All Hallows' tide – 1d.
Item for timber and workmanship of the desk – 2s 6d.
Sum – 4s 5d.
Sum total this side – 11s 10 $\frac{1}{2}$d.

fo 4v
Repairs on the hall window in T. Snygge's house
In primis for 50 laths – 3 $\frac{1}{2}$d.
Item delivered a plumber 26 lb lead. Received of him 47 lb lead. Sum with the casting 15 $\frac{1}{2}$d, the fault of the which lead was the rotting of the rester and would have been the confusion of the house, sum – 15 $\frac{1}{2}$d.
Item paid for a load of stones with the hauling – 16d.
Item paid 2 carpenters for 2 $\frac{1}{2}$ days' – 2s 8 $\frac{1}{2}$d.
Item paid for the principal rester – 7d.
Item for 4 *mownells* – 6d.
Item paid the tiler and his man for 2 days' – 2s 2d.
Item paid for tile pins – 3d.
Item my brother Pernaunt for boards and nails – 3s 2d.
Item paid for 3 foot glass to the window – 18d.
Item paid a tiler for his labours – 10d.
Item paid for mending a gutter in Thomas Went's house – 12d.
Item allowance for drinking money to the tenants – 16d.
Sum – 14s 4d.

Here follows that I have paid Richard clerk every quarter for his wage
Item paid for Our Lady quarter – 21d.
Item paid for Midsummer quarter – 8d.
Item paid for Michaelmas quarter – 12d.
Sum – 3s 5d.

Amount this side – 17s 9d.

fo 5
Memorandum that by [word illegible] Sir Raffe is from whom [?home]
that the dinner of Our Lady Feast is prolonged till he comes whom
[?home], which dinner cost the last – 4s 6d.

Sum total repairs and other ordinary costs and payments – £8 14s 7d.

Item paid for a bolt of iron to Thomas Snygge's hall window – 4d.
Item paid for cleaning the hearse cloth – 3d.
Item paid for making this book – 12d.
Item for paper – 1 ½d.
Sum – 20 ½d.

Item received of ?now lord of ?Tewkesbury for John Steynar's bequest –
9s 8d.

Sum the whole receipts – £13 9s 8 ½d.
Sum the whole payments – £8 18s 3 ½d.

[Different hand] So rest that Thomas Snygge owes to the church at the day
of account – £4 13s 5d.
The which money the said Thomas Snygge delivered and paid to the
pareschsoners at the aforesaid day of account.

[1505–1506]

fo 1
[In dark ink: Ao dm 1505   John Dee]
Here follows the rental of the church of All Hallows' of Bristol with
allowance, repairs, costs and expenses with customable charges done,
from the feast of the Annunciation of Our Lady in the year of Our Lord
God 1505, John Dee and Thomas Pacye for that year proctors of the said
church unto the same feast next following in the year of Our Lord 1506,
then being mayor Master Roger Dawse, Thomas Smith and John Hare
sheriffs.

Rent assize by the year
In primis of Paul James – 3s 4d.
Item of John Carlyon – 4s.
Item of Rawlyn Cocke – 2s 6d.
Item of Richard Erle – 12d.
Item of the master of the Tailors – 12s.
Item of Master Croft – 6d.
Item of John Shipward – 2s.
Sum – 25s 4d.

In High Street by the year
Thomas Snygge – £3 6s 8d.
Item of Thomas Pernaunt – £4.
Item of Thomas Newton – 16s.
Item of Thomas Went – 13s 4d.
Item of Sir William Woode for his chamber – 6s 8d.
Item John Cokks – 20d.
Item of Thomas Cook – £4.
Sum – £13 4s 4d.

Sum total the rent of the church – £14 9s 8d.

fo 1v
The receipts of customable duties belonging to the church
In primis received upon Palm Sunday – 2s 7d.
Item on Shere Thursday – 10d.
Item on Good Friday – 2s 6d.
Item on Easter eve – 10d.
Item on Easter day – 7s 2d.
Item received for William Thomas' grave – 6s 8d.
Item received for Master Pernaunt's wife's burial – 6s 8d.
Item received for Richard Crakyngthorp's grave – 6s 8d.
Item received of William Apowell and his wife for their pews – 12d.
Item received of John Marten and his wife for their pews – 12d.
Item received of Master Monose for Thomas Cock's house – 7s 1d.
Item received of Henry Esterfeld and his wife for their pews – 2s.
Item received of Thomas Kere and his wife for their pews – 12d.
Item received of Alice Penke for her grave – [blank]
Item received of Master John Baten – £10 [sum in different hand]
Sum – £12 7s
Rest clear to the church – £26 16s 8d.

Vacations following
In primis of [scored: Richard Erle].

Item of Master Crofte's in St Peter's parish – 6d.
Item of John Shipward for a house in Marsh Street – 2s.
[Scored: Item of Paul James for a house that late he held – 3s 4d.]
Item of John Cocks – 20d.
Item of the house that Thomas Cook dwelt – £4.
Sum vacations – £4 4s 2d.

Rest of this side – £22 12s 6d.

fo 2
Thomas Fylour's obit
In primis to the vicar for his wax to burn at dirige and at mass – 12d.
Item to the 7 priests – 2s 8d.
Item to the clerk – 14d.
Item to the vicar for his oversight and bede roll – 12d.
Item to the bellman – 2d.
Item for bread to the poor people – 5s.
Item to the 2 proctors for their labour – 12d.
Sum – 12s.

William Newbery's obit
Item to the vicar for his wax and dirige – 16d..
Item to the 5 priests – 20d.
Item to the clerk – 10d.
Item for bread to the poor people – 2s.
Item to the bellman – 2d.
Item for offering – 1d.
Sum – 6s 1d.

Harry Chestre's obit
Item to the vicar for his wax to burn at dirige and at mass – 12d.
Item to the vicar and 5 priests – 2s.
Item to the clerk – 12d.
Item to the bellman – 4d.
Item for bread to the poor people – 2s 8d.
Item for offering – 1d.
Sum – 7s 1d.

Sum total of this side – 25s 2d.

fo 2v
Costs and payments customable
In primis for besoms – 1d.
Item paid to the suffragan for his year's wages – 20s.

Item for coals – 2d.
Item for scouring the candlesticks – 2s.
Item for washing the church cloths – 2s 4d.
Item for watching the sepulchre – 12d.
Item to [the] raker for his year's wages – 8d.
Item for making the rent roll – 6d.
Item for the supper at the accounts – 2s 9d.
Item paid the proctors of Our Lady Worcester – 8d.
Item for bearing the banners – 4d.
Item for a pottle of wine on Palm Sunday – 6d.
Item for hanging up the Dance of Pauls – 16d.
Item paid for candles to set about the church on Christmas Day – 4d.
Item paid upon Palm Sunday to Sibble for her children – 2d.
Item paid for mending an alb – 2d.
Item paid for washing the *kercher* to the *schryne* – 2d.
Item paid for mending of the blue copes – 4d.
Item paid for half a hide of leather *hongrye* – 22d.
Item paid for 6 girdles to the priests – 3d.
Item paid for a new key to the coffer that the jewels are in – 6d.
Item paid for making 3 baldrics and for 2 *boculls* [?buckles] – 14d.
Item for mending Master vicar's surplice – 14d.
[Scored: Item paid for bearing the banners in the Rogation week – 4d.
Item paid for making the rent roll – 6d.]
Item paid for making of the clerk's collar of his surplice – 4d.
Item paid for the dinner of Our Lady Mass – 7s 4d.
Sum of this side – 46s 1d.

fo 3
Costs upon Corpus Christi day
Item paid to 2 friars to bear the shrine – 8d.
Item to Master vicar – 4d.
Item to *Pollys* priest – 4d.
Item to 2 priests of the Kalendars – 8d.
Item to Sir Richard and to Sir John my lady priests – 8d.
Item to Sir William Wode – 4d.
Item to the clerk – 4d.
Item to the suffragan for bearing the cross – 4d.
Item a pottle of wine – 4d.
Item to the children for bearing the candlesticks – 3d.
Item for bearing up the copes – 3d.
Item paid for another priest – 4d.
Sum – 4s 10d.

Repairs upon the church and the tower

In primis for 2 tilers a day – 12 $\frac{1}{2}$d.
Item for half a load of stones – 8d.
Item for tile pins – 3d.
Item for 2 sacks of lime – 2d.
Item for a board – 1d.
Item for 4 *cressys* [?crests] – 4d.
Item paid a plumber for soldering of 13 *skares* upon the tower upon the church – 2s 2d.
Item for 15 lb solder – 3s 9d.
Item paid for workmanship, lead and solder for the church part done betwixt the church and the Kalendars – 18d.
Item paid for mending 2 pews – 10d.
Item for a lamp – 1d.
[Scored: Item paid for 7 gallons and a pottle of lamp oil – 8s 9d.]
Item paid for dressing the bells – 26s 8d.
[Different hand: Item paid for pulleys to the bells – 2s 4d.]
Sum – 39s 10 $\frac{1}{2}$d.
Sum of this side – 44s 8 $\frac{1}{2}$d.

fo 3v
Costs of the obit for all good doers
In primis to the vicar and 4 priests – 15d.
Item to the clerk – 14d.
Item for 2 bushels meal – 20d.
Item for an ounce of saffron – 2s 8d.
Item for a quart of oil – 5d.
Item for a gallon of osey – 16d.
Item for *barme* – 4d.
Item for baking – 6d.
Item for 2 dozen ale – 3s 4d.
Item for divers wines – 3s 10d.
Item for bread to the poor people – 8d.
Item for offering – 1d.
Sum – 16d 5d.

Here follows the parcels of wax
In primis delivered 13 square tapers weighing 73 lb
Item received the said 13 tapers weighing 95 $\frac{1}{4}$ lb
Item in new wax there is 22 $\frac{1}{4}$ lb – 12s $\frac{1}{2}$d.

Item delivered the paschal taper weighing 30 lb
Item received the said taper again weighing 34 lb
Item so there is in new wax – 4 lb – 2s 2d.

Item delivered 15 round tapers weighing 22 lb
Item received the said tapers again weighing 30 $\frac{3}{4}$ lb
Item so there is in new wax 8 $\frac{3}{4}$ lb – 4s 8 $\frac{1}{2}$d.

Item delivered the font taper weighing 3 $\frac{1}{2}$ lb
Item received the said taper again weighing 4 lb
Item received 4 small tapers weighing 1 lb in new wax 1 $\frac{1}{2}$ lb – 9 $\frac{3}{4}$d.

Item delivered 15 round tapers weighing 20 $\frac{1}{2}$ lb
Item received the same again 31 lb
Item so there is in new wax 10 $\frac{1}{2}$ lb – 5s 8d.

Sum of the new wax is 47 lb at 6 $\frac{1}{2}$d the pound. Sum – 25s 5 $\frac{1}{2}$d.

Item paid for making of the new wax at both the times – 3s 4d.

Sum total – 41s 10d.

fo 4
Repairs done upon Thomas Snygge's house
In primis for spike nails paid – 2d.
Item for board nails – 2d.
Item paid to a mason for a day's work – 6d.
Item paid to a labourer for a day's work – 4 $\frac{1}{2}$d.
Item more to a labourer for half a day's work – 2d.
Item paid to 2 carpenters for 4 days' wages – 4s 4d.
Item paid for the church part for a partible beam – 14d.
Item paid for a wall plate – 12d.
Item paid for lead 31 lb – 11d.
Item paid for hauling of timber – 1d.
Item paid for a load of stones – 14d.
Item paid for 10 feet of gutter case which is betwixt Master Pernaunt and Master Snygge – 11d.
Item paid for 7 feet of gutter case – 8d.
Item paid more for 4 feet of gutter case – 6d.
Item paid to 2 tilers for a whole week's work – 6s 6d.
Item paid to a labourer for 5 days' work – 22d.
Item paid for ?3000 tile pins and for *mosse* – 16d.
Item paid for 500 tile stones – 2s 6d.
Item paid to a carpenter for a day's work – 6 $\frac{1}{2}$d.
Item paid to a labourer for 4 days' work – 16d.
Item paid for 4 rafters – 16d.
Item paid for a floor beam – 8d.
Item 50 board nails – 2 $\frac{1}{2}$d.

Item for half hatch nails – 1 $\frac{1}{2}$d.
Item paid for 100 laths – 6d.
Item paid for board nail – $\frac{1}{2}$d.
Sum of this side – 29s 4d.

fo 4v
Thomas Snygge's house
Item paid for hauling 5 loads of stones – 8d.
Item for hauling a piece of timber – 1d.
Item paid for 100 feet of boards – 2s.
Item paid for 2 loads of tile stones – 2s 6d.
Item paid for 6 studs – 12d.
Item paid for a piece of timber – 2s.
Item paid to 2 carpenters for working 200 feet of board – 19 $\frac{1}{2}$d.
Item paid to a tiler for a day's work – 6 $\frac{1}{2}$d.
Item to a labourer for a day's work – 4 $\frac{1}{2}$d.
Item paid to a tiler for 2 $\frac{1}{2}$ days' work – 16d.
Item paid for 100 feet of board – 2s.
Item delivered in partible lead betwixt Master Pernaunt and Master Snygge and for other necessaries about their gutters one ?hundredweight and 96 lb.
Received in new lead, 2 cloths weighing 2 $\frac{1}{2}$?hundredweight and 13 lb.
So we paid to the plumber for a ?hundredweight *faute* 6 lb – 4s.
Item paid for casting the foresaid lead – 2s 2d.
Item paid for solder and 2 *skares* – 9d.
Item delivered in old lead partible between Master Harvey and the church 1 $\frac{1}{2}$?hundredweights and 19 lb.
Received in new lead with a *cestorn* [?cistern] 1 $\frac{3}{4}$?hundredweights 11 $\frac{1}{2}$ lb.
So paid to the plumber for 20 $\frac{1}{2}$ lb and 9 pennyweights, which came to our part – 4 $\frac{1}{2}$d.
Item paid for casting the same lead for the church part – 9d.
Item paid for soldering the *cestorn* and 2 *skares* and 4 lb solder for the church part – 10d.
Item paid for 100 tile stones – 7d.
Item paid for 10 crests – 10d.
Item paid for 2 carpenters for a week's work – 3s 4d.
Sum of this side – 27s 9d.

fo 5
Thomas Snygge's house
Item paid for workmanship of 100 feet of board – 9d.
Item paid for 2 pieces of timber for a ceiling and for a ground seal – 13 $\frac{1}{2}$d.

Item paid for 304 feet of board and for hauling – 5s 6d.
Item paid to a tiler for 4 $\frac{1}{2}$ days' plastering – 2s 4d.
Item paid to a labourer for 2 $\frac{1}{2}$ days' work – 11d.
Item paid for 3 weys of lime – 2s 6d.
Item paid for a load of tile stones – 15d.
Item paid for hauling tile stones – 7d.
Item paid for hauling 10 vats of rubble – 8d.
Item paid to Master Pernaunt for timber laths and nails which was occupied about the said house – 18s 7d.
Sum – 34s 2 $\frac{1}{2}$d.

Thomas Snygge
Item I paid to him for repairs that he did for the church which he had forgotten at his account – 12d.
Item more paid to him for certain stuff that he had of Master Pernaunt for the church work – 12d.
Item paid to 2 masons and a labourer and for cleansing a gutter in the said house – 3s 4d.
Item paid for a load of stones and for hauling – 18d.
Item paid for lime and for sand – 14d.
Item paid for a gutter case which as yet is not occupied – 12d.
Item paid to a plumber for casting a pipe of lead weighing 51 lb and for soldering a *skare* and for 2 $\frac{1}{2}$ lb of solder and for dressing the same pipe in a *drawgtht* in the back chamber of the said house – 2s $\frac{1}{2}$d.
Sum – 11s $\frac{1}{2}$d.
Sum of this side – 45s 3d.

fo 5v
Repairs done on the lands of the church
In primis paid for mending a pipe in Master Pernaunt's gutter and for 2 *skares* and 2 lb of solder – 10d.
Item paid for making a window and for stuff to the same in Thomas Went's house – 8d.
Item allowance for drinking money – 16d.
Item paid for paper – 1d.
Item paid for making this book – 12d.
Item paid 3 long ?studs William Wood's house – 9d.
Item for a bundle and a half of laths to the same – 4 $\frac{1}{2}$d.
Item paid for calf foot nails – 1 $\frac{1}{2}$d.
Item paid for 3 sacks of lime – 3d.
Item paid for a day's work to a tiler – 6 $\frac{1}{2}$d.
Item for a labourer a day – 5d.
Sum – 5s 4 $\frac{1}{2}$d.

Sum total of all the costs payments and repairs aforesaid – £13 6s 5 ½d.

[Remainder of the account in a different hand] Item paid hereof to John Lord – 52s 2d.
Rest £6 13s 10d.

Item received of John De the day and year aforesaid – £5 22d.
Rest 32s.

Item John De hath delivered a pledge ?surety of the foresaid 32s, a standing mazer weighing 10 ½ oz.

[1507–1508; very different hand to previous and subsequent accounts; small, spidery writing]

fo 1
Jhus Maria

Here after follows the rental of the church of All Hallows' of Bristol with allowance, repairs, expenses with customable charges done from the feast of the Annunciation of Our Blessed Lady in the year of Our Lord God 1507, Thomas Pernaunt and Thomas Barber for that year being proctors of the aforesaid church, unto the feast next following in the year of Our Lord God 1508, then being mayor Master John Vaghan, ?John Edwards and Symond Gerves sheriffs.

Rents of assize by the year
Item the good Powll – 3s 4d.
Item Thomas Gellett's house – 4s.
Item of Rawlyn Coke – 2s 6d.
Item Richard Erle – 12d.
Item the master of Tailors – 12s.
Item of Master Croft's house – 6d.
Item George Chepward – 2s.
Sum – 25s 4d.

The High Street by the year
Item Thomas Snygge – £3 6s 8d.
Item Thomas Pernaunt – £4.
Item Edmond Newton – 16s.
Item Went tailor – 13s 4d.
Item Sir ?John's chamber – 6s 8d.
Item the shop in the churchyard – 20d.

Item the house in Broad Street – £4.

Sum total – £14 9s 8d.

fo 1v
Jhu
The vacations following
Richard Erle's house – 12d.
Item the master of the Tailors – 12s.
Item the house in Broad Street – £4.
Item the shop in the churchyard – 20d.
Sum the vacations – £4 13s 8d.
So amounts the clear receipts of the church rents, the vacations abated
clear – £9 15s.

fo 2
Jhu
The receipts of customable duties to the church
Item received on Palm Sunday – 2s 6d.
Item on Sheer Thursday I received – 11 $\frac{1}{2}$d.
Item on Good Friday received – 23d.
Item received on Easter eve – 15 $\frac{1}{2}$d.
Item received on Easter day – 6s 10d.
Item received of Thomas Pace that was proctor the last year – 18s 10d.
Item received of the masters of the parish to bestow in repairs – £4 2s.
Received for 100 laths that I sold of the church's – 6d.
Item received of John Heows for a priest that died in his house – 6s 8d.
Item received of the good wife Stevens for her husband's grave – 6s 8d.
Item received for a ?vat that ?was ?delivered out of Thomas Coke's house
– 5s.
Item received of the good wife Stevens for her husband's bequest – 10s.
Item received of Humphrey Bradly for the house that ?he dwelt in –
33s 4d.
Item received for a gilt cup that was a ?posset, of John Dee – 31s.
Item received of ?William Appowell for his wife's grave – 6s 8d.
Item received of Master Snygge for his mother and his daughter's grave –
13s 4d.
Item received of the goodwife Walsall ?rest for her seat – 8d.
Item received of John Heows for the bequest of the priest that died in his
house – 12d.
Item received of Watkyn Coke for 100 laths – 6d.
Sum – £11 9s 8d.

Sum total clear – £21 4s 8d.

fo 2v

Jhu

Hereafter follow the obits

William Newbery's obit

In primis paid to Master vicar for his wax and his duty – 16d.

Item paid to 5 priests – 20d.

Item paid to the clerk – 10d.

Item for bread – 2s.

Item for the bellman – 2d.

Item for offering – 1d.

Sum – 6s 1d.

Thomas Fylour's obit

Item paid to Master vicar for his wax at dirige and at Mass – 12d.

Item paid to 8 priests – 2s 8d.

Item paid to the clerk – 14d.

Item paid to Master vicar for the bede roll – 12d.

Item the bellman – 2d.

Item for bread – 5s.

Item for the proctors' oversight – 12d.

Sum – 12s.

Harry Chestre's obit

Item paid to Master vicar for his wax – 12d.

Item paid to Master vicar and 5 priests – 2s.

Item paid to the clerk – 12d.

Item paid the bellman – 4d.

Item paid for bread – 2s 8d.

Item offering – 1d.

Sum – 7s 1d.

Sum this side – 25s 2d.

fo 3

Jhu

The obit of Thomas Spicer and Dame Maud his wife

In primis paid to master vicar and 5 priests – 2s.

Item paid for 4 tapers of 2 lb apiece to burn at dirige and at Mass – 2s.

Item paid to Master vicar for his oversight – 12d.

Item paid to the clerk for his bells and dirige – 14d.

Item to the bellman – 4d.

Item the sexton – 1d.

Item offering – 1d.

Item bread to the poor people – 2s 4d.

Sum – 10s.

The obit of all good doers
Item paid to the vicar and for 4 priests – 15d.
Item paid the clerk for his labour and his bells – 14d.
Item paid for 2 bushels of meal – 20d.
Item paid for an ounce of saffron – 14d.
Item a pottle osey – 6d.
Item the cakes' baking – 6d.
Item a dozen double ale and a dozen single ale – 2s 6d.
Item the wines – 3s.
Item offering – 1d.
Item for spices to the ale and cakes – 6d.
Item for bread – 8d.
Sum – 13s

Sum total of this side – 23s.

fo 3v
Jhu
Costs of Corpus Christi day
In primis paid to Master vicar – 4d.
Item paid to 4 priests – 16d.
Item paid for bearing the shrine – 10d.
Item for bearing the cross – 4d.
Item for bearing 2 candlesticks – 4d.
Item paid to the clerk – ?2d.
Item for bearing the candlesticks, censers, torches and copes, to lads – 8d.
Item for wine – 4d.
Item paid for bearing a banner in Rogation week – 4d.
Sum – 4s 8d.

fo 4
Jhu Maria
Hereafter follows the parcels of wax
Item delivered 13 square tapers weighing 75 lb for the rood loft.
Received them weighing 86 lb; so there is 11 lb new wax at 6d a pound –
5s 6d.
Item delivered 15 round tapers, 19 lb; received them weighing 31 lb; so
there is received of new wax, 12 lb at 6d the pound – 6s.
Item delivered the paschal weighing 32 lb; received weighing 32 ½ lb –
3d.
Item received 4 tapers for 4 angels of the sepulchre of 1 lb – 6d.
Item delivered the said tapers weighing 3 lb 6 oz; received them weighing

4 lb; so there is received of new wax 10 oz – 3 ½d.

Item delivered against our Dedication day 15 square tapers weighing 18 lb; received them weighing 31 lb, so there is received of new wax 13 lb – 6s 6d.

[Scored: Item delivered for Halleway 2 tapers weighing 13 lb; received them weighing 16 lb; received of new wax 3 lb at 6d a lb – 18d.]

The new wax is 40 lb 2 oz at 6d a lb – 20s 6 ½d.

Item for making the old wax by the year – 3s 4d.

Sum total – 22s 4 ½d.

fo 4v

Jhu

The customable payments

In primis paid for besoms – 1d.

Item paid to Nicholas for his wages – 20s.

Item paid to 2 friars on Palm Sunday – 8d.

Item paid for a pottle of wine – 6d.

Item for coals – 2d.

Item for mending a banner – 4d.

Item paid for scouring – 2s.

Item paid for hauling away the dust – 8d.

Item paid for watching the sepulchre – 12d.

Item paid to the church of Our Lady in Worcester – 8d.

Item for mending a lock in the churchyard door – 3d.

Item for making 3 bowls to a censer – 7d.

Item for hanging up the Dance of Pauls – 16d.

Item paid to the priests for the lenten dinner – 3s 4d.

Item paid for 2 surplices for 2 lads – 3d.

Item paid for washing the church cloths – 2s 4d.

Item paid for mending the clapper of the 3rd bell – 16d.

Item paid to the clerk that he lacked of his wages – 16d.

Item for ?pins to hang the pans in the church – 1d.

Sum this side – 39s 8d.

fo 5

Jhu

Certain payments

Item paid to John Solby for his allowance for painting the rood loft – 10s.

Item for mending the glass windows to John Brown, glazier – 4s.

Item for mending the lead on the charnel house – 20d.

Item for making the rent roll – 6d.

Item for candles on Christmas day – 4d.

Item paid for a supper at the day of our account – 21d.

Item for making this book – 12d.
Item for 7 gallons and a pottle lamp oil at 14d a gallon – 8s 9d.
Sum – 28s.

The costs to take down the house in Broad Street
Item paid for 3 labourers for 4 days' – 3s 8d.
Item paid for 2 tilers to take down the tile and the ?timber – 6s 6d.
Item for mending a twist and a lock – 4d.
Item for mending a stable in the same house – 4d.
Sum – 10s 10d

Sum this side – 38s 10d.

fo 5v
Jhu
The repairs of ?Morse Payn's house that my lady gave to the church
Item paid for nails for the said house – 13d.
Item paid for a bundle of laths – 3d.
Item paid for 2 lb solder for the glazier – 8d.
Item paid for casting 30 feet of lead – 5s.
Item paid to the plumber for casting 24 lb of old lead and 10 lb of new
lead – 3s.
Item paid for 4 ½ days' to a mason – 2s 6d.
Item for the said mason's labourer – 18d.
Item for 2 weys of lime – 20d.
Item paid for 4 ½ days' to a carpenter – 2s.
Item paid for mending a *stapull* and sheeting of 2 bars – 2d.
Item paid for mending the glass – 16d.
Item for carrying a draught of rubble – 1d.
Item for a ?plane to mend a window – 8d.
Item paid to Hugh Carpenter for his labour – 8d.
Sum – 20s 7d.

fo 6
Jhu
Hereafter follow the costs done on certain tenements
Item paid for a pavier for mine own kitchen – 6d.
Item for mending a gutter in mine own house – 20d.
Item for mending a chimney in Newton's house – 3d.
Item for gift money to the tenants – 16d.
Item for paper to make this book – 1d.

[Different hand: Amount total the ordinary costs and payments –
£8 18s 1d.]

[Original hand: Sum total of the receipts – £21 4s 8d.]

[Next lines scored:
Sum total of costs and payments – £8 19s 7 $\frac{1}{2}$d.
So the proctors owe to the church – £12 5s 2 $\frac{1}{2}$d.
Abate for the chantry – £8 2s 6d.
So the receipts clear that the proctors must bring in the sum of –
£4 2s 7 $\frac{1}{2}$d.]

[Another hand: Received of Master Batten 28th day of March in part of
payment of a more sum – 30s. Anno 1508.]

[The remainder in another hand]
Sum total of the receipts – £22 14s 8d.

Memorandum lent unto Arnold Stewte, beer brewer, 18th day of March
1507 [words unintelligible] doth appear – £7 by a notification and by the
consent of the which *parsse* [parish] so that the foresaid Arnold do pay
every year 20s and till the sum of £5 be paid; William Whalsalle to pay at
the ?year's end – 20s; Thomas Taverner to pay at the year's end – 20s.
Sum – 40s.
Item received at the day of audit for Thomas Pace for the stable in the
house of John – 2s.
Received of Thomas Pernaunt and of Thomas Barber for the present year
– £4 4s 6d.

[1509–10]

fo 1
Jhu
[In darker ink: Ao 1509   Thomas Spicer]

Here after follows the rental of the church of All Hallows' in Bristol with
the allowance, reparations, expenses with customable charges done from
the feast of the Annunciation of Our Lady in the year of Our Lord God
1509, Thomas Spicer and John Reynold being proctors for the year unto
the feast next following in the year of Our Lord God 1510, Master Cabell
then being mayor, John Williams and John Chapman being sheriffs.

Rent assize by the year
In primis the good wife Powle – 3s 4d.
Item Thomas Gylett's house – 4s.
Item Rawlyn Coke – 2s 6d.

Item Richard Erle – 12d.
Item the master of the Tailors – 12s.
Item of Master Croft's house – 6d.
Item of George Schepward – 2s.
Sum – 25s 4d.

The High Street
Item John Snygge by the year – £3 6s 8d.
Item my lady Pernaunt by the year – £4.
Item Edmond Newton by the year – 16s.
Item Thomas Went, tailor – 13s 4d.
Item Sir John Murell's chamber – 6s 8d.
Item the shop in the churchyard – 20d.
Item the house in Broad Street – £4.
Sum – £13 4s 4d.

Sum total – £14 9s 8d.

fo 1v
Small Street
Morys Payn by the year – 26s 8d.

Wynch Street
John Tank, smith, by the year – 30s.

Sum – 56s 8d.
Sum total of the rents – £17 6s 4d.

The vacations following
In primis Thomas Cokys house the whole year – £4.
John Tank, smith, the whole year – 30s.
The master of the Tailors – 12s.
The beer house – 20d.
Sir John Muryell the whole year – 6s 8d.
Item Richard Erle – 12d.
Item of Master Costys house – 6d.
Item George Schipward the whole year – 2s.
Sum – £6 13s 10d.

Sum total of the rents, the vacations allowed – £10 12s 6d.

fo 2
The receipts of customable duties to the church
In primis on Palm Sunday – 2s 4d.

Item on Sheer Thursday – 20d.
Item on Good Friday – 2s 3 ½d.
Item on Easter eve – 15 ½d.
Item on Easter day – 6s 7 ½d.
Item received of the proctors of Jesus – 10s 1d.
Item Richard Whalle and his wife for their pews – 16d.
Item John Maunsell and his wife for their pews – 16d.
Item received of Humphrey Brown for Joan Steven's grave – 6s 8d.
Sum – 33s 7 ½d.
Sum total of all my receipts – £12 6s 1 ½d.

Item received of Thomas Pace for the stable in Thomas Coke's house – 4s.

Sum total of all receipts – £12 10s 1 ½d.

fo 2v
The obit of William Newbery
In primis paid to Master vicar for his wax and dirige – 16d.
Item paid to 5 priests – 20d.
Item paid to the clerk – 10d.
Item paid for bread – 2s.
Item paid to the bellman – 2d.
Item paid for offering – 1d.
Sum – 6s 1d.

The obit of Thomas Fylour
Item paid to Master vicar for his wax and his dirige – 12d.
Item paid to 8 priests – 2s 8d.
Item paid to the clerk – 14d.
Item paid to Master vicar for the bede roll – 12d.
Item paid to the bellman – 2d.
Item paid for bread – 5s.
Item paid to the proctors for their oversight – 12d.
Sum – 12s.

The obit of Harry Chestre
In primis paid to Master vicar for his wax and dirige – 16d.
Item paid to 5 priests – 20d.
Item paid to the clerk – 12d.
Item paid to the bellman – 4d.
Item paid for bread – 2s 8d.
Item paid for offering – 1d.
Sum – 7s 1d.

fo 3

The obit of Thomas Spicer and Dame Maud his wife

In primis paid to Master vicar and to 5 priests – 2s.

Item paid for 4 tapers of 2 lb apiece to burn at dirige and mass – 2s.

Item paid to Master vicar for his oversight – 12d.

Item paid to the clerk – 14d.

Item paid to the bellman – 4d.

Item paid to the sexton – 1d.

Item paid for offering – 1d.

Item paid for bread – 2s 4d.

Sum – 9s.

The General Mind

Item paid to Master vicar and to 4 priests – 15d.

Item paid to the clerk for his labour and his bells – 14d.

Item paid for 2 bushels of meal – 20d.

Item paid for saffron – 14d.

Item paid for a pottle osey – 6d.

Item paid for baking the cake – 6d.

Item for 1 dozen of double ale and 1 dozen of single ale – 2s 6d.

Item for divers wines – 3d.

Item for spice to the ale and cakes – 6d.

Item for bread – 8d.

Item the offering – 1d.

Sum – 13s.

Sum total – 22s.

fo 3v

Costs on Corpus Christi day

In primis paid to Master vicar – 4d.

Item paid to 4 priests – 16d.

Item paid for bearing the shrine – 10d.

Item paid for bearing the cross – 4d.

Item to the clerk – 2d.

Item for bearing the candlesticks, censers, torches and copes – 8d.

Item for wine – 4d.

Item for bearing the banner in Rogation week – 4d.

Item for bearing 2 tunicles – 4d.

Sum – 4s 8d.

The parcels of wax

In primis delivered unto John Waxmaker 13 square tapers weighing 62 ½ lb, received them weighing 86 lb, so amount in new wax 23 ½ lb at 6d the pound, sum – 11s 9d.

Item delivered 15 round tapers weighing 24 lb, received them weighing 31 lb, so amount in new wax 7 lb at 6d the pound, sum – 3s 6d.

Item delivered the paschal and font taper weighing 29 lb, received them weighing 39 lb, so amount in new wax 10 lb at 6d the pound – 5s.

Item received 4 quarter tapers to the sepulchre, sum – 6d.

Item delivered against our Dedication day 14 round tapers weighing 15 ½ lb, received them weighing 32 lb, so amount in new wax 16 ½ lb at 6d the pound, sum – 8s 3d.

Item paid to John Waxmaker for making wax for the whole year – 3s 4d.

Sum – 32s 4d.

fo 4

Payments following

In primis paid for besoms – 1d.

Item paid for a pottle of wine upon Palm Sunday – 5d.

Item paid to 2 friars for bearing the sacrament on Palm Sunday – 8d.

Item paid for coals – 2d.

Item paid for scouring – 2s.

Item paid to the raker for carrying away the church dust – 8d.

Item paid for watching the sepulchre – 12d.

Item paid to Our Lady church of Worcester – 8d.

Item paid for Our Lady Mass in Lent – 3s 4d.

Item paid for supper at the day of accounts – 18d.

Item paid for mending the copes – 23s 4d.

Item more paid for ribbons, *maillis*, buckram and his labour – 20d.

Item paid for hanging up the Dance of Pauls – 16d.

Item paid for washing the church gear – 2s 4d.

Item paid to Nicholas suffragan for his year's wages – 20s.

Item paid to my lady Pernaunt for 8 gallons of lamp oil at 14d the gallon – 9s 4d.

Item paid for pins on All Hallows' eve – 1d.

Item paid for a new *sapur* dish – 10d.

Item paid for candles upon Christmas day – 3d.

Item paid for the key of the treasure coffer – 2d.

Item paid for a new key and mending the lock of the enterclose door – 4d.

Item paid to the old clerk for his table [for] 4 Saturdays at the commandment of the *parische* – 12d.

Item paid for ringing at the death of the king – 10d.

Item paid for 6 threaded girdles – 4d.

Item paid to the town clerk for overseeing the deeds of Master Snygge's house – 12d.

Item paid to Richard Sommer and Hugh Mason – 12d.

Item paid for cleansing Ardnoll Stowt's wells – 13s 4d.

Item paid to the old clerk for lacking his wages of midsummer quarter – 23d.

Item paid to Lambert for lacking his wages of Michaelmas quarter – 15d.

Item more paid unto him for lacking his wages of Christmas quarter – 12d.

Item paid to Robert Byrell for lacking his wages of Our Lady quarter by the commandment of the parish – 9s 2d.

Item paid for mending the conduit – 12d.

Item paid unto my lady Pernaunt for nails – 3s 1d.

Item paid unto Thomas Barbar for candles that was not set in his book of account – 3d.

Sum of this side – £5 5s 4d.

fo 4v

Item allowance to the tenants at the receiving of the rents – 16d.

Item for making this book – 12d.

Sum – 2s 4d.

Repairs of my Lady Pernaunt's house

Item paid for solder 12 ¼ lb – 2s 9d.

Item paid for soldering 8 ¼ *skarys* – 16 ½d.

Item paid for casting 2 ¾ hundredweights of lead – 2s 9d.

Item paid to a tiler for 11 ½ days' – 6s 1d.

Item paid for tile pins – 2d.

Item paid for 3 staves of ?moss – 3d.

Item paid to a labourer for 2 days' work – 8d.

Item paid for 23 feet gutter case – 2s 10 ½d.

Item paid for 4 sacks fine lime – 4d.

Item paid for a stone and laying [it] in her hall – 9d.

Item paid for boards and nails that were occupied upon the repair of her gutter – 2s 10d.

Sum – 20s 10d.

Moris Payne's house

Item paid for 3 sacks of fine lime – 3d.

Item paid to a mason for a day's work – 5d.

Sum – 8d.

fo 5

Costs of the church

In primis paid for 1 ¼ lb of solder – 3d.

Item paid for soldering 1 ?stair – 2d.

Sum – 5d.

Costs done at Thomas Coke's house

Item paid for taking down the tile and timber – 14s 4d.
Item paid for taking down the timber of the fore part – 12d.
Item paid for mending my lord of St Austin's house – 5 $\frac{1}{2}$d.
Item paid to Moris Tiler for himself and his 3 men for 4 $\frac{1}{2}$ days', paying 5 $\frac{1}{2}$d a day – 8s 3d.
Item more paid to Moris for himself 3 $\frac{1}{2}$ days' – 19d.
Item paid for 2500 tile pins – 7 $\frac{1}{2}$d.
Item paid to a mason for making the new wall – 5s 5d.
Item paid for lime – 3s 4d.
Item paid for 6 loads of sand – 5d.
Item paid to a labourer for 3 $\frac{3}{4}$ days' – 12 $\frac{1}{2}$d.
Item paid for mending the walls by the mill – 8d.
Item paid for half a wey of lime – 4 $\frac{1}{2}$d.
Sum – 37s 6d.

[Remainder of account in different hand]
Sum total of all payments – £12 11s 4d.

So the payments amount more than the receipts – 13 $\frac{1}{2}$d.

Memorandum that in the day of this account we of the parish received of Thomas Apprice, Master of the Tailors – 3s 4d for the arrears of a quit rent for 3 years past, 12s by the year, of a house in Baldwin Street, the residue we forgive to the Tailors for as much as for the said 3 years the said house was vacant from *on tenare* and the said Thomas promised to pay at Michaelmas next 3s and so forth according to the rent vz 12s yearly.
Ete solum

fo 5v
Item the said day Thomas Pace paid for the grave of his sister Joan buried in the church – 3s 4d.
The which 3s 4d so also the 3s 4d received of the said Thomas Apprice was put into the treasure coffer.

[Written in bold hand on the end page of the booklet: The Book of the Account of the Church of Allhallon yn Brystow]

[1510–11; the following employs a system of accounting dots in the margins for purposes of addition]

fo 1
Anno dm 1510
The church book

John Baten

fo 2
Here after follows the rental of the church of All Hallows' in Bristol with the allowance, reparations, expenses with customable charges done from the feast of the Annunciation of Our Lady in the year of Our Lord God 1510, John Baten and John Rainnold being proctors, unto the feast next following in the year of Our Lord God 1511, then being mayor Master Popeley, Raff Apprice and Robert Hutton sheriffs.

Rents assize by the year
In primis of Poule James wife [superscript: for a gutter going through the church ground] – 3s 4d.
Item Thomas Gillet's house – 4s.
Item Rawlyn Coke's house – 2s 6d.
Item Richard Erle – 12d.
Item the master of the Tailors – 12s.
Item of Master Croft's house – 6d.
Item of George Sheppard – 2s.
Sum – 25s 4d.

The High Street rents
Item John Snygge by the year – £3 6s 8d.
Item my lady Pernaunte by year – £4.
Item Edmond Newton by year – 16s.
Item Thomas Went, tailor – 13s 4d.
Item Sir John Muriell's chamber – 6s 8d.
Item the shop in the churchyard – 20d.
Item the house in Broad Street – £4.
Sum – £13 4s 4d.

Small Street
Maurice Payne by year – 26s 8d.

Wynch Street
John Tank, smith, by the year – 30s.
Sum – 56s 8d.

Sum total of the rents – £17 6s 4d.

Vacations following
Item Thomas Coke's house the whole year – £4.
Item John Tank, smith, the whole year – 30s.
Item the master of the Tailors, void half year – 6s.
Item the beer house in the churchyard – 20d.
Item Richard Erle – 12d.
Item of Master Croft's house – 6d.
Item of George Shepward the whole year – 2s.
Sum – £6 14d.

Sum total of the rents the vacations allowed – £11 5s 2d.

Receipts of customable duties to the church
In primis on Palm Sunday, Sheer Thursday, Good Friday, Easte eve and Easter day – 14s.
Item of the proctors of Jesus – 11s.
Item of Thomas Spicer's bequest – £4.
Item for his grave in the church – 6s 8d.
Item for a pew to Jois a Barrow and his wife – 12d.
Item [for a pew] to Andrew Hillary and his wife – 12d.
Item [for a pew] to Thomas Yonge and his wife – 16d.
Item [for a pew] to Richard Buke maker – [blank].
Sum – £5 15s.

Item received of Thomas Pacy for a stable in Coke's house – 4s.

Sum total receipts amounts clear, sum – £17 4s 2d.

The obit of William Newbery
In primis to Master vicar for his wax and dirige – 16d.
Item to 5 priests – 20d.
Item to the clerk – 10d.
Item paid for bread – 2s.
Item to the bellman – 2d.
Item for offering – 1d.
Sum – 6s 1d.

The obit of Thomas Fylour
Item paid to Master vicar for his wax and his dirige – 12d.

Item to 8 priests – 2s 8d.
Item to Master vicar for the bede roll — 12d.
Item to the bell man – 2d.
Item for bread – 5s.
Item to the proctors for their oversight – 12d.
Sum – 12s.

The obit of Harry Chestre
Item paid to the vicar for his wax and dirige – 16d.
Item to 5 priests – 20d.
Item to the clerk – 12d.
Item to the bellman – 4d.
Item for bread – 2s 8d.
Item for offering – 1d.
Sum – 7s 1d.

The obit of Thomas Spicer and Dame Maud his wife
Item to Master vicar and 5 priests – 2s.
Item for 4 tapers of 2 lb apiece to burn at dirige and Mass – 2s.
Item to Master vicar for oversight – 12d.
Item to the clerk – 14d.
Item to the bellman – 4d.
Item to the sexton – 1d.
Item for offering – 1d.
Item for bread – 2s 4d.
Sum – 9s.

Sum this side – 34s 2d.

fo 3v
The general mind
Item paid to 4 priests – 12d.
Item to clerk for his labour and his bells – 14d.
Item for 2 bushels meal – 20d.
Item for saffron – 14d.
Item for a pottle of osey – 6d.
Item for baking the cake – 6d.
Item for 2 dozen of ale, one single and another double – 2s 6d.
Item for divers wines – 3s.
Item for spices to ale and cake – 6d.
Item for bread – 8d.
Item for offering – 1d.
Sum – 12s 9d.

Costs on Corpus Christi day
[Scored] In primis paid to master vicar – 4d.
Item to 4 priests – 16d.
Item for bearing the shrine – 10d.
Item to the clerk – 2d.
Item for bearing of censer, candlesticks, torches and tapers – 8d.
Item for wine – 4d.
Item for bearing the banner in Rogation week – 4d.
Item for bearing 2 tunicles – 4d.
Sum – 4s 4d.

The parcels of wax
In primis received the paschal weighing 30 lb.
Item delivered the same weighing 31 lb – 6d.
Item received the font taper weighing 3 lb, delivered 4 lb – 6d.
Item received 13 square tapers weighing 70 lb, delivered 82 lb – 11s.
Item delivered 4 tapers weighing 1 lb – 6d.
Received 15 round tapers weighing 16 lb, delivered 31 lb – 10s.
Item for making the church wax for the whole year – 3s 4d.
Item for 2 new torches – 10s.
Sum – 35s 10d.

Sum total this side – 52s 11d.

fo 4
Payments follow
In primis paid for besoms – 1d.
Item for a pottle of wine on Palm Sunday – 5d.
Item to 2 friars for bearing the sacrament on Palm Sunday – 8d.
Item for coals – 2d.
Item for scouring – 2s.
Item to the raker for carrying the dust of the church – 8d.
Item for watching of the sepulchre – 12d.
Item to Our Lady church of Worcester – 8d.
Item for Our Lady Mass in Lent – 3s 4d.
Item for the supper at the day of account – 2s 10d.
Item for hanging up the Dance of Pauls – 16d.
Item for washing the church gear – 2s 4d.
Item to Nicholas Sexten for his year's wages – 20d.
Item for lamp oil – 10s 10d.
Item for a cord and a lamp – 2d.
Item for 3 lb of tallow candle – 3d.
Item for 5 girdles to the priests – 2 $\frac{1}{2}$d.
Item for pins on All Hallows' eve – 1d.

Item for the clapper of the 3rd bell – 18d.
Item for a baldrick – 4d.
Item for glue and leather to the organs – 2d.
Item for mending the holy water tinnell – 8d.
Item for a new tinnell – 3s 4d.
Item allowance to the tenants at receiving the rent – 16d.
Item for making this book – 12d.
Item for a quarter of linen cloth to make sleeves for an alb – 2d.
Item for making the same with surplice and rochets – 4d.
Item for 9 ells of cloth at 9 $\frac{1}{2}$d the ell, amount – 7s 1 $\frac{1}{2}$d.
Item for making the same – 3s.
Item for ringing at the coming of the bishop – 8d.
Item paid to William Clarke for lacking of his wages 2 quarters – 3s 4d.
Sum – £3 10s 3d.

fo 4v
Repairs of John Snygge's house
In primis to 2 tilers 4 days' – 4s 4d.
Item to 3 tilers half a day – 9d,
Item to 2 tilers a quarter of a day – 6d.
Item for 2500 tile pins – 7 $\frac{1}{2}$d.
Item to a tiler 2 days' – 13d.
Item to 3 tilers 3 days' – 4s 10 $\frac{1}{2}$d.
Item to a tiler 2 days' – 13d.
Item for 14 crests – 7d.
Item for boards – 3d.
Item for a wey and a half of lime – 15d.
Item for hauling tile stones – 4d.
Item to 2 tilers a day – 13d.
Item for nails – 15d.
Sum – 18s.

My lady Pernaunt's house
Item for a load of pendant stone with haulage – 18d.
Item to a mason 2 days' about a chimney – 13d.
Item to a labourer 2 days' – 13d.
Item for 7 feet of free stone to the same – 14d.
Sum – 4s 5d.

Arnold Stout's house
[Entries scored, note in margin 'to the chantry book']
Item to a tiler 5 days' and 50 tile pins – 2s 9 $\frac{1}{2}$d.
Item for lime – 2s 6d.
Item for 4 lb of solder and 3 skares – 18d.

Sum – 6s 9 ½d.

Item to Maurice Payne's house 1 ½ lb of solder and 2 *skarys* – 8 ½d.
Item upon the church 2 ½ lb of solder and 3*skarys* – 13 ½d.
Sum – 22s.

Sum this side – 24s 3d.
fo 5
Sum total payments and repairs – £9 19d.

And so rest that the receipts is more than the payments – £8 2s 7d.
[The remainder in a different hand:]The which was received by the vicar
and all the *p[ar]yshon* and put in to the treasure coffer the 8th day of May,
Anno domini 1511. [Added:] except 11s which was put into the purse of
Jesus the same day and year.

Memorandum that on the day of our account which was the 8th day of
May A.D. 1511 that where Thomas Went paid for the rent of his house
yearly but 13s 4d, so by the agreement of Master vicar, Master Batten
[and] John Waxmaker proctors, with all the whole *p[ar]ashe*, that from
midsummer quarter next following the said Thomas Went to pay yearly
?16s and so to continue as long as it shall please the parish to the church
advantage – 16s.

Memorandum paid of this money afore written unto John Lamberd being
clerk, sum – 10s 1d, for that he was to paying of his wages.

[At foot of end page: Item for wine on Corpus Christi day – 4d.]

[1511–12]

fo 1
Anno dm 1511

John Baten
The Church Book

fo 2
Here after follows the rental of the church of All Hallows' in Bristol with
the allowance of reparations, expenses, with customable charges done
from the feast of the Annunciation of Our Lady in the year of Our Lord
God 1511 unto the same feast 1512 next following, John Baten and
Thomas Davy barber proctors, then being mayor Master John Rowland,
John Hutton and Humphrey Brown sheriffs.

Rent assize by the year
In primis of Paul James' wife for a gutter going through the church ground
– 3s 4d.
Item Thomas Gillet's house – 4s.
Item Rawlyn Cokes' house – 2s 6d.
Item Richard Erle – 12d.
Item the master of the Tailors – 12s.
Item of Master Croft's house – 6d.
Item George Sheppard – 2s.
Sum – 25s 4d.

The High Street rents
Item John Snygge by the year – £3 6s 8d.
Item my lady Pernaunt by the year – £4.
Item Edmund Newton by the year – 16s.
Item Thomas Wente, tailor – 13s 4d.
Item Sir John Muriell's chamber – 6s 8d.
Item the shop in the churchyard – 20d.
Item the house in Broad Street – £4.
Sum – £13 4s 4d.

Small Street
Maurice Payne by the year – 26s 8d.

Wine Street
John Tanke, smith, by the year – 30s.
Sum – 56s 8d.

Sum total of the rents – £17 6s 4d.

fo 2v
Vacations following
In primis Thomas Coke's house the whole year – £4.
Item the house John Tanke dwelt in the whole year – 30s.
Item the beer house in the churchyard – 20d.
Item Richard Erle – 12d.
Item of Master Croft's house – 6d.
Item of George Shepperd the whole year – 2s.
Sum – £5 15s 2d.

Sum total of the rents, the vacations allowed – £11 11s 2d.

Receipts of customable duties to the church

In primis received on Palm Sunday, Sheer Thursday, Good Friday, Easter
eve and Easter day – 14s.
Item received of the proctors of Jesus – 21s 2d.
Sum – 35s 2d.

Item received of John Colles for a stable in Coke's house – 4s.

Sum total with receipts amounts clear – £13 10s 4d.

[Different hand: Paid to the Prior of St James – 2s.]

fo 3
The obit of William Newbery
In primis to Master vicar for his wax and dirige – 16d.
Item to 5 priests – 20d.
Item to the clerk – 10d.
Item for bread to poor people – 2s.
Item to the bellman – 2d.
Item for the offering – 1d.
Sum – 6s 1d.

The obit of Thomas Fylour
In primis to Master vicar for his wax and dirige – 12d.
Item to 8 priests – 2s 8d.
Item to the clerk – 14d.
Item to the vicar for the bede roll – 12d.
Item the bellman – 2d.
Item for bread – 5s.
Item the proctors for their oversight – 12d.
Sum – 12s.

The obit of Harry Chestre
In primis to the vicar for his wax and dirige – 16d.
Item to 5 priests – 20d.
Item the clerk – 12d.
Item to the bellman – 4d.
Item for bread to poor people – 2s 8d.
Item for offering – 1d.
Sum – 7s 1d.

The obit of Thomas Spicer and Dame Maud his wife
In primis to the vicar and 5 priests – 2s.
Item for 4 tapers of 2 lb apiece to burn at dirige and Mass – 2s.
Item to the vicar for oversight – 12d.

Item to the clerk – 14d.
Item to the bellman – 4d.
Item to the sexton – 1d.
Item the offering – 1d.
Item for bread to poor people – 2s 4d.
Item to the 2 proctors for gathering the rent and see[ing to] repairs of the
?land and payments of the obit – 2s.
Sum – 11s.

Sum of this side – 36s 2d.

fo 3v
The General Mind
In primis paid 4 priests – 12d.
Item to the clerk for his labour and his bells – 14s.
Item 2 bushels meal – 2s 1d.
Item an ounce of saffron – 14d.
Item a pottle of osey for the cakes – 6d.
Item for baking the cakes – 6d.
Item for 2 dozen ale, one single and another double – 3s.
Item 2 gallons of osey – 2s.
Item for 2 gallons of claret wine – 16d.
Item for spices to ale and the cakes – 6d.
Item for bread to poor people – 8d.
Item the offering – 1d.
Sum – 14s.

The costs on Corpus Christi day
In primis master vicar – [blank]
Item 4 priests – 16d.
Item bearing the shrine – 10d.
Item bearing the cross – 4d.
Item the clerk – 2d.
Item for bearing censer, candlesticks, torches and copes – 8d.
Item for a pottle of wine in the *marsche* – 4d.
Item for bearing 2 tunicles – 4d.
Sum – 4s.

The parcels of wax against Easter
Item delivered a paschal at Easter weighing 26 lb; received of him a
paschal weighing 31 lb, so rest owing 5 lb – 3s 4d.
Item delivered John Waxmaker 13 square tapers weighing 58 lb; received
of him the same tapers weighing 72 $\frac{1}{2}$ lb – 7s 4d.
Item more delivered the same John 15 round tapers weighing 16 lb;

received of him the same tapers weighing 31 lb, amount the same – 10s.
Item delivered the same John Waxmaker a font taper of 2 lb; received a
font taper weighing 4 lb, amount the same – 16d.
Item a little taper of a pound for the sepulchre – 8d.
Sum – 22s 8d.

Sum of this side – 40s 8d.

fo 4
The costs in wax against our Dedication day
Item delivered to John Waxmaker against our Dedication day 15 round
tapers weighing 18 lb; received of him the same tapers weighing 29 $\frac{1}{2}$ lb at
6d the pound, amount the whole – 5s 9d.

Item the making of wax for the whole year – 3s 4d.
Sum – 9s 1d.

Payments following
In primis paid for besoms – 1d.
Item for a pottle and a pint of wine on Palm Sunday – 5d.
Item for 2 friars to bear the sacrament in the shrine on Palm Sunday – 8d.
Item for a load of coals – 3d.
Item for half an ell of lockeram – 2 $\frac{1}{2}$d.
Item for mending 2 surplices – 8d.
Item a supper [on] the day of our account – 3s 4d.
Item for scouring – 2s.
Item to the raker to haul away the church dust – 8d.
Item to Our Lady church of Worcester – 8d.
Item for washing the church cloths – 2s 4d.
Item allowance to tenants – 16d.
Item for bearing the banner in Rogation week – 4d.
Item for hanging the Dance of Pauls – 16d.
Item a baldric to the great bell – 18d.
Item paid for mending the baldric of the second bell – 2d.
Item paid for lamp oil this present year – 10s 6d.
Item paid to my lord Wulffe for hallowing 6 altar cloths and corporals –
16d.
Item paid for a key for the evidence coffer – 5d.
Item for mending of the sleeves of the best suit – 6d.
Item for pins – $\frac{1}{2}$d.
Item a ?free mason to bolt a hoop of iron on Our Lady Assumption in
Jesus Gild – 4d.
Item 3 lb of tallow candles – 3d.
Item Nicholas suffragan for his whole year's wages – 20s.

Item paid the clerk to make up his wages quarterly 2s, amount the whole year – 8s.
Sum – ?58s 4d.

Sum total of this side – £3 7s 5d.

fo 4v
Repairs in the High Street
In primis my lady Pernaunt's house
Item a board of oak 16 feet length – 8d.
Item a carpenter to dress 2 windows there – 4d.
Item a mason to ?bolt a stone on the overchimney with 4 posts of stone – 4d.
Sum – 16d.

Repairs of John Snygge's house
In primis 37 lb in bars of iron for a window – 3s 8d.
Item 2 sacks of lime – 2d.
Item to Thomas Benett, mason, 3 days' – 19 ½d.
Item Thomas Birte and Davy and 2 labourers 2 days' – 2s 8d.
Item for a window of free stone of 19 feet and 8 inches at 3d the foot, amount the whole – 4s 9d.
Item more half a wey of lime – 5d.
Item for 2 studs – 2 ½d.
Item one plasterer – 8d.
Item for hair – ½d.
Item 7 ½ feet of new glass and mending the old glass – 4s.
Item a labourer to make mortar – 1d.
Sum – 18s 2 ½d.

Item the mending of the best pax
In primis an ounce of silver – 3s 2d.
Item a *crusadowe* to gild it – 4s 6d.
Item the working thereof – 2s 4d.
Item the mending and soldering the chain of Thomas Spicer's censer – 12d.
Sum – 11s.

Sum of this side – 30s 6 ½d.

fo 5
Repairs of the Brew House in Broad street [added: otherwise pulling down the said house]
In primis 2 labourers 2 days', 4d a day a man, amount – 16d.

Item 4 labourers for 4 days' – 5s 4d.
Item for 2 cords – 1d.
Item 4 labourers 2 $\frac{1}{2}$ days' – 3s 4d.
Item a carpenter to pull down the mill – 8d.
Item 4 labourers 4 $\frac{1}{2}$ days' – 5s 4d.
Item 1 labourer 1 $\frac{1}{2}$ days' – 6d.
Item 2 panniers to bear rubble – 6d.
Item more 5 labourers 2 days' – 3s 4d.
Item paid a sergeant to ?fet[ch] Robert Wryter to the mayor – 2d.
Item a ?hurdle to cast rubble – 2d.
Item for a pair panniers – 5d.
Item more 4 labourers 4 days' – 5s 4d.
Item 2 labourers half a day – 4d.
Item 2 labourers half a day to pull down a chimney – 4d.
Item 2 masons 2 days' – 13d.
Item 2 labourers and a half – 20d.
Item a wey of lime and 3 sacks of lime – 9d.
Item calf-foot nails to make a scaffold – 1d.
Sum – 30s 9d.

[Remainder in different hand]
Sum total of all payments – ?£9 13s 8 $\frac{1}{2}$d.
and so rest clear to the church – £3 4s 9 $\frac{1}{2}$d.

For making of this book – 6d.
Received of Mistress Baten widow on our day of accounts – 4s 9d
[$\frac{1}{2}$d scored].
So rest to pay £3 for the ?wage £3 we the p[ar]reschsons received off her
a flat cup overgilt in pledge weighing 20 $\frac{1}{2}$ ounces.
Item the said 4s 9d was delivered among priests and clerks for Our Lady
Mass kept in Lent by the priests and clerks.

[1512–13]

fo 1
Anno dm 1512
The Church Book
Thomas Davy, barber

fo 2
Here follows the rental of the church of All Hallows' in Bristol with the
allowance of reparations, expenses with customable charges done from the
feast of the Annunciation of Our Blessed Lady in the year of Our Lord

God 1512 unto the same feast in the year of Our Lord God 1513, Thomas
Davy barber and Thomas Pacy proctors, then being mayor John Elyot,
Thomas Dale and Thomas Broke sheriffs.

Rents of assize by the year
In primis Paul James for a gutter going through the church ground, not
rent of assize – 3s 4d.
Item Thomas Gelett's house by the year – 4s.
Item Ralyn Coke's house by the year – 2s 6d.
Item Richard Erle by the year – 12d.
Item for a house in Baldwin Street of the master of the Tailors – 12s.
Item of Master Croft's house by the year – 6d.
Item of George Schepwarde's house in Marsh Street – 2s.
Sum – 25s 4d.

The High Street
Item John Snygge for his house by the year – £3 6s 8d.
Item my lady Pernaunt by the year for her house – £4.
Item Mawdeleyne Abynton by the year for her house – 16s.
Item Thomas Hossyar for his house by the year – 16s.
Item Sir John Muryell for his chamber by the year – 6s 8d.
Item the shop in the churchyard by the year – 20d.
Item the old house in Broad Street – £4.
Item Robert Coke in Small Street yearly – 26s 8d.
Item John Tank's house in Wine Street yearly – 30s.
Item John Collis for a stable yearly – 4s.
Sum – £17 17s 8d.

Sum total of the whole rents – £19 3s.

fo 2v
Vacations following
In primis Thomas Coke's house – £4.
Item John Tank's house – 30s.
Item the house in the churchyard – 20d.
Item Richard Erle's house – 12d.
Item Master Croft's house – 6d.
Item George Shipward's house – 2s.
Item Robert Coke's house, a quarter – 6s 8d.
Sum – £6 22d.

Paid to the prior of St James – 2s.[figure scored]
Sum of whole rents and vacations abated – £13 14s.

Receipts of customable duties of the church
Item received on Palm Sunday [added: to the sexton] – 2s 6d.
Item received on Sheer Thursday [added: to the pascal] – 10 ½d.
Item received on Good Friday [added: to the jewels] – 2s 4 ½d.
Item received on Easter eve [added: to the wax of the the church] – 12d.
Item received on Easter day [added: to the wax of the church] – 6s 1d.
Item received of Richard Coke for his pew – 8d.
Item received of Richard Bokbynder for his pew – 8d.
Item received of Harry Hyggyns for his pew – 16d.
Item received of Thomas Cortes for his pew – 16d.
Item received of John Aylworth for his pew – 16d.
Item received of the *p[ar]reschsyons* – £3.
Item received of the proctors of Jesus – 17s.
Sum of all receipts – £4 15s 3d.

Sum of this side – £17 16s 5d.

Item received of Went's wife, a spoon of silver.
Item received of Master Baten, a whole cloth, *p'ce* – 4 marks.

fo 3
The obit of William Newbery
In primis to Master vicar for his wax and dirige – 16d.
Item to 5 priests – 20d.
Item to the clerk – 10d.
Item for bread to poor people – 2s.
Item to the bellman – 2d.
Item for offering – 1d.
Sum – 6s 1d.

The obit of Thomas Fylour
In primis to Master vicar for his wax and dirige – 12d.
Item to 8 priests – 2s 8d.
Item to the clerk – 14d.
Item to the vicar for the bede roll – 12d.
Item to the bellman – 2d.
Item for bread for poor people – 5s.
Item to the proctors for the oversight – 12d.
Sum – 12s.

The obit of Harry Chestre
In primis to the vicar for his dirige and wax – 16d.
Item to 5 priests – 20d.
Item to the clerk – 12d.

Item to the bellman – 4d.
Item for bread to poor people – 2s 8d.
Item for offering – 1d.
Sum – 7s 1d.

The obit of Thomas Spicer and Dame Maud his wife
In primis to the vicar and 5 priests – 2s.
Item for 4 tapers of 2 lb apiece and have ?at dirige and Mass – 2s. [added: for bede roll – 4d].
[Scored: Item to the vicar for his oversight – 12d.]
Item to the clerk – 14d.
Item to the bellman – 4d.
Item to the sexton – 1d.
Item for offering – 1d.
Item to the proctors for their oversight and labour – [scored: 12d. 2s.] 12d.
Item for bread to poor people – 2s.
Sum – 11s [possibly altered to 10s.]

Sum of this side – 36s 2d.

fo 3v
The obit for *algooddoars*
In primis paid to 4 priests – 12d.
Item paid to the clerk for his dirige and bells – 14d.
Item for offering – 1d.
Item paid for a pottle of osey to the cake – 6d.
Item paid for 2 $\frac{1}{2}$ bushels of meal – 3s 4d.
Item paid for a quart of oil – 4d.
Item paid for $\frac{1}{2}$ lb of sugar – 4d.
Item paid for 2 gallons and a pottle of osey – 2s 6d.
Item paid for malmsey a pottle – 6d.
Item paid for ?romney a gallon – 10d.
Item paid for saffron ?2 oz – 20d.
Item paid for $\frac{1}{2}$ dozen of bread – 6d.
Item paid for a dozen ?$\frac{1}{2}$ of double ale – 2s 3d.
Item paid for a dozen of single ale – 13d.
Item paid for baking of the cake – 12d.
Sum – 17s 1d.

The costs of Corpus Christi day
Item paid to Master vicar – ?nychil.
Item paid to 4 priests – 16d.
Item paid for bearing the shrine – 10d.
Item paid for bearing the cross – 4d.

Item paid to the clerk – 2d.

Item paid for bearing censers, torches, candlesticks – 8d.

Item paid for bearing 2 tunicles – 4d.

Item paid for a pottle of wine in the *mersche* – 4d.

Sum – 4s.

Sum of this side – 21s 1d.

fo 4

Here follows parcels of wax

In primis delivered to the waxmaker 13 square tapers weighing 58 lb; received them again weighing 77 lb; so there is in new wax 19 lb at 7d the pound, sum – 11s 1d.

Item delivered the round tapers weighing 20 lb; received them again weighing 29 $\frac{1}{2}$ lb; so there is in new wax 9 $\frac{1}{2}$ lb – 6s 6 $\frac{1}{2}$d. [altered to 5s 6d]

Item delivered the paschal taper weighing 30 lb; received him again weighing 34 lb; so there is in new wax 4 lb – 2s 4d.

Item delivered the font taper weighing 2 lb; received him again weighing 4 lb; so there is in new wax 2 lb – 14d.

Item more received 4 tapers weighing 1 lb – 7d.

Item paid for making all the said wax – 3s 4d.

Item delivered the round tapers weighing 18 $\frac{1}{2}$ lb; received them again 31 lb, so there is in new wax 13 $\frac{1}{2}$ lb at 7d, sum – 7s 10 $\frac{1}{2}$d.

Sum – 32s 11d. [altered to 31s 11d].

Item I bought 2 torches weighing 40 lb at 4d the pound, sum – 13s 4d.

Sum this side – 46s 3d [altered to 45s 3d.]

fo 4v

Item paid for besoms – 1d.

Item paid for a pottle of wine on Palm Sunday – 6d.

Item paid to 2 friars for bearing the shrine – 8d.

Item paid coals a load – 3d. [altered to 2d.]

Item paid for watching the sepulchre – 12d.

Item paid for the supper at our day of account – 18d.

Item paid for scouring the church stuff – 2s.

Item paid to the raker – 8d.

Item paid to Our Lady church of Worcester – 8d.

Item paid for washing the church stuff – 2s 4d.

Item paid for allowance to the tenants – 16d.

Item paid for bearing the banner in Rogation week – 4d.

Item paid for hanging the Dance of Pauls – 16d.

Item paid for lamp oil this present year – 10s 6d.

Item paid for 3 lb candles – 3d.

Item paid to Nicholas our sexton his year's wages – 20s.

Item paid for 8 ½ ells of holland to make our clerk a surplice at 7d the ell, sum – 4s 11 ½d.

Item paid for making of the same surplice – 2s 8d.

Item paid for pins – ½d.

Item paid for mending of the church windows – 2s 4d.

Item paid to the clerk for that he lacked of his wage – 11s 5d.

Item paid for mending John Hugh's pew door – 3d.

Item paid for mending a key to the treasure coffer – 3d.

Item paid for hallowing altar cloths – 8d.

Item paid for mending 7 albs – 12d.

Item paid for removing stones to the church garden – 4d.

Item paid for pins to the censer – 1d.

Item paid for a piece of iron to the new work – 6d.

Item paid to Nicholas for carrying away the rubble – 12d. [figure scored]

Item paid to Nicholas for carrying of stones – 8d.

Item paid for paper to make the book – 1d.

Item paid for 1 lb of *corten* rings – 6d.

Sum of this side – £3 9s 2d.

fo 5

Reparations done in the High Street

Reparations done on my lady Pernaunt's house

Item paid to 2 tilers for 4 days' work – 4s 4d.

Item paid to 2 tilers for 2 days' work – 2s 2d.

item paid for 6 crests – 3d.

Item paid to a plumber for 7 ¼ lb of solder and for soldering 5*skarys* – 2s 8d.

Item paid for 200 laths – 12d.

Item paid to 2 tilers for 2 days' work – 2s 2d.

Item paid for lath nails – 2 ½d.

Item paid for tile pins – 2d.

Item paid for hauling 2 loads of tile stones – 4d.

Item paid to a carpenter for oak boards and for his men's wages – 5s.

Item paid for 1000 lath nails – 12d.

Item paid for 200 ?hook nails – 6d.

Item paid for board nails and for calf foot nails – 5 ½d.

Item paid for hair – ½d.

Item paid for 7 sacks of fine lime and 3 sacks coarse lime – 8 ½d.

Item paid to a mason for his labour – 2s 4d.

More paid to 2 tilers for 1 day's labour – 12d.

Sum – 24s 4d.

Reparations done on Richard Abynton's garden
Item paid for board nails and lath nails – 9d.
Item paid for hauling of a load of tile stones – 2d.
Item paid for 6 crests – 3d.
Item paid for tile pins – 1d.
Item paid for lime – 3d.
Item paid to 2 tilers for their labour – 15d.
Item paid for a load of tile stones – 16d.
Sum – 4s 1d.
Item paid for making this book – 6d.
Sum of this side – 28s 11d.

Sum total of all costs and reparations done this present year – £10 6d.
So rest that the proctors owe the church – £7 15s 11d, a spoon and a cloth.
Dysacownte of this sum which is charged in the chantry book for this year,
which now the chantry owes to the church – £4 17s 9d.

fo 5v
Item the proctors must bring to the church for this present year, all costs
[and] repairs allowed them – 58s 3d. A spoon and a whole cloth.

Item abate of the said sum for Paul James' house – 3s 4d.
Also abate for ?Jenet's house – 3s 4d.
Also 4d, and for a lock 10d – 14d.

So the proctors now owe to the church – 50s 4d.
Also Thomas Barber owes for Raffe Sankye – 8s 3d.
And he to pay it at St James' tide Anno 1513.

Item Thomas Barber paid to the *p[ar]reschsons* at the day of account
which was on the 21st day of April 1513 – 50s 4d.
Item he delivered a spoon which was of Thomas Went's gift.

Of the which money was paid to the priests and clerks for keeping Our
Lady Mass – 3s 4d.

Rest in money that Thomas Barber brought in to the church – 47s and a
spoon, which money and spoon was delivered Thomas Pacy also a whole
cloth which is in Jerome ?Green's hands.

[Next entries scored: So Thomas Barber must pay for Raffe Sanky as is
afore said – 8s 3d.
A quarter rent for the garden – 22d.]

[Different hand: Paid to Thomas Pace by Master Sanky for the 2 ?things aforewritten – 6s 8d.]

[1514–1515; the right edge of this account is slightly damaged]

fo 1
Anno domini 1514

The Church Book
John Snygge

fo 2
ihu
Here after follows the rental of the church of All Hallows' in Bristol which is the allowance, expenses, reparations and customable charges done from the feast of the Annunciation of Our Lady in the year of Our Lord God 1514 unto the [?] feast being 1515, then being proctors [erased: Thomas] John Snygge and Richard Wale, also Master Robert Thorne then mayor, John Ware and Richard Tennell sheriffs.

Rents of assize per annum
In primis Johanne James widow per annum – 3s 4d.
Item Robert Barbor's house per annum – 4s.
Item John Waters cook for the baste door per annum – 2s 6d.
Item Richard Erle per annum – 12d.
Item the master of the Tailors per annum – 12s.
Item Croft's house in St Peter's parish per annum – 6d.
Item George Sheppard for a house in Marsh Street – 2s.
Sum – 25s 4d.

Rents in the High Street per annum
Item of my lady Pernaunt per annum – £4.
Item John Snygge per annum – £3 6s 8d.
Item Thomas Williams tailor afore the tolsell – 16s.
Item Harry Brewster next to the same per annum – 16s.
Item Sir John Coke for his chamber per annum – 6s 8d.
Item the shop under the said chamber – 20d.
The old house in the Broad Street – £4.
Item Master Blisse *fycssissoner* [physician] in Small Street per annum – 26s 8d.
Item John Colls for a stable per annum – 4s.
Sum – £14 17s 8d.

Sum total this side – £16 3s.

Vacations following
In primis the old house in Broad Street – £4.
Item the shop in the churchyard – 20d.
Item Richard Erle – 12d.
Item Master Croft's house – 6d.
Item George Sheppard's house – 2s.
Item Johanne James widow – 20d.
Sum – £4 6s 10d.

Sum the whole rents, vacations abated – £11 16s 2d.

The receipts of the customable duties
Item received on Palm Sunday for the sexton's wages – 3s.
Item received on Palm Sunday and Sheer Thursday of *howsellyng* people – 14d.
Item received on Good Friday to the jewels, sum – 2s 1d.
Item received on Easter eve and on Easter day to the paschal – 8s 3 $\frac{1}{2}$d.
Item received of John Lord's wife for his bequest – 30s.
Item received of John Lord's wife for his grave – 6s 8d.
Item received of the proctors of Jesus – 18s 9d.
Item received of a plumber for occupying Arnold's house – 14d.
Item received for a barrel *or a oxed* [?or a hogshead] of Arnold's house – 4d.
Item received of Thomas Barber for a hogshead – 6d.
Sum – £3 11s 5 $\frac{1}{2}$d.
Sum clear to the church vacations abated – £15 7s 7 $\frac{1}{2}$d.

The obit of William Newbery
In primis paid to Master vicar for his wax and dirige – 16d.
Item paid to 5 priests for their dirige – 20d.
Item paid to the clerk – 10d.
Item paid to the bellman – 2d.
Item paid for bread to poor people – 2s.
Item paid to the offering – 1d.
Sum 6s 1d.

The obit of Thomas Fylour
In primis paid to Master vicar for his wax and dirige – 12d.
Item paid to 8 priests – 2s 8d.
Item paid to the clerk – 14d.

Item paid to Master vicar for the bede roll – 12d.
Item paid to the bellman – 2d.
Item paid for bread for poor people – 5s.
Item paid to the 2 proctors for their oversight – 12d.
Sum – 12s.

The obit of Harry Chestre
Item paid to Master vicar for his wax and dirige – 16d.
Item paid to 5 priests – 20d.
Item paid to the clerk – 12d.
item paid to the bellman – 4d.
Item paid for bread to poor people – 2s 8d.
Item paid for offering – 1d.
Sum – 7s 1d.

The obit of Thomas Spicer and Dame Maud his wife
Item paid to Master vicar and to 6 priests for dirige and Mass – 2s 4d.
Item paid to Master vicar for 4 tapers of 2 lb ?apiece to have about the
hearse at dirige and Mass – 2s.
Item paid to Master vicar for the bede roll – 4d.
Item paid to the clerk – 14d.
Item paid to the bellman – 4d.
Item paid to the sexton – d.
Item paid for offering – 1d.
Item paid for bread to the poor people – 3d.
Item paid to the proctors for their oversight – 12d.
Sum – 10s 4d.

Sum this side – 29s 5d.

fo 3v
The obit for all good doers
In primis paid to 5 priests for dirige and Mass – 15d.
Item paid to the clerk for dirige and his bells – 14d.
Item paid for offering – 1d.
Item for 3 quarts osey to the cake – 9d.
Item for *mete* oil to the same – 1d.
Item for 2 bushels of meal for the cake – 20d.
Item for ?2 dozen ale – 3s.
Item for saffron to the cake, 2 oz – 18d.
Item for baking the cake – 12d.
Item for Gascon wine, 2 gallons – 16d.
Item for osey, 2 ¼ gallons – 2s 3d.
Item for malmsey and ?rommey – 16d.

Sum – 16s.

The costs done on Corpus Christi day
Item paid to Master vicar – [blank].
Item paid to 4 priests – 16d.
Item paid for bearing the shrine – 10d.
Item paid for bearing the Cross – 4d.
Item paid for bearing 2 torches – 4d.
Item paid the clerk – 2d.
Item paid for bearing censers and candlesticks – 4d.
Item paid to 4 children for singing *salve festa dies* – 4d.
Item paid for a pottle of wine – 4d.
Sum – 4s 4d.

Sum – 20s 4d.

fo 4
Here follow the parcels of wax
In primis delivered to the waxmaker 13 square tapers weighing 69 lb.
Received them again weighing 78 lb. So there is in new wax 9 lb at 6 ½d
the pound, sum – 4s 10 ½d.
Item delivered the waxmaker in round tapers weighing 16 lb. Received
them again weighing 31 lb. So there is in new wax 15 lb at 6 ½d, sum – 8s
1 ½d.
Item delivered the waxmaker the paschal weighing 28 lb. Received [of]
him again weighing 30 ¾ lb. So there is in new wax 2 ¾ lb, at 6 ½d the
pound, sum – 18d.
[Margin: for the chantry][Scored: Item delivered the waxmaker 12 lb wax.
Received of him 16 lb. So there is in new wax 4 lb, at 6 ½d the pound, sum
– 2s 2d.]
Item delivered the font taper weighing 3 ½ lb. Received [of] him again
weighing 4 lb. So there is in new wax ½ lb, sum – 3 ¼d.
Item received of the waxmaker 4 tapers weighing 1 lb – 6 ½d.
Item delivered 15 round tapers weighing 15 lb. Received them again
weighing 31 lb. So there is in new wax 16 lb at 6 ½d the pound, sum – 8s
8d.
Item paid for making the said stuff – 3s 4d.
Sum the church wax – 27s 3 ¾d.

Sum this parcel – 27s 3 ¾d.

[Scored: Sum total the rents, vacations abated, and obits with other
ordinary costs aforesaid – £19 11s 7 ¼d.]

fo 4v

Payments

In primis paid for a pottle of wine on Palm Sunday – 6d.

Item paid for besoms for the church – 1d.

Item paid the raker for the whole year – 8d.

Item paid for 2 sacks coals on Shere Thursday – 2 $\frac{1}{2}$d.

Item paid for a rope for the paschal – 6d.

Item paid for storing the church stuff – 2s.

Item paid Nicholas for watching the sepulchre – 12d.

Item paid for washing the church stuff – 2s 4d.

Item paid for bearing the banners in the Rogation week – 4d.

Item paid for making a baldric for the 2nd bell – 18d.

Item for *sipers* [?cyprus] to the shrine by Nicholas – 2s 4d.

Item for pins that same time – 1d.

Item paid William ?Repock for mending the vestments – 3s 4d.

Item allowance of our tenants – 16d.

Item paid for hanging the dance of Pauls – 16d.

Item paid for making the ?*lre* to my lord of Winchester – 8d.

Item paid John Ricarts for his labour, attendance and for costs of ?bate here and for a reward, sum – 6s 8d.

Item for mending the glass windows – 4d.

Item for mending the *lasse* standards [superscript: candlesticks] – 8d.

Item paid for mending the great organs to Sir John Toby – 9d.

Item paid Thomas Barbor for allowance of his account [superscript: at our cost] – 30s.

Item paid Thomas Pacy for that the church owed him by his account – 13s 4d.

Item paid for candles against Christmas – 3d.

Item paid for pins against Christmas – $\frac{1}{2}$d.

Item paid for lamp oil this present year – 14s.

Item paid for making the rent roll – 4d.

Item paid the sexton for his year's wages – 20s.

Item paid the clerk for that he lacked of his wages – 29s 7d.

Item paid for paper for this book – 1d.

Item paid for making this book – 6d.

Item paid for mending 2 cruets and the ship – 3s 2d.

Item paid for making a key of silver for a box called the *pycks* and for mending it – 6d.

Item paid for *frenshe* [?fringe] to the *lenton* banner and for making it 2s 8d.

Item paid for a key to the *bessett* belonging to John Lord's priest – 2d.

Sum this side – £7 15d.

fo 5

Repairs done in my lady Pernaunt's house

In primis 1 bundle of laths – 3d.

Item boards for the same – 4d.

Item paid for a pipe of lead weighing $\frac{3}{4}$ [of a hundred weight?] and 10 lb at 1d the pound, sum – 7s 3d, of the which he allowed me for the old pipe weighing $\frac{3}{4}$ and 26 lb at $\frac{1}{2}$d the pound, sum – 3s 7 $\frac{1}{2}$d. So I paid him clear – 3s 3d.

Item paid for 1 $\frac{3}{4}$ lb of solder – 7d.

Item for boards to make a door – 6d.

Item for nails to the same – 3d.

Item for *legges* to the door – 3d.

Item for twists to the same – 6d.

Item paid the carpenter – 8d.

Sum – 6s 7d.

Repairs done on John Snygge's house

Item paid for 2 studs for the stairs – 7d.

Item paid for 1 seme of boards to the same – 7d.

Item paid for nails, calf-foot nails and board nails – 5d.

Item paid for workmanship of the same – 2s 4d.

Item paid for planks for the steps of the same – 2s 10d.

Item paid for soldering the gutter between Master Harvey and the church over the ?pillar, sum our part – 3d.

Item paid for laths and lime to stop a hole between Rankyn and ?me – 2d.

Item paid for lath nails – 1d.

Sum – 7s 3d.

Repairs done on Master ?Blisse's house

In primis paid to 2 labourers for voiding and mending of a privy – 20d.

Item for lyme *de way* [?half a wey] – 6d.

Item for hauling the same [word illegible] away – 3d.

Item for soldering our gutter of lead – 2d.

Item for mending a stair in the same house – 7d.

Sum – 3s 2d.

Sum this side – 17s.

fo 5v

Repairs to Harry Brewster's house

In primis paid for ?cleaning his *drauft* – 12d.

Item paid for mending a gutter of Thomas Grenefeld – 3d.

Sum – 15d.

Sum of all payments and allowances for this year passed – £12 2s 8 ¾d.

Rest owing the church by the proctors – £3 4s 10 ¾d.

[Remaining entries in different hand:] Also the proctors paid for repairs done on the chantry lands this year more than was received – 29s 6d.

Which proctors were paid before the *p[ar]reschesons* on the day of the accounts of the church's money. So the chantry owes to the church the said – 29s 6d.

And also the proctors have brought in to the church the rest of the money, sum – 35s 4 ½d.

Item allowed by the *p[ar]reschesons* to the proctors for *pok's* cellar – 8d.

Also allowed them for Raynnold Tailor's house for half year – 8s.

So the *p[ar]resschesons* have received to the use of the church – 26s 8 ¾d.

Of the which money the *p[ar]resschesons* paid to the clerk for keeping Our Lady Mass – 3s 4d.

So rest to the church clear – 23s 4d.

Which money was delivered by the said *p[ar]reschsons* to Richard Wale and he to bring it in to the church the next day of his account – 23s 4d.

Also Ralyng Webe has promised to be proctor the next year.

[1515–1516]

fo 1
Anno domini 1515
Richard Wale
The Church Book

fo 1v
Jhu
Here after follows the rental of the church of All Hallows' in Bristol with the allowances, expenses, reparations, and customable charges done from the Feast of the Annunciation of Our Lady in the year of Our Lord God 1515 unto the same Feast being 1516, then being proctors Richard Wale and Thomas Yonge, also Master Roger Dawys then Mayor, Richard Abyngton and William Vaghan sheriffs.

Rent of assize per annum
In primis Johanne James widow per annum – 3s 4d.
Item Robert Barbor's house per annum – 4s.
Item John Watson cook for the baste door per annum – 2s 6d.
Item Richard Erle per annum – 12d.
Item the master of the Tailors per annum – 12s.

Item Croft's house in St Peter's parish per annum – 6d.
Item George Schypard for a house in Marsh Street per annum – 2s.
Sum – 25s 4d.

Rents in the High Street
Item of my lady Pernaunt per annum – £4.
Item of John Snyg per annum – £3 6s 8d.
Item Thomas Williams tailor afore the tolsell – 16s.
Item Harry Brewster next to the same – 16s.
Item Sir John Coke for his chamber per annum – 6s 8d.
Item the shop under the said chamber – 20d.
Item the old house in the Broad Street – £4.
Item Master Blysse *fyessission* [physician] in Small Street – 26s 8d.
Item John Colle for a stable per annum – 4s.
Sum – £14 17s 8d.

Sum total this side – £16 3s.

fo 2
Vacations following
In primis the old house in Broad Street – £4.
Item the shop in the churchyard – 20d.
Item Richard Erle – 12d.
Item Master Croft's house – 6d.
Item George Schepard's house – 2s.
Item Johanna James widow – 20d.
Sum – £4 6s 10d.

Sum the whole rents, vacations abated – £11 16s 2d.

The receipts of customable duties
Item received on Palm Sunday for the sexton's wages – 3s 2d.
Item received on Palm Sunday, Shere Thursday of houselling people – 12d.
Item received on Good Friday to the jewels – 2s 4d.
Item received on Easter eve and on Easter day to the paschal – 8s $\frac{1}{2}$d.
Item received of the proctors of Jesus – 38s 2d.
Item received of the man of Lichfield that died at the *new ende* toward the gilding of the high altar and for the cross and 2 copes, amount all – 11s.
Item received of John Jervys for his pew – 16d.
Item received of Katherine Dee for her pew – 8d.
Item received of Thomas Dale for his father's legacy – £4 6s 8d.
Item saved of my lady Spicer's obit – 4d.
Item of John Bancke for his pew – 8d.
Item received of the clerk for Richard Booksyller's gown – 16s.

Item received the day of our account last past of the parish – 23s 4d.
Item received of Phelyp Meyssary for her pew – [blank].
Sum – £9 12s 8 ½d.
[In margin: Sum total of all the receipts of this present year –
£21 8s 10 ½d.]

The obit of William Newbery
In primis paid to Master vicar for his wax and dirige – 16d.
Item paid to 5 priests for the dirige – 20d.
Item paid to the clerk – 10d.
Item paid to the bellman – 2d.
Item paid for bread to poor people – 2s.
Item paid to the offering – 1d.
Sum – 6s 1d.

fo 2v.
The obit of Thomas Fylour
In primis paid to Master vicar for his wax and dirige – 12d.
Item paid to 8 priests – 2s 8d.
Item paid to the clerk – 14d.
Item paid to Master vicar for the bede roll – 12d.
Item paid to the bellman – 2d.
Item paid for bread to poor people – 5s.
Item paid to the 2 proctors for their oversight – 12d.
[Different ink: Item paid for offering – 1d.]
Sum – 12s 1d.

The obit of Harry Chestre
Item paid to Master vicar for his wax and dirige – 16d.
Item paid to 5 priests – 20d.
Item paid to the clerk – 12d.
Item paid to the bellman – 4d.
Item paid for bread to poor people – 2s 8d.
Item paid for offering – 1d.
Sum – 7s 1d.

The obit of Thomas Spicer and Dame Maud his wife
In primis paid to Master vicar and to 6 priests for dirige and Mass – 2s 4d.
Item paid to Master vicar for 4 tapers of 2 lb apiece to have about the
hearse at dirige and Mass – 2s.
Item paid to Master vicar for the bede roll – 4d.
Item paid to the clerk – 14d.
Item paid to the bellman – 4d.
Item paid to the sexton – 1d.

Item paid for offering – 1d.
Item paid for bread to the poor people – 3s.
Item paid to the proctors for their oversight – 12d.
Sum – 10s 4d.

Sum this side – 29s 5d.

fo 3
The obit for all good doers
In primis paid to 5 priests dirige and Mass – 15d.
Item paid to the clerk for dirige and Mass – 14d.
Item for offering – 1d.
Item for *met* oil for the cake – 3d.
Item for 2 bushels of meal for the cake – 2s 2d.
Item for 2 oz of saffron for the said cake – 22d.
Item for 2 dozen ale, 1 of them double ale – 3s 1d.
Item for baking 13 dozen cakes – 13d.
Item for half a dozen bread for poor people – 6d.
Item for 2 gallons of Gascon wine 16d.
Item for a quart of malmsey – 3d.
Item for a gallon and a pottle of romney – 12d.
[Added: Item for 1 gallon of osey – 12d.]
Sum – 15s.

Costs done on Corpus Christi Day
In primis for bearing the shrine to 2 friars about the parish – 6d.
Item to the priests – 4d.
Item to the clerk, for him and his children – 4d.
Item to the sexton for bearing the cross – 1d.
Sum – 15d.
Sum this side – 16s 3d.

Sum total for all obits – 51s 9d.

fo 3v
Here follow the parcels of wax
In primis delivered to the waxmaker 13 square tapers weighing 56 lb;
whereof we have received the said 13 tapers weighing 83 lb; so rests of
new wax 27 lb, amount – 15s 9d.
Item delivered him the paschal weighing 26 lb; received of him again 29
lb; so rests 3 lb of new wax, amount – 21d.
Item delivered him 15 round tapers weighing 15 lb; received the same
again weighing 31 lb; rests 16 lb of new wax at 7d – 9s 4d.
Item delivered in old wax 2 lb a fan taper [font taper] and received 4

tapers for the angels, 5 lb; rests of new wax 3 lb, amount – 21d.
Item delivered 15 round tapers weighing 13 lb; received 31 lb; rests of
new wax 18 lb at 8d the pound – 12s.
Item for making the church wax – 3s 4d.
Sum – 43s 11d.

Payments
In primis paid for a pottle of wine on Palm Sunday – 6d.
Item paid for besoms to the church – 1d.
Item paid to the raker for the whole year – 8d.
Item for 2 sacks of coals on Shere Thursday – 2 ½d.
Item for scouring the church stuff – 2s.
Item for watching the sepulchre – 12d.
Item for washing the church stuff – 2s 4d.
Item for bearing the banner in Rogation week – 4d.
Item allowance for our tenants – 16d.
Item for hanging the Dance of Pauls – 16d.
Item paid for candles against Christmas – 3d.
Item paid for lamp oil for the whole year – 13s.
Item paid for making the rent roll – 4d.
Item paid for the sexton's wages – 20s.
Item paid the clerk to make up his full wages – 22s 2d.
Item paid for paper [scored: for both books] – 1d.
Item for mending a censer – 12d.
Item for mending the lock to the font – 2d.
Item for mending the clerk's surplice – 1d.
Item for mending the *bynche* at the church door with 2 sacks of lime – 5d.
Item paid to the plumber for mending the conduit 2 times – 20d.
Item paid for a key to the conduit head – 3s.
Item paid for making these books – 6d.
Item paid unto Thomas Owen and to Raffe Hoper for the *vevynge* of such
stuff as belongs unto the church – 20d.
[Line added: Chantry house in Lewinsmede in which house John Awode
dwells.]
Sum – £3 11s 4 ½d.

fo 4
Reparations done in my lady Pernaunt's house
In primis for cleaning a gutter there for 2 men a day – 12d.
Item for 2 sacks of lime to the same – 2d.
Item paid a tiler for a day's labour to the same house – 5d.
Sum – 19d.

Reparations done upon John Snygge's house

Item for soldering a gutter, to the plumber – 6d.

Reparations of Master Blysse's house
Item paid to John Brown glazier for mending his glass windows in Small Street – 4d.

Reparations done on Harry Bryster's house
Item for a table stone before the hearth of 3 feet – 4d.
Item for a firestone for the hearth – 4d.
Item for a sack of fine lime and another of coarse to the same – 1 $\frac{1}{2}$d.
Item for the man's labour for a day there – 5d.
Sum – 14 /12d.

Item for soldering of 6 *skarys* and for 8 lb of solder partible between the church and Walssall's *yn* [?inn] – 3s, so amounts the church's part – 18d, and more for wood, amount all – 19d.
[Addition: ?Know that this repair of 19d should whole be written in the chantry book.]
Sum – 7s 2 $\frac{1}{2}$d.

Sum total of all obits, reparations and other payments – £8 14s 3d.
Sum of all rents and receipts of this present year, obits and payments abated – £12 14s 7 $\frac{1}{2}$d.
Item the proctors have paid this year of the church's money in reparations on the chantry's lands – £8 14s 9 $\frac{1}{2}$d, which the chantry owes for this year to the church.

fo 4v
So rest that the proctors must bring in to the church of this account aforesaid for this present year – £3 19s 10d.

Item received on the said day of our account of the foresaid proctors – £3 19s 10d.
Which money the *p[ar]reschsons* delivered it unto Thomas Snygge and to Thomas Pacy and they to bestow it on the reparations on All Hallows' conduit.
And also the said *p[ar]reschsons* have assigned the said Thomas Snyg and Thomas Pacy to receive of Thomas Yonge in money – 6s 10d
to make up the sum of £4 6s 8d and all to be bestowed on the abovesaid conduit.
Also this year Master Humfrey Harvey's executors gave us the house in the High Street that John Repe grocer now holds, yearly rent – 40s.
And Thomas Young at his day of accounts to answer the whole year's rent
And also we the *p[ar]reschsons* gave then to Master Harvey's burial –

[blank].

[1518]

fo 1
The Church Book
Rawlyn Webb Anno Domini 1518

fo 2
The accounts of Rawlyn Webbe and John Hewes proctors of the church of All Hallows' in Bristol of and for the lands and other receipts of the said church made in the year of our lord God 1518, then being mayor John Jay, John Drewes and John Repe sheriffs

Receipts of the church for customable duties
In primis received on Palm Sunday for the sexton's wages – 2s 10 $\frac{1}{2}$d.
Item received on Palm Sunday for the Paschal – 9d.
Item received on Shere Thursday – 22d.
Item received on Good Friday to the reparation of the jewels – 2s 11d.
Item received on Easter eve and Easter day – 7s 11d.
Item received of Master [superscript: Richard Bromefelde] vicar's gift unto the church – 20s.
Item received of the proctors of Jesus – 52s 3d.
Item received of my lady Pernaunt [superscript: for part of the 40s bequeathed by Sir John Thomas] – 20s.
Item received of Thomas Yonge last proctor – £6.
Item received for a *clavey of ffreston* [?a measure of free stone] – 2s 4d.
Item received for old timber – 40s.
Item received of Thomas Yonge for his wife's grave – 6s 8d.
Sum – £13 17s 6 $\frac{1}{2}$d.

fo 2v
Receipts of the church rent by the year
Rent assize
In primis of John Watson cook for his back door – 2s 6d.
Item Richard Erle in Lewins Mead – 12d.
Item of Robert Barbor for his house – 4s.
Item of the master [superscript: with the fellowship] of the Tailors for a tenement in Baldwin Street – 12s.
Item of Master Croft for a house in St Peter's parish – 6d.
Item of George Shepard for a house in Marsh Street – 2s.
Item for a gutter from Paul James' house – 3s 4d.
Sum – 25s 4d.

High Street
John Snygge for a tenement by year – £3 6s 8d.
Item of my lady Pernaunt for a tenement by year – £4.
Item of Harry Brusestur clerk – 16s.
Item Thomas Williams tailor – 16s.
Item Sir John Cook for his chamber – 6s 8d.
Item the great house in Broad Street – £4.
Item Blisse in Small Street for a tenement by year – 26s 8d.
Item John Colls for a garden [superscript: and stable] – 4s.
Item John Repe for a tenement – 40s.
[Different ink: Item Sir John Cooke for the school house or beer house in the churchhouse [sic] – 20d.
Sum – £16 17s 8d.

Sum total of the whole rents – £18 3s.
[Margin: Sum of the whole rents and other receipts – £32 6 ½d.]

Vacations and allowance of rent following
In primis of Richard Erle in Lewins Mead – 12d.
Item of the master of the Tailors for a house in Baldwin Street – 12s.
Item of Master Croft for a house in St Peter's parish – 6d.
Item of George Sheppard for a house in Marsh Street – 2s.
Item the great house in Broad Street void – £3 17s 6d.
Item allowance for a gutter from Paul James' house – 20d.
[Different ink: Item for the school house or beer house in the churchyard[sic] – 20d.
Sum – £4 16s 4d.

[Scored: Sum total received, vacations allowed and deducted – £26 17s 6d.]
Sum total of the rents and receipts, vacations allowed and deducted – £27 4s 2 ½d.

fo 3
Costs and payments of the church
In primis paid for a pottle of wine on Palm Sunday – 6d.
Item for nails to the sepulchre – 1d.
Item paid to the raker – 8d.
Item for watching the sepulchre – 12d.
Item to a carpenter for dressing the sepulchre – 2d.
Item for a *Bonde* to the clerk's surplice – 2d.
Item for a line to the lent cloth – 2d.
Item paid to the clerk for Our Lady Mass – 4s.

Item for pins and earnest to the suffragan – 1 ½d.

Item for coals and besoms – 3 ½d.

Item for a line to a cloth before the cross – 2d.

Item for a lamp to the high altar – 1d.

Item for mending the locks to the copes and the coffer in the chancel and the enterclose door – 4d.

Item paid for a *haspe*, keys and 2 locks to the font – 4d.

Item paid for a clamp and mending a bolt to the enterclose door – 3d.

Item for making 2 iron bars for the charnel house – 7d.

Item for 5 ells of cloth for a surplice to the suffragan – 20d.

Item for making the same – 10d.

Item for 3 quarters of cloth for an amice and hemming the same – 3 ½d.

Item for making 3 rochets – 9d.

Item paid to George Badrod for 31 ells of Normandy canvas at 5d an ell to cover the high altar – 12s 11d.

Item to Joan Bromwell for making the same – 2s.

Item for curtain rings – 6d.

Item for lines to draw the said cloth – 5d.

Item for *lyre* – 2d.

Item for a small line for the middle of the same cloth – 1d.

Item for 4 *shevers* for the pulleys – 2d.

Item for making pulleys and for setting up the same and the cloth – 8d.

Item for lamp oil – 12s 4d.

Item paid to the steward for seeing deeds – 12d.

Item for making clean the church roof and the walls – 10d.

Item for making clean the tower – 4d.

Item for *wyngis* and besoms – 2d.

Item for bearing banners in Rogation week – 4d.

Sum – 44s 4 ½d.

fo 3v

Item for washing the church stuff – 2s 4d.

Item for scouring – 2s.

Item paid to Nicholas sexton for his wages – 3s 4d.

Item paid to Watkyn sexton for 3 quarters – 15s.

Item paid to the clerk more than could be gathered in the parish the whole year – 22s 3d.

Item paid for curtain wire to the high altar – 2s.

Item for mending the branch before Jesus – 3d.

Item for 12 hooks for the great image – 4d.

Item for 20 hooks for the small image – 3d.

Item for a baldric to 1 of the bells – 12d.

Item for hanging up the Dance of Pauls 2 times – 16d.

Item paid to the waxmaker for the church the whole year as appears by parcel – 46s 9 $\frac{1}{2}$d.

Item to the waxmaker for his labour the whole year – 3s 4d.

Item paid to a carpenter for mending of a board in the belfry – 1d.

Item to John Collis for the overseeing of the deeds of the great house in Broad Street – 20d.

Item for our supper at the day of account – 14d.

Item allowance for our tenants – 16d.

Item to Our Lady of Worcester – 8d.

[Three items scored: Item for board nail and calf-foot nail – 3d.

Item for board nail, stone nail and hair – 3d.

Item for a carpenter 2 $\frac{1}{2}$ days' – 16d.]

Item for a lock and a key and a chain to the *bere* – 4d.

Item for making the rent roll – 4d.

Item for paper – 2d.

Item for making this book – 8d.

Sum – £5 6s 7 $\frac{1}{2}$d.

fo 4

The obit of William Newbury

In primis to Master vicar for wax and dirige – 16d.

Item to 5 priests – 20d.

Item to the clerk – 10d.

Item to the bellman – 2d.

Item for bread to the poor people – 2s.

Item for offering – 1d.

Sum – 6s 1d.

The obit of Thomas Fylour

In primis to Master vicar for his dirige and wax – 12d.

Item to 8 priests – 2s 8d.

Item to the clerk – 14d.

Item to Master vicar for the bede roll – 12d.

Item to the bellman – 2d.

Item for bread to poor people – 5s.

Item for offering – 1d.

Item to the 2 proctors for their attendance – 12d.

Sum – 12s 1d.

The obit of Harry Chestre and Humfrey Hervey

In primis to Master vicar for his wax and dirige – 16d.

Item to 5 priests – 20d.

Item to the clerk – 12d.

Item to the bellman – 4d.

Item for bread to poor people – 3s 8d.

Item to the sexton – 2d.
Item for offering – 1d.
Item to the proctors for their labour – 8d.
Sum – 8s 11d.

The obit of Thomas Spicer and Dame Maud his wife
In primis to Master vicar and 6 priests for dirige and Mass – 2s 4d.
Item to Master [vicar] for tapers of 2 lb apiece about the hearse – 2s.
Item to Master vicar for the bede roll – 4d.
Item to the clerk – 14d.
Item to the bellman – 4d.
Item to the sexton – 1d.
Item for offering – 1d.
Item for bread to the poor people – 3s.
Item to the 2 proctors for their attendance – 12d.
Sum – 10s 4d.

Sum total this side – 37s 5d.

fo 4v
The obit of good doers
[Added: Item to Master vicar – 4d.]
In primis to 5 priests – 15d.
Item to the clerk – 14d.
Item for offering – 1d.
Item for *mete* oil for the cakes – 3d.
Item for 2 bushels of meal for cakes – 22d.
Item for 2 oz of saffron – 2s 4d.
Item for 2 dozen of ale, 1 double and another single – 3s 1d.
Item for baking the cakes – 13d.
Item for half a dozen bread to poor people – 6d.
Item for 2 gallons of wine – 16d.
Item for a quart of malmsey – 3d.
Item for 3 pottles of Romney – 12d.
Item for 3 pottles of osey – 18d.
Sum – 15s 8d.

Corpus Christi day
In primis to Master vicar – [blank]
Item to 6 priests – 2s.
Item for bearing 2 torches – 4d.
Item to the sub deacon – 2d.
Item to the clerk – 4d.
Item for a pottle of wine in the Marsh – 4d.

Item to the children that sang – 9d.
Item for bearing the candlesticks – 2d.
Item for bearing up the copes – 4d.
Item for bearing the shrine – 12d.
Item for bearing the cross – 4d.
Sum – 5s 9d.

The obit of [scored: Harry Chestre and Alice] [inserted: Humfrey Hervey and Ann] his wife
In primis to the vicar or his deputy and 6 priests – 2s 4d.
Item to the vicar for his wax – 8d.
Item for offering – 1d.
Item to the clerk for his bells – 12d.
Item to the bellman – 4d.
Item for bread to Newgate – 20d.
Item for bread to the almshouse in All Hallows' parish – 4d.
Item for bread to poor people in Long Rewe – 4d.
Item for [?bread] to the Bright bowe – 4d.
Sum – 7s 1d.

Sum this side – 28s 6d.

fo 5
Reparations of the conduit
In primis paid for cleansing the gutter of the pipe and removing the stone before the *trowe* – 6d.
Item paid to the plumber for a ?pitch cloth – 3d.
Item for mending of the pipe with 3 lb of solder on the grey friars – 14d.
Item paid to the plumber for 2 *fawts* [faults] in Broad Street – 6d.
Sum – 2s 5d.

[In margin against the following section: My lady Pernaunt]
Item paid to the plumber for 4 *scarys* in my lady Pernaunt's house partible – 8d.
Item for soldering a *scare* in the same house – 5d.
Item paid to a tiler in my lady Pernaunt's house and John Snygge's house for a tiler for 3 $\frac{1}{2}$ days' – 22 $\frac{1}{2}$d.
Item to his apprentice 3 $\frac{1}{2}$ days' – 10 $\frac{1}{2}$d.
Item to a labourer half a day – 2d.
Item for half a wey of lime – 5d.
Item paid to 2 tilers 2 days' – 2s 2d.
Item to an apprentice 2 days' – 6d.
Item for lath nail – 1d.
Item for hauling 2 vats of stones – 4d.

Item for 3 lb of solder and 3 *scarys* – 15d.
Item for mending a chimney – 2d.
Item for mending a form in Nicholas Sexton's – 1d.
Sum – 9s.

Item for cleaning 2 gutters in Blysse's house – 2s 8d.
[In margin against rest of section: Windows in the tower]
Item for 6 sacks of lime – 5d.
Item for dressing the windows in the tower – 6d.
Item for 2 bundles of laths – 6d.
Item for nails – 5d.
Item to a carpenter for his handy work – 9d.
Item for 2 hooks and a staple – 1 ½d.
Item for mending a gutter in Harry Brustar's and Thomas William's house – 2s 4d.

[In margin against following section: Sir John Cook's chamber]
Item paid for a wey of lime for Sir John Coke's house – 10d.
Item to a mason 3 days' at 6 ½d the day – 19 ½d.
Item to another mason 2 days' at 5 ½d the day – 11d.
Item to a mason, 3 days' – 15d.
Item to a labourer, 3 days' – 12d.
Item for hauling 4 vats of stones and a vat of rubble – 5d.
Item paid for a cover to a chimney – 3d.
Item to a tiler, half a day – 3d.
Sum – 14s 3d.

Sum this side – 25s 8d.

fo 5v
Reparations on the house in Broad Street
Item to 3 labourers for ridding the ground, a day – 12d.
Item to a carpenter and a tiler, 5 ½ days' at 6 ½d a day – 4s 10d.
Item to 5 labourers on Tuesday – 20d.
Item of Wednesday, Thursday, Friday and Saturday, every day 3 labourers – 3s 6d.
Item for 1400 laths – 7s.
Item for 7500 lath nails – 7s 9 ½d.
Item for 10 weys lime – 8s 4d.
Item for 3500 tile pins – 10d.
Item for 800 stone nails – 2s.
Item for board nail, calf-foot nail and hair – 6d.
Item to a carpenter, 2 ½ days' – 16d.
Item to a tiler, 3 ½ days' – 22d.

Item to a tiler for 4 days' – 2s 2 ½d.
Item to a labourer, 3 ½ days' – 14d.
Item for board nail and calf-foot nail – 5d.
Item to a carpenter, a day and a half – 9 ½d.
Item for board nail – 2d.
Item for 2 hooks, 2 twists and 2 staples – 4d.
Item for a seme of boards – 7d.
Item for calf-foot nail and board nail – 2d.
Item to a labourer, half a day – 2d.
Item for calf-foot nail – 3 ½d.
Item to a labourer, a day – 4d.
Item for 4 lb of solder – 12d.
Item for 2 *skares* – 4d.
Item for board nail – 2d.
Item for hair and stone nail – 3d.
Item to 2 tilers for a whole week – 6s 6d.
Item to a carpenter, 3 days' – 19 ½d.
Item for 4 hooks, 2 staples and 2 twists – 5d.
Item for 50 board nails – 2d.
Item for calf-foot nail – 4d.
Item for hair – 1d.
Item to a carpenter, 2 days' – 13d.
Item to a tiler, 2 ½ days' – 2s 5d.
Item to his apprentice, 2 ½ days' – 12d.
Item for stone nail and hair – 1 ½d.
Item paid to a tiler's apprentice for 4 days' – 18d.
Item for a lock and a key to a door – 5d.
Sum this side – £3 3s 8d.
fo 6
Item to a labourer, 2 ½ days' – 10d.
Item for 100 board nails – 5d.
Item to a tiler, 3 ½ days' – 22d.
Item to a tiler, 2 ½ days' – 16d.
Item to a carpenter, a day and a half – 9d.
Item to 2 labourers, a day and a half – 12d.
Item for tile pins – 3d.
Item for calf-foot nail – 3d.
Item for 6 bewdley boards – 18d.
Item to a tiler, 2 days' – 13d.
Item to his apprentice, 2 days' – 9d.
Item to John the labourer, a whole week – 22d.
Item for calf-foot nail and hair – 2 ½d.
Item for 2 sacks of lime – 2d.
Item for 2 staples – 1d.

Item to a carpenter, 2 $\frac{1}{2}$ days' – 16d.
Item to a labourer – 4d.
Item for tile pins – 1 $\frac{1}{2}$d.
Item to a carpenter, a day – 6 $\frac{1}{2}$d.
Item to a carpenter, a day and a half – 9 $\frac{1}{2}$d.
Item to 2 labourers, 2 days' – 2s.
Item for 50 board nail – 2 $\frac{1}{2}$d.
Item for 3 sacks of lime – 2 $\frac{1}{2}$d.
Item to a carpenter, 3 days' – 19 $\frac{1}{2}$d.
Item for *rakhoks* – $\frac{1}{2}$d.
Sum – 19s 6d.

[Following in inferior hand:] Sum total payments – £16 5s 9d.
And so rest clear owing to the church – £10 18s 5 $\frac{1}{2}$d.

Memorandum that Ralyn Wode senior proctor paid to the *p[ar]reschsons*
at his day of his account in money – £8 18s 5 $\frac{1}{2}$d.
So he owes to the church of this account for old timber – 40s.
Which 40s he must pay to John Hewes and he to bring it into the church at
his next accounts.

fo 6v
[Scored: Item received for Thomas Yong's wife's grave – 6s 8d.]

Item that the Master of St John's gave unto ? to our reparations ?10,000
tile pins.

[Following two entries in neat hand:] Memorandum that John Hewes
proctor has received the day of this account £4, which sum he must bring
in at the time of his accounts.
Moreover the same John Hewes must bring in at his accounts 40s that he
shall receive of Rawlyn Cooke *al* Webb.

[At foot of page in inferior script: Memorandum delivered to Rawlyn
Webbe at the day of account in [word illegible] money 10s to be paid at
[words illegible].

[1519]

fo 1
The Church Book
John Hewes Anno dm 1519

fo 1v

The account of John Hewes and John Maunsell proctors of the church of All Hallows' in Bristol of and for the lands and other receipts of the said church made in the year of Our Lord God 1519, then being mayor John Edwards, William Cale and John Hall sheriffs

Receipts of the church for customable duties
In primis received on Palm Sunday – 2s 6d.
Item received on Sheer Thursday – 20d.
Item on Good Friday to the reparation of the jewels – 2s 4d.
Item on Easter eve – 18d.
Item on Easter day – 7s.
Item received of Master Snygge for the blindman's pew – 4d.
Item received of Thomas Apowell's bequest – 20d.
Item received of John Davies for Richard Wall's bequest – 10s.
Received more of him for his wife's grave – 6s 8d.
Received more of Rawlyn Webbe at the day of his account – £4.
[Following in different ink:] Received of Rawlyn Webbe for church timber – 40s.
Received of Robert Barbar for his wife's grave – 6s 8d.
Received of Gerram Grene and Harry Hyggons for Jesus brotherhood for this present year – 38s 11d.
Sum – £9 19s 3d.

fo 2

Receipts of the church rents
In primis of John Watson cook for his back door – 2s 6d.
Item Richard Erle in Lewins Mead – 12d.
Item of Thomas Ven for his house – 4s.
Item of the master and fellowship of the Tailors for a tenement in Baldwin Street by the year – 12s.
Item of Master Croft for a house in St Peter's parish – 6d.
Item of George Shepard for a house in Marsh Street – 2s.
Item for a gutter from Paul James' house – 3s 4d.
Sum – 25s 4d.

The High Street
Item John Snygge for a tenement by the year – £3 6s 8d.
Item of my lady Pernaunt for a tenement by the year – £4.
Item of a tenement that Thomas Smethe late held – 16s.
Item of Thomas Williams tailor – 16s.
Item of Sir John Cooke for his chamber – 6s 8d.
Item of the great house in Broad Street – £4.
Item of Blisse's house in Small Street by the year – 26s 8d.

Item of John Colls for a garden and a stable – 4s.
Item of Roger Phelpott for a *vavte* [?vault] by the year – 6s.
Item of John Vaghan for a chamber by the year – 6s 8d.
Item of William Pewterer for a stable the year – 6s 8d.
[Different hand: Item received of John Repe for a tenement – 40s.
Item received of Sir John Cook for the beer house – 20d.]
Sum of this side – £19 2s 4d.

Sum total of rents and other receipts amounts – £29 19d.

fo 2v
Vacations and allowances of the rents following
Item of Richard Erle in Lewins Mead – 12d.
Item of the master of the Tailors – 12s.
Item of Master Croft for a house in St Peter's parish – 6d.
Item of the great house in Broad Street – £3 5s 6d.[sic]
Item of George Sheppard for a house in Marsh Street – 2s.
Item of allowance for a gutter in the good wife Powll's house – 20d.
Item for the beer house or school house – 20d.
Item for half a year of William Pewterer's stable – 3s 4d.
Item for half a year of the house that Thomas Smith held afore the Tolsey
– 8s.
[Different hand: Item for a quarter of Roger Phylpot's ?vault – 18d.
Sum of the vacations with the allowances – £4 17s 2d.

Sum of the whole receipts, the vacations abated – £24 4s 5d.

Costs and payments of the church
Item paid for a pottle of osey on Palm Sunday – 6d.
Item paid to the raker for carrying away the church dust – 8d.
Item paid for the watching the sepulchre – 12d.
Item paid for ?pulley – 2d.
Item paid for besoms – 2d.
Item for washing the church stuff – 2s 4d.
Item paid for scouring – 2s.
Item paid to Watkyn the sexton for his year's wages – 20s.
Item paid to the clerk more than could be gathered in parish the whole
year – 29s 6d.
Item paid for hanging up the Dance of Pauls – 16d.
Item to Our Lady of Worcester – 8d.
[Different hand: Item paid to ?Fraunssre for binding a *prossesseor* and a
book at the organs – 2s.]
Sum of this side – 51s 4d.

fo 3

Repprashyngs of the blue copes and the white copes

Item paid for 3 ½ yards of buckram – 21d.

Item paid for 2 ½ yards of ribbons – 5d.

Item paid for thread – 3d.

Item paid for setting on the clasps on the blue copes – 10d.

Item paid to an embroiderer for his handiwork to mend the said copes – 5s 8d.

Sum – 8s 11d.

Item paid for a mat before the high altar – 3s 6d.

Item paid to a labourer to clean the leads over the charnel house – 2d.

Item paid to the sexton for making clean the ?corner over the charnel house – 1d.

Item paid for mending of the lamp in the choir – 2d.

Item paid for making clean the churchyard – 2d.

Item paid for hauling away 2 vats of rubble out of the churchyard – 2d.

Item paid for a board for the sepulchre – 6d.

Item for mending the cope coffer lock in the vestry – 2d.

Item paid for the cope press lock in the choir and a new key – 3d.

Item paid for a new baldric for the second bell – 12d.

Item paid ?to Thomas Ker's servant for dubbing the other 3 baldrics [erased: clappers] – 16d.

Item paid for 2 staples and 2 *forloks* for the great bell – 4d.

Item paid for ?stopping the scaffold holes at the high altar – 4d.

Item paid for mending a lock and making a new key and for nails for the church door in the south side – 8 ½d.

Item paid for ?sweeping the church gutters – 2d.

Item paid for 39 quarts of lamp oil – 13s ?d

Sum of this side – 30s 11 ½d.

fo 3v

Item paid to John Waxmaker for the church wax the whole year as it appears by his book and mine – 50s 7d.

Item paid for making the church wax – 3s 4d.

Item paid for supper at the day of our account – 20d.

Item for making the rental – 4d.

Item for paper – 2d.

Item making this book – 8d.

Item paid to Roger Pekeryng for his wages from St John's tide to Christmas – 4s 4d.

Item paid for bearing the banners in Rogation week – 4d.

Sum – £3 17d.

Costs on Corpus Christi day
Item to Master vicar – [blank].
Item to 6 priests – 2s.
Item for bearing 2 torches – 4d.
Item paid to the sexton – 2d.
Item paid to the clerk – 4d.
Item paid to 2 children that bore the candlesticks – 2d.
Item paid to the children that did bear up the copes – 4d.
Item paid for bearing the bell and the censers – 3d.
Item paid to 2 friars for bearing [the] shrine – 12d.
Item paid for bearing the cross – 4d.
Item for a pottle of claret wine in the Marsh – 4d.
Sum – 5s 1d.

Sum of this side – £3 6s 6d.

fo 4
[In different hand: Memorandum that the obit of William Newbury lacks here]

The obit of Thomas Fylour
Item to Master vicar for his dirige and wax – 12d.
Item to 8 priests – 2s 8d.
Item to the clerk – 14d.
Item to Master vicar for the bede roll – 12d.
Item to the bellman – 2d.
Item for offering – 1d.
Item for bread for poor people – 5s.
Item to the proctors for their attendance – 12d.
Sum 12s 1d.

Item the obit of Harry Chestre and Humfrey Harvey
Item to Master vicar for wax and dirige – 16d.
Item to 5 priests – 20d.
Item to the clerk – 12d.
Item to the bellman – 4d.
Item for bread to poor people – 3s 8d.
Item to the sexton – 2d.
Item for offering – 1d.
Item to the 2 proctors for their attendance – 8d.
Sum – 8s 11d.

Sum of this side – 21s.

fo 4v.

The obit of Thomas Spicer and Dame Maud his wife
Item to Master vicar and to 6 priests for dirige and Mass – 2s 4d.
Item to Master vicar for 4 tapers of 2 lb apiece about the hearse – 2s.
Item to Master vicar for the bede roll – 4d.
Item to the clerk – 14d.
Item to the bellman – 4d.
Item for offering – 1d.
Item for bread to poor people – 3s.
Item to the proctors for their attendance – 12d.
Sum – 10s 4d.

The [obit] of all good doers
[Margin, in different hand: Memorandum that it is agreed that the 2
proctors shall not exceed 14s upon this obit]
Item to Master vicar – 4d.
Item to 5 priests – 15d.
Item for offering – 1d.
Item to the clerk – 14d.
Item for *mette* oil for the cakes – 3d.
Item for 3 bushels of meal at 10d the bushel – 2s 6d.
Item 2 oz of saffron – 2s.
Item for 2 dozen of ale, one of double and another single – 3s 1d.
Item for baking cakes – 13d.
Item for half a dozen bread for poor people – 6d.
Item Gascon wine – 16d.
Item for osey, malmsey and romney – 2s 8d.
Sum – 16s 3d.
Sum of this side – 26s 7d.

fo 5

The obit of Umfre Hurvi and Anne his wife
Item to Master vicar or his deputy – 4d.
Item to 6 priests – 2s.
Item to the vicar for his wax – 8d.
Item for offering – 1d.
Item to the clerk – 12d.
Item to the bellman – 4d.
Item for bread to poor people – 2s 8d.
Sum 7s 1d.

Reparations in the great house in Broad Street
Item paid to 4 labourers for to rid the *vavt* for Roger Pylpot and the ground
for William Pewterer's stable, a day – 16d.

Item paid to a carpenter to make *dernyey* and doors for the said stable for
2 days' – 13d.
Item paid to a mason to make the wall at both the ends of the stable, for 13
perches at 4d the perch, sum – 4s 4d.
Item paid for the one half of the workmanship to make the wall of the
pavement – 2s 8d.
Item paid for planks for the same stable – 2s.
Item paid for the manger – 8d.
Item paid for the *rake* – 8d.
Item paid to a carpenter to lay the planks and to make the floor overhead
in the same stable for 4 days' at 6 ½d the day, sum – 2s 2d.
Sum – 14s 11d.

Sum of this side – 22s.

fo 5v
Reparations in John Reppe's house, paving his water place and mending
the gutter
Item paid for a load of paving stones and for the hauling – 17d.
Item to a mason to hew the same stones for 2 days' at 6 ½d the day, sum –
13d.
Item paid for boards to mend the ?floor under the paving – 5d.
Item paid to a mason to lay the said paving for a day – 6 ½d.
Item paid to a labourer to serve him and to make him mortar, a day – 4d.
Item paid for ?using 2 ¼ hundredweights and 14 lb of lead at 12d the
hundredweight – 2s 4d.
Sum – 6s 1 ½d.

Reparations on Thomas Williams ?house, paving his kitchen
Item paid for a load of paving stones and for the hauling – 17d.
Item paid for laying the boards in the kitchen floor to a man, a day –
6 ½d.
Item paid to a mason to hew the paving for 2 days' at 5 ½d the day – 11d.
Item paid to a mason to lay the same stones and to ?pitch the chimney in
the same kitchen – 11d.
Item paid to a labourer to serve the mason and to rid the ground for 3
days' at 4d the day – 12d.
Item paid for a load of clay – 2d.
Item paid for casting of 2 ¾ hundredweight of lead at 12d the
hundredweight – 2s 9d.
Sum – 8s 10 ½d.

Sum of this side – 15s

fo 6

The house next the chandler's shop

Item paid for a seme of welsh boards – 8d.

Item paid to a carpenter to make the *skreine* over the window and to mend the great door in Broad Street – 6d.

Item paid for making a hook for the same door – 1d.

Sum – 15d.

Reparations of my lady's kitchen chimney and mending the paving

Item paid for a load of *penantte* – 16d.

Item for hauling them – 2d.

Item paid to a mason to hew the said stones and for pitching the chimney and mending the floor for 3 days' at 6 ½d the day, sum – 19 ½d.

Item paid to a labourer to ?break the chimney and to serve the mason for 3 days at 4d the day, sum – 12d.

Sum – 4s 1 ½d.

Item paid for making a wall between my lord Lylle and our ground in Broad Street as it does appear by the *baylly ys* [?bailiff's] bill, and so it amounts to our part – 5s 4 ½d.

Sum of this side 10s 9d.

fo 6v

Reparations of the church roof and Thomas William's house and Thomas ?Sith's house

Item paid for a load of tile and the hauling – 17d.

Item paid for hauling a vat of old tiles from the stair house – 2d.

Item paid to a tiler for 8 days' at 5 ½d the day, sum – 3s 4
8d.

Item paid to his lad for 5 days' at 3 ½d the day, sum – 15 ½d.

Item paid for 100 laths – 6d.

Item paid for ? tile pins – 3d.

Item paid for 2 crests – 1d.

Sum – 7s 6 ½d.

Nails

Item for nails for the churchworks the whole year as it appears in John Maunsell's book and by my bill – 2s.

Item paid for nails that were [word unintelligible] and in ?William [words illegible] – 5 ½d.

Sum – 2s 5 ½d.

Lime

Item for lime for the church works for the whole year as it doth appear by a score endentured between Julyn a Channer and me for the churchworks – 11s 8d.

Sum 11s 8d.

Sum of this side – 21s 8d.

fo 7

Item paid for cleaning Master Blysse's gutter that goes out of his kitchen – 2s.

Item paid for cleaning of a gutter between my lady Pernaunt's and John Maunsell for our part – 10d.

Sum – 2s 10d.

Sum total of payments – £13 8s 7 $\frac{1}{2}$d.

[Remainder in different hand:] So rest clear to the church (the 32s 8d of the arrearages of the chantry allowed) – £9 3s 1 $\frac{1}{2}$d.

The which sum the said accountant has delivered to the *parisshons* the day of his accounts, the 13th day of the month of May the year of Our Lord God 1519 and so he is clearly discharged.

Item delivered to John Maunsell senior proctor of the said sum – £5 3s, he to bring it in again at his account.

And the rest, that is to say £4, is put in the treasure coffer in the presence of the said *parisshons*.

[1520]

fo 1

Jhu

The Church Book

John Mawncell 1520

fo. 2

Ihu

Here after follows the rentals of the church of All Saints' in Bristol with the allowances, repairs, expenses, with customable charges done from the feast of the Annunciation of Our Lady in the year of Our Lord God 1519, John Mawncell and Robert Barbur for the year being proctors, to the feast next after ensuing, that is to say the year of Our Lord God 1520, then being mayor John Williams, Clement Basse and Robert Sawyrge *strenys*.

The Rent Assize
In primis Jenat Powll for a gutter – 3s 4d.
Item of Thomas Ven – 4s.
Item of Rawlyng Webbe – 2s 6d.
Item of Richard Eryll – 12d.
Item of the master of the Tailors – 12s.
Item of Master Croft's house in St Peter's parish – 6d.
Item for a house in Marsh Street of George Schyppard's – 2s.
Sum – 25s 4d.

fo 2v
Ihu
The Church rents here in the High Street
Item of John Snygge by the year – £3 6s 8d.
Item of my lady Pernaunt – £4.
Item of Nicholas Jenys – 16s.
Item of Thomas Williams – 16s.
Item of the chantry priest – 6s 8d.
[Insert: Item the beer house – 20d.]
Item the house in Broad Street – £4.
Item of Master Blysse for a house in Small Street – 26s 8d.
Item of John Collys for a garden and a stable – 4s.
Item of Roger Felpot for a vault – 6s.
Item for a cellar John a Vaughn late held – 6s 8d.
Item of William Pewterer for a stable – 6s 8d.
Item for a loft over the store house – 2s.
Item of Master Reppe – 40s.
Item of John a London for a garden in the old market place – 2s.
Sum – £18 12d.

Sum the whole rent – £19 6s 4d.

Vacations
Item for Richard Erlys house in Lewins Mede – 12d.
Item of the master of the Tailors – 12s.
Item of Master Croft's house in St Peter's parish – 6d.
Item of the great house in Broad Street – £4.
Item of George Schyppard's house in Marsh Street – 2s.
Item for the allowance of a gutter in Jenat Polly's house – 20d.
Item for Nicholas Jenys' house – 9s.
Item for John Agham's chamber in the old house in Broad Street – 3s 4d.
Item for a beer house in the churchyard – 20d.
Sum – £5 11s 2d.

Sum the rents the vacations abated – £13 15s 2d.

fo 3
Ihu

The receipts of customable duties
In primis received on Palm Sunday – 2s 3d.
Item received on Sheer Thursday of *howselyng* [houselling] people – 14d.
Item received on Good Friday – 2s 6d.
Item received on Easter eve – 16d.
Item received on Easter day – 7s.
Item received of Newton of the Gyllows for his wife's grave – 6s 8d.
Item received of Harry Hyggyns and George Badram, Jesus proctors –
£3 15d.
Item received for stones that was broken down of the oven in Chamber's
house, ?tanner – 2s.
Item received of Leonard Osborne for his pew and his wife's – 16d.
Item received of George Badram for his maid's grave – 6s 8d.
Item received of Robert Poll for his wife's grave – 6s 8d.
Item of Master Ryppe for a fine of his house – 20s.
Item received of the masters of the parish at the last day of the account –
£5 3s.
Item received for Our Lady of Worcester – 10 ½d.
Sum – £11 2s 8 ½d.

Sum total of the receipts of rents and casualties, the vacations abated – £24
17s 10 ½d.

fo 3v
Ihu

The payments
In primis paid for a pottle of *malvasey* of our Palm Sunday – 8d.
Item for mending of a silver cruet – 8d.
Item for scouring stone and oil to the sexton – 3d.
Item to the sexton 2 lines for the cloth at the high altar and 14 yards of *lere*
– 8d.
Item for scouring – 2s.
Item for watching the sepulchre – 12d.
Item for besoms and coals – 4d.
Item for Wattyr, his wages – 20s.
Item to the raker – 8d.
Item to the clerk for Our Lady Mass – 4s.
Item for setting the board at the day of accounts – 2d.
Item for a cord for the sanctus bell – 4d.
Item for bearing banners in Rogation week to St Austin's – 4d.

Item delivered [to] John Goldsmith 2 ¾ oz of silver to make a chain for the cope for the sacrament and 3 pins for the oil fat. Received of the church's broken silver 1 ¾ ozs less a ?groat weight. Rest of mine own silver the which I set to it 1 oz and a groat weight – 3s 4d.

Item for a silver pin to the oil fat and making of all – 2s 4d.

Item for gilding a chalice – 3s 4d.

Item paid to the smith for 2 irons [added: on the high altar] – 12d.

Item paid for 2 new keys, 1 for the sexton's *bysset*, another for the ladders – 4d.

Item to the chancellor's clerk – 1d.

Item to Our Lady of Worcester – 8d.

Item for hanging up and taking down the Dance of Pauls – 2s.

Item for a fire pan – 8d.

Item for mending a glass window by the organs and the mending all the others about the church – 6s.

Item delivered to the sexton at divers times in nails, *rechokys*, pins for the altars and mending of the albs – 6d.

Item for candles on Christmas day – 4d.

Sum this side – 51s 8d.

fo 4

Ihu

Item for a paring shovel for the church – 7d.

Item for 2 *maylyng* cords for the paschal and the lamp before the high altar – 6d.

Item I paid William Clerk more than I gathered in the parish – 18s 10d.

Item paid to Wat for boarding the window in the organ loft – 16d.

Item paid for a pole and a cord that hang up the *scheen* – 3d.

[Hand and ink colour alters at this point] Item for wine at the Boar's Head when the masters took possession – 8d.

Item for a cord for the use of the lamp before the high altar, and a lamp and 2 staples, cost – 4d.

Item for staining the Lent cloth for the crucifix – 4d.

Item for mending the Lenten cross – 8d.

Item for gilting a foot to set the best cross in – 7s.

Item for [superscript: part] the organs – £3.

Item for the carriage of the same – 13s 4d.

Item for 2 cords for the bellows – 1d.

Item for hauling from Saint Peter's Cross – 2d.

Item for wire to mend 2 lamps, 1 in the Jesus aisle, another before [word illegible] the high altar and mending – 4d.

Item for mending and cleaning the tower and the church gutter – 4d.

Item paid for 41 quarts of lamp oil at 16d a quart – 13s 8d.[sic]

Item paid costs done upon Master Harvy for Master Rep's house – 37s 1d.

Item for rope the which cost me 3s 8d the which I have a bill – 2s.
Item for parchment paper and making of this book – 14d.
Item the sexton's wages – 16d.
Item for mending the chain of the book in the choir and a new [word illegible] – 2d.
Sum – £8 3s 11d.

Wax

Item 13 square tapers 74 lb; received them 105 lb; rest 32 lb.
Item the round light 18lb; received them 31 lb; rest 13 lb.
Item the paschal 18 lb; received 25 $\frac{1}{2}$ lb; rest 7 $\frac{1}{2}$ lb.
Item the font taper 2 $\frac{1}{4}$ lb; received 4 lb; rest 1 $\frac{3}{4}$ lb.
Item for making of the same wax – 3s 4d.
Item for 6 candle tapers – 6d.
Sum 54 $\frac{1}{4}$ lb at 9d a pound amounts to 40s 7 $\frac{1}{4}$d.
Sum – 44s 2 $\frac{1}{4}$d.
Item at All Hallows' tide 15 tapers weighing 18 lb. Received them 31 $\frac{3}{4}$ lb. Rest 13 $\frac{3}{4}$ lb. At 10d a pound – 11s 5 $\frac{1}{2}$d.
Sum the wax – 55s 11 $\frac{3}{4}$d.

Sum this side – £10 19s 10 $\frac{3}{4}$d.

fo 4v
Ihu
Costs on Corpus Christi day
Master Vicar good reward him
Item 6 priests – 2s.
Item for bearing 2 torches – 4d.
Item paid Watkin – 2d.
Item paid the clerk – 4d.
Item paid 9 children that sang – 9d.
Item for bearing 2 candlesticks – 2d.
Item 4 that bore up the copes – 4d.
Item for bearing 2 censers and the bell – 3d.
Item paid to 2 friars that bore the shrine – 12d.
Item for bearing the cross – 4d.
Item a pottle of wine – 4d.
Sum – 6s.

Memorandum this was done for W Newberry's mind when it was used.
Item to master vicar 16d for wax and dirige. Item 5 priests – 20d. The clerk – 10d. The bellman – 2d. Bread to poor – 2s. Offering – 1d. Sum – 6s 1d.

Memorandum that this is the third year that we be unpaid of the Tailors.

The obit of Thomas Fylour
Item Master vicar for dirige and wax – 12d.
Item 8 priests – 2s 8d.
Item the clerk – 14d.
Item Master vicar for the bede roll – 12d.
Item the bellman – 2d.
Item offering – 1d.
Item for 2 proctors for their attendance – 12d.
Item in bread to poor people – 5s.
Sum – 12s 1d.

The obit of Harry Chestre and Humfrey Harvy
Item for Master vicar for wax and dirige – 16d.
Item 5 priests – 20d.
Item the clerk – 12d.
Item the bellman – 4d.
Item bread to the poor, cost – 3s 8d.
Item paid the sexton – 2d.
Item offering – 1d.
Item 2 proctors for their attendance – 8d.
Sum – 8s 11d.

Sum this side – 27s.

fo 5
Ihu
Obit Thomas Spicer and Dame Maud his wife
Item to master vicar and 6 priests – 2s 4d.
Item to master vicar for 4 tapers for the hearse – 2s.
Item to master vicar for the bede roll – 4d.
Item to the clerk – 14d.
Item to the bell man – 4d.
Item to the sexton – 1d.
Item offering – 1d.
Item for bread to the poor – 3s.
Item for the 2 proctors for their labour – 12d.
Sum – 10s 4d.

The obit of all good doers
Item master vicar – 4d.
Item 6 priests – 18d.
Item for offering – 1d.

Item paid the clerk – 14d.

Item a quart *met* oil – 4d.

Item 3 bushels of meal – 4s.

Item 2 oz of saffron – 2s 6d.

Item for baking the cakes – 13d.

Item half dozen bread for the poor people – 6d.

Item for Gascon wine – 16d.

Item for osey, *melvesey* and rommey – 2s 8d.

Item paid for a dozen double ale and a dozen single – 3s 2d.

Sum – 18s 8d.

The obit of Humfrey Harvy

Item to master vicar or his deputy – 4d.

Item 6 priests – 2s.

Item to master vicar for his wax – 8d.

Item for offering – 1d.

Item to the clerk for his duty – 12d.

Item to the bellman – 4d.

Item for bread to the poor – 2s 8d.

Sum – 7s 1d.

Sum this side – 36s 1d.

fo 5v

Ihu

The repairing of the church roof and tiling the same

In primis for 3000 tile stones – 15s.

Item for 3000 laths at 4s 4d the thousand – 13s.

Item for hauling and for piling this and bearing in the laths in[to] the store house – 2s 10d.

Item to Hugh Carpenter's wife for ?studs and such stuff that the tiler occupied – 2s 9d.

Item 4 semes of boards at 8d a seme – 2s 8d.

Item paid for 2000 large lath nails – 2s 8d.

Item paid for 800 ?big stone nails – 2s 1 $\frac{1}{2}$d.

Item paid for 16 feet of gutter case – 2s $\frac{3}{4}$d.

Item 200 board nails at – 8d.

Item for 100 calf foot nails – 12d.

Item more in calf foot nails – 2 $\frac{1}{2}$d.

Item 7000 forrest nails at 10d the thousand – 5s 10d.

Item 2 dozen crests at – 10d.

Item 150 hatch nails – 4 $\frac{1}{2}$d.

Item for 38 bundles of ?moss – 3s 2d.

Item for 9000 tile pins at 3d the thousand – 2s 3d.

Item for 3 weys of lime, fine lime – 2s 6d.
Item 2 weys of coarse lime – 5d.
Item paid 2 tilers for 2 days', 6 ½d a day – 2s 2d.
Item the Monday before St Lawrence day paid 4 tilers 6 ½d a day – 2s 2d.
Item on Saint Lawrence's eve for 4 tilers three-quarters of a day, 4 ¾d apiece – 19d.
Item the Thursday after Saint Lawrence's day for 5 tilers – 2s 8 ½d.
Item the same day for an apprentice – 5 ½d.
Item the Friday following, 5 tilers – 2s 8 ½d.
Item an apprentice – 5 ½d.
Item the Saturday for 5 tilers – 16 ¼d.
Item this apprentice for half a day – 2 ¾d.
Item the Tuesday after the Assumption of Our Lady, 4 tilers – 2s 2d.
Item 2 apprentices at 5 ½d a day – 11d.
Item the Monday following, 4 tilers – 2s 2d.
Item 2 apprentices – 11d.
Item Thursday, the same 4 tilers – 2s 2d.
Item 2 apprentices – 11d.
Item the Friday, 4 tilers – 2s 2d.
Item 2 apprentices – 11d.
Item the Saturday, 4 tilers, half a day – 13d.
Item 2 apprentices – 5 ½d.
Item the next week following, 4 tilers, 5 days' – 10s 10d.
Item 2 apprentices, 5 days' – 4s 7d.
Item paid to a tiler and his man and his apprentice, the last day – 18d.
Item for hauling away the rubble that was left of stones and laths – 2s 6d.
Item paid to the plumber for 6 lb of solder and 4 *skarys* – 2s 3 ½d.
Sum this side – £5 9s 10 ½d.

fo 6
Ihu
Reparations of John Snygg's house
Item paid for 15 feet of gutter case – 23d.
Item 2 studs – 4d.
Item a load of tile stones – 16d.
Item for hauling – 2d.
Item a seme of boards – 8d.
Item in board nails, calf-foot nails and hatch nails – 9d.
Item lath nails 1000 and a pennyworth – 11d.
Item paid to a tiler for 4 days', 5 ½d a day – 22d.
Item his man for 4 days' – 20d.
Item his apprentice 4 days' – 16d.
Sum – 10s 10d.

To the same house the old lead of a gutter weighing 1 $\frac{1}{2}$ hundredweights and 20 lb; received of new lead 2 $\frac{1}{2}$ hundredweights and 21 lb; rest 1 hundredweight and 1 lb – 5s $\frac{1}{2}$d.

Item 3 $\frac{1}{4}$ lb of solder at – 9 $\frac{1}{2}$d.

Item the workmanship of 3 *skarys* – 8d.

Received this and the casting of this lead before rehearsed, the which is 18d the casting. So amounts the whole – 8s.

Memorandum that I John Mauncell received this 8s in part payment of a more sum that the said W [William Plumber] owed unto the church.

Memorandum I paid him for all other things that he did in that here save only 8s.

My lady Pernaunt

Item paid for the mending of the gutter between my lady and me 2s 6d, the our church part came to – 15d.

Sum this side the plumber's work except – 12s 2d.

fo 6v

Ihu

The church door[1]

Item 3 boards – 12d.

Item a stud – 1d.

Item board nails – 2d.

Item for making 6 ?iron *pekes* and mending 2 twists – 6d.

Item a new lock and a key – 6d.

Item for 11 lb of new lead and the casting – 10d.

Item for making a key and mending another – 3d.

Item for making the door – 6d.

Sum – 3s 10d.

Memorandum about 40 ells of camas, cost 20s to *holle the hows be cawsseyt was met for hortyng of the selling.*

Item for allowance for giving money and expenses to the tenants when I received the rent – 6s.

[Rest of account in different hand] Sum this side – 9s 10d.

Sum total of all payments – £23 6s 6 $\frac{1}{2}$d.

So rest clear to the church of this account – 31s 4 $\frac{1}{4}$d.

The which sum the said accountant has delivered to the *parisshons* the day of his account, 26 April 1520, and so he is clearly discharged.

Memorandum that the said accountant is allowed of the said sum 13s 2 $\frac{3}{4}$d for arrearage of Halleway's chantry as it appears in the book of accounts of the said chantry. So rests clear to the church 18s 2d, which sum was delivered to Robert Hanworth proctor the said day and time in the presence of the *parisshons*.

---

[1] The following section is repeated, written 'in rough', on the back page of the booklet.

fo 7

Memorandum that William Plumber received of Thomas Pacye and
Thomas Barbor proctors in the year of Our Lord God 1513 in lead 16 $\frac{1}{4}$
hundredweights and 21 lb whereof they received for Robert Cook's
kitchen in Small Street 6 hundredweights of lead less 12lb.
So rested that year in his hands 10 $\frac{1}{2}$ hundredweights and 5 lb.
Of the which John Mawnsell proctor received in his year. A.D. 1519 for
John Snygge's house as it appears in this book before in lead and in his
workmanship – 8s.

[1521]

fo 1

The Church Book
[Scored: Harry Hichyns] 1521
Robert Hamworth

fo 2

Jesus Maria. Omnes Sancti orate pro nobis
18th day of April AD 1521.
The accounts of Robert Hanworth and Harry Hychyns proctors of the
parish church of All Saints in Bristol for their receipts of the rents with
other profits belonging to the same church for a whole year, that is to say
from the feast of the Assumption of Our Lady in the year of Our Lord God
1520 unto the same feast of Our Lady in the year of Our Lord God 1521.
Roger Daws being mayor; William Shipman and Robert Avyntree sheriffs.

The rent assize
In primis the tenement that Jone Powll holds for a gutter – 3s 4d.
Item of the tenement that Thomas Ven holds by All Hallows pipe – 4s.
Item of the tenement that John Watson holds for his back door – 2s 6d.
Item of a tenement of Richard Erle in Lewins Mede [superscript: Christ
Church] – 12d.
Item of the master and fellowship of the Tailors for a tenement in Baldwin
Street – 12s.
Item of a tenement of Master Crofte in St Peter's parish – 6d.
Item of a tenement of Master Sheparde in Marsh Street – 2s.
Sum – 25s 4d.

Sum this side – 25s 4d.

fo 2v
The rents belonging to the church by the year.

In primis of the tenement that John Snygge holds – £3 6s 8d.
Item of the tenement that my lady Pernaunt holds – £4.
Item of the tenement that John Rope holds – 40s.
Item of the tenement that Nicholas Jenyns holds – 16s.
Item of the tenement that Thomas Williams holds – 16s.
Item of the tenement that Sir John Cooke holds – 6s 8d.
Item of the beer house in the churchyard – 20d.
Item of the tenement that Master Blisse holds in Small Street – 26s 8d.
Item of the great tenement in Broad Street – £4.
Item of a stable and a garden that John Colle holds in the same house – 4s.
Item of a vault in the said house that Roger Felpot holds – 6s.
Item of a loft over the same vault that John Mawncell holds – 6s 8d.
Item of a stable in the same house that William Eascrean pewterer holds – 6s 8d.
Item of a loft over our store house there that the same William holds – 2s.
Item of a garden that John of London holds in the old market place – 2s.
Sum – £18 12d.

Sum the whole rents – £19 6s 4d.

fo 3
The vacations and decays
In primis of the tenement of Richard Erle in Lewins Mede – 12d.
Item of the master and the fellowship of the Tailors for a tenement in Baldwin Street – 12s.
Item of a tenement of Master Crofte in St Peter's parish – 6d.
Item of the great house in Broad Street – £4.
Item of the loft over the vault in the same house that John Mawncell holds – 20d.
Item for 3 quarters vacation of the same loft – 3s 9d.
Item of the tenement of Master Shephard in Marsh Street – 2s.
Item of the gutter in Jone Powll's house – 20d.
Item of the tenement that Nicholas Jenyns late held – 2s.
Item of the beer house in the churchyard – 20d.
Sum – £5 6s 3d.

Sum the rents, the vacations abated – £14 1d.

fo 3v
The receipts of customable duties belonging to the church
In primis on Palm Sunday – 2s 3d.
Item on Shere Thursday – 16d.
Item on Good Friday to the repairs of the jewels – 23d.
Item on Easter eve – 16d.

Item on Easter day for duty of them that were houselled – 5s 10d.
Item for Our Lady of Worcester – 16d.
Item received the day of the account – 18s 2d.
Item received of Master vicar and of Master Pacy of that they gathered towards the new organs – 50s.
Item received of George Badram for the brotherhood of Jesus – 40s.
Item received of Wate the sexton for old timber – 2s.
Item of Sir John Carleon for his father's grave – 3s 4d.
Item of William Eyrworth for his wife's pew – 8d.
Sum – £6 8s 2d.

Sum total of the receipts of rents and casualties, the vacations abated – £20 8s 3d.

fo 4
Payments that yearly be accustomed and other casualties that grow in ornaments or jewels of the church.
In primis a pottle of osey on Palm Sunday – 6d.
Item to the raker – 8d.
Item for watching the sepulchre – 12d.
Item for coals – 2 ½d.
Item for besoms – 2d.
Item for washing the church stuff – 2s.
Item for oil and stone to scour – 3d.
Item for scouring – 2s.
Item for reward to tenants at their payments – 12d.
Item to the clerk for his whole year's wage more than the taxation of the *parishons* amounts – 17s 5d.
Item to Water the sexton for his year's wage – 20s.
Item for hanging up and taking down the Dance of Pauls – 2s.
Item to my lady Pernaunt for 48 quarts of oil as it appears before at 4d the quart, amount the whole – 16s.
Item of Our Lady of Worcester's money – 8d.
Item to the clerk for keeping Our Lady Mass in Lent – 4s.
Item for costs to the church on the day of account at supper – 2s 4d.
Item for bearing the banners in Rogation week – 4d.
Item to Roger Pickring for his wage – 16d.
Item for making the book of accounts – 20d.
Sum – £3 13s 6 ½d.

fo 4v
Payments for the church
In primis for 2 little wheels for the lamp in the choir – 20d.
Item for 2 pieces of lead to the new organs using 42 lb – 2s 4d.

Item for making 2 new forms in the choir for children and for a new desk – 22d.

Item paid for a towel of silk to bear the oil vat at Easter – 16d.

Item for mending the best pax – 4d.

Item for a new bottom of lead to the holy water stock at the south door – 9d.

Item to Roger the sexton for his attendance at the accounts – 4d.

Item to Wate the sexton for making the foot of the image that St George stands upon – 9d.

Item paid for 8 ½ ells of Holland for a surplice to the clerk at 7 ½d the ell, the whole amounts – 5s 4d.

Item for making the same surplice – 2s.

Item for a surplice to Water the sexton – 3s 4d.

Item for a new bond for the same surplice – 4d.

Item for 4 keys to the chest that Master Pacye gave to the church – 8d.

Item for nails to the same – ½d.

Item for a board to make a *bissett* in the same chest – 2d.

Item more for nails to the same *bissett* – 1d.

Item for workmanship of the *bissett* – 4d.

Item to 3 men that did help the chest up into the tower – 3d.

Item to Wate the sexton for bringing the chest through the high loft into the treasure house – 3d.

Item for nails to nail the boards of the loft again – 1d.

Item to John Plumber for 5 *scares* in the lead upon the tower and over the charnel house – 10d.

Item for 9 lb of solder to the same – 2s 3d.

Sum this side – 25s 3 ½d.

fo 5

Payments for the church

Item to 3 masons for mending the door by the Jesus altar – 19 ½d.

Item for half a wey of lime – 5d.

Item for a *trene* shovel – 1 ½d.

Item for *turing* [?turning] the cords of the new organs and for a plank and a stool for the same – 9d.

Item to the turner for 2 *shevers* to the organs – 1 ½d.

Item for the making of a *quietance* [?quittance] to my lady Pernaunt for money that she paid to the church – 2d.

Item for a plank of wainscot to make a new wheel to the first bell – 12d.

Item for nails to the same – 1d.

Item for mending iron work to the wheel – 1d.

Item to Wate the sexton for workmanship on the same wheel for 2 ½ days' – 15d.

Item for a board to make the door by the Jesus altar – 12d.

Item for 50 board nails – 2d.

Item for a lock and a key to the same door – 8d.

Item for nails to the same – 1d.

Item for making 2 hinges – 2d.

Item to Wate the sexton for 1 ½ days' work about the same door – 9 ½d.

Item paid for half a seme of welsh board [for] the bottom of the new organs – 4d.

Item for 3 lb of lead to mend a pipe in Thomas William's house – 2d.

Item for wood to heat the plumber's irons – 1d.

Item to the chancellor and his officers for his writing ?sealed concerning the residence of the master of the Kalendars – 12s.

Item for stuff and making of a new *beere* – 2s 8d.

Item for a cord to the paschal – 4d.

Item for Master Hervy's costs when he brought the evidence of John Rep's house – 4s 4d.

Item for a cover of canvas to St Thomas's altar – 6d.

Item for candles and holly – 4d.

Item to Master Hervy at his father's obit, a pottle of wine – 4d.

Sum this side – 29s 6 ½d.

fo 5v

Payments on Corpus Christi day

In primis to Master vicar – nil

Item to 5 priests wearing copes – 20d.

Item to 2 friars for bearing the shrine – 12d.

Item to them that did wear tunicles – 4d.

Item for bearing the best cross – 4d.

Item to the clerk and 6 singing children – 10d.

Item to Wate the sexton – 2d.

Item to 9 children bearing up the copes, censers, candlesticks and the bell – 9d.

Item for bearing 2 torches – 4d.

Item for a pottle of Gascon wine in the Mersh – 4d.

Item for packthread to fasten the jewels in the shrine – ½d.

Item for a pair of gloves to the sexton to dress the shrine – 1d.

Sum – 5s 10 ½d.

Wax for the church the whole year

In primis delivered to John Reynald, waxmaker, 13 square tapers weighing 76 lb; received 100 lb; so rests in new wax 24 lb.

Item delivered the paschal weighing 23lb; received 25 ½ lb; so rests in new wax 2 ½ lb.

Item delivered 15 round tapers weighing 18 lb; received 31 lb; so rests in new wax 13 lb.

Item delivered the font taper weighing 3 lb; received 4 lb; so rests in new wax 1 lb.

Also delivered against our Dedication day 15 round tapers weighing 16 lb; received 32 lb; so rests in new wax 16 lb.

So amounts all the new wax for the whole year 56 ½ lb at 10d every lb, amount the whole – 47s 1d.

Item for making all the said wax – 3s 4d.

Item for 6 prickets of wax for the angels – 6d.

Item for a link of torch to go with the sacrament in visitation – 9d.

Sum – 51s 8d.

Sum this side – 57s 6 ½d.

fo 6

The obit of William Newbery held in this church the 10th day of May

[Bracketed against the entries for this obit are the words *Vacat nunc*:]

In primis to Master vicar for dirige and wax – 16d.

Item to 5 priests – 20d.

Item to the clerk for ringing and his labour – 10d.

Item to the bellman – 2d.

Item in bread to poor people – 2s.

Item in offering at Mass – 1d.

Sum – 6s 1d.

Memorandum that this is the fourth year that we have lacked our payment of the Tailors.

The obit of Thomas Fylour and Agnes his wife held the 20th day of November

In primis to Master vicar for wax – 12d.

Item to 8 priests – 2s 8d.

Item to Master vicar for the bede roll – 12d.

Item to the clerk for his labour and for ringing – 14d.

Item to the bellman – 2d.

Item in offering at Mass – 1d.

Item to the proctors for their intendance – 12d.

Item in bread to poor people – 5s.

Item to the sexton to lay the hearse – 2d.

Sum – 12s 3d.

Sum this side – 12s 3d.

fo 6v

The obit of Harry Chestre and Humfrey Hervy, their wives with their other friends, held the 14th day of February

In primis to Master vicar – 12d.
Item to 6 priests – 2s.
Item to the clerk – 12d.
Item to the bellman – 4d.
Item in offering at Mass – 1d.
Item to the proctors – 8d.
Item to the sexton – 2d.
Item to the prisoners of Newgate in bread – 20d.
Item to our almshouse in bread – 4d.
Item to the lazar house at Bright bowe in bread – 4d.
Item to the almshouse in the Long Rowe in bread – 4d.
Sum – 7s 11d.

The obit of Thomas Spicer and Dame Maud his wife, held the 15th day of February
In primis to Master vicar and to 6 priests – 2s 4d.
Item to Master vicar for 4 tapers – 2s.
Item to Master vicar for the bede roll – 4d.
Item to the clerk – 14d.
Item to the 2 proctors for their intendance – 12d.
Item to the bellman – 4d.
Item to the sexton – 1d.
Item in offering at Mass – 1d.
Item in bread to poor people – 3s.
Sum – 10s 4d.

Sum this side – 18s 3d.

fo 7
The obit of good doers
In primis to Master vicar – 4d.
Item to 4 priests, every priest 3d – 12d.
Item in offering at Mass – 1d.
Item to the clerk – 14d.
Item for 3 bushels of wheat – 5s 3d.
Item for grinding the wheat – 3d.
Item for 2 oz of saffron – 20d.
Item for a quart of *mete* oil – 6d.
Item for malvesey, osey and romeney – 17 $\frac{1}{2}$d.
Item for Gascon wine – 2s.
Item for bread – 6d.
Item for 2 dozen of double ale – 4s.
Item for baking the cake – 16d.
Sum – 19s 6 $\frac{1}{2}$d.

The second obit of Harry Chestre and Humfry Hervy *cum ?et ut supra*
['with those above'] held the 4th day of March
In primis to Master vicar – 12d.
Item to 6 priests – 2s.
Item to the clerk – 12d.
Item to the bellman – 4d.
Item in offering at Mass – 1d.
Item to the proctors – 8d.
Item to the sexton – 2d.
Item to the prisoners of Newgate in bread – 20d.
Item to our almshouse in bread – 4d.
Item to the lazar house at Bright bow in bread – 4d.
Item to the almshouse in the Long Row in bread – 4d.
Sum – 7s 11d.

Sum this side – 27s 5 $\frac{1}{2}$d.

fo 7v
Repairs in Sir John Coke's house
In primis paid for half a load of paving stone – 7d.
Item for hauling the same stones – 1d.
Item for a board to the same work – 2d.
Item for nails – $\frac{1}{2}$d.
Item for 2 loads of clay – 4d.
Item for a load of sand – 1d.
Item 4 sacks of lime – 4d.
Item paid to the paviour for his handiwork – 17d.
Item to a carpenter for a day's work mending the stair – 6d.
Item for nails to the same stair – 4d.
Item for other repairs a *?mister* to remain in the house – 20d.
Sum – 5s 6 $\frac{1}{2}$d.

John Repe's house
Item paid for a board to mend the pentys and for workmanship of the same
– 8d.
Sum – 8d.

Item John Snygge's house
Item paid for mending the chimney – 4d.
Sum – 4d.

Sum this side – 6s 6 $\frac{1}{2}$d.
Sum total of payments this year – £12 10s 5d.

fo 8
So rests clear to the church of this account – £7 17s 10d.
Which sum the said accountant delivered to the *parisshons* the day of his
account, the 18th day of April in the year of Our Lord God 1521. So he is
clearly discharged.

Memorandum Master Pacy has paid the day of this account to the church
for certain wood that he had of Arnold Stowte – 5s.
Memorandum also that there remains of the church lead in William
Plumber's hand 10 $\frac{1}{2}$ hundredweights and 5 lb as it appears more plainly in
John Mawncell's book of account.
Memorandum that the day of this account Harry Hickyns received of the
parisshons – £3 10s 6d, he to bring it in again at the day of his accounts.
Memorandum also that there remains in Thomas Snygge's hands of his
father's legacy £5 10s as appears in the testament, which is now contented
and paid, as it appears in the account of [sic].

[1522]

fo 1
The Church Book
Anno Domini 1522
Harry Hickyns

fo 2
Jesus Maria
The accounts of Harry Hickyns and Jerome Grene proctors of the parish
church of All Saints', Bristol, for their receipts of the rents with other
profits belonging to the same church for a whole year, that is to say from
the feast of the Annunciation of Our Lady in the year of Our Lord God
1521 unto the same feast of Our Lady in the year of Our Lord God 1522,
John Shipman being mayor, Robert Eliott and Roger Cooke sheriffs.

The rent of assize
In primis of the tenement that Jone Powll holds for a gutter – 3s 4d.
Item of the tenement that Thomas Ven late held by All Hallows pipe – 4s.
Item of the tenement that John Watson holds for his back door – 2s 6d.
Item of Christ Church for a tenement of Richard Erle in Lewins Mede –
12d.
Item of the master and fellowship of the Tailors for a tenement in Baldwin
Street – 12s.
Item of a tenement of Master Crofte in St Peter's parish – 6d.

Item of a tenement of Master Shepherde in Marsh Street – 2s.
Sum – 25s 4d.

Sum – 25s 4d.

fo 2v
The rents belonging to the church by the year
In primis of the tenement that John Hoper holds – £3 6s 8d.
Item of the same John Hoper for part of the tenement belonging to the Abbey of Tewkesbury – 53s 4d.
Item of the tenement that my lady Pernaunt holds – £4.
Item of the tenement that John Rope holds – 40s.
Item of the tenement that Nicholas Jenyns holds – 16s.
Item of the tenement that Andrew Page holds – 16s.
Item of the tenement that Sir John Cooke holds – 6s 8d.
Item of the beer house in the churchyard – 20d.
Item of the tenement that Thomas Marmen holds in Small Street – 26s 8d.
Item of the great tenement in Broad Street – £4.
Item of a stable and a garden that Master Townclerk holds in the same house – 4s.
Item of a vault there that Roger Filpott holds – 6s.
Item of a loft over the same vault that John Mawncell holds – 6s 8d.
Item of a stable there that William Eascran holds – 6s 8d.
Item of a loft over our store house there that the same William holds – 2s.
Item of a garden in the market place that John of London late held – 2s.
Sum – £20 14s 4d.

Sum the whole rents – £21 19s 8d.

fo 3
The defaults, vacations and decays
In primis of Richard Erle's tenement in Lewins Mead – 12d.
Item of the master and fellowship of the Tailors for the tenement in Baldwin Street – 12s.
Item of a tenement of Master Crofte in St Peter's parish – 6d.
Item of the great house in Broad Street – £4.
Item of the loft over the vault there that John Mawncell holds – 20d.
Item of the tenement of Master Shepherde in Mersh Street – 2s.
Item of the gutter in Joan Powll's house – 20d.
Item of the tenement that Andrew Page holds – 2s.
Item of the beer house in the church yard – 20d.
Item of John Snygge [superscript: John Hoper's] house for a quarter – 16s 8d.
Item of the part of the same tenement that belongs to the Abbot and

convent of Tewkesbury – 40s.
Item of the tenement that Andrew Page holds, a quarter – 3s 6d.
Sum – £8 2s 8d.

Sum the rents, the vacations abated – £13 17s.

fo 3v
Receipts of customable duties belonging yearly to the church
In primis of Palm Sunday – 2s 6d.
Item on Shere Thursday – 6d.
Item on Good Friday to the reparations of the jewels – 2s 1d.
Item on Easter eve of them that were houselled – 19d.
Item on Easter day of them that were houselled – 7s.
Item to Our Lady of Worcester – 21d.
Item received the last day of accounts of the church money – £3 10s 6d.
Item received of Andrew Elisworthye for the brotherhood of Jesus – 47s.
Item received of William Eireworth for the fine of his house – £6 13s 4d.
Item of John Hoper and his wife for their pews – 20d.
Item of Symon Hancok and his wife for their pews – 16d.
Item of William Webly and his wife for their pews – 16d.
Item of Wat Fillips and his wife for their pews – 12d.
Sum – £13 11s 7d.

Sum total of the receipts of rents and casualties, the vacations abated –
£27 8s 7d

fo 4
Payments that yearly be accustomed and other and other casualties that
grow in ornaments and jewels of the church
In primis for a pottle of osey on Palm Sunday – 6d.
Item to the raker – 8d.
Item for watching the sepulchre – 12d.
Item for coals – 2 ½d.
Item for besoms – 2d.
Item for washing the church stuff – 2s.
Item for reward to tenants at their payment – 12d.
Item to Wat the sexton for his year's wages – 20s.
Item for hanging and taking down the Dance of Pauls – 2s.
Item to Our Lady of Worcester – 8d.
Item to the clerk for keeping Our Lady Mass in Lent – 4s.
Item towards the cost of our supper on the day of accounts – 2s 4d.
Item for bearing the banners in Rogation week – 4d.
Item to Roger Pyckring for his wage – 16d.
Item for making the book of accounts – 20d.

Item for scouring – 2s.
Item for oil and stone – 3d.
Item to the clerk for his year's wages more than the taxation of the parish – 16s 8d.
Sum – 56s 9 ½d.
Item to Mistress Hervy for her part of the tenement that John Hoper holds, for a quarter's rent – 10s.
Sum – 10s.

Sum this side – £3 6s 9 ½d.

fo 4v
Payments for the church
In primis for a pole to make a ladder for the church – 8d.
Item for making the same ladder – 9d.
Item for hooks and nails to the sepulchre – 1d.
Item to the under sexton for his attendance in the day of accounts – 4d.
Item for a skin to make *lyfte* to the cover of the shrine – 2d.
Item for linen cloth to the same – ½d.
Item for 450 card nails to the same – 4 ½d.
Item for mending the same cover – 6d.
Item for making the great iron bar in the rood loft weighing 88 lb, at ½d the pound, the workmanship amounts – 3s 6d.
Item for ½ a hundredweight of new iron to perform the same bar with 2 standards of iron to stay him – 2s 6d.
Item for workmanship of the same half hundredweight of iron, at ½d the lb, amounts – 2s 4d.
Item to Mistress Hervy for the years of Tewkesbury's [word illegible] in John Hoper's house – £3.
Item for hallowing 2 corporases – 8d.
Item for 10 ells and half a yard of Holland at 10d the ell, amounts – 8s 8d.
Item for making the same cloth in a surplice for master vicar – 3s 4d.
Item to Nicholas Adams for mending the *vice* of the best candlestick – 12d.
Item for half a wey of lime to the south aisle – 5d.
Item to a tiler for 3 ½ days' – 22 ½d.
Item to a labourer for 3 ½ days' – 14d.
Item for a rope to the paschal and another rope to the morrow mass bell – 19d.
Item to my lady Pernaunt for lamp oil as it appears by a ?score – 10s.
Item for a key to the churchyard door – 4d.
Item for a hook of iron to hang the new ladder – 4d.
Sum – £5 7 ½d.

fo 5

Payments on Corpus Christi day
Item paid to Master vicar – nil
Item to 5 priests wearing copes – 20d.
Item to 2 friars bearing the shrine – 12d.
Item to 2 deacons – 4d.
Item for bearing the cross – 4d.
Item to the clerk and 6 singing children – 11d.
Item to Wat the sexton – 2d.
Item to 11 children to bear up copes with others – 11d.
Item for bearing 2 torches – 4d.
Item for a pottle of claret wine – 4d.
Item for a pair of gloves to the under sexton – 1d.
Sum – 6s 1d.

Wax for the church the whole year
In primis delivered to John Reynold, waxmaker, 13 square tapers
weighing 80 lb; received in new [sic] wax 111 lb; so amounts in new wax
31 lb.
Item delivered the paschal weighing 21 $\frac{1}{2}$ lb; received 27 $\frac{3}{4}$ lb; so amounts
in new wax 6 $\frac{1}{4}$ lb.
Delivered 15 round tapers weighing 29 lb; received 33 lb; so amounts in
new wax 4 lb.
Delivered the font taper weighing 2 $\frac{1}{2}$ lb; received 4 $\frac{1}{4}$ lb; so amounts in
new wax 1 $\frac{3}{4}$ lb.
Received 6 tapers for the angels over the sepulchre weighing $\frac{3}{4}$ of a lb.
Delivered against our Dedication day in old wax 15 round tapers weighing
20 lb; received 32 lb; so amounts in new wax 12 lb.
So amounts all the new wax for the whole year – 55 $\frac{3}{4}$ lb.
At 9 $\frac{3}{4}$d every pound, amounts to – 45s 5 $\frac{3}{4}$d.
Item paid for making the same wax for all the year – 3s 4d.
Sum – 48s 9 $\frac{3}{4}$d.

Sum this side – 54s 10 $\frac{3}{4}$d.

fo 5v

The obit of William Newbery held in the church the 10th day of May
[Bracketed against the entries in margin the words *vacat nunc*]
In primis to master vicar for dirige and wax – 16d.
Item to 5 priests – 20d.
Item to the clerk for the bells and his labour – 10d.
Item to the bellman – 2d.
Item in bread to poor people – 2s.
Item in offering at Mass – 1d.

Sum – 6s 1d.

Memorandum that this is the fifth year that we have lacked our payment of the Tailors.

The obit of Thomas Fylour and Agnes his wife held the 20th day of November
In primis to Master vicar for wax – 12d.
Item to 8 priests – 2s 8d.
Item to Master vicar for the bede roll – 12d.
Item to the clerk for the bells and for his labour – 14d.
Item to the bellman – 2d.
Item in offering at Mass – 1d.
Item to the proctors for their labour and intendance – 12d.
Item in bread to poor people – 5s.
Item to the undersexton for laying the hearse – 2d.
Sum – 12s 3d.

Sum this side – 12s 3d.

fo 6
The obit of Harry Chestre and Humphrey Hervey, their wives with other friends, held the 14th day of February
In primis to Master vicar – 12d.
Item to 6 priests – 2s.
Item to the clerk – 12d.
Item to the bellman – 4d.
Item in offerings at Mass – 1d.
Item to the proctors – 8d.
Item to the sexton – 2d.
Item to the prisoners of Newgate in Bristol – 20d.
Item to our almshouse in bread – 4d.
Item to the lazar house at Bright bowe – 4d.
Item to the almshouse in the Long Rowe in bread – 4d.
Sum – 7s 11d.

The obit of Thomas Spicer and Dame Maud his wife, held the 15th day of February
In primis to Master vicar and 6 priests – 2s 4d.
Item to Master vicar for 4 tapers – 2s.
Item to Master vicar for the bede roll – 4d.
Item to the clerk – 14d.
Item to the proctors – 12d.
Item to the bellman – 4d.
Item to the sexton – 1d.

Item in offering at Mass – 1d.
Item in bread to poor people – 3s.
Sum – 10s 4d.

Sum this side – 18s 3d.

fo 6v
The obit of good doers
In primis to Master vicar – 4d.
Item to 4 priests, every priest 3d – 12d.
Item in offering at Mass – 1d.
Item to the clerk – 14d.
Item for 3 bushels of wheat at 23d the bushel, amounts – 5s 9d.
Item for the grinding – 3d.
Item for 2 oz of saffron – 20d.
Item for a quart of *mete* oil – 6d.
Item in malvesey and osey – 2s 8d.
Item for 3 pottles of claret wine – 15d.
Item for *barme* – 3d.
Item in bread – 6d.
Item for 2 dozen of double ale – 4s.
Item for baking the cakes – 16d.
Sum – 20s 9d.

The second obit of Harry Chestre and Humphrey Hervy, held the 4th day
of March
In primis to Master vicar – 12d.
Item to 6 priests – 2s.
Item to the clerk – 12d.
Item to the bellman – 4d.
Item in offering at Mass – 1d.
Item to the proctors – 8d.
Item to the sexton – 2d.
Item to the prisoners of Newgate in bread – 20d.
Item in bread to our almshouse – 4d.
Item to the lazar house of Bright bowe – 4d.
Item to the almshouse in the Long Row in bread – 4d.
Sum – 7s 11d.

Sum this side – 28s 9d.

fo 7
Reparations
The house that Thomas Marmyn dwells in in Small Street

In primis paid for 11 semes of Welsh board at 5d the seme, amounts – 4s 2d.

Item for 300 board nails – 13 $\frac{1}{2}$d.

Item for 300 hatch nails – 9d.

Item for 2 studs – 4d.

Item to a carpenter for 3 $\frac{1}{2}$ days' at 6 $\frac{1}{2}$d the day, amounts – 22 $\frac{1}{2}$d.

Item for a stud, a board and legs for a window – 3d.

Item for hinges and hooks to the same – 3d.

Item for 50 board nails – 2 $\frac{1}{2}$d.

Item for 50 hatch nails – 1 $\frac{1}{2}$d.

Item a seme of Welsh board – 5d.

Item for 50 hatch nails – 1 $\frac{1}{2}$d.

Item to a carpenter for 4 days' – 2s 2d.

Item for half a wey of lime – 5d.

Item for lath nails – 2d.

Item to a labourer for cleaning the house – 2d.

Item for hauling 3 vats of rubble – 3d.

Item for another half wey of lime – 5d.

Item for 2 loads of sand – 2d.

Item for 2 loads of ?pendant – 2s 4d.

Item for hauling them – 4d.

Item for 1 $\frac{1}{2}$ days' to a mason – 9 $\frac{1}{2}$d.

Item to a labourer for 1 $\frac{1}{2}$ days' – 6d.

Item for 2 $\frac{1}{2}$ weys of lime – 2s 1d.

Item to a mason for 3 days' work – 19 $\frac{1}{2}$d.

Item to a labourer for 3 days' work – 12d.

Item in nails – 1d.

Item for 500 lath nails – 6d.

Item for hair – $\frac{1}{2}$d.

Item to a tiler to [word illegible] hair lime for 1 $\frac{1}{2}$ days – 9d.

Item for 100 laths – 6d.

Sum this side – 23s 11 $\frac{1}{2}$d.

fo 7v

Reparations upon Thomas Marmen's house

Item for a load of tile stones – 14d.

Item for hauling them – 2d.

Item for 4 crests – 2d.

Item for 3 $\frac{3}{4}$ lb of solder for our own gutter – 11d.

Item for soldering a pipe in the kitchen and a skare – 6d.

Item for wood – 1d.

Item for 3 $\frac{3}{4}$ lb of solder for the *parteable* gutter and for soldering 3 *skares* – 17d.

Item for wood – 1d.

Item to a tiler for 3 ½ days' at 6 ½d the day – 22 ½d.
Item for 8 ½ foot of new glass at 6d the foot – 4s 3d.
Item for mending the same windows – 6d.
Item for hauling a load of stones to the store house – 1d.
Item for hauling of 2 vats of rubble – 2d.
Item to a labourer to clean the house and fill the vats – 3d.
Sum – 11s 7 ½d.

Sum total the reparations of the same house – 35s 7d.

fo 8
Reparations done upon the houses that Nicholas Jenyns and Andrew Page hold
In primis for a seme of Welsh board for the windows in the shop – 6d.
Item for 100 board nails – 4 ½d.
Item for 100 hatch nails – 3d.
Item for hasps and staples to the windows – 2 ½d.
Item for a weather board of oak – 10d.
Item for 4 semes of Welsh board at 6d the seme – 2s.
Item for 2 elm boards for legs and to mend other ?faults – 8d.
Item for 200 board nails and 300 hatch nails – 18d.
Item to a carpenter for 2 days' work – 13d.
Item for calf-foot nails – 3d.
Item for a seme of Welsh board – 6d.
Item to 3 carpenters for a day's work – 19 ½d.
Item for 200 lath nails – 2 ½d.
Item for half a wey of lime – 5d.
Item for hair – ½d.
Item to a tiler for his day's work – 6 ½d.
Sum – 11s.

Reparations on the charnel house
Item paid for paving stones and ?pendant – 15d.
Item for hauling – 2d.
Item to a mason for 2 days' work – 13d.
Item to a labourer a day and a half – 6d.
Sum – 3s.

Sum this side – 14s.

fo 8v
Reparations done upon John Rep's house
In primis to a mason for mending a gutter – 5d.
Item for lime – 2d.

Item for a load of paving stones for the kitchen with hauling them – 16d.
Item for 53 feet of oak boards for the floor – 14d.
Item for 100 board nails – 4 ½d.
Item for 3 loads of clay and a load of sand – 7d.
Item for ½ a wey of lime – 5d.
Item to a mason for 2 days' work – 13d.
Item to a labourer for 2 days' – 8d.
Item for a load of clay and a load of sand – 3d.
Item for an oaken board for the stair – 2d.
Item to a mason for 1 ½ days' work – 9 ½d.
Item to a labourer for a day's work – 4d.
Item for casting 1 hundredweight and 2 lb of lead – 6d.
Item for wood – 1d.
Item for a load of *pendante* – 14d.
Item for hauling them – 2d.
Item for free stones to the hearth – 16d.
Item for hauling – 1d.
Item for a wey of lime – 10d.
Item for hatch nails – ½d.
Item for a load of sand – 1d.
Item to a mason for 2 ½ days' – 16d.
Item to a labourer for 2 ½ days' – 10d.
Item for 1 ½ weys of lime at the turning of the stairs – 15d.
Item to a mason for 2 days' work – 13d.
Sum – 16s 6 ½d.

Sum this side – 16s 6 ½d.

fo 9
Reparations on the house that John Hoper holds
In primis for a wey of lime – 10d.
Item for hair – ½d.
Item for a load of tile stones – 14d.
Item for hauling – 2d.
Item for soldering 2 *scaris* that are partible between my lady Pernaunt and
us, for our part with the solder – 4 ½d.
Item to a tiler for 5 ½ days' at 6 ½d the day – 2s 11 ½d.
Item to his servant for 2 ½ days' at 5d the day – 12 ½d.
Item for 100 board nails – 4 ½d.
Item for ½ a wey of lime – 5d.
Item for 500 lath nails – 6d.
Item for 100 laths – 6d.
Item for calf-foot nails – 3d.
Item for 100 hatch nails – 3d.

Item for 100 ?crash nails – 2 ½d.
Item for 2 studs – 2d.
Item for a wey of lime – 10d.
Item to a carpenter for 1 ½ days' – 9 ½d.
Item for 2 loads of sand – 2d.
Item to a tiler for 6 days' at 6 ½d the day – 3s 3d.
Item to a labourer for 6 days' – 2s.
Item for 100 board nails and 100 lath nails – 10d.
Item for 100 hatch nails and 100 tack nails – 5 ½d.
Item for 105 feet of elm board – 3s.
Item for a wey of lime – 10d.
Item for 150 elm boards for the buttery floor at 2s 8d the 100, amounts to – 4s.
Sum this side – 25s 11d.

fo 9v
Reparations done upon the house that John Hoper holds
Item for hauling the same board – 1d.
Item for 100 calf-foot nails – 10d.
Item for 100 board nails – 4 ½d.
Item for 100 tack nails – 2 ½d.
Item for a wey of lime – 10d.
Item for 2 loads of sand – 2d.
Item for hauling boards – 1d.
Item for hauling 2 vats of rubble – 2d.
Item for a wey of lime – 10d.
Item for hair – ½d.
Item for 100 hatch nails – 3d.
Item for 3 studs – 13d.
Item for a board – 6d.
Item for 3 studs – 6d.
Item for 3 semes of Welsh board at 7d the seme – 21d.
Item for 2 weys of lime for the buttery – 20d.
Item for 200 laths – 12d.
Item for 500 lath nails – 11d.
Item for 3 studs – 11d.
Item for hair – 1d.
Item for a load of paving stone for the kitchen – 16d.
Item for hauling – 2d.
Item for a board to the [word illegible] – 3d.
Item for a wey of lime – 10d.
Item for 500 lath nails – 5 ½d.
Item for hauling a vat of rubble – 1d.
Item for 75 boards for the little *aller* – 2s.

Item for 100 board nails – 4 ½d.
Item to a mason for 5 days' work at 6 ½d the day – 2s 8 ½d.
Sum this side – 20s 6d.

fo 10

Item to 2 tilers for 5 days' at 6 ½d the day – 5s 5d.
Item to 2 labourers for 5 days' – 3s 4d.
Item to a carpenter for 5 days' – 2s 8d.
Item to a tiler for 5 days' – 2s 8 ½d.
Item to a labourer for days' – 20d.
Item for hauling 2 vats of rubble – 2d.
Item for 3 *drawts* hauling to the stone house – 3d.
Item to *formasse* – 1d.
Item for a pair of twists to the door at the stair foot – 6d.
Item for 2 pairs of twists and hooks for 2 doors in the loft – 9d.
Item for mending twists and hooks to the door in the ?entry – 3d.
Item for twists and hooks to the gutter window – 2 ½d.
Item for mending an iron *crowe* that John Howse lent us – 1d.
Item for a *crampet* of iron for the post in the entry – 2 ½d.
Item for 2 weys of lime to the entry – 20d.
Item for a bundle of laths – 3d.
Item for 6 spikes – 2d.
Item for 6 ½ feet of new glass for the windows in the hall and in the
parlour, and repairs to the same – 6s 8d.
Item to a carpenter for 5 days' – 2s 8 ½d.
Item to 2 labourers for 5 days' – 3s 4d.
Item to another carpenter for 5 days' – 2s 8 ½d.
Item to a tiler for 3 days' – 19 ½d.
Item for hauling 5 vats of rubble – 5d.
Item for 100 board nails – 4 ½d.
Item for 100 hatch nails – 3d.
Item to a tiler for 3 days' – 19 ½d.
Item to another tiler with him for 2 days' – 13d.
Item to a carpenter for 2 days' – 13d.
Sum this side – 42s 3d.

fo 10v

Item to a labourer for a day – 4d.
Item to another labourer for 4 days' – 16d.
Item for 250 laths – 15d.
Item for 1000 lath nails – 11d.
Item for small nails – ½d.
Item for 6 pairs of *gymose* [hinges] for the lattice windows – 13d.
Item to the painter for dressing the lattice windows and for the colours –

2s 4d.

Item for 2000 tile pins – 5d.

Item to a carpenter for a day's work – 6 ½d.

Item for 15 ½ feet of new lattice at 2 ¼d the foot – 3s 2 ¼d.

Item to a tiler for a day on the parlour chamber and the ?pentys – 6 ¼d.

Item for a new pipe of lead set in, my lady Pernaunt *paymente* [?pavement], weighing 107 lb at 1d the pound, amounts – 8s 11d.

Item for 2 lb of solder – 6d.

Item for a *skarr* – 2d.

Item for dressing 2 pipes in John Hoper's pavement – 6d.

Item for 4 ½ lb of solder – 13 ½d.

Sum – 23s 2 ½d.

Sum total of the reparations on that house – £5 11s 10 ½d.

Sum this side – 23s 2 ½d.

fo 11

Reparations done to a stable that William Glastren holds

Paid to a tiler for a day's work – 6 ½d.

Sum – 6 ½d.

Paid for 40,000 tile pins to be in store for the church – 5s 2d.

Sum – 5s 2d.

Sum total payments this years amounts to – £23 5s 3 ¼d.

Sum resting clear to the church at this account – £4 3s 3 ¾d.

Of the which sum the said accountant asks to be allowed – 5s 10d, which he has paid more than he has received of the emoluments of the chantry as it appears more plainly in the book of the chantry this year. So there rests clear

to the church – £3 17s 2 ¾d, which sum the said accountant delivered to the *parisshyns* on the day of his account, the 15th day of May, the year of Our Lord God 1522. So he is clearly discharged.

fo 11v

Memorandum that there remains of the church's lead in William Plomer's hands 10 ½ hundredweights and 5 lb, as appears more plainly in John Mawncell's book of accounts, of the which he has delivered to Harry Hickyns in his year ½ a hundredweight. So rests yet clearly in his hands at this account 10 hundredweights and 5 lb.

Memorandum that the day of the accounts Jerome Grene received of the *parisshons* – £3 17s 2d he to bring it in again at the day of his accounts.

Memorandum that there remains in Thomas Snygge's hands of his father's bequest – £5, *ut apparet in testamente ipsius.*

[1523]

fo 1
The Church Book
Anno Domini 1523
Jerome Grene

fo 2
Jesus Maria
The accounts of Jerome Grene and Master Thomas Passy, proctors of the parish church of All Saints', Bristol, for their receipts of the rents with other profits belonging to the same church for a whole year that is to say from the feast of the Annunciation of Our Lady in the year of Our Lord God 1522 unto the same feast of our Lady in the year of Our Lord God 1523, William Wosley being mayor, Gilbert Cogan and William Chestyr sheriffs.

The rents of assize
In primis of the tenement that Joan Poll holds for a gutter – 3s 4d.
Item of the tenement that the shoemaker dwells in by All Hallows' pipe – 4s.
Item of the tenement that John Watson holds for his back door – 2s 6d.
Item of Christ Church for a tenement of Richard Erle in Lewins Mead – 12d.
Item of the master and fellowship of the Tailors for a tenement in Baldwin Street – 12s.
Item of a tenement of Master Croft in St Peter's parish – 6d.
Item of a tenement of Master Shepherd's in Marsh Street – 2s.
Sum – 25s 4d.

Sum this side – 25s 4d.

fo 2v
The rents belonging to the church by the year
In primis of the tenement that John Hoper holds – £3 6s 8d.
Item of the same John Hoper for part of the tenement belonging to the Abbey of Tewkesbury – 53s 4d.
Item of the tenement that my lady Pernaunt holds – £4.
Item of the tenement that John Repe holds – 40s.
Item of the tenement that Nicholas Jenyns holds – 16s.

Item of the tenement that Andrew Page holds – 16s.
Item of the tenement that Sir John Cooke holds – 6s 8d.
Item of the beer house in the churchyard – 20d.
Item of the tenement that Thomas Marmen holds in Small Street – 26s 8d.
Item of the great tenement in Broad Street – £4.
Item of a stable and a garden that Master Townclerk holds in the same house – 4s.
Item of a vault there that Roger Filpott holds – 6s.
Item of a loft over the said vault that John Mawncell holds – 6s 8d.
Item of a stable that John Hoppar holds – 6s 8d.
Item of a loft over the store house – 2s.
Item of a garden in the market place that a tiler now holds – 2s.
Sum – £20 14s 4d.

Sum the whole rents – £21 19s 8d.

fo 3

The defaults, vacations and decays
In primis of Richard Erle's tenement in Lewins Mead – 12d.
Item of the master and fellowship of the Tailors for the tenement in Baldwin Street – 12s.
Item of a tenement of Master Croft in St Peter's parish – 6d.
Item of the great house in Broad Street – £4.
Item of the loft over the vault there that John Mawncell holds – 20d.
Item of the tenement of Master Shepherd in Marsh Street – 2s.
Item of the gutter in Joan Poll's house – 20d.
Item of the tenement that Andrew Payge holds – 2s.
Item of the beer house in the churchyard – 20d.
Sum – £5 2s 6d.

Sum of the rents, the vacations abated – £16 17s 2d.

fo 3v

Receipts of customable duties belonging yearly to the church
In primis on Palm Sunday – 2s.
Item on Shere Thursday – 12d.
Item on Good Friday to the repair of the jewels – 2s 4d.
Item on Easter eve of them that were houselled – 15d.
Item on Easter day of them that were houselled – 5s 7d.
Item to Our Lady of Worcester – 17 ½d.
Item received on the last day of account of the church money – £3 17s 2d.
Item received of John Jervys for the brotherhood of Jesus – 50s 9d.
Sum – £7 18 ½d.

Sum total receipts of rents and casualties, the vacations abated –
£23 18s 8 ½d.

fo 4
Payments that are yearly accustomed and other casualties that grow in
ornaments and jewels of the church
In primis for a pottle of osey on palm Sunday – 6d.
Item watching the sepulchre – 12d.
Item for coals – 2 ½d.
Item for besoms – 3d.
Item for washing the church stuff – 2s.
Item for rewards to the tenants [for] their payments – 12d.
Item to Walter the sexton for his year's wages – 20s.
Item for hanging up the Dance of Pauls – 2s.
Item to Our Lady of Worcester – 8d.
Item to the clerk for keeping Our Lady Mass in Lent – 4s 4d.
Item towards the costs of our supper on the day of account – 3s 4d.
Item for bearing the banners in Rogation week – 4d.
Item to Roger Pyckryng for his wages – 5s.
Item for making the book of accounts – 20d.
Item for scouring – 2s.
Item for oil and stone – 3d.
Item to the clerk for his year's wages more than the taxation of the parish
– 28s 7d.
[Different ink, smaller script: Memorandum for lamp oil]
Sum – £3 13s 9 ½d.

Item to Mistress Hervy for her part of the tenement that John Hopper
holds – 40s.

Sum of this side – £5 13s 9 ½d.

fo 4v
Payments for the church
In primis for a small line for the cloth that hangs before the rood – 4d.
Item for *reke* hooks occupied in the church – 1d.
Item to Walter for mending the sepulchre – 18d.
Item to the under-sexton for his attendance at the day of account – 4d.
Item to ?Rorar for making the baldric of the first bell – 4d.
Item to Kery's wife for leather for the same – 3d.
Item for nails for mending the bier – 1d.
Item for *machys* [?matches] for the lamp – 1d.
Item in thread and pins – 2 ½d.
Item mending the lock on the churchyard door – 3d.

[The seven items following have been lightly scored, and bracketed with the words *Vacat nunc* in the margin]

Item for 500 lath nail for mending the stable that John Hoppar holds in Broad Street – 5 ½d.

Item for board nail for the same – 1d.

Item for hair – ½d.

Item for a wey of lime – 10d.

Item for a piece of timber for the said stable – 4d.

Item for a board for the said stable – 4d.

Item to a tiler for 3 days' on the said stable and on Nicholas Jennyn's house – 19 ½d.

Item for the overplus of iron and for making a *gymmow* [hinge] for the churchyard door – 12 ½d.

Item to a mason for setting the hook to hang the door, and mending the churchyard wall – 2d.

Item for lead for fastening the said hook, 6 lb – 3d.

Item for nails for the said door – 1d.

Item to the plumber for ridding the pipe by the steeple – 4d.

Item to a tiler for ridding the church wall next [to] Jesus – 3d.

Item for making 2 surplices for children – 2d.

Item in *rekhoks* – ½d.

Item for a pottle of wine that was given to the steward – 4d.

Item for help hanging the choir against All Hallows' tide – 2d.

Item for thread to ?Rorar for his labour for mending the albs – 2 ½d.

Sum of this side – 6s 6d.

fo 5

Payments on Corpus Christi day

In primis to master vicar – [blank]

Item to 4 priests wearing copes – 16d.

Item to 2 friars bearing the shrine – 12d.

Item to 2 torch bearers – 3d.

Item for bearing the cross – 4d.

Item to the clerk and his children – 11d.

Item to Walter the sexton – 2d.

Item to the children that bore the candlesticks and the censers and the copes – 7d.

Item to the 2 deacons – 2d.

Item to 2 others that helped to sing – 2d.

Item for a pair of gloves for the sexton – 1d.

Item for a pottle of claret wine – 5d.

Sum – 5s 5d.

Wax for the church, the whole year
In primis [given] to John Reynold waxmaker 13 square tapers weighing
92 $\frac{1}{4}$ lb; received in new wax 117 $\frac{3}{4}$ lb; so amount in new wax –
25 $\frac{1}{2}$ lb.
Item [given] the paschal weighing 19 $\frac{1}{4}$ lb; received 26 lb; so amount in
new wax – 6 $\frac{3}{4}$ lb.
[Item given] 15 round tapers weighing 29 $\frac{1}{2}$ lb; received 31 $\frac{3}{4}$ lb; so
amount in new wax – 2 $\frac{1}{4}$ lb.
[Item given] the font taper weighing 2 $\frac{1}{2}$ lb; received 4 lb; so amount in
new wax 1 $\frac{1}{2}$ lb.
Item received 4 small tapers weighing $\frac{1}{2}$ lb for the sepulchre.
[Item given] against our dedication day in old wax 15 round tapers
weighing 17 $\frac{3}{4}$ lb; received 32 lb; so amount in new wax, 14 $\frac{1}{4}$ lb.
So amount all new wax for the whole year 50 $\frac{3}{4}$ lb, at 10d the pound,
amounts to – 41s 10 $\frac{1}{2}$d.
Item paid for making the said wax for the whole year – 3s 4d.
Sum – 45s 2 $\frac{1}{2}$d.

Sum this side – 50s 7 $\frac{1}{2}$d.

fo 5v
The obit of William Newbury held in the church the 10th day of May
[Bracketed against the entries for this obit are the words *Vacat nunc*:] In
primis to Master vicar for dirige and wax – 16d.
Item to 5 priests – 20d.
Item to the clerk for the bell and his labour – 10d.
Item to the bellman – 2d.
Item in bread to poor people – 2s.
Item in offering at Mass – 1d.
Sum – 6s 1d.
Memorandum that this is the 6th year that we have lacked our payment of
the Tailors.

The obit of Thomas Fyler and Agnes his wife held the 20th day of
November
In primis to Master vicar for wax – 12d.
Item to 8 priests – 2s 8d.
Item to master vicar for the bede roll – 12d.
Item to the clerk for the bell and his labour – 14d.
Item to the bellman – 2d.
Item in offering at Mass – 1d.
Item to the proctors for their labours [superscript: in attendance] – 12d.
Item in bread to poor people – 5s.
Item to the under sexton for laying the hearse – 2d.

Sum – 12s 3d.

Sum this side – 12s 3d.

fo 6
The obit of Harry Chestre and Humfrey Hervey and their other friends
held the 14th day of February
In primis to Master vicar – 12d.
Item to 6 priests – 2s.
Item to the clerk – 12d.
Item to the bellman – 4d.
Item in offering at Mass – 1d.
Item to the proctors – 8d.
Item to the sexton – 2d.
Item to the prisoners of Newgate in Bristol – 20d.
Item to our almshouse in bread – 4d.
Item to the lazar house at Brightbowe – 4d.
Item to the almshouse in the Longrewe in bread – 4d.
Sum – 7s 11d.

The obit of Thomas Spicer and Dame Maud his wife held the 15th day of
February
In primis to Master vicar and 6 priests – 2s 4d.
Item to Master vicar for 4 tapers – 2s.
Item to Master vicar for the bede roll – 4d.
Item to the clerk – 14d.
Item to the proctors – 12d.
Item to the bellman – 4d.
Item to the sexton – 1d.
Item in offering at Mass – 1d.
Item in bread to poor people [superscript in different ink: and the
?prisoners] – 3s.
Sum – 10s 4d.

Sum of this side – 18s 3d.

fo 6v
The obit of the good doers
In primis to Master vicar – 4d.
Item to 4 priests, every priest 3d – 12d.
Item in offering at Mass – 1d.
Item to the clerk – 14d.
Item for 3 bushels of wheat at 10d the bushel – 2s 6d.
Item for the grinding – 3d.

Item for saffron, 2 oz at 13d the ounce – 2s 2d.
Item for cloves – 6d.
Item for *moskadell* for the cake – 8d.
Item in claret wine 3 pottles – 12d.
Item for *barme* – 2d.
Item in bread – 6d.
Item for sack, 3 gallons – 3s.
Item for baking the cakes – 16d.
Item for a dozen of double ale and another of single ale – 3s.
Sum – 17s 8d.

The second obit of Harry Chestre and Humphrey Hervy held the 4th day
of March
In primis to Master vicar – 12d.
Item to 6 priests – 2s.
Item to the clerk – 12d.
Item to the bellman – 4d.
Item in offering at Mass – 1d.
Item to the proctors – 8d.
Item to the sexton – 2d.
Item to the prisoners of Newgate in Bristol in bread – 20d.
Item in bread to our almshouse – 4d.
Item to the lazar house at Brightbowe – 4d.
Item to the almshouse in the Long Rowe in bread – 4d.
Sum – 7s 11d.

Sum this side – 25s 7d.

fo 7
Reparations
The stable in the great house in Broad Street that John Hopper holds
In primis for 500 lath nail – 5 ½d.
Item in board nail and hair – 1 ½d.
Item in lime a wey – 10d.
Item a piece of timber – 4d.
Item a plank – 4d.
Item to a tiler for 3 days' – 19 ½d.
Item for a key to the great door for J. Hoppar – 2d.
Sum – 3s 10 ½d.

Reparations done on the church roof
In primis for 50 laths – 2 ½d.
Item for nails – 1d.
Item for 3 boards – 3d.

Item for a wey of fine lime and coarse – 4d.
Item for a large cornish tile – 2d.
Item a mason for one day and a labourer for another day – 10 $\frac{1}{2}$d.
Item to a tiler for the said work – 10d.
Item for 2 $\frac{1}{2}$ lb of solder – 6d.
Item to the plumber for mending 3 *skarys* – 8d.
Sum – 3s 11d.

More payments for the church
Item for mending a key of a coffer in the treasure house – 2d.
Item for candles against Christmas, 4 lb – 5d.
Item for holly against Christmas – 1d.
Item to the ?summoner for his labour – 3d.
Sum – 11d.

Sum this side – 8s 8 $\frac{1}{2}$d.

fo 7v
Reparations upon the tenement that John Hoppar holds in the High Street
In primis for removing 2 panes of glass and for mending it – 5d.
Item for 4 lb of solder – 12d.
Item for mending 4 $\frac{1}{2}$ *skarys* – 9d.
Sum – 2s 2d.

Sum total of the payments this year amounts to – £11 17s 10 $\frac{1}{2}$d.
Sum resting clear to the church at this account – £12 10d.

Of the which sum the said accountant has delivered to the *parisshons* – £4 10d in money, and for the rest, the sum of £8, *he hath browte in for posett*, a standing cup whole gilt, a *flatt* cup parcel gilt, a salt parcel gilt, a flat cup parcel gilt, 12 silver spoons with lions gilt.

Memorandum that master Thomas Pacy senior proctor has received of the church money £4. He to bring the said money in again at his account; which money was delivered to him by the whole *parishons* the day of this said account, and the same day 23s 8d was brought into the treasure coffer and the said *posett* of plate.

[Following entry in different ink:] Memorandum that the said standing cup whole gilt, 25 oz; the *flatt* cup 8 $\frac{1}{2}$ oz; the salt parcel gilt 10 oz; the 12 spoons with lions gilt 14 oz.

[1523–1524; outer cover page torn off and missing]

fo 1

Jhu

The accounts of Thomas Pacy and John Gerves proctors of the parish church of All Saints' in Bristol for their receipts of the rents with other profits and charges belonging to this same church for a whole year, that is to say from the feast of the Annunciation of Our Blessed Lady in the year of Our Lord God 1523 unto this same feast of Our Lady in the year of Our Lord God 1524, John Wylkyns then being mayor, Robert Chapman and John Davys sheriffs.

Rents of assize

In primis out of the tenement that Joan Poll holds for a gutter going through the church's ground – 3s 4d.

Item out of the *cornell* house next our conduit – 4s.

Item out of the tenement that John Watson now holds for his back door – 2s 6d.

Item for a tenement of Richard Erle in Lewins Mead that Christ Church holds – 12d.

Item of the master and fellowship of the Tailors for a tenement in Baldwin Street – 12s.

Item of a tenement of Master Croft in St Peter's parish – 6d.

Item of a tenement of Master Shipwarde in Marsh Street – 2s.

Sum – 25s 4d.

Sum of this side – 25s 4d.

fo 1v

Receipts belonging to the church by the year

In primis of the tenement that John Hoper now holds – £3 6s 8d.

Item of the same John Hoper for part of his house belonging to the Abbey of Tewkesbury – 53s 4d.

Item for a tenement that my lady Pernaunt holds – £4.

Item for a tenement that John Repe holds – 40s.

Item for a tenement that Nicholas Jennyns late held – 16s.

Item for a tenement that Andrew Page now holds – 16s.

Item for a tenement that Sir John Cooke now holds – 6s 8d.

Item for the beer house in the churchyard – 20d.

Item for a tenement that Thomas Mervyn late held in Small Street – 26s 8d.

Item for the great house in Broad Street – £4.

Item for a stable and a garden that John Collis holds – 4s.

Item for a vault and a loft that John Mawncell holds – 12s 8d.

Item for a stable that John Hoper now holds – 6s 8d.
Item for a loft over the store house by the year – 2s.
Item for a garden in the market place that William Schiperd tiler now holds – 2s.
Sum – £20 14s 4d.

Sum the whole receipts – £21 19s 8d.

fo 2
The defaults, vacations and decays
In primis of Richard Erle's house in Lewins Mead – 12d.
Item of the master and fellowship of the Tailors for the tenement in Baldwin Street – 12s.
Item for a tenement of Master Croft in St Peter's Street – 6d.
Item for the great house in Broad Street – £4.
Item for the loft over the vault that John Mawnsell holds – 20d.
Item for a tenement of Master Shipward in Marsh Street – 2s.
Item for the gutter of Joan Poll's house – 3s 4d.
Item for Andrew Page's house – 2s.
Item for the house that Nicholas Jenyns late held – 16s.
Item for the beer house – 20d.
Item Thomas Mervyn's house a quarter – 6s 8d.
Sum – £6 6s 10d.

Sum the whole rents, the vacations and decays abated – £15 12s 10d.

Receipts of customable duties belonging yearly to the church
In primis received on Palm Sunday of the parish – 2s 5d.
Item received on Shere Thursday towards the paschal – 14d.
Item received on Good Friday towards the repairs of the jewels – 2s 4d.
Item received on Easter eve towards the paschal – 13d.
Item received on Easter day towards the paschal and for Our Lady of Worcester – 8s 6d.
Item received of the parish at the day of account – £4.
Item received of the proctors of Jesus – 29s 5 $\frac{1}{2}$d.
Item received for Andrew Elysworthy's grave – 6s 8d.
Item received for Russell's pew for him and his wife – 8d.
Item received of Davy Laurence for his pew and his wife's – 16d.

fo 2v
Receipts
Item I received for 5 lb of old lead – 2 $\frac{1}{2}$d.
Item received for the ends of 4 rafters – 4d.
Item received also out of the treasure coffer towards the buying of a new

cross and a new cope and for other necessaries for the church as the parish agreed for the parcels of plate, in silver plate – 20 oz.

Item in gilt plate of an old chalice 14 oz and a mazer with the ?tree, this – 11 oz.

Also I received in plate that laid in pledge to the church – £20.

Item received for a paving stone that was naught – 1d.

Item received at St James' tide for the hire of Nicholas Jenyns house – 8d.

Item received for an old coffer that stood in the vestry – 6d.

Item received of 11 ells of ?dolas that was left from the albs – 5s 9d.

Sum of all the receipts – [erasures] £27 14d.

Sum total of the receipts, rents and casualties, the vacations abated – £42 14s.

fo 3

Payments that are yearly accustomed with other casualties that grow in ornaments and jewels of the church

In primis paid for a pottle of wine on Palm Sunday – 6d.

Item paid for watching the sepulchre – 12d.

Item paid to the raker – 8d.

Item paid for coals – 2 $\frac{1}{2}$d.

Item paid for besoms – 3d.

Item paid for washing the church stuff – 2s.

Item paid for rewards to tenants at their payments – 12d.

Item paid to Walter Carpynter for his year's wages – 20s.

Item paid for hanging up the Dance of Pauls – 2s.

Item paid to Our Lady of Worcester – 8d.

Item paid to the clerk for keeping Our Lady Mass – 4s 4d.

Item paid towards the supper at the day of our accounts – 22d.

Item paid for bearing the banner in Rogation week – 4d.

Item paid for Roger Pykryng's house the whole year – 6s 8d.

Item paid to him besides his wages – 5s 4d.

Item paid for making the book of accounts – 20d.

Item paid for scouring the church stuff – 2s.

Item paid for oil and scouring stone – 3d.

Item paid to the clerk for his year's wages more than the taxation of the parish – 26s 2d.

Item paid to William Groth for 3 quarters of lamp oil – 12d.

Item paid to John Mawnsell for 13 $\frac{3}{4}$ gallons of lamp oil – 18s 4d.

Item paid to Mistress Hervy for her part of the house that John Hoper now holds – 40s.

Item paid to the sexton for a pair of gloves for Easter – 2d.

Item paid to him for his attendance at the day of account – 4d.

Item paid for making the rental – 2d.

Item paid for matches – 1d.
Item paid for pins – 2d.
Item paid for small nails – 1d.
Item paid to *wone* [?one] to help to hang the choir – 2d.
Sum – £6 17s 4 ½d.

fo 3v
Payments
Item paid for candles and holly against Christmas – 6d.
Item paid for mending a candlestick before Our Lady of Pity – 4d.
Item paid for staining 2 cloths for the sepulchre and for *vysse* – 2s.
Item paid for 100 [word illegible] of fine gold – 7s.
Item for making 4 *spors* and painting them and to bells for the same for the paschal – 4d.
Item paid for mending a vestment – 2d.
Item paid for mending the organs in the choir – 2s.
Item paid for mending our old organs – 16d.
Item paid for a parchment skin to cover the statutes of the Kalendars in – 4d.
Item paid for 2 yards of hair for St Thomas' altar – 10d.
Item paid for 2 oz of gold for the cloth that covers the sacrament – 4s.
Item paid for silk for the fringe to the same and for fringe to the frontel of the high altar – 4s 8d.
Item paid for a yard of buckram – 6d.
Item paid for making and workmanship of this same – 16d.
Item paid for mending an old alb – 4d.
Item paid for mending Master vicar's surplice – 5d.
Item paid for making 6 new albs and 6 amices – 4s.
Item paid for half a piece of *dolas* for the same – 22s.
Item paid for mending the chain to the sacrament – 1d.
Item paid for making 6 surplices made of the old albs – 2s.
Item paid for mending the churchyard wall – 3d.
Item paid for the new cross besides the plate had out of the treasure coffer – £3 10s 2d.
Item paid for another cope of white damask with an orfras [?orfrey] of red velvet – £4 6s 8d.
Item paid for hallowing the albs – 12d.
Item paid for a new wheel to the morrow mass bell – 2s 8d.
Item paid for nails and iron work to the same – 4 ½d.
Item paid for mending 2 locks of the *byssetts* in the choir – 3d.
Item paid to the collectors for the king – 36s.
Sum of this side – £12 11s 6 ½d.

fo 4

Payments on Corpus Christi day
In primis paid to Master vicar – nil.
Item paid to 4 priests wearing copes – 16d.
Item paid to 2 friars bearing the shrine – 12d.
Item paid to 2 torch bearers – 4d.
Item paid for bearing the cross – 4d.
Item paid for a pottle of wine – 6d.
Item paid to Walter Carpynter – 2d.
Item paid to children for bearing candlesticks, copes and censers – 4d.
Item paid to 2 deacons – 2d.
Item paid to the clerk and his children – 12d.
Sum – 5s 2d.

Costs on the wax for the church
In primis delivered to the waxmaker 13 square tapers, weight with their
?trees 103 lb. Received them again weighing 116 $\frac{1}{2}$ lb. So weight in new
wax 13 $\frac{1}{2}$ lb, at 10d the pound, sum – 11s 3d.
Also delivered to him 13 round tapers, weight 17 $\frac{3}{4}$ lb; and another 2
tapers, 2 lb 7 oz. Received them again weighing 30lb, so there is in new
wax 9 lb 13 oz, at 10d the pound, sum – 8s 2 $\frac{1}{2}$d.
Paid for 4 prickets for 4 angels – 4d.
Delivered the paschal taper with the tree, weight 23 $\frac{1}{2}$ lb. Received it again
weighing 27 $\frac{1}{2}$ lb, so there is in new wax 4 lb at 10d the pound, sum – 3s
4d.
Delivered the font taper, weight 3 lb. Received it again at 4 lb – 10d.
Paid for making the old wax – 3s 4d.
Item allowed for waste of old wax, 4lb – 3s 2d.
Delivered 15 round tapers, weight 13 $\frac{1}{2}$ lb. Received them again – 32 lb, so
there is in new wax 18 $\frac{1}{2}$ lb at 9d the pound, sum – 13s 10 $\frac{1}{2}$d.
Sum – 44s 4d.

Sum of this side – 49s 6d.

fo 4v

The obit of William Newbery held on the 10th day of May
[Bracketed against the entries for this obit is the word *Vacat*:] In primis to
Master vicar for dirige and wax – 16d.
Item to 5 priests – 20d.
Item to the clerk for the bells and his labour – 10d.
Item to the bellman – 2d.
Item in bread to poor people – 2s.
Item for offerings at Mass – 1d.
Sum – 6s 1d.

Memorandum that this is the 7th year that we have lacked our payment of the master and fellowship of the Tailors.

The obit of Thomas Fyler and Agnes his wife held on the 20th day of November
In primis to Master vicar for wax – 12d.
Item to 8 priests – 2s 8d.
Item to Master vicar for the bede roll – 12d.
Item to the clerk for the bells and his labour – 14d.
Item to the bellman – 2d.
Item for offering at Mass – 1d.
Item to the proctors for their labour and attendance – 12d.
Item in bread for poor people – 5s.
Item to the sexton for laying the hearse – 2d.
Sum – 12s 3d.

fo 5
The obit of Harry Chestre and Humphrey Hervy and other of his friends held on the 14th day of February
In primis to Master vicar for wax – 12d.
item to 6 priests – 2s.
Item to the clerk – 12d.
Item to the bellman – 4d.
Item for offering at Mass – 1d.
Item to the proctors for oversight and labour – 8d.
Item to the sexton – 2d.
Item to the prisoners in Newgate in bread – 20d.
Item to our almshouse in bread – 4d.
Item to the lazar house at Brightbowe in bread – 4d.
Item to the almshouse at the Long Row in bread – 4d.
Sum – 7s 11d.

The obit of Thomas Spicer and Dame Maud his wife held on the 15th day of February
In primis to Master vicar and 6 priests – 2s 4d.
Item to Master vicar for 4 tapers – 2s.
Item to Master vicar for the bede roll – 4d.
Item to the clerk for the bells and dirige – 14d.
Item to the proctors for their labour and attendance – 12d.
Item to the bellman – 4d.
Item for offering at Mass – 1d.
Item to the sexton for laying the hearse – 1d.
Item in bread to prisoners and to poor people – 3s.
Sum – 10s 4d.

fo 5v

The obit for all good doers

In primis to Master vicar – 4d.

Item to 4 priests, every priest 3d, sum – 12d.

Item for offering at Mass – 1d.

Item to the clerk for the bells and dirige – 14d.

Item paid for 3 bushels of wheat – 2s 9d.

Item paid for grinding the same – 3d.

Item paid for saffron, 2 oz – 4s 4d.

Item for cloves – 6d.

Item for osey [scored: a pottle] – 8d.

Item for bread – 6d.

Item for barme – 2d.

Item for 3 gallons of sack – 2s 6d.

Item for baking the cake – 12d.

Item for ale, single and double, 2 dozen – 3s.

Item for a pottle of malmsey – 8d.

Sum – 18s 11d.

The second obit of Harry Chestre and Humphrey Hervy held on the 4th day of March

In primis to master vicar for wax – 12d.

Item 6 priests – 2s.

Item to the clerk for the bells – 12d.

Item to the bellman – 4d.

Item for offering at Mass – 1d.

Item to the proctors for their labour and attendance – 8d.

Item to the sexton for laying the hearse – 2d.

Item to the prisoners of Newgate in bread – 20d.

Item in bread to our almshouse – 4d.

Item to the lazar house in Brightbowe in bread – 4d.

Item to the almshouse at the Long Row in bread – 4d.

Sum 7s 11d.

fo 6

Repairs done on the tower

In primis paid for 1000 tile stones – 5s.

Item paid for hauling the same stones – 9d.

Item paid to 2 tilers for hewing the same stones for 2 days and for 3 parts of a day – 2s 8d.

Item paid for 500 laths – 20d.

Item paid for 1000 lath nails – 11d.

Item paid for 200 stone nails – 6d.

Item paid to 2 tilers for 4 $\frac{1}{2}$ days' work – 2s 5d.

Item more paid for 1 tiler for 3 $\frac{1}{2}$ days' work – 22 $\frac{1}{2}$d.

Item delivered to a plumber in old lead, 386 lb. Received in new lead again, 545 lb. So there is in new lead, 159 lb, at 4s 4d the hundredweight, sum – 6s 2d.

Item paid for casting this same – 5s.

Item paid for hauling the said lead – 1d.

Item paid for 10 lb of solder at 3d the pound, sum – 2s 6d.

Item paid for soldering 2 *skarys* – 4d.

Item paid for an oaken board for the one side of the gutter – 5d.

Item paid for board nails and calf-foot nails – 2 $\frac{1}{2}$d.

Item paid to a tiler for 2 $\frac{1}{2}$ days' work – 22 $\frac{1}{2}$d.

Item paid to 2 tilers for 2 $\frac{1}{2}$ days' work – 2s 8 $\frac{1}{2}$d.

Item more paid for 100 stone nails – 3d.

Item paid more for 500 lath nails – 5 $\frac{1}{2}$d.

Item paid to a labourer for a day's work – 4d.

Item paid for hauling away 4 vats of rubble – 4d.

Item more I paid for hauling of a load of tile stones – 2d.

Item paid for a piece of timber for the *groundsyll* [grounsell] to the tower window – 1d.

Sum of this side – 36s 8 $\frac{1}{2}$d.

fo 6v

Repairs on the tower

Item paid for hauling a load of tile stones – 2d.

Item more paid for 1000 tile stones – 5s.

Item paid for a wey of lime of fine and coarse – 9d.

Item paid for moss – 7d.

Item paid to 4 tilers for 3 days' work – 6s 6d.

Item paid for $\frac{1}{2}$ a seme of boards – 3d.

Item paid for 6 crests – 2 $\frac{1}{2}$d.

Item paid for hatch nails and board nails – 2d.

Item paid to 2 labourers for 2 days' work to rid and to make clean the tower – 16d.

Item paid for hauling 2 loads of tile stones – 4d.

Item paid for hauling away 5 vats of rubble – 5d.

Item paid to 2 tilers for 2 $\frac{1}{2}$ days' work – 3s 3d.

Item paid for 1000 tile pins – 3d.

Item paid for 1 $\frac{1}{2}$ lb of solder – 4 $\frac{1}{2}$d.

Item paid for soldering 1 $\frac{1}{2}$ *skares* – 3d.

Sum – 19s 10d.

Repairs done on the house that Nicholas Jennyns late held

In primis paid for 2 keys, 1 for the hall door and another to the cellar door and for a hook to the hall door and nails – 8 $\frac{1}{2}$d.

Item paid for ledges and for workmanship to the cellar door – 5d.
Item more for nails to the same – 2d.
Sum – 15 ½d.
Sum of this side – 21s 1 ½d.

fo 7
Repairs done on the churchyard
In primis paid for 2 loads of paving stones to the churchyard and for 1
[for] the *chanell* [charnel] house – 2s 8d.
Item paid for hauling [word illegible] of the same – 4d.
Item paid for 4 loads of sand – 4d.
Item paid for 2 loads of clay – 4d.
Item paid for a wey of lime – 10d.
Item paid to 2 masons for 2 ½ days' work – 2s 8d.
Item more paid for 2 loads of sand – 2d.
Item paid to a labourer for 1 ½ days' work – 6d.
Item more for a load of paving stones – 16d.
Item I paid for hauling of this same – 2d.
Item I paid to the labourer for 2 ½ days' work – 10d.
Item I paid for 2 loads of sand – 2d.
Item I [paid] to 2 masons for 4 days' work – 4s 4d.
Item paid for 4 weys of fine lime – 3s 4d.
Item paid to 2 masons, 1 for 3 days' work and the other for 1 ½ days' work
– 2s 5d.
Item paid to a labourer for 2 ½ days' work – 10d.
Item paid for a wey of lime – 10d.
Item more paid for a load of paving stones – 16d.
Item paid for hauling this same – 2d.
Item paid more for 2 loads of sand – 2d.
Sum – 23s 9d.

fo 7v
Repairs done of John Hoper's house
In primis paid for 50 laths – 3d.
Item paid for 250 lath nails – 3d.
Item paid for a tiler for 1 ½ days' – 8d.
Item paid for 4 sacks of lime – 4d.
Item paid for hair – ½d.
Item I paid for a load of paving stones – 16d.
Item I paid for hauling the same – 2d.
Item I paid to 2 masons for 2 days' work – 2s 2d.
Item paid for lime fine and coarse – 9d.
Item paid to 2 masons for cleaning a gutter going out of the buttery under
his kitchen chimney – 2s.

Item more for cleaning another gutter partible between the church and John Davis, for our part – 12d.

Item paid to a carpenter for a day's work – 6d.

Item paid for 50 board nails – 2 ½d.

Item paid for a wey of lime fine and coarse – 4 ½d.

Item paid for another gutter partible between John Davis and the church, for our part – 12d.

Item paid to 2 masons for 1 ½ days' work, for the church's part – 9d.

Item paid to the carpenter for the sawing of a post end – 1d.

Item paid for 2 loads of sand – 2d.

Item paid for 4 loads of wall stones – 2s 6d.

Item paid to a mason for a whole week's work – 3s 3d.

Item paid for the church's part of 9 ¼ weys of lime – 3s 10d.

Item paid to a labourer for 5 ½ days' work – 22d.

Item paid for 2 *drawght* boards – 5d.

Item paid for board nails and hatch nails – 1 ½d.

Item paid for hauling away a *drawght* of rubble – 1d.

Sum of this side – 24s 1d.

fo 8

More repairs on John Hoper's house

Item paid for hauling away 8 loads of wall stones for our part – 8d.

Item paid for hauling away 4 vats of rubble – 4d.

Item more paid for hauling 4 loads of wall stones – 8d.

Item paid to 2 masons for 1 ½ days' work – 11d.

Item paid to a carpenter for a day's work – 7d.

Item paid for a stud – 3d.

Item paid for shingle stones – 14d.

Item paid for soldering 9 *scarys* partible between John Hoper and William ?Droth and for solder, for the church's part – 15d.

Sum – 5s 10d.

Repairs done on John Hoper's stable

In primis paid for 5 planks at – 2s 4d.

Item paid for a stud and nails – 6d.

Item paid to a carpenter for a day's work – 6d.

Sum – 3s 4d.

Item paid for a new cross staff and for his *knotts* – 5d.

Item paid for painting this same staff – 2s 8d.

Item paid for the exchange of a taper that was broken in the choir – 1d.

Sum – 3s 2d.

Sum of this side – 12s 4d.

fo 8v

Costs done on the new press made in the vestry for the copes
In primis paid for *wentchecot* timber for the press – 6s 8d.
Item paid for hauling thereof – 1d.
Item more paid for timber – 16d.
Item paid for 2 semes of boards – 14d.
Item paid for ?10 bewdeley boards – 2s 6d.
Item paid for an elm board for the same – 4s.
Item paid for 100 board nails and hatch nails – 3 $\frac{1}{2}$d.
Item paid for a seme of boards – 6d.
Item paid for *gemmowes* [hinges] and locks and bars – 2s 8d.
Item paid to Walter for timber and boards – 3s 4d.
Item more paid for 2 locks and a pair of *gemmowes* with a ring – 2s 4d.
Item more for timber and boards to Walter – 4s.
Item paid to Walter for his handiwork – 26s 8d.
Item paid to a labourer to help him in the vestry for 3 $\frac{1}{2}$ days' – 14d.
Item paid for calf-foot nails and board nails – 8d.
Sum – 57s 4 $\frac{1}{2}$d.

Costs to the new frame with mysters in the vestry for vestments and
surplices and other things
In primis paid for timber to Walter Carpynter – 22d.
Item paid for 100 board nails – 5d.
Item paid for candles and nails – 2 $\frac{1}{2}$d.
Item paid for 3 semes of boards – 20d.
Item paid for a long elm board to hang by it – 22d.
Item paid for hooks and *gemmowes* and rings with a stay – 2s 4d.
Item paid for 12 days' work – 6s 6d.
Sum – 14s 10 $\frac{1}{2}$d.

Sum of this side – £3 12s 2d.

fo 9

Repairs done of the store house
In primis paid for a new key to the door – 2d.
Item paid for stopping up the ?stone door – 5d.
Item paid for 3 sacks of lime – 3d.
Item more paid for the pulling of an old wall – 4d.
Item paid for mending the outer door – 2d.
Sum – 16d.

Repairs on John Mawnsell's house
Item paid for boards to make a door to the vault – 6d.
Item paid for a ?fillet and a stock lock to the same – 2 $\frac{1}{2}$d.

Item paid for twists and hooks for the same – 8d.
Item paid for nails – 2d.
Item paid to Walter for 1 $\frac{1}{2}$ days' work – 9 $\frac{1}{2}$d.
Item paid for a lock and a staple for the same door – 8d.
Item paid for a piece of timber to William Tyllar's garden door – 3d.
Sum – 3s 3d.

Repairs on Andrew Page's house
In primis paid for nails to mend his stair and his hall window – 1 $\frac{1}{2}$d.
Item paid to the carpenter for a ledge and a board for the window – 4d.
Item more for 4 bewdeley boards – 12d.
Item paid for 50 board nails – 2 $\frac{1}{2}$d.
Sum – 20d.
Sum of this side – 6s 3d.

Sum total of all payments this year – £34 12s 2d.
So rests clear that the aforesaid accountant owes to the church by this account – £8 1s 10d.
Which money he has paid unto the *p[ar]reschons* at the day of his account – £8 1s 10d.

[Remainder of account in darker ink and various hands] Memorandum that at this account the said John Gervis has received the sum £3 18s 11d as it appears more plainly in the foot of the chantry book, and he is to bring it in again to the use of the church at his account.
Also delivered to the said John Gervis all Thomas Snygge's plate being pledged to the church to furnish money necessary to the church's use and to bring it in his accounts.
Also delivered [by] him a great maser weighing with the tree 11 oz to be sold to the said use of the church.

fo 9v
The parcels of all Thomas Snygge's plate pledged to the church with the weight of the same
In primis a nutte with a cover whole gilt weighing without the shell – 24 $\frac{3}{4}$ oz.
Item flat piece with his cover parcel gilt weighing – 31 oz.
Item a *birrell* goblet with his cover whole gilt – 12 oz.
Item 6 spoons of silver weighing – 8 $\frac{3}{8}$ oz.
Sum – £13 6s 8d.

Memorandum that John a Wood beer, brewer, is bound to pay to the church at Michaelmas next coming as it appears by his obligation – 40s.
John Folke tanner being bound with him in the same obligation.

And so every quarter following 10s til £8 be fully paid.

Also William a Chamber, tanner, with other sureties be bound by their obligations to pay at Midsummer next 10s, and so every year following at Midsummer 10s, til 40s be fully paid.

[1524–25]

fo 1
John Gervys
The Church Book
Anno Domini 1525

fo 2
The account of John Gervys and Thomas Yonge proctors of the parish church of All Saints' in Bristol for their receipts of the rents with other profits and charges belonging to the same church for a whole year, that is to say from the feast of the Annunciation of Our Blessed Lady in the year of Our Lord God 1524 unto the same feast of Our Lady in the year of Our Lord God 1525, Thomas Hutton then being mayor and Thomas Geoffreys and John Sprynge sheriffs.

Receipts of rents of assize
In primis received of Joan Poll for a gutter going through the church's ground by the year – 3s 4d.
Item of the *cornell* house next our conduit by year – 4s.
Item of the tenement that John Watson by year – 2s 6d.
Item of the tenement that [?was] Richard Erle's in Lewins Mead that Christ Church holds by year – 12d.
Item of the master and fellowship of the Tailors for a tenement in Baldwin Street – 12s.
Item of a tenement of Master Croft in St Peter's parish – 6d.
Item of a tenement of Master Shypwarde in Marsh Street – 2s.
Sum – 25s 4d.

Sum of this side – 25s 4d.

fo 2v
Rents of the church
Item of John Hoper for a tenement by year – £3 6s 8d.
Item the same John for part of his house belonging to Tewkesbury – 53s 4d.

Item of my lady Pernaunt for a tenement by year – £4.
Item of a tenement that John Repe holds by year – 40s.
Item of a tenement that Nicholas Jennyns late held by year – 16s.
Item of a tenement that Andrew Page now holds – 16s.
Item of a tenement that Sir John Cooke holds – 6s 8d.
Item of a tenement the beer house in the churchyard – 20d.
Item of a tenement that Thomas Mervyn late held in Small Street – 26s 8d.
Item of the great house in Broad Street – £4.
Item of a stable and a garden that John Collis holds by year – 4s.
Item of a vault and a loft that John Mawncell holds – 12s 8d.
Item of a stable that John Hoper holds by year – 6s 8d.
Item of a loft over the store house by year – 2s.
Item of a garden in the market place that William Shepard tiler holds by year – 2s.
Sum – £20 14s 4d.

Sum the whole rents – £21 19s 8d.

fo 3
Vacations and decays
In primis of Richard Erle's house void the year – 12d.
Item of the master of the Tailors the year [inserted: for the tenement in Baldwin Street] – 12s.
Item of Master Croft's house void the year – 6d.
Item of the great house in Broad Street void the year – £4.
Item of the tenement of Master Shipward void the year – 2s.
Item of the gutter of Joan Poll's house void the year – 3s 4d.
Item of Andrew Page's house void the year – 2s.
Item of the house the turner holds void three quarters – 12s.
Item of the beer house void the year – 20d.
Item of Thomas Marmyn's house void the year – 26s 8d.
Item of John Mawnsell's house void – 2s 8d.
Item of the little loft void three quarters – 19d.
Sum is – £7 5s 5d.

Sum total of the rents, and the vacations abated – £14 13s 3d.

Receipts of the church
Item received upon Palm Sunday towards the sexton's wages – 2s 8d.
Item received to the paschal on Shere Thursday and Easter eve and Easter day – 8s 2d.
Item received of Our Lady at Worcester that belongs to the church – 14d.
Item received upon Good Friday to the repairs of the jewels – 2s 9d.
Item received at the day of account – £3 18s 11d.

Item received of the proctors of Jesus – 28s 6d.

Item received of Thomas Yate for the loan of the candlesticks for a Spaniard's burial – 4d.

Item received of William Bregeman's wife for the cellar that the tanners dwell in – 10d.

Item received for the cross that the man of *brynte* marsh holds – 4d.

Item received of the parish at the day of account, all Master Snygge's plate that I have sold, sum – £13 6s 8d.

Item received of Thomas Snygge for part of his father's legacy to the church – £3 6s 8d.

Item received a mazer weighing 11 oz with the tree, the which I sold for – 25s.

Sum of this – £24 2s.

fo 3v

Receipts of pews

Item received of Robert Byrke and his wife for their pews – 8d.

Item received of Thomas Asshehurst for their pews – 8d.

Item received of William Garon for their pews – 8d.

Item received of Richard Johan for their pews – 8d.

Item received of Thomas Torner for his pew – 4d.

Item received of William Mashall for his pew – 3d.

Sum of this – 3s 3d.

Sum total of the receipts, rents and casualties, the vacations abated – £38 19s 6d.

fo 4

Payments of the church

In primis paid for a pottle of muscadel upon Palm Sunday – 8d.

Item paid for watching the sepulchre – 12d.

Item paid to the raker – 8d.

Item paid for coals – 2 ½d.

Item paid for besoms – 3d.

Item paid for washing the church stuff – 2s.

Item paid for rewards among the tenants – 12d.

Item paid to Walter Jones for his year's wages – 20s.

Item paid for hanging up the Dance of Pauls – 2s.

Item paid to Our Lady of Worcester – 8d.

Item paid to William Clerke for keeping Our Lady Mass – 5s.

Item paid to the sexton for attendance at the day of account – 4d.

Item paid for our supper at the day of account – 3s 1d.

Item paid for bearing the banners in Rogation week – 4d.

Item paid to Roger Pekeryn for his house the year – 6s 8d.

Item paid to him [scored: besides; superscript: to] his wage – 5s 4d.
Item paid for making this book of account – 20d.
Item paid for scouring church stuff – 2s.
Item paid for oil and scouring stone – 3d.
Item paid to the clerk for his wages more than we received of the parish – 27s 11d.
Item paid for 13 gallons of lamp oil, 16d the gallon – 17s 4d.
Item paid to the prior of St James for his part of the [superscript: rent of the] house that John Hoper now holds – 40s.
Item paid to the sexton for a pair of gloves at Easter – 2d.
Item paid for making the rent roll – 2d.
Item paid for matches – 1d.
Item paid for pins – 2d.
Item paid to a man to hang the choir – 2d.
Item paid to Master Pase to make up the full payment of the lands that we bought of Master Hervey's executors – 43s 9d.
Sum of this side – £9 2s 10 $\frac{1}{2}$d.

fo 4v
Payments
Item paid for candles and holly against Christmas – 6d.
Item paid for rats' bane – 1d.
Item paid for board nails – 1d.
Item paid for white liming the church – 13s 4d.
Item paid for 4 bushels of lime stones – 8d.
Item paid to William Tyler for pointing the church – 12d.
Item paid for a sack of lime – 1d.
Item paid for a line to draw the curtain at the Jesus altar – 1d.
Item paid for a cord to hang the paschal – 1d.
Item paid to Harry Hegens for part that he laid out when he was proctor for ridding a gutter in my lady Parnell's house – 2s 1d.
Item paid for 2 antiphonars – £11.
Item paid to Master vicar towards his costs for buying them – 3s 4d.
Item paid for the carriage of the 2 books – 10d.
Item paid for the carriage up of the money – 4d.
Item paid to the sexton for the *regestyen* of the same books – 4d.
Item paid to the sexton for [scored: white liming; superscript: making clean of the white lime] of the church – 4d.
Item paid for an iron shovel – 4d.
Item paid for a *pykys* [pick axe] weighing 6 lb – 9d.
Item paid for a gallon of muscadel to my lord of St Austin's and his company at John Hoper's – 16d.
Item paid to the town clerk for [scored: writing] making [scored: and other; insert: of] writing with the *seychment* [superscript: of master

Hawke's lands] – 13s 4d.
Item paid to Master Mayor for the seals – 6d.
Item paid at John Hoper's for drinking the same time – 8d.
Item paid for a *whyskare* to the church – 1d.
Item paid for mending the glass windows – 3s 4d.
Item paid for a bell to hang in the tower upon the Dedication day – 2d.
Item paid for 8 lb of lead to mend the case of the morrow mass bell and solder to the same – 7d.
Item paid for a rope to the same bell – 6d.
Item paid for mending Katherine Dye's pew – 1 ½d.
Item paid for a new key to Elizabeth Gyllet's hall door – 2d.
Sum of this – £13 5s ½d.

fo 5
Payments
Item paid for 2 locks for the treasure *besset* in the tower – 11d.
Item paid for setting the 2 locks – 2d.
Item paid for a baldric for the second bell – 8d.
Item paid for mending the lock on the church door next to the street – 4d.
Item paid for a new key to the vestry door and mending the lock – 4d.
Item paid for mending the organs – 12d.
Item paid to Master vicar and to Master Collys when they rode to master Harvy's with the copies of the writings of Master Hauk's lands, for wine and other pleasures – 23d.
Item paid to Master vicar for the fine that he paid to John Gervys for Mistress Harvey – 53s 4d.
Item paid to Fraunces for binding all the books of accounts – 8d.
Item paid to the Prior of St James for a state that we have in part of John Hoper's house – £4 6s 8d.
Item paid to John Byche for pricking 5 *carell* books – 5s.
Item paid for paper *ryoll* for the same books – 8d.
Item paid to John Corner of the Gaunts for pricking 5 books of songs of square note – 6s 8d.
Item paid for paper *ryoll* for the same books – 8d.
Item paid for 2 *stolys* in the choir – 14d.
Item paid for ringing at the procession at the commandment of the king for taking of the French king – 8d.
[Scored: Item paid to the ?factors of Mistress Haukys otherwise called Harvey – 43s 9d.]
Item paid for hauling a vat of rubble at the church end – 2d.
Item paid to John Ayleworth and Thomas Smyth collectors – 36s.
Item paid for mending the iron over the high altar to draw the curtain upon – 7d.
Item paid to the smith for *shuttyng* the iron – 2d.

Item paid to Roger to help make the scaffold – 3d.
Sum of this – [written over an erasure: £9 23s [sic]]

fo 5v
Costs of the wax
Item delivered to the waxmaker 13 square tapers with the trees, weighing 100 lb. Item received in new wax with the old, 114 lb. And so received in new wax 14 lb at 8d the pound, sum – 9s 4d.
Item more given to him 15 round tapers weighing 21 lb. Item received them again, weighing 30 lb. So there is in new wax 9 lb at 8d the pound, sum – 6s.
Item delivered a paschal weighing with the tree 25 $\frac{1}{2}$ lb. And so received him again, weighing 28 $\frac{1}{2}$ lb. So rests in new wax 3 lb at 8d the pound, sum – 2s.
Item paid for 4 prickets for the 4 angels – 4d.
Item given the font taper weighing 3 $\frac{1}{2}$ lb. Received again 4lb. In new wax $\frac{1}{2}$ lb – 4d.
Item paid for making all the old wax – 3s 4d.
Item allowance of the waste of the old wax, 4 lb – 2s 8d.
Item delivered 15 round tapers weighing 18 lb. Received again 31 lb. So there is in new wax 13 lb at 7 $\frac{1}{2}$d the pound, sum – 8s 1 $\frac{1}{2}$d.
Sum of this – 32s 1 $\frac{1}{2}$d.

Payments of Corpus Christi day
Item paid to Master vicar – nil
Item paid to 4 priests wearing the copes – 16d.
Item paid to 2 friars to bear the shrine – 12d.
Item paid to 2 torch bearers – 4d.
Item paid for bearing the cross – 4d.
Item paid for a pottle of wine – 6d.
Item paid to Walter [scored: Carpynter; superscript: the second clerk] – 2d.
Item to the children for bearing the candlesticks and the censers and copes – 4d.
Item paid to 2 deacons – 2d.
Item paid to the clerk and his children – 12d.
Sum – 5s 2d.

Sum of this side – 37s 3 $\frac{1}{2}$d.

fo 6
The obit of William Newbery held the 10th day of May
[Bracketed against the entries for this obit in the margin are the words *vacant nunc:*] In primis to Master vicar for his dirige and wax – 16d.
Item paid to 5 priests – 20d.

Item paid to the clerk for the bells and his labour – 10d.
Item paid to the bellman – 2d.
Item paid for bread to the poor people – 2s.
Item paid for the offering at Mass – 1d.
Sum – 6s 1d.

Memorandum that this is the 8th year that we lacked our payments of the master of the Tailors and his fellowship

The obit of Thomas Fylour and Agnes his wife held the 20th day of November
In primis paid to Master vicar for wax – 12d.
Item paid to 8 priests – 2s 8d.
Item paid to Master vicar for the bede roll – 12d.
Item paid to the clerk for the bells and his labour – 14d.
Item paid to the bellman – 2d.
Item paid for offering at Mass – 1d.
Item paid to the proctors for their labour and attendance – 12d.
Item paid for bread to the poor people – 5s.
Item paid to the sexton laying the hearse – 2d.
Sum of this – 12s 3d.

Sum of this side – 12s 3d.

fo 6v
The obit of Harry Chestre and Humfrey Hervy and his friends held the 14th day of February
In primis paid to Master vicar for wax – 12d.
Item paid to 6 priests – 2s.
Item paid to the clerk – 12d.
Item paid to the bellman – 4d.
Item paid for offering at Mass – 1d.
Item paid to the proctors for their labour – 8d.
Item paid to the sexton – 2d.
Item paid to the prisoners of Newgate in bread – 20d.
Item paid to our almshouse in bread – 4d.
Item paid to the lazar house at Bright Bowe in bread – 4d.
Item paid to the almshouse at the Long Rewe in bread – 4d.
Sum is – 7s 11d.

The obit of Thomas Spicer and Dame Maud his wife held the 15th day of February
In primis paid to Master vicar and 6 priests – 2s 8d.
Item paid to Master [vicar] for 4 tapers – 2s.

Item paid to Master vicar for the bede roll – 4d.
Item paid to the clerk for bells and dirige – 14d.
Item paid to the proctors for their labour and attendance – 12d.
Item paid to the bellman – 4d.
Item paid for offering at Mass – 1d.
Item paid to the sexton for laying the hearse – 1d.
Item paid for bread to the prisoners and to the poor people – 3s.
Sum is – 10s 4d.

Sum of this side – 18s 3d.

fo 7
The obit for all good doers
In primis paid to Master vicar – 4d.
Item paid to 4 priests, each of them 4d – 12d.
Item paid for offering at Mass – 1d.
Item paid to the clerk for the bells and his dirige – 14d.
Item paid for 3 bushels of wheat – 2s 3d.
Item paid for grinding the same – 3d.
Item paid for 2 oz of saffron – 2s 6d.
Item paid in cloves – 6d.
Item paid for a pottle of osey – 8d.
Item paid in bread – 6d.
Item paid for balm – 2d.
Item paid for baking the cake – 12d.
Item paid for single ale and double ale, 2 dozen – 3s.
Item paid for a pottle of malmsey – 8d.
Item paid for 2 gallons of claret wine – 2s.
Item paid for 3 pottles of romney – 18d.
Item paid to the sexton for laying the hearse – 2d.
Sum is – 17s 9d.

The obit of Harry Chestre and Humfrey Hervey held the 4th day of March
Item paid to Master vicar for wax – 12d.
Item paid to 6 priests – 2s.
Item paid to the clerk for the bells – 12d.
Item paid to the bellman – 4d.
Item paid for offering at Mass – 1d.
Item paid to the proctors for their labour – 8d.
Item paid to the sexton for laying the hearse – 2d.
Item paid to the prisoners in Newgate in bread – 20d.
Item paid to the almshouse in bread – 4d.
Item paid to the Bright Bowe in bread – 4d.
Item paid to the almshouse in the Long Rowe in Bread – 4d.

Sum is – 7s 11d.

Sum of this side – 25s 8d.

fo 7v
Repairs and paving the churchyard
Item paid for a load of paving stones – 14d.
Item paid for hauling the same – 2d.
Item paid for 2 weys of fine lime – 20d.
Item paid for 7 loads of sand – 6d.
Item paid for ½ a wey of coarse lime – 2d.
Item paid for 2 loads of sand – 2d.
Item paid for a load of paving stones – 14d.
Item paid for hauling them – 2d.
Item paid to a mason for 2 ½ days' – 16d.
Item paid to a labourer for 2 ½ days' – 10d.
Item paid for ½ a wey of fine lime – 5d.
Item paid to a mason for 3 days' – 19 ½d.
Item paid to a labourer for 3 days' – 12d.
Item paid for hauling 6 butts of rubble and stones – 6d.
Sum is – 10s 10 ½d.

Repairs, mending the window and the dormer and the gutter
Item paid for a load of stones – 14d.
Item paid for ½ a wey of lime – 5d.
Item paid for nails – 1d.
Item paid for hauling the stones – 2d.
Item paid for timber – 10d.
Item paid for nails – 1d.
Item paid for 100 lathes – 5d.
Item paid for moss at – 1d.
Item paid to a tiler for 3 ½ days' – 22 ½d.
Item paid for 500 lath nails – 5d.
Item paid for 3 lb of solder to mend the gutter – 9d.
Item paid for soldering 2 ½ *skarys* and for wood – 5 ½d.
Sum is – 6s 9d.

Sum of this side – 17s 7 ½d.

fo 8
For making an altar in the vestry and other repairs
Item paid for boards – 2s 2d.
Item paid for 50 board nails – 2d.
Item paid for timber to ?safe the bell ropes – 3d.

Item paid for spike nails – 1d.
Item paid for hatch nails – 1d.
Item paid for *busshell* nails – 1d.
Item paid for spike nails and calf-foot nails – 1 ½d.
Item paid for a studd to make the *barkylment* over the altar – ½d.
Item paid to Walter Jones for 3 ½ days' – 19 ½d.
Item paid 3 feet of new glass – 18d.
Item paid for cleaning and setting 6 feet of old glass – 12d.
Sum is – 7s 2 ½d.

For sealing the vestry
Item paid for 200 laths – 10d.
Item paid for 1500 lath nails – 15d.
Item paid for 2 weys of fine lime – 20d.
Item paid for ½ a bushel of lime stones – 1d.
Item paid to a tiler for 7 ½ days' – 4s 1d.
Sum is – 7s 11d.

Repairs to Master Ryppe's house
Item paid for 300 boards – 7s 3d.
Item paid for hauling the same – 1d.
Item paid for 100 board nails – 4d.
Item paid for half a wey of lime – 5d.
Item paid for 50 calf-foot nails – 5d.
Item paid for 50 board nails – 2d.
Item paid for calf-foot nails – 1d.
Item paid for nails at – 1d.
Item paid to a carpenter for 4 ½ days' – 2s 5d.
Item paid for a seme of welsh boards – 6d.
Item paid for 2 ½ lb of solder – 7 ½d.
Item paid for 3 *skarys* – 6d.
Item paid to a tiler for a day – 6 ½d.
Sum of this – 13s 5d.

Sum of this side – 28s 6 ½d.

fo 8v
Repairs of John Hoper's house
Item paid for mending a *pentes*, 6 joysse [?joists] – 12d.
Item paid for hatch nails and board nails and calf-foot and moss – 2 ½d.
Item paid for 50 laths – 2 ½d.
Item paid to a carpenter for ½ a day – 3d.
Item paid for 3 sacks of fine lime and 1 of coarse – 3 ½d.
Item paid for 500 lath nails – 5d.

Item paid for 200 cornish tiles – 10d.
Item paid to a tiler for 1 $\frac{1}{2}$ days' – 9 $\frac{1}{2}$d.
Item paid for 2 $\frac{3}{4}$ lb of solder – 8d.
Item paid for 4 *skarys* – 8d.
Item paid to a tiler for 2 $\frac{1}{2}$ days' – 12 $\frac{1}{2}$d.
Sum is – 6s 4 $\frac{1}{2}$d.

Repairs of Thomas Torner's house and Andrew Page's house
Item paid for 2 loads of sand – 2d.
Item paid for a wey of lime – 10d.
Item paid for candles and nails – 1 $\frac{1}{2}$d.
Item paid to John Power for cleaning and making clean the 3 gutters, 3 $\frac{1}{2}$ days' at 8d the day – 2s 4d.
Item paid to a labourer for 3 $\frac{1}{2}$ days' at 5d the day – 17 $\frac{1}{2}$d.
Sum is – 4s 11d.

Item paid for the repairs of the same house for a load of stones – 14d.
Item paid for hauling the same – 2d.
Item paid for 100 laths – 5d.
Item paid for 200 lath nails – 2d.
Item paid for a seme of boards – 6d.
Item paid for board nails and hatch nails – 2 $\frac{1}{2}$d.
Item paid for a 14 foot lattice at 3d the foot – 3s 6d.
Item paid to Watyr [for] 1 $\frac{1}{2}$ days' to mend things about the house – 9 $\frac{1}{2}$d.
Item paid for nails and crests – 4 $\frac{1}{2}$d.
Item paid to a tiler for 4 days' – 2s.
Item paid for 8 sacks of lime – 7d.
Item paid for making a new lock to the shop door – 4d.
Item paid for mending the lock of the hall door and making a key to the trap-door – 3d.
Sum – 10s 5 $\frac{1}{2}$d.

Sum of this side – 21s 9d.

fo 9
Repairs of the great door in Broad Street
Item paid to a carpenter for 2 days' – 11d.
Item paid to Thomas Carpenter for his laths and bolts – 4d.
Item paid for hauling them – 1d.
Item paid getting rid of the dung at the door – 1d.
Item paid for 50 board nails – 2d.
Sum is – 19d.

Sum total of all payments this year – £40 13s 10 $\frac{1}{2}$d.

So rest that the church owes to the accountant [erased: £3 13s 7 ½d] clear of this count – 29s 4 ½d.

[The following entries on the side are each in differing hands] This account was made before the vicar and *parisshons* by the said accountant the 4th day of May in the year of Our Lord God 1525, and so it appears that the church owes the said accountant – 29s 4 ½d.
Received the 6th day of May by me John Gervys then being proctor – 29s 4 ½d.

Memorandum that we have delivered the day of this account to Thomas Young senior proctor one obligation upon John a Wood's beer house and William Chambre ?turner and he to bring them in again at his account.

fo 9v
Memorandum the last day of the month of May in the year of Our Lord God 1524 in the presence of the vicar and of the whole *paryshons* all such plate as was in pledge to the church by Master Thomas Pacy and by Jerome Grene (as it appears by their bill) was delivered to the said vicar, to Thomas Pacy and Davy Lawrens, and also at the same time was delivered to them a basin and ewer of silver and a standing cup of silver parcel gilt, a small nut whole gilt, a spice dish of silver parcel gilt, and the same vicar, Thomas Pacy and Davy Lawrens promised to discharge the said church and *p[ar]issons* against the Abbot and Convent of St Austins of Bristol of £45 and against the vicar and *p[ar]ishons* of St Leonards of £22 10s for the sales of Master Hawkes lands which the *paryshons* of the said church have bought; the spice dish weighs 7 ½ oz at 3s 6d the oz., amounting to 26s 3d, the nut weighs 13 ¼ oz at 3s 4d the oz. with the shell, amounting to 44s 2d, the basin and the ewer and the standing cup weigh 80 oz at 3s 4d the oz., amounting to £13 6s 8d. Master Thomas Pacy's plate lies for £20. Jerome Grene's plate lies for £25. At the same was delivered to the vicar [and] to Thomas Pacy and Davy Lawrens of the church money – 29s 2d. Item the same vicar, Thomas and Davy must recover of this church's duty of Richard Harvy – 40s. Sum – £65 6s 3d. More the said vicar, Thomas and Lawrens must recover of John Gervys proctor – 43s 9d, the which money was paid on the 25th day of June anno 1524 by the hands of Thomas Younge.

[Different ink:] Memorandum that it is condescended and agreed the day of this general account by the vicar and *parisshons* that from henceforward the senior proctor shall be allowed at his account yearly – 6s 8d, for gathering the church and chantry rents, for making the book of accounts and for reward money to the tenants at the payment of their rents.
Per me prefatum vicar in [sic].

[The following account is not a churchwardens' account; it would appear to be a record kept by two of the parish elite of the work that they had supervised on the tenements and property which comprised the lands bought from Hawks – which land had previously been the Haddon chantry endowment]

fo 1
Anno Domini 1525
The rental of certain lands and tenements belonging to the parish church of All Saints' in the town of Bristol made at the feast of the Annunciation of Our Blessed Lady in the year of Our Lord God 1525.

The High Street
Item John Gerves for his house by the year – £3.

The Pithay
Item John Gerves for a garden by the year – 5s.
Item Harry Foxholl for his house and garden by the year – 32s.
Item John Howell for his house and garden by the year – 24s.
Item Roger Philpot for a garden by the year – 5s.
Item Thomas Hawkyns for a garden by the year – 6s.
Item Robert Ellyote for a garden by the year – 8s.
Item Master Vicar of All hallows for a garden by the year – 8s.
Item Thomas Browne *potecare* [apothecary] for a garden by the year – 8s.
Sum – £7 16s.

Receipts received by the hands of Thomas Pacy for 3 quarters rent, that is for Midsummer, Michaelmas and Christmas as it appears by the old rental, sum – £5 7s 6d.

More received of William a Chamber tanner in part payment of an obligation of a greater sum – 10s.
Also received of John a Woode beer brewer at Michaelmas – 40s.
More received of him on Christmas eve – 10s.
More received of him on the eve of Our Lady's Annunciation – 10s.
Sum of these receipts – £3 10s.

Sum total of the rents received with these other receipts – £8 17s 6d.
[Different hand and ink: Sum total of the receipts – £8 17s 6d.]

fo 1v
Repair done on the tenements in the Pithay by Thomas Pacy and John Hewis
In primis paid to a carpenter for hire of his timber to underset the house

while they were repairing – 20d.
Item paid for the hauling thither and home again of the said timber – 4d.
Item paid for hauling 3 draughts of timber – 3d.
Item paid to 5 labourers to help to take down the tile – 5d.
Item more paid for hauling 2 draughts of timber – 2d..
Item paid for 100 board nails – 4d.
Item paid for calf-foot nails – 1d.
Item paid to 2 carpenters for 2 days' work – 2s 3d.
Item paid for 100 calf-foot nails – 10d.
Item paid for 100 hatch nails – 3d.
Item paid for 50 board nails – 2d.
Item paid for 5 pieces of timber to the flooring of Harry Foxhall's kitchen – 2s 1d.
Item paid for 16 pieces of timber – 6s 8d.
Item paid to a mason for 2 $\frac{1}{2}$ days' work – 16d.
Item paid for hauling 200 boards – 1d.
Item paid for 200 feet of oaken boards – 6s.
Item paid to a labourer for 2 $\frac{1}{2}$ days' work – 10d.
Item paid for 1 $\frac{1}{2}$ weys of fine lime – 15d.
Item paid for $\frac{1}{2}$ a wey of coarse lime – 2 $\frac{1}{2}$d.
Item paid for 8 floor beams – 4s.
Item paid to a carpenter for 3 days' work – 21d.
Item paid to another carpenter for 2 days' work – 13d.
Item paid to a tiler for 2 $\frac{1}{2}$ days' work – 16d.
Item paid for 3 lb of spoke nails – 4 $\frac{1}{2}$d.
Item paid for a seme to ?fyste sand – 1 $\frac{1}{2}$d.
Item paid for hauling a draught of timber – 1d.
Sum of this side – 33s 11 $\frac{1}{2}$d.

fo 2
Item paid for 500 laths – 22d.
Item paid for hauling them – 1d.
Item paid for 1000 lath nails – 10d.
Item paid for 3 *crampets* of iron, weight 14 lb – 21d.
Item paid more for 1 *crampet*, weight 4 lb – 6d.
Item paid for 50 calf-foot nails – 5d.
Item paid for 100 stone nails – 3d.
Item paid to a labourer for a day's work – 4d.
Item paid for 2 loads of paving stones – 2s 6d.
Item paid for hauling them – 4d.
Item paid for a load of tile stones – 15d.
Item paid for hauling them – 2d.
Item paid for 1 lb of spoke nails – 1 $\frac{1}{4}$d.
Item paid for 350 board nails – 14d.

Item paid for 1000 lath nails – 10d.
Item paid for 200 calf-foot nails – 20d.
Item paid to a mason for a whole week's work – 3s 3d.
Item paid to a labourer for a whole week's work – 2s.
Item paid to a tiler for a whole week's work – 3s 3d.
Item paid to his man for 5 $\frac{1}{2}$ days' work – 3s.
Item paid to a carpenter for a whole week's work – 3s 6d.
Item paid to his man for a whole week's work – 3s 3d.
Item paid for 2000 tile pins – 6d.
Item paid for 300 feet of elm board and planks – 7s.
Item paid for other timber – 2s 6d.
item paid for 6 loads of clay – 12d.
Item paid for 3 $\frac{1}{2}$ weys of fine lime – 2s 11d.
Item paid for hauling boards and timber – 2d.
Item paid to master vicar for timber – 6s 8d.
Sum of this side – 53s $\frac{1}{2}$d.

fo 2v
Item paid for 4 semes of Welsh boards – 2s.
Item paid to a labourer for 2 $\frac{1}{2}$ days' work – 10d.
Item paid for 200 stone nails – 6d.
Item paid for a load of pendant stone – 13d.
Item paid for hauling them – 2d.
Item paid for a load of tile stones – 15d.
Item paid for hauling them – 2d.
Item paid more for 2 pieces of timber and 3 boards – 11d.
Item paid to a carpenter for 4 days' work – 2s 4d.
Item paid to his man for 4 days' work – 2s 2d.
Item paid more for a load of tile stones – 15d.
Item paid for hauling them – 2d.
Item paid to a tiler for 5 days' work – 2s 8 $\frac{1}{2}$d.
Item paid to a mason for 4 days' work – 2s 2d.
Item paid for 1 $\frac{1}{2}$ weys of fine lime – 15d.
Item paid for a seme of Welsh boards – 6d.
Item paid for 2 loads of clay – 4d.
Item paid for 300 board nails – 12d.
Item paid for wood to make keys of, for the carpenter – 2d.
Item also delivered to the plumber 25 lb in old lead. Received again in
new lead 91 lb. So is clear in new lead 66 lb – 3s 2d.
Item paid for casting the old lead – 3d.
Item paid for 100 *bosschell* nails – 2d.
Item paid for 200 feet of boards – 4s 8d.
Item paid for hauling them – 1d.
Item paid for moss – 12d.

Item paid more for a load of tile stones – 15d.
Item paid to a mason for 4 ½ days' work – 2s 5d.
Item paid to a labourer for 5 ½ days' work – 22d.
Sum of this side – 35s 9 ½d.

fo 3
Item paid for 3 lb of spikes – 4d.
Item paid for 4 weys of lime – 3s 4d.
Item paid for 9 loads of sand – 9d.
Item paid for 300 board nails – 12d.
Item paid for 150 hatch nails – 4 ½d.
Item paid for 900 lath nails – 9d.
Item paid for 50 calf-foot nails – 5d.
Item paid for 100 laths – 5d.
Item paid for 7 semes of welsh board – 3s 6d.
Item paid to a carpenter for 4 ½ days' work – 2s 8d.
Item paid to his man for 4 ½ days' work – 2s 5d.
Item paid for hooks – 1d.
Item paid to a tiler for 4 ½ days' work – 2s 5d.
Item paid more to a tiler for 3 days' work – 19d.
Item paid for 100 board nails – 4d.
Item paid for hauling a load of stones – 2d.
Item paid more to the tiler for 4 ½ days' work – 4s 10d.
Item paid more to 2 labourers for 4 ½ days' work – 3s.
Item paid for 1000 tile pins – 3d.
Item paid for hauling 15 draughts of lime and sand – 15d.
Item paid to a mason for 4 ½ days' work – 2s 5d.
Item paid to a carpenter for 4 ½ days' work – 2s 8d.
Item paid to his man for 4 ½ days' work – 2s 5d.
Item paid for 4 loads of sand – 4d.
Item paid for a *crampet* of iron – 11d.
Item paid for a seme of boards – 6d.
Item paid for 300 feet of boards – 7s.
Item paid for floor beams and for studs – 2s.
Item paid for 6 ½ weys of lime – 5s 5d.
Sum of this side – 53s 6 ½d.

fo 3v
Item paid for calf-foot nails and lath nails – 4d.
Item paid for 150 board nails – 6d.
Item paid more for 100 calf-foot nails – 10d.
Item paid for 200 board nails – 8d.
Item paid for 1,000 lath nails – 10d.
Item paid for hauling 2 draughts of boards – 2d.

Item paid for 100 hatch nails – 3d.
Item paid for 6 crests – 2 ½d.
Item paid for moss – 10d.
Item paid more for 3 loads of sand – 3d.
Item paid to 2 tilers for 4 ½ days' work – 4s 10d.
Item paid to a mason for 4 ½ days' work – 2s 5d.
Item paid to a labourer for 4 ½ days' work – 14d.
Item paid for hair – 1d.
Item paid for 3 ½ weys of lime – 2s 11d.
Item paid for ½ wey of coarse lime – 2 ½d.
Item paid for 500 lath nails – 5d.
Item paid to a tiler for 5 ½ days' work – 2s 8d.
Item paid for hauling boards – 2d.
Item paid for hauling 8 vats of stone and rubble – 8d.
Item paid for 500 laths – 2s 6d.
Item paid more for 4 loads of sand – 4d.
Item paid to a labourer for 2 hours' labour – 1d.
Item paid to a carpenter for a whole week's work – 3s 6d.
Item paid to his man for a whole week's work – 3s 3d.
Item paid to a labourer for a whole week's work – 2s.
Item paid for 200 board nails – 8d.
Item paid for 300 hatch nails – 9d.
Item paid for 700 lath nails – 7d.
Item paid for calf-foot nails – 2d.
Sum of this side – 34s 3d.

fo 4
Item paid 50 calf-foot nails – 5d.
Item paid for 100 board nails – 4d.
Item paid for 100 hatch nails – 3d.
Item paid for a load of paving stones – 15d.
Item paid for hauling them – 2d.
Item paid for 12 ½ semes of Welsh boards – 4s 10d.
Item paid for posts and studs – 20d.
Item paid for 125 boards – 2s 11d.
Item paid to a labourer for 4 ½ days' work – 18d.
Item paid for 4 loads of sand – 4d.
Item paid to a mason for cleaning gutters and paving, for 4 ½ days' work –
2s 7d.
Item paid for a stone for a *kackerell* – 3d.
Item paid to a tiler for 3 days' work – 18 ½d.
Item paid for 500 hatch nails – 15d.
Item paid for 300 lath nails – 3d.
Item paid for board nails and calf-foot nails – 2d.

Item paid to a carpenter for 4 ½ days' work – 2s 7d.
Item paid to his man for 4 ½ days' work – 2s 5d.
Item paid for 19 ½ weys of fine lime – 16s 3d.
Item paid for hauling away rubble – 11d.
Item paid to a mason for 4 days' work – 2s 2d.
Item paid to a labourer for 4 days' work – 16d.
Item paid more for 200 laths – 10d.
Item paid to a smith for hasps, hooks and twists – 16d.
Item paid for 2 loads of sand – 2d.
Item paid for a key to the outer door – 2d.
Item paid for mending 2 doors and for 1 board and nails – 2d.
Item paid for a key to John Gerves' back door – 4d.
Item paid for mending the lock with a new key to ?Mother Flogh – 4d.
Sum of this side – 48s 8 ½d.

fo 4v
Item paid for wood to make *sclabbis* and 1 crest – 1d.
Item paid for calf-foot nails and lath nails – 2 ½d.
Item paid for lath nails and board nails – 1 ½d.
Item paid for 50 laths – 3d.
Item paid to a tiler for 3 days' work – 16d.
Item paid for lime – 1 ½d.
Item paid for cleaning a gutter on John Gerves' back side, for the church's part – 4d.
Item paid for cleaning the almshouse gutter at Robert Ellyott's garden and for lime and candles – 21 ½d.
Sum of this side – 4s 3d.

Sum total of the repairs and payments – £13 3s 6 ½d.
Sum total of the receipts – £8 17s 6d.
So the repairs and payments amount above the receipts at this account –
£4 6s ½d.

[Different hand: This account was made before the vicar and *parisshons* by the said accountant, the 4th day of May in the year of Our Lord God 1525 so it appears that the church owes to the said accountant –
£4 6s ½d.]

[Original hand: Which £4 6s ½d I the said accountant acknowledge that I am fully content and paid by the vicar and the *p[ar]reschesons*, and so the church to be discharged and quit thereof.]

[1525–1526; outer page has been lost from front of booklet. Note that the rental of the following is augmented by the property mentioned (and, in part, repaired) in the previous account, which the church had obtained from the Hawkes' estate by purchase.]

fo 1

The accounts of Thomas Young and Davy Lawrens proctors of the parish church of All Saints' in Bristol for their receipts of the rents with other profits and charges belonging to the same church for a whole year, that is to say from the feast of the Annunciation of Our Blessed Lady in the year of Our Lord God 1525 unto the same feast of Our Lady in the year of Our Lord God 1526, Richard Abyngton then being mayor, Henry Whyt and John Gervys sheriffs.

Receipts of rent assize
In primis of Joan Poll for a gutter going through the church ground, by the year – 3s 4d.
Item of Cornell Hows next our conduit, by the year – 4s.
Item of the tenement that John Watson holds, by the year – 2s 6d.
Item of a tenement that [?was] Richard Erle's in Lewins Mead that Christ Church holds, by the year – 12d.
Item of the master and fellowship of the Tailors for a tenement in Baldwin Street, by the year – 12s.
Item of a tenement of Master Crofts in Saint Peter's parish – 6d.
Item of a tenement of Master Shipward's in Marsh Street – 2s.
Sum of this side – 25s 4d.

fo 1v
Rents of the church
Item received of John Hoper for a tenement by the year – £3 6s 8d.
Item received of the same John for the south part of the same house belonging to *tuoxbery* [Tewkesbury] by the year – 53s 4d.
Item received of my Lady Pernaunt for a tenement by the year – £4.
Item received of John Repe for a tenement by the year – 40s.
Item received of Thomas Kempe for a tenement by the year – 14s.
Item received of Andrew Page for a tenement by the year – 14s.
Item received of a tenement that Sir John Coke holds – 6s 8d.
Item received of the beer house in the church yard – 20d.
Item received of a tenement that Thomas Marmyn late held in Small Street – 26s 8d.
Item received of the great house in Broad Street – £4.
Item received of a stable and a garden that Colls holds by the year – 4s.
Item received of John Mansell for a vault by the year – 3s 4d.
Item received of John ?Heyd for a house and a loft by the year – 6s.

Item received of John Hoper for a stable by the year – 6s 8d.
Item received of the same John for a little loft – 20d.
Item received of W. Scheperd, tiler, for a garden in the old market – 2s.
Item received of Master Gervys for the south side of his house – £3.
Item received more for a garden in the *Pety* [Pithay], by the year – 5s.
Item received of Henry Foxole for a tenement by the year – 32s.
Item received of John Howell by the year for a tenement – 24s.
Item received of Roger Phylpot for a garden by the year – 5s.
Item received of Thomas Hawkyns for a garden by the year – 6s.
Item received of Master Robert Ellyot for a garden by the year – 8s.
Item received of Master vicar of All Hallows' for a garden – 8s.
Item received of Thomas Browne for a garden by the year – 8s.
Sum these rents – £28 2s 8d.

Sum the whole rents – £29 8s.

fo 2
Vacations and debts
Item of Joan Poll for a gutter, void by the year – 3s 4d.
Item of Richard Erle's house in Lewins Mead, void by the year – 12d.
Item of the master of the Tailors for the tenement in Baldwin Street, void the year – 12s.
Item of Master Croft's house in St Peter's parish, void – 6d.
Item of Master Shipward in Marsh Street, void the year – 2s.
Item of the beer house, void the year – 20d.
Item of Thomas Marmen's house, void the year – 26s 8d.
Item of the great house in Broad Street, void the year – £4.
Sum – £6 7s 2d.

Sum total of the rents, and the vacations abated – £23 10d.

Receipts of the church
Item received on Palm Sunday towards the sexton's wages – 2s 6d.
Item received to the paschal on Shere Thursday and Easter day and Easter eve – 9s 3 $\frac{1}{2}$d.
Item received for Our Lady of Worcester that belongs to the church – 7 $\frac{1}{2}$d.
Item received on Good Friday to the repairs of the jewels – 2s 4d.
Item received of John Whoper for the fine of his house – 26s 8d.
Item received of Agnes Waxmaker for the ?loan of a cellar – 12d.
Item received of a skinner for the ?loan of our storehouse – 20d.
Item received of John Hews for 100 cornish tiles – 5d.
Item received of William Chand, tanner – 10s.
Item received of John a Wood – 30s.

Item received of the proctors of Jesus – 28s 4d.
Item received of Gryffyth Barber for his wife's grave – 6s 8d.
Item received of Thomas Snygge in full payment for his father's legacy to the church – 33s 4d.
Sum – £7 12s 10d.

fo 2v
Receipts of pews
Item received of William Yong and his wife for their pews – 16d.
Item received of Alice Pacy for her pew – 4d.
Item received of Gryffyth Barber for his pew – 8d.
Sum – 2s 4d.

Sum total of the receipts, rents and casualties, the vacations abated – £30 16s.

fo 3
Payments of the church
In primis for a pottle of muscadel on Palm Sunday – 8d.
Item paid for watching the sepulchre – 12d.
Item paid to the raker – 8d.
Item paid for coals – 2 ½d.
Item paid for besoms – 3d.
Item paid for washing the church stuff – 2s.
Item paid for gathering the church and the chantry rents and for making the book of accounts and rewards to the tenants – 6s 8d.
Item paid to Walter Jones for his year's wages – 20s.
Item paid for hanging up the Dance of Pauls – 2s.
Item paid to Our Lady of Worcester – 8d.
Item paid to Thomas Hervyst for keeping Our Lady Mass – 5s.
Item paid to the sexton for attendance at the day of account – 4d.
Item paid for our supper at the day of account – 2s 10d.
Item paid for bearing the banner in Rogation week – 4d.
Item paid to Roger Pekeryng for his house the year – 6s 8d.
Item paid to him to his wage – 5s 4d.
Item paid for scouring of the church stuff – 2s.
Item paid for oil and scouring stone – 3d.
Item paid to T. Hervyst for his wages more than we received of the parish – 25s 9d.
Item paid for 11 gallons of lamp oil at 18d the gallon – 16s 6d.
Item paid to the Prior of St James for his part of the south side of the house that John Hoper now holds – 40s.
Item paid for a pair of gloves to the sexton at Easter – 2d.
Item paid for making the rent roll – 2d.

Item paid for matches – 1d.
Item paid for pins – 2d.
Item paid to a man to hang the *quere* – 2d.
Item paid for candles and holly against Christmas – 6d.
Sum of this – £7 [scored: 3s] 4 ½d.

fo 3v
Item paid for 1266 feet of elm board at 23d the 100 feet, sum – 24s 3d.
Item paid for hauling – 8d.
item paid to 2 labourers to bring them in the store house – 4d.
Item paid for 125 *rent* board – 25s.
Item paid for 212 feet of oak boards at 2s 4d [the 100 feet], sum – 4s 11d.
Item paid for hauling – 4d.
item paid for 2000 laths – 6s 8d.
Item paid for hauling – 2d.
Item paid to the chamberlain [superscript: for the rent of assize of the gardens in the Pithey] – 12d.
Item paid to Master vicar in part payment – £5 13s 4d.
Item paid to John Torner for pricking of ?songs – 2s.
Item paid for mending 2 hinges in the choir – 1d.
Item paid to Master vicar for saving of *tymer* [?timber?] – 10d.
Item paid for hauling – 1d.
Item paid for 3000 cornish tiles – 9s.
Item paid for hauling 6 draughts – 12d.
Item paid for bearing them into the storehouse – 4d.
Item paid for making a new collar in Thomas Hervyst's surplice and mending it – 6d.
Item paid for gilding the *bagyll* that serves on St Nicholas's night – 14d.
Item paid for a key to Elizabeth Gyllet's hall door – 2d.
Item paid for pricking 2 masses of 5 parts – 3s.
Item paid for a 16 foot gutter case to the tailor's house in the Pit Hey – 2s.
Item paid for *lynnys* [?lines] – 6d.
Item paid for a twist to Henry Foxole's stair door – 3d.
Item paid for *clapsyng* 3 processionals and for binding 1 of them – 12d.
Sum of this side – £9 18s 7d.

fo 4
Repairs
Payment
Master Gervys House
Item paid to a mason for 4 days' – 2s 2d.
Item paid for undersetting the house – 20d.
Item paid to 2 labourers for 4 days' – 2s 8d.
Item paid to a labourer for 1 ½ days' – 6d.

Item paid for hauling 4 vats of sand – 4d.

Item paid for hauling a piece of ?timber – 2d.

Item paid for nails to the scaffold – 1d.

Item paid to 2 masons for 4 $\frac{1}{2}$ days' – 3s 10 $\frac{1}{2}$d.

Item paid to 2 labourers for 4 $\frac{1}{2}$ days' – 3s.

Item paid to a labourer for 3 days' – 12d.

Item paid to a labourer for 2 $\frac{1}{2}$ days' – 10d.

Item paid for hauling 41 vats of stones and sand – 3s 5d.

Item paid for a pannier to bear sand and rubble – 3d.

Item paid to 2 masons for 2 $\frac{1}{2}$ days' – 2s 8 $\frac{1}{2}$d.

Item paid to 2 labourers for 2 $\frac{1}{2}$ days' – 20d.

Item paid for hauling 5 draughts of stones – 5d.

Item paid for [hauling] 4 vats of rubble – 4d.

Item paid for 20 weys of lime at 10d the wey, sum – 16s 8d.

Item paid to 2 tilers for a day – 13d.

Item paid for a load of paving stones – 16d.

Item paid to a mason for 2 days' – 13d.

Item paid to a labourer for 2 days' – 8d.

Item paid to 2 masons for a day – 13d.

Item paid for [hauling] 3 vats of rubble – 3d.

Item paid for hauling a load of paving stones – 2d.

Item paid for taking down a window in the back side and for mending it – 2s.

Item paid for 3 weys of lime – 2s 6d.

Item for a twist to the back door – 5 $\frac{1}{2}$d.

Item paid to a carpenter for 2 days' – 12d.

Item paid for a board to make legs – 6d.

Item paid for a load of paving – 16d.

Item paid for hauling – 2d.

Sum of this side – 56s 4 $\frac{1}{2}$d.

fo 4v

Repairs

Payments

Master Gervys house

Item paid in ale to the workmen at ?times – 2d.

Item paid for half the soldering of 3 *skarrys* betwixt the chamberlain and us – 3d.

Item paid to our part for 2 $\frac{1}{4}$ lb of solder – 6d.

Item more paid for half 2 $\frac{1}{2}$ lb of solder and for soldering 2 *skarrys* – 5d.

Item paid for mending a gutter between Master Pacy and us, to our part – 14d.

Item paid to a labourer for a day – 4d.

Item paid for clay and sand – 3d.

Item paid for cleaning another gutter in the back side – 12d.
Item paid to a labourer – 7 $\frac{1}{2}$d.
Item paid for 2 twists, 2 hooks and 4 staples weighing 22 lb at 1 $\frac{1}{4}$d the pound, sum – 2s 3 $\frac{1}{2}$d.
Sum – 7s.

The great house in Broad Street
Item paid for a new door, for boards and for making – 4s.
Item paid for 100 calf-foot nails – 10d.
Item paid for the repair of a twist – 3d.
Item paid for mending a wall – 12d.
Sum – 6s 1d.

Sum of this side – 13s 1d.

fo 5
Repairs Payments
Henry Foxoll's chimney and the Tailors
Item paid to John ?Poor for 5 days' at 6 $\frac{1}{2}$d, sum – 2s 8 $\frac{1}{2}$d.
Item paid to John Badkok for 6 days' at 6 $\frac{1}{2}$d, sum – 3s 3d.
Item paid to 2 labourers for 5 days' – 3s 4d.
Item paid for a load of stones called *tavellyng* – 16d.
Item for hauling – 2d.
Item paid for 7 loads of stones to the prior of St James – 4s 8d.
Item paid for calf-foot nails – 1d.
Item paid to 2 masons for 6 days' – 6s 6d.
Item paid to 2 labourers for 6 days' – 4s.
item paid for hauling 3 vats of sand and a vat of stones – 4d.
Item paid for a *reddyll* – 1 $\frac{1}{2}$d.
Item paid to 2 masons for 4 days' – 4s 4d.
Item paid to 2 labourers for 4 days' – 2s 8d.
Item paid for a load of tile – 14d.
Item paid for hauling – 2d.
Item paid for 4 crests – 2d.
Item paid for 15 weys of lime at 10d the wey, sum – 12s 6d.
Item paid for 100 *sowght* [?salt (for chimney)] stones – 6d.
Item paid to a tiler for 3 days' – 19 $\frac{1}{2}$d.
Item paid for 200 lath nails – 2 $\frac{1}{2}$d.
Item paid for 600 tile pins – 2d.
Item paid to a labourer – 1d.
Item paid for a piece of timber for the chimney – 12d.
Item paid for [hauling] 12 vats of rubble – 12d.
Sum of this side – 52s 1d.

fo 5v

Costs of the wax

Item delivered to the waxmaker 13 square tapers weighing 3 quarters and 13 lb [95 lb].

Item received in new wax with the old 111 $\frac{1}{2}$ lb and so received in new wax 26 $\frac{1}{2}$ lb at 7d, sum – 15s 5 $\frac{1}{2}$d.

Item delivered 15 round tapers weighing 15 lb.

Item received them again at 30 $\frac{1}{2}$ lb, and so there is in new wax 15 $\frac{1}{2}$ lb at 7d, sum – 9s $\frac{1}{2}$d.

Item more delivered a paschal and the font taper weighing 26 $\frac{1}{2}$ lb, and so received them again with 4 prickets [weighing] 28 $\frac{1}{4}$ lb, and so received in new wax 1 $\frac{3}{4}$ lb at 7d, sum – 12 $\frac{1}{2}$d.

Item delivered 15 round tapers weighing 15 lb and received them again at 31 lb, and so there is in new wax 16 lb at 7d the pound, sum – 9s 4d.

Item paid for making all the old wax – 3s 4d.

Sum – 38s 2 $\frac{1}{2}$d.

Item for 2 torches weighing 34 lb at 4d, sum – 11s 4d.

Payments of Corpus Christi day

Item paid to Master vicar – nil.

Item paid to 4 priests – 16d.

Item paid to 2 friars to bear the shrine – 12d.

Item paid to 2 torch bearers – 4d.

Item paid for bearing the cross – 4d.

Item paid for a pottle of wine – 6d.

Item paid to Walter the second clerk – 2d.

Item paid to the children for bearing the candlesticks, censers and copes – 4d.

Item paid to the sub deacon – 2d.

Item paid to the clerk and his children – 12d.

Sum – 5s 2d.

Sum of this side – 54s 8 $\frac{1}{2}$d.

fo 6

The obit of William Newbery, held the 10th day of May

[Bracketed to the entries for the obit in the margin, *Vacat nunc*:]

Item paid to Master vicar for his dirige and wax – 16d.

Item paid to 5 priests – 20d.

Item paid to the clerk for his bells and his dirige – 10d.

Item paid to the bellman – 2d.

Item paid for bread to the poor people – 2s.

Item paid for offering at Mass – 1d.

Sum – 6s 1d.

Memorandum that this is the 9th year that we lacked our payments of the master and fellowship of the Tailors.

The obit of Thomas Fylour and Agnes his wife, held the 20th day of November.
In primis to Master vicar for wax – 12d.
Item paid to 8 priests – 2s 8d.
Item paid to Master vicar for his bede roll – 12d.
Item paid to the clerk for his bells and his labour – 14d.
Item paid to the bellman – 2d.
Item paid for offering at Mass – 1d.
Item paid to the 2 proctors for their labour and attendance – 12d.
Item paid for bread to the poor people – 5s.
Item paid to the sexton laying out the hearse – 2d.
Sum – 12s 3d.

fo 6v
The obit of Harry Chestre and Humfrey Hervy and his friends, held the 14th day of February.
In primis paid to Master vicar for wax – 12d.
Item paid to 6 priests – 2s.
Item paid to the clerk – 12d.
Item paid to the bellman – 4d.
Item paid for offering at Mass – 1d.
Item paid to the proctors for their labour – 8d.
Item paid to the sexton – 2d.
Item paid to the proctors of Newgate in bread – 20d.
Item paid to our almshouse in bread – 4d.
Item paid to the lazar house at Bright Bowe in bread – 4d.
Item paid to the almshouse at the Long Rowe in bread – 4d.
Sum – 7s 11d.

The obit of Thomas Spicer and Dame Maud his wife, held the 15th day of February.
In primis paid to Master vicar and 6 priests – 2s 8d.
Item paid to Master vicar for 4 tapers – 2s.
Item paid to Master vicar for the bede roll – 4d.
Item paid to the clerk for bells and dirige – 14d.
Item paid to the proctors for their labour and attendance – 12d.
Item paid to the bellman – 4d.
Item paid for offering at Mass – 1d.
Item paid to the sexton for laying out the hearse – 1d.
Item paid for bread to prisoners and to poor people – 3s.
Sum – 10s 4d.

Sum of this side – 18s 3d.

fo 7
The obit of all good doers
In primis paid to Master vicar – 4d.
Item paid to 4 priests – 12d.
Item paid for offering at Mass – 1d.
Item paid to the clerk for the bells and dirige – 14d.
Item paid for 3 bushels of wheat – 23d.
Item paid for grinding the same – 3d.
Item paid for 2 oz of saffron – 2s.
Item paid for 1 oz of cloves – 5d.
Item paid for a pottle of osey – 6d.
Item paid for bread – 6d.
Item paid for balm – 2d.
Item paid for baking the cake – 12d.
Item paid for 2 dozen ale – 2s.
Item paid for a pottle and a pint of malmsey – 10d.
Item paid for 2 gallons of claret wine – 16d.
Item more paid for 2 gallons and a pottle of osey – 2s 6d.
Item paid to the sexton for laying out the hearse – 2d.
Sum – 16s 2d.

The obit of Henry Chestre and Humfrey Harvy, held the 4th day of March.
Item paid to Master vicar for wax – 12d.
Item paid to 6 priests – 2s.
Item paid to the clerk for the bells – 12d.
Item paid to the bellman – 4d.
Item paid for the offering at Mass – 1d.
Item paid to the proctors for their labour – 8d.
Item paid to the sexton for laying out the hearse – 2d.
Item paid to the prisoners in Newgate in bread – 20d.
Item paid to our almshouse in bread – 4d.
Item paid to the Bright Bowe in bread – 4d.
Item paid to the almshouse in the Longe Rowe in bread – 4d.
Sum – 7s 11d.

Sum of this side – 24s 1d.

fo 7v
For cleaning a gutter in Sir John Kok's chamber
Item paid to a mason for 2 days' – 16d.
Item paid to a labourer for 2 days' – 8d.
Sum – 2s.

Repairs to the little vestry
Item paid for 2 $\frac{1}{4}$ lb of solder – 6d.
Item paid for soldering 2 *skarrys* – 4d.
Item paid for making 2 bolts to the vestry door and a staple to set the cross staff in – 3d.
Item paid for a *pypyd* key to the vestry door – 4d.
Item paid for a key to the tower door – 2d.
Sum – 19d.

Sum of this side – 3s 7d.

fo 8
Sum total of all payments this year – £28 13s 4 $\frac{1}{2}$d.

So rests that the accountant owes of this account to the church – 42s 7 $\frac{1}{2}$d.

[Remainder of side in different hand:] This account was made before the vicar and *parisshons* by the said accountant the 26th day of April in the year of Our Lord 1526 and so it appears that the said accountant owes to the church this year – 42s 7 $\frac{1}{2}$d.
Which sum the said accountant has brought into the said church before the said vicar and *parisshons* the day and year above written and so he is dismissed quietly.

Memorandum that David Lawrence has received the day of this account 4s 10 $\frac{1}{2}$d, which money he must bring in to the church at the day of his account – 4s 10 $\frac{1}{2}$d.

Memorandum also that Thomas Yong of Bristol, grocer, has paid to David Lawrence proctor of the said church in part payment of the legacies of John Wale late apprentice to the said Thomas Yong, [on] the day of this account – £3.

[1527]

fo 1
Master David Lawrence
Anno Domini 1527
The Church Book

fo 2
The accounts of David Lawrence and Roger Filpott proctors of the parish

church of All Saints' in Bristol for their receipts of the rents with other profits belonging to the same church for a whole year that is to say from the feast of the Annunciation of Our Lady in the year of Our Lord God 1526 unto the same feast of Our Lady in the year of Our Lord God 1527, Thomas Brooke then being mayor, the above named David Lawrence and George Badram sheriffs.

Rents of assize by the year
In primis received of Joan Powle [superscript: John Alye] for a gutter that goes through the church ground that Thomas Prene barber holds – 3s 4d.
Item received of the Cornell house next to All Hallows' conduit – 4s.
Item received of the tenement that John Watson holds for his back door – 2s 6d.
Item received of Christ church for a tenement in Lewins Mead that was Richard Erle's – 12d.
Item received of the master and fellowship of the Tailors for a tenement in Baldwin Street that John Northall, pewterer, now holds – 12s.
Item received of a tenement that was Master Croft's in Saint Peter's parish – 6d.
Item received of a tenement in Marsh Street that was Master Shipward's – 2s.
Sum – 25s 4d.

Sum this side – 25s 4d.

fo 2v
Rents of the church by the year
In primis received of my Lady Pernaunt for a tenement – £4.
Item received of John Hoper for a tenement – £3 6s 8d.
Item received of Hoper again for the south side of the same tenement which we hold of the monastery of Tewkesbury – 53s 4d.
Item received of Master John Repe for a tenement – 40s.
Item received of Master John Gervis for a tenement – £3.
Item received of Thomas Prene, barber, for a tenement – 14s.
Item received of Andrew Page for a tenement – 14s.
Item received of Sir John Cooke for a tenement – 6s 8d.
Item received of the beer house in the churchyard – 20d.
Item received of Mistress Hoobby for a tenement in Small Street – 26s 8d.
Item received of the great house in Broad Street – £4.
Item received of John Collys for for a stable and a garden in the same house – 4s.
Item received of John Mawncell for a vault there – 3s 4d.
Item received of John Hyed, skinner, for a work-house there with a loft – 6s.

Item received of John Hooper for a stable there – 6s 8d.
Item received of John Hooper also for a little loft there – 20d.
Item received of William Shepward, tiler, for a garden in the old market place – 2s.
Item received of Master John Gervis for a garden in the Pithey – 5s.
Item received of Harry Foxole for a tenement there – 32s.
Item received of John Howell for a tenement there – 24s.
Item received of Roger Filpott for a garden there – 5s.
Item received of Thomas Hawkyns, merchant, for a garden there – 6s.
Item received of Robert Helyott, merchant, for a garden there – 8s.
Item received of the vicar of All Hallows for a garden there – 8s.
Item received of Thomas Browne, apothecary, for a garden there – 8s.
Sum the rents – £28 2s 8d.

Sum the whole rents – £29 8s.

fo 3
The vacations and decays
In primis Joan Powll [superscript: John Alye] for a gutter through the church ground – 3s 4d.
Item Richard Erle's tenement in Lewins Mead that Christ church should pay – 12d.
Item the master and fellowship of the Tailors for a tenement in Baldwin Street that John Northhall, pewterer, holds, now 10 years behind – 12s.
Item Master Croft's tenement in Saint Peter's parish – 6d.
Item Master Shipward's tenement in Marsh Street – 2s.
Item the beer house in the churchyard – 20d.
Item the tenement that Master Hobby holds in Small Street, half a year – 13s 4d.
Item the great house in Broad Street – £4.
Sum – £5 13s 10d.

Sum total of the rents, the vacations and decays abated – £23 13s 2d.

The receipts of customable duties belonging to the church
In primis received on Palm Sunday towards the sexton's wages – 2s 10d.
Item received on Shere Thursday, Easter eve and Easter day towards the paschall – 8s 6d.
Item received on Good Friday towards the repair of the jewels – 2s 6d.
Item received on Easter Day for Our Lady of Worcester – 12 ½d.
Item received of Thomas Yong for part of John Wale's bequest to the church – £3.
Item received of John Davis, beer brewer, for the full payment of the said bequest – 40s.

Item received of John a Wood beer brewer – 40s.
Item received the day of the last account – 4s 10 $\frac{1}{2}$d.
Item received of the proctors of the fraternity of Jesus – 20s 10d.
Item received of Thomas Prene, barber, [for] his pew and for his wife's pew – 16d.
Item received of Robert Byrkyn for Griffith Barber's grave – 6s 8d.
Item received of [scored: Katherine Kere for her husband's grave] Rawlyn Webbe for his wife's grave – 6s 8d.
Item received of John a Chamber, tanner, at midsummer – 10s.
Item received of Morgan Thomas, whittawer – 10s.
Item received a standing cup of silver and parcel gilt of Griffith barber, weighing 17 oz at 3s 5d the oz., amounting to – 58s 1d.
Sum – £13 13s 4d.

Sum total of the receipts of rents and casualties, the vacations and decays abated – £37 7s 6d.

fo 3v
Payments that yearly be accustomed and other casualties that grow to the charge of the church
In primis paid on Palm Sunday for a pottle of *mosfardel* – 8d.
Item paid for watching the sepulchre – 12d.
Item paid to the raker – 8d.
Item paid for coals – 2 $\frac{1}{2}$d.
Item paid for besoms – 3d.
Item paid for washing the church cloths – 2s.
Item paid for gathering the rents, making the book of accounts and for rewards to tenants – 6s 8d.
Item paid to Wat Jones the second clerk for his year's wages – 25s.
Item paid for hanging up the Dance of Pauls – 2s.
Item paid to Our Lady of Worcester – 8d.
Item paid to Thomas Harvist, clerk, for keeping Our Lady Mass – 5s.
Item paid more to the same Thomas for his wages more than taxation of the parish – 23s 6d.
Item paid to the sexton for his attendance at the day of the accounts – 4d.
Item paid towards our supper at the day of the accounts – 2s 8d.
Item paid for bearing the banners in Rogation week – 4d.
Item paid to Roger Pickring, sexton, for his house rent – 6s 8d.
Item paid to the same Roger for his year's wage – 5s 4d.
Item paid for scouring the church stuff – 2s.
Item paid for oil and scouring stone – 3d.
Item paid for lamp oil to William Enworth amounting to 12 gallons and a pottle at 18d the gallon – 18s 9d.
Item paid to the Prior of St James for the south part of the tenement that

John Hooper holds – 40s.
Item paid for a pair of gloves to the sexton at Easter – 2d.
Item paid for making the rent roll – 2d.
Item paid for matches – ½d.
Item paid for pins – 2d.
Item paid for candles and holly against Christmas – 6d.
Item paid for washing the shrine cloth – 2d.
Sum – £7 5s 2d.

fo 4
Payments for the church
Item paid to the organ maker for new reforming the organs – 23s 4d.
Item paid to the clerk of St Thomas for 5 pricksong books containing 8
Masses – 6s 8d.
Item paid to John ?Bech for pricking 4 books of masses and anthems *of
the trebuls and meanes* for the children – 8s 10d.
Item paid for paper for that book – 5d.
Item paid to Jerome Grene by agreement of Master vicar and the parish –
50s 6d.
Item paid to Thomas Yong for the funeral expenses of John Wale – 10s 6d.
Item paid for 8 ells of *dowles* to make a surplice for the clerk at 6[d] the
ell – 4s.
Item paid for making the same surplice – 2s.
Item paid for making 4 surplices to the children – 2s.
Item paid for a rope to the morrow mass bell – 15d.
Item paid for a line to draw the curtains at the Jesus altar – 1d.
Item paid to John Power, mason, to make 2 places in the choir to put 2
bars of iron to stay the standards – 4d.
Item paid to a smith for making the same bars of iron – 5d.
Item paid for mending the pulleys over the high altar – 4d.
Item paid for 4 cords for the cloths at the high altar – 4d.
Item paid for a quire of paper to ?perform the said pricksong book – 3 ½d.
Item paid for 2 desks, 1 for the high altar and another for St Thomas's altar
– 16d.
Item paid for mending the wheel of the great bell – 16d.
Item paid for fetching a ladder at the White Friars – 2d.
Item paid to the Morrow Mass priest for 2 quarters from Michaelmas to
the feast of the Annunciation of Our Lady last past – £3.
Item paid to the clerk of St Thomas for binding a book – 4d.
Item paid for 2 curtains hanging at the enterclose of the choir – 16d.
Item paid to Master vicar the day of the last account in full payment of all
such money as the church owed him – 52s 8d.
Sum – £11 8s 5 ½d.

fo 4v
Payments on Corpus Christi Day
In primis paid to Master vicar – nil.
Item paid to 4 priests – 16d.
Item paid to 2 friars to bear the shrine – 12d.
Item paid to 2 torch bearers – 4d.
Item paid for bearing the cross – 4d.
Item paid for 3 quarters of wine – 6d.
Item paid to Wat the second clerk – 2d.
Item paid to the children that bore candlesticks, censers and copes – 4d.
Item paid to the sub deacon – 2d.
Item paid to the clerk and to his children – 12d.
Sum – 5s 2d.

Costs of the wax for the church
In primis the waxmaker delivered 13 square tapers weighing 106 lb.
Item he delivered a paschal weighing 22 lb.
Item he delivered a font taper weighing 3 lb.
Item he delivered 15 round tapers weighing 31 lb.
Item he delivered 15 round tapers at All Hallowstide weighing 31 lb.
Item he delivered 2 standards weighing 5 lb.
Amount the new wax 10 score and 10 lb

Item he received 13 square tapers weighing 102 lb.
Item he received a paschal weighing 21 lb.
Item he received a font taper weighing 2 $\frac{1}{2}$ lb.
Item he received 15 round tapers weighing 16 lb.
Item he received 15 round tapers at All Hallowstide weighing 11 lb.
Item he received 2 standards weighing 2 $\frac{1}{4}$ lb.
Amount the old wax 7 score and 14 $\frac{3}{4}$ lb.

So it appears that the new wax amounts above the old wax 55 $\frac{1}{4}$ lb at 7d
the pound, sum – 32s 2 $\frac{1}{2}$d.
Item for a torch for to go in visitation with the sacrament weighing 7 $\frac{1}{4}$ lb
at 4d the pound, amount – 2s 5d.
Item paid for 4 tapers for the angels – 4d.
Item paid for making the whole wax all the year – 3s 4d.
Sum total – 38s 3 $\frac{1}{2}$d.

Sum this side – 43s 5 $\frac{1}{2}$d.

fo 5
The obit of William Newbery, held the 10th day of May
[In margin, bracketed against the entries for the obit: Vacant nunc]

Item paid to Master vicar for his labour and wax – 16d.
Item paid to 5 priests – 20d.
Item paid to the clerk for his labour and bells – 10d.
Item paid to the bellman – 2d.
Item paid for bread for poor people – 2s.
Item paid for offering at Mass – 1d.
Sum – 6s 1d.

Memorandum that this is the 10th year that we lack our payment of the master and fellowship of the Tailors.

The obit of Thomas Fyler and of Agnes his wife, held the 20th day of November.
Item paid to Master vicar in wax – 12d.
Item paid to 8 priests – 2s 8d.
Item paid to Master vicar for his bede roll – 12d.
Item paid to the clerk for his labour and bells – 14d.
Item paid to the bellman – 2d.
Item paid for offering at Mass – 1d.
Item paid to the 2 proctors for their labour and intendance – 12d.
Item paid for bread to poor people – 5s.
Item paid to the sexton for laying out the hearse – 2d.
Sum – 12s 3d.

Sum this side – 12s 3d.

fo 5v
The obit of Harry Chestre and Humfrey Hervy with their friends, held the 14th day of February.
Item paid to Master Vicar for wax – 12d.
Item paid to 6 priests – 2s.
Item paid to the clerk for his labour and bells – 12d.
Item paid to the bellman – 4d.
Item paid for offering at Mass – 1d.
Item paid for the 2 proctors' labour and intendance – 8d.
Item paid to the sexton for laying out the hearse – 2d.
Item paid to the prisoners of Newgate in bread – 20d.
Item paid to our almshouse in bread – 4d.
Item paid to the lazar house at Bright Bowe in bread – 4d.
Item paid to the almshouse in the Long Rowe in bread – 4d.
Sum – 7s 11d.

The obit of Thomas Spicer and Dame Maud his wife, held the 15th day of February

Item paid to Master vicar and 6 priests – 2s 8d.
Item paid to Master vicar for 4 tapers – 2s.
Item paid to Master vicar for the bede roll – 4d.
Item paid for the clerk's labour and bells – 14d.
Item paid to the proctors for their labour and intendance – 12d.
item paid to the bellman – 4d.
Item paid for offering at Mass – 1d.
Item paid to the sexton for laying out the hearse – 1d.
Item paid for bread to the prisoners and other poor people – 3s.
Sum – 10s 4d.

Sum this side – 18s 3d.

fo 6
The obit of all Good doers
Item paid to Master vicar – 4d.
Item paid to 4 priests, every priest 3d – 12d.
Item paid for offering at Mass – 1d.
Item paid to the clerk for his labour and bells – 14d.
Item paid for 3 bushels of wheat – 23d.
Item paid for grinding the same – 3d.
Item paid for 2 oz of saffron – 2s.
Item paid for cloves and *mases* – 5d.
Item paid for a pottle of osey for the cake – 6d.
Item paid in bread – 6d.
Item paid in balm – 2d.
Item paid for baking the cake – 12d.
Item paid for 2 dozen ale – 2s.
Item paid for a pottle and a pint of malmsey – 10d.
Item paid for 2 gallons of claret wine – 16d.
Item paid for 2 gallons and a pottle of osey – 2s 6d.
Item paid to the sexton for laying out the hearse – 2d.
Sum – 16s 2d.

The second obit of Humfrey Hervy and Harry Chestre, held the 4th day of March.
Item paid to Master vicar for wax – 12d.
Item paid to Master vicar and 5 priests – 2s.
Item paid to the clerk for his labour and bells – 12d.
Item paid to the bellman – 4d.
Item paid for offering at Mass – 1d.
Item paid to the proctors for their labour and intendance – 8d.
Item paid to the sexton for laying out the hearse – 2d.
Item paid to the prisoners of Newgate in bread – 20d.

Item paid to our almshouse in bread – 4d.
Item paid to the lazar house at Bright Bowe in bread – 4d.
Item paid to the almshouse in the Longe Rewe – 4d.
Sum – 7s 11d.

Sum this side – 24s 1d.

fo 6v
Repairs done upon John Hooper's house
Item paid to John Power for ridding a gutter, there working 4 days – 2s 8d.
Item paid to 2 labourers for 4 days' – 2s.
Item paid for lime to the same – 16d.
Item paid to the raker for hauling away 6 vats of rubble – 6d.
Item paid for making a pipe of lead into a *drawte* – 13d.
Item paid to John Plummer for mending a *scare* in the gutter – 4d.
Sum – 7s 11d.

Repairs done upon Mistress Hobbe's house
Item paid to the tiler for a day's work – 6 $\frac{1}{2}$d.
Item paid for 6 lb of solder – 18d.
Item paid for mending 5 *scares* – 8d.
Item paid for 37 lb of lead for the gutter – 23d.
Item paid for tile pins – 1d.
item paid for nails – 1d.
Item paid for 4 sacks of lime – 4d.
Item paid to 2 tilers for a day's work – 10d.
Sum – 5s 11 $\frac{1}{2}$d.

Item paid for hauling away 7 vats of rubble that lie before my lady
Pernaunt's garden door – 7d.
Sum – 7d.

Sum this side – 14s 5 $\frac{1}{2}$d.

Sum total of the payments – £24 6s 1 $\frac{1}{2}$d.

fo 7
So it appears that the receipts of this year amount above the payments –
£13 16d.
Which sum of money the said accountant has brought into the church at
this his account, held the 16th day of the month of May in the year of Our
Lord God 1527 in the presence of the vicar and *parisshons*, and so he is
dismissed and clearly discharged.

Memorandum that the chantry owes the church this year, as it appears in the chantry book – 19s 8d.

Which money the said accountant has received the day of this account of the church money.

Memorandum that of the £13 16d above written the said accountant has delivered to Roger Felpott proctor a standing cup of silver parcel gilt weighing 17 oz for the sum of 58s 1d; and the same accountant is allowed of the said 19s 8d for the chantry; and so it appears that he has brought in at this account in ready money – £9 3s 9d, of the which money we have put into the church coffer the day of this account – £6 13s 4d; and the above named Roger Felpott has received at this account in money – 50s 5d, which money he must bring into the church again at his account. And also the same Roger has the said standing cup to deliver to him to the intent that he shall make sales thereof to the most advantage of the church and to bring in to the church the money coming of the same sales at his account with the said 50s 5d. *Solute at sic quiete recessit.*

[1528]
fo 1
Roger Felpott
Anno 1528
The Church Book

fo 2
The accounts of Roger Felpott and Symond Hancocke, proctors of the parish church of All Saints', Bristol, for their receipts of the rents with other profits belonging to the same church for a whole year, that is to say from the feast of the Annunciation of Our Lady in the year of Our Lord God 1527 unto the same feast of Our Lady in the year of Our Lord God 1528, John Ware then being mayor, David Hutton and Thomas Marshe sheriffs.

Rents of Assize by the year
In primis of Joan Polle for a gutter that goes through the church grounds that Thomas Prene, barber, holds – 3s 4d.
Item of the Cornell house next to All Hallows' conduit – 4s.
Item of the tenement that John Watson holds for his back door – 2s 6d.
Item of Christchurch for a tenement in Lewins Mead that was Richard Erle's – 12d.
Item of the master and fellowship of the Tailors for a tenement in Baldwin Street that John Marshall, pewterer, now holds – 12s.
Item of a tenement that was Master Croft's in St Peter's parish – 6d.

Item of a tenement in Marsh Street that was Master Shipward's – 2s.
Sum – 25s 4d.

fo 2v
Rents of the church by the year.
Item my lady Parnant for a tenement by the year – £4.
Item John Hoper for a tenement – £3 6s 8d.
Item John Hoper again for the south side of the same tenement which we
hold of the monastery of Tewkesbury – 53s 4d.
Item Master John Repe for a tenement – 40s.
Item Master John Gervys for a tenement – £3.
Item Thomas Prene, barber, for a tenement – 14s.
Item Andrew Page for a tenement – 14s.
Item Sir John Coke for a tenement – 6s 8d.
Item the beer house in the churchyard – 20d.
Item the surgeon in Small Street for a tenement – 26s 8d.
Item the great house in Broad Street – £4.
Item John Collys for a stable and a garden in the same house – 4s.
Item John Collys for a house and a loft there – 6s.
Item John Hoper for a stable there – 6s 8d.
Item John Hoper for a little loft there – 20d.
Item John Rychards, tailor, dwelling in Baldwin Street, for a garden in the
old market place – 20d.
Item Master John Gervys for a garden in the Pyte – 5s.
Item Harry Foxoll for a tenement there – 32s.
Item John Howell for a tenement there – 24s.
Item Roger Felpott for a garden there – 5s.
Item Thomas Hankyns for a garden there – 6s.
Item Robert Elyott for a garden there – 8s.
Item Master Thomas Parsye for a garden there – 8s.
Item Thomas Browne, apothecary, for a garden there – 8s.
Item Richard Skynar for a vault in the old house in Bread Street – 5s.
Sum of the rents – £28 4s.

Sum of the whole rents – £29 9s 4d.

fo 3
The vacations and decays
Item Joan Polle for a gutter that goes through the church ground – 3s 4d.
Item Richard Erle's tenement in Lewins Mead that Christchurch should
pay – 12d.
Item the master and fellowship of the Tailors for a tenement in Baldwin
Street that John Northall, pewterer, holds now 11 years – 12s.
Item Master Croft's tenement in St Peter's parish – 6d.

Item Master Shipward's tenement in Marsh Street – 2s.
Item the beer house in the churchyard – 20d.
Item the tenement that Mistress Holbye held in Small Street 1 quarter of a year – 6s 8d.
Item the great house in Broad Street – £4.
Item the vault there for half a year – 2s 6d.
Sum – £5 9s 8d.

Sum total of the rents, the vacations and decays abated – £23 19s 8d.

The receipts of the customable duties belonging to the church
In primis on Palm Sunday towards the sexton's wages – 2s 8d.
Item on Sheer Thursday towards the paschal – 21d.
Item on Good Friday likewise towards the repairs of the jewels – 2s 9d.
Item on Easter eve towards the paschal – 11d.
Item on Easter day towards the paschal – 6s 3d.
Item on Easter day for Our Lady of Worcester – 12d.
Item of John a Wood, beer brewer – 20s.
Item of John Mawnsell [added: for a quarter's rent for the vault] – 10d.
Item of the tanner upon the Were [added: John a Chambyr] – 10s.
Item of Jesus proctors – 22s.
Item of Master Parsye for a bewdley board – 3d.
Item of Walter sexton for 9 bewdley boards – 22d.
Item of the parish towards the clerk's wages – £3 7s 3d.
Sum – £6 17s 6d.

fo 3v
More receipts of customable duties belonging to the church
Item of Master Abynton for 131 feet of board – 3s 6d.
Item of Joan Tyson's son upon an obligation – 3s 4d.
Item of the good wife Kere for her husband's grave – 6s 8d.
Item of Thomas Polsam for his wife's grave – 6s 8d.
Item of Franks for his wife's pew – 8d.
Item of Katherine Mylward for her pew – 8d.
Item of John Mawnsel, his mother's pew – 8d.
Item of William Ayre, for his pew and his wife's pew – 16d.
[Erased: Item received a standing cup of silver parcel gilt at 3s 6d an ounce.]
Item received at the last day of accounts in money – 50s 5d.
Item received a standing cup of silver parcel gilt weighing 17 oz, which was sold for 3s 6d an ounce, amount – 59s 6d.
Item received of Master Thomas Parsye for 48 bewdley boards, at 20s the 100, amount – 8s 10d.
Item of John Tailor for ?550 cornish tiles – 22d.

Item of Master Pacy for 1000 cornish tiles – 3s.
Item of William Eruth for 50 cornish tiles – 2d.
Item of the bequest of John Watson – 20s.
Item of the bequest of John Pooke – 3s 4d.
Item of Thomas a Pulton for his pew and his wife's – 12d.
Sum – £8 11s 7d.
Sum of the whole customable receipts – £15 9s 1d.

Sum total of the receipts, of the rents and casualties, the vacations and decays abated – £39 8s 9d.

fo 4
Payments that be yearly accustomed and other casualties that grow to the charge of the church
In primis on Palm Sunday for a pottle of muscadel – 8d.
Item for watching the sepulchre – 12d.
Item to the vicar – 8d.
Item for coals – 3d.
Item for besoms – 2d.
Item for washing the church cloths – 2s.
Item for gathering rents, for making books of accounts and for rewards to tenements [sic] – 6s 8d.
Item to Walter Jones [superscript: second clerk] for his year's wages – 26s 8d.
Item for hanging up the Dance of Pauls – 2s.
Item to Our Lady of Worcester – 8d.
Item to Thomas Harvyst for keeping our Mass – 5s.
Item to Sir Nicholas for a quarter's wages – 31s 4d.
Item to Sir John Jeffries for a quarter's wages – 30s.
Item to Thomas Harvyst for his year's wages – £4 13s 4d.
Item to the sexton for his attendance at the day of accounts – 4d.
Item paid over the receipt of our supper of our day of account – 3s 5d.
Item paid for bearing the banner in Rogation week – 4d.
Item to Roger Pykeryn, sexton, for his house rent – 6s 8d.
Item to the same Roger for his year's wages – 5s 4d.
Item for scouring the church stuff – 2s.
Item for oil and scouring stone – 3d.
Item for 12 gallons and a quart of lamp oil at 16d – 16s 4d.
Item to the Prior of St James for the south part of the tenement that John Hoper holds – 40s.
Item for a pair of gloves to the sexton at Easter – 2d.
Item for making the rent roll – 2d.
Item for matches – ½d.
Item for pins – 2d.

Item for candles and holly against Christmas – 6d.
Item for washing the shrine cloths – 1d.
Sum – £13 16s 2 ½d.

fo 4v
Payments of the church
In primis to Robert Ruffin for 175 planks at 2s 8d the 100, amount – 4s 8d.
Item 8 ells of *doles* to make a surplice at 6d the ell – 4s.
Item for making the same surplice – 2s.
Item for thread – 2d.
Item for mending 2 surplices, 1 for Master vicar and the other for Thomas Harvyst – 5d.
Item to Frauncs for mending the pricksong books – 2s 4d.
Item on Palm Sunday in singing bread – ½d.
Item in nails – ½d.
Item a banner staff – 4d.
Item to Roger for cleaning the gutter over the charnel house – 1d.
Item for curtain rings – 2d.
Item for a spade tree – 1d.
Item a shovel – 1d.
Item a rope for the paschal – 10d.
Item a dozen girdles – 20d.
Item for hallowing the same dozen girdles – 4d.
Item for laying the stone upon the tailor's house in the Pyte – 6d.
Item for mending a lock of the store house door in Broad Street – 2d.
Item for mending the churchyard stile – 7d.
Item to William Harrys for his labour to Salisbury – 4s.
Item to Brandon for his costs – 2s 8d.
Item for hallowing of 2 corporas [erased: cases] – 4d.
Item for a *pypyd* key to John Hyde's house in Broad Street – 3d.
Item for a lamp – 1d.
Item for pricking an anthem – 12d.
Item for paper – 2d.
Item for a yard of buckram to mend the vestment – 6d.
Item paid for the *sytacyon* [citation] [superscript: with other fees for Robert ?Birky] – 3s 4d.
Item for hauling a draught of planks to the ?store house – 2d.
Item for cleaning the great house in Broad Street – 1d.
Sum – 31s 1d.

Sum total of the church payments – £15 7s 3 ½d.

fo 5
Payments of the church

In primis for carriage of the *sartyffycathe* [?certificate] to Worcester – 4d.
Item for mending a candlestick – 4d.
Item a chain for the Morrow Mass bell – 2d.
Item to John Beche for pricking a song against St Nicholas night – 4d.
Item for making and pricking a part which was lost – 12d.
Item for paper – 2d.
Item for 1 $\frac{1}{2}$ oz of silk for the fringe for the high altar – 18d.
Item for making the fringe – 8d.
Item to Master vicar for costs [superscript: of the suit of Robert ?Birky] of the church – 2s 8d.
Sum – 7s 2d.

Payments on Corpus Christi Day
Item to Master vicar – nil.
Item to 4 priests – 16d.
Item to 2 friars to bear the shrine – 12d.
Item to 2 torch bearers – 4d.
Item for bearing the cross – 4d.
Item for 3 quarts of wine – 6d.
Item to Walter the second clerk – 2d.
Item to the children that bore the candlesticks, censers and copes – 4d.
Item to the subdeacon – 2d.
Item to the clerk and his children – 12d.
Sum – 5s 2d.

Sum this side – 12s 4d.

fo 5v
Costs of the wax for the church
In primis delivered to the waxmaker 13 square tapers weighing – 98 lb.
Item 15 tapers weighing – 14 lb.
Item the font taper and the paschal weighing – 17 $\frac{1}{2}$ lb.
Item 15 tapers weighing – 14 $\frac{1}{2}$ lb.
Sum of the old wax – 7 score and 4 lb.

Received of the wax maker 13 square tapers weighing 114 $\frac{1}{4}$ lb –
114 $\frac{1}{4}$ lb.
Received 15 tapers weighing – 29 lb.
Received the font taper and the paschal taper weighing – 24 lb.
Received 15 tapers weighing – 31 $\frac{1}{2}$ lb.
Sum of the new wax – 9 score and 18 $\frac{3}{4}$ lb.

So it appears that the new wax amounts above the old wax – 54 $\frac{3}{4}$ lb.
At 6 $\frac{1}{2}$d the pound – 29s 7 $\frac{1}{2}$d.

Item 4 tapers for the angels – 4d.
Item a taper of a pound – 6 ½d.
Item the making of the whole wax at the year – 3s 4d.
Sum total – 33s 10d.

fo 6
The obit of William Newbery held the 10th day of May
[Bracketed against the entries of the obit: *vacat nunc*]Item to Master vicar
for his labour and wax – 16d.
Item to 5 priests – 20d.
Item to the clerk for his labour and bells – 10d.
Item to the bellman – 2d.
Item for bread for poor people – 2s.
Item for offering at Mass – 1d.
Sum – 11s 1d.

Memorandum that this is the eleventh year that we lacked our payment of
the master and fellowship of the Tailors.

The obit of Thomas Fyler and Agnes his wife held the 20th day of
November.
Item to Master vicar for wax – 12d.
Item to 8 priests – 2s 8d.
Item to Master vicar for his bede roll – 12d.
Item to the clerk for his labour and bells – 14d.
Item to the bellman – 2d.
Item for offering at Mass – 1d.
Item to the 2 proctors for their labour and attendance – 12d.
Item for bread to poor people – 5s.
Item to the sexton for laying out the hearse – 2d.
Sum – 12s 3d.

fo 6v
The obit of Harry Chestre and Humfrey Hervey with their friends held the
14th day of February.
Item to Master vicar for wax – 12d.
Item to 6 priests – 2s.
Item to the clerk for his labour and bells – 12d.
Item to the bellman – 4d.
Item for offering at Mass – 1d.
Item to the 2 proctors for their labour and attendance – 8d.
Item to the sexton for laying out the hearse – 2d.
Item to the prisoners at Newgate in bread – 20d.
Item to our almshouse in bread – 4d.

Item to the lazar house at Brightbowe in bread – 4d.
Item to the almshouse in the Long Rewe in bread – 4d.
Sum – 7s 11d.

The obit of Thomas Spicer and Dame Maud his wife held the 15th day of February.
Item to Master vicar and 6 priests – 2s 8d.
Item to Master vicar for 4 tapers – 2s.
Item to Master vicar for the bede roll – 4d.
Item to the clerk for his labour and bells – 14d.
Item to the 2 proctors for their labour and attendance – 12d.
Item to the bellman – 4d.
Item for offering at Mass – 1d.
Item to the sexton for laying out the hearse – 1d.
Item for bread to the prisoners and other poor people – 3s.
[Erased: Sum – 10s 4d] Sum – 10s 8d.

Sum of this side – 18s 3d.

fo 7
The obit of all good doers
Item to Master vicar – 4d.
Item to 4 priests, every priest 3d – 12d.
Item for offering at Mass – 1d.
Item to the clerk for his labour and bells – 14d.
Item for 3 bushels of wheat – 5s 6d.
Item for grinding the same – 3d.
Item for 2 oz of saffron – 3s 4d.
Item a pottle of osey for the cake – 8d.
Item in bread – 6d.
Item in balm – 2d.
Item for baking the cakes – 12d.
Item for 2 dozen ale – 3s 6d.
Item for a pottle and a pint of malmsey – 10d.
Item for 2 gallons of claret wine – 2s.
Item for 2 gallons and a pottle of osey – 3s 4d.
Item to the sexton for laying out the hearse – 2d.
Item in *clowys and massys* [cloves and mace] – 6d.
Sum – 24s 4d.

The second obit of Humfrey Hervey and Harry Chestre held the 4th day of March
Item to Master vicar for wax – 12d.
Item to Master vicar and 5 priests – 2s.

Item to the clerk for his labour and bells – 12d.
Item to the bellman – 4d.
Item for offering at Mass – 1d.
Item to the proctors for their labour and attendance – 8d.
Item to the sexton for laying out the hearse – 2d.
Item to the prisoners of Newgate – 20d.
Item to our almshouse in bread – 4d.
Item to the lazar house at Bright bowe in bread – 4d.
Item to the almshouse in the Long Rewe in bread – 4d.
Sum – 7s 11d.

Sum of this side – 32s 3d.

fo 7v
Repairs upon John Hoper's house
In primis 2 masons 11 days' – 6s 5d.
Item a labourer 5 ½ days' – 22d.
Item to 3 men an morning before day [sic] – 6d.
Item for 3 loads of stones – 4s 1d.
Item for an *aftyr* stone – 16d.
Item for a vat of stones – 6d.
Item for a draught [of] single stones – 8d.
Item for hauling 3 loads of stones from St Peter's cross – 6d.
Item for hauling a vat of stones – 2d.
Item for hauling a stone from Redcliffe gate – 2d.
Item to a tiler for plastering the *buttre* – 6d.
Item for 4 weys and 4 sacks of lime – 3s 8d.
Item for 4 loads of sand – 4d.
Item in nails – 2d.
Item for covering a draft – 2d.
Item for candles – 2 ½d.
Item to John Plommer for mending and soldering gutters – 22d.
Item for hair – ½d.
Item for hauling 3 vats of rubble – 3d.
Item delivered to John Plommer in old lead, 23 lb. Received in new lead,
25 lb. Amount above the old, 2 lb – 2d.
Item for casting the same lead for a pipe for a draft – 10d.
Item 2 lb of solder – 6d.
Item for soldering a *skare* – 2d.
Item for a clamp of iron to hold the pipe – 3d.
Sum – 25s 3d.

fo 8
Repairs done upon the house in Small Street

In primis delivered to John Plommer in old lead for a pipe, 32 $\frac{1}{2}$ lb.
Received in new lead, 35 lb. Amount above the old, 2 $\frac{1}{2}$ lb – 2 $\frac{1}{2}$d.
Item for casting the same pipe – 15d.
Item for $\frac{3}{4}$ lb of solder – 2d.
Item for 2 keys – 4d.
Item for a *pypyd* key – 3d.
Item for keys and locks which Master Davy Waxmaker should have paid – 16d.
Item to the glazier for mending the glass in divers places – 20d.
Item to a workman for a day and a half – 9 $\frac{1}{2}$d.
Item to a labourer for a day – 4d.
Item for half a wey of lime – 5d.
Item for a quarter of lath nails – 3d.
Item for hair – $\frac{1}{2}$d.
Item for hauling a vat of rubble – 1d.
Sum – 7s 1 $\frac{1}{2}$d.

Repairs done upon Master John Repe's house
Item paid for leading 6 feet of glass – 12d.
Item for a foot of new glass – 6d.
Sum – 18d.

Sum of this side – 8s 7 $\frac{1}{2}$d.

fo 8v
Thomas Prene barber, his house.
Item to a carpenter half a day – 3d.
Item for a pair of twists [hinges] for a window – 3d.
Item in nails – $\frac{1}{2}$d.
Item for mending the goodwife Gyllet's hall windows – 3d.
Item for mending her chimney – 2d.
Item for nails – $\frac{1}{2}$d.
Sum – 12d.

Repairs done upon Master Gervys's house.
In primis for nails – 1 $\frac{1}{2}$d.
Item for hatch nails and lath nails – 2d.
Item for 7 feet of gutter case – 11d.
Item for 2 sacks of fine lime and 1 of coarse – 2d.
Item for moss – 1d.
Item for 2 men for a day – 12d.
Item delivered to John Plommer in old lead, 1 hundredweight. Received in new lead, 1 hundredweight and 2 lb – 1d.
Item for casting the same – 12d.

Sum – 3s 6 ½d.

Repairs done on Harry Foxoll's house.
Item for 2 hinges and hooks – 6d.
Item to a carpenter – 3d.
Item for nails – 2d.
Item for laying a stone upon the tailor's chimney, next door to the same –
[Erased: 6d].
Sum – [Erased: 17d] 11d.

Sum of this side – 5s 5 ½d.

fo 9
Seymans Lane
[The following section has been scored lightly, with the phrase 'The
Chantry' in the left-hand margin].
Item for casting 52 lb of lead over the *stryng* house – 6d.
Item for 4 ¾ lb of solder – 14 ½d.
Item for soldering 4 *skares* – 8d.
Item to a tiler for a day and a half – 9d.
Item in wood – ½d.
Item for a lock for John Jay's house – 5s.
Item for a key to the storehouse door – 3d.
Itemfor a lock to William ?Yerath's cellar door – 5d.
[Scored: Sum – 4s 3d.]

The great house in Broad Street
Item to a carpenter for mending the ?outerpart – 3d.
Item to a smith for mending the lock to the ?outer door and 2 *pypyd* keys –
7d.
Item to a labourer to clean the door – 1d.
Sum – 11d.

Repairs done in Thomas Hawkyn's garden.
Item to a labourer for 3 days' – 12d.
Item to a labourer 7 days' – 2s 4d.
Item for half a wey of lime – 5d.
Item for half a wey of coarse lime – 3d.
Item for 4 paving stones – 6d.
Item to a labourer for a day and a half – 6d.
Sum – 5s.

Sum of this side – 5s 11d.

fo 9v
Repairs done in Roger Mylward's garden
Item for making a new door with a lock and nails, with carpenter's wages,
hinges and hooks – 17d.
Item for calf-foot nails – 3d.
Sum – 20d.

Sum total of the payments this year – £23 3s 1 ½d.
So it appears that the receipts of this year amount above the payments –
£16 5s 7 ½d.

Which sum the said accountant has brought into the church [on] the day of
his account, the 5th day of May in the year of Our Lord God 1528 in the
presence of the vicar and *parisshons* and so he is dismissed and clearly
discharged.

Memorandum that Walter Jones our second clerk has borrowed from the
church stock – £4 of lawful money [on] the day of this account, and he is
to pay again thereof yearly at the feast of the Annunciation of Our Lady –
26s 8d, til the said £4 be fully contented and paid as by his obligation
more clearly appears.
[Signature: By me Walter Jones]

Memorandum also that Simon Hancok, proctor, has received the day of
this account before hand of the church money – £4, and he is to bring that
money in again at his accounts the next year.
Memorandum also that we have paid the day of this account of the sum
above written to Roger Filpott for 11 hundredweight, 3 quarters and 20
pounds of lead – 56s 2 ½d, and so the said lead is clear to the church.

So of the said sum remains now in the church the day of this account – £6,
which sum we put into the treasure coffer in the presence of the vicar and
p[ar]isshons.

[1529]

fo 1
Simon Hancoke
Anno 1529
The Church Book

fo 2
The accounts of Simon Hancoke and John Hoppar, proctors of the parish

church of All Saints' in Bristol, for their receipts of the rents and other
profits belonging to the same church for a whole year that is to say from
the feast of the Annunciation of Our Lady in the year of Our Lord God
1528 unto the same feast of Our Lady in the year of Our Lord God 1529.
Richard Tonell mayor, and Nicholas Thorne and John Thorne sheriffs. [NB
dates are written in arabic numerals]

Rents of assize by the year
In primis of Joan Powlle for a gutter that goes through the church rent that
Thomas Pryne now dwells in – 3s 4d.
Item of a tenement next to All Hallows' conduit – 4s.
Item of the tenement that Rawlyn Webbe now holds for his back door – 2s
6d.
Item of Christchurch for a tenement in Lewinsmead – 12d.
Item of the master and fellowship of the Tailors for a tenement in Baldwin
Street that John Northealle, pewterer, now dwells in – 12s.
Item of a tenement that was master Croft's in St Peter's parish – 6d.
Item of a tenement that was Master Shipward's in Marsh Street by the year
– 2s.
Sum – 25s 4d.

fo 3
Rents of the church by the year
In the High Street
Item my Lady Parnaunt for a tenement by the year – £4.
Item John Hopper for a tenement by the year – £3 6s 8d.
Item John Hopper again for the south side of the same tenement which we
hold of the monastery of Tewkesbury – 53s 4d.
Item John Reppe for a tenement – 40s.
Item John Gervys for a tenement – £3.

Corn Street
Item Thomas Prene, barber, for a tenement – 14s.
Item Andrew Page for a tenement by the year – 14s.
Item Sir John Coke for a tenement – 6s 8d.
Item the beer house in the churchyard – 20d.

Small Street
Item a house that the surgeon late held by the year – 26s 8d.

In Broad Street
Item the great house by the year – £4.
Item John Colles for a stable and a garden in the same house – 4s.
Item John Colles for a house and a loft there – 6s.

Item John Hoppar for a stable there – 6s 8d.
Item of the same John Hoppar for a little loft there – 20d.
Item for a vault in the same house – 5s.
Item John Richard in Baldwin Street for a garden in the marketplace by the year – 20d.
Sum of this side – £23 8s.

fo 3v
Rents of the church by the year in the Pitte
Item John Jervys for a garden there by the year – 5s.
Item Harry Foxholle for a tenement by the year – 32s.
Item John Howelle for a tenement by the year – 24s.
Item Roger Phyllpot for a garden – 5s.
Item Thomas Hawkyns for a garden – 6s.
Item Robert Elyott for a garden by the year – 8s.
Item Thomas Passye for a garden there – 8s.
Item Thomas Browne, apothecary, for a garden – 8s.
Sum – £4 16s.

Sum [of the] rents of the church amounts – £28 4s.

Sum the whole rents – £29 9s 4d.

The vacations and decays
Item Joan Powlle for a gutter through the church ground – 3s 4d.
Item Richard Erle's tenement in Lewinsmead – 12d.
Item the master and fellowship of the Tailors for a tenement in Baldwin Street that John Northe, pewterer, now dwells in, to pay 12 years by the year – 12s.
Item Master Croft's tenement in St Peter's parish – 6d.
Item Master Shipward's tenement in Marsh Street – 2s.
Item the beer house in the churchyard – 20d.
Item the house in Broad Street – £4.
Item the house in Small Street void a quarter – 6s 8d.
Item corner house by the conduit – 4s.
Sum of the vacations – £5 11s 2d.

Sum total of the rents, the vacations and decays abated amounts – £23 18s 2d.

fo 4
The receipts of customable duties belonging to the said church.
In primis received on Palm Sunday towards the sexton's wages – 2s 3d.
Item received on Sheer Thursday towards the paschal – 13 ½d.

Item received on Good Friday towards the repair of the jewels – 2s 3d.
Item received on Easter eve towards the paschal – 16d.
Item received on Easter day – 6s 10 ½d.
Item received of Our Lady of Worcester's money – 14 ½d.
Item received for a ring of silver that I received of Master vicar
[superscript: that Thomas ?Polsom's wife gave to the church] – 18d.
Item received of John Hewys in part payment of 35s for Robert Byrke – 21s.
Item received of Walter Sexton [superscript: in part payment of a more sum] – 20s.
Item received at the reckoning day at the board in money – £4.
Item received for the door in the Pitte – 12s.
Item received of Master Jervys for his wife's grave and for his servant's grave – 13s 4d.
Item received of Mistress Lawrance for her husband's grave – 6s 8d.
Item received of the *paryshesyns* towards the clerk's wages as it does appear in my roll – £3 6s 8d.
Item received of the proctors of Jesus – 20s.
Sum of the receipts of the customable duties – £12 16s 2 ½d.

Sum total of the receipts of the rents and casualties, the vacations and decays abated – £36 14s 4d.

fo 4v
Payments that are yearly accounted and other casualties that grow to the charges of the church
In primis on Palm Sunday for a pottle of muscadel – 8d.
Item for watching the sepulchre – 12d.
Item for coals – 2d.
Item paid to the raker – 8d.
Item paid for washing the church cloths – 2s.
Item paid for gathering the rents and making the book of accounts and for rewards to tenants – 6s 8d.
Item paid to Walter Jones, second clerk, for his wages – 26s 8d.
Item paid for hanging up the Dance of Pauls – 2s.
Item paid to Our Lady of Worcester – 8d.
Item paid to the sexton for his wages – 5s 4d.
Item paid to the sexton for cleaning the vestry – 2d.
Item paid for registers for the books in the choir – 5d.
Item paid for laying out the hearse on All Hallows' day – 2d.
Item paid to the sexton for his attendance upon our day of account – 4d.
Item paid at the supper upon the day of our account more than was gathered – 4s 1d.
Item paid for 4 keys for *bessetts* in the church – 9d.

Item paid for nails – ½d.
Item paid to the sexton for scouring – 2s.
Item paid for bearing the banner in Rogation week – 4d.
Item paid for the sexton's house rent – 6s 8d.
Item paid to the Prior of St James for the south side of John Hopper's house – 40s.
Item paid for a pair of gloves for the sexton at Easter – 2d.
Item paid for making the rent roll – 2d.
Item paid for pins – ½d.
Item paid for candles and holly at Christmas – 6d.
Item paid for washing the shrine cloth – 2d.
Sum of this side – £5 22d.

fo 5
Payments following
Item paid for mending 2 surplices – 4d.
Item paid for ?ropes to the bellows of the organs – 2d.
Item paid to the chancellor – 7s 6d.
Item paid for horse hire and expenses going to the chancellor – 10d.
Item paid to his ?workmen – 8d.
Item paid for a *kyer* that was give to the chancellor – 10d.
Item paid for the carriage of the same *kyer* – 6d.
Item paid for hauling ?bores to the store house – 4d.
Item paid to John Phelippes for Our Lady quarter – 20s.
Item more paid to him for half a quarter – 10s.
Item paid to Brandon for half Midsummer quarter – 11s 8d.
Item paid to Brandon for Michaelmas quarter – 23s 4d.
Item paid to William ?Mothe for 12 ¼ gallons of lamp oil at 16d the gallon, amounts – 16s 4d.
Item paid for a sergeant to go with me when I did ?distrain the surgeon's house in Small Street – 2d.
Item paid for mending a lock upon the vestry door – 1d.
Item paid for nails – ½d.
Item paid for making a baldric for the second bell – 12d.
Item paid for ?tacks for the rood loft – 1 ½d.
Item paid for a rope for the morrow Mass bell – 3d.
Item paid for washing 12 albs – 12d.
Item paid for washing 13 corporases – 6d.
Item paid for 9 ells of *dolas* at 6d the ell, amounts – 4s 6d.
Item paid for making 3 rochets – 18d.
Item paid to Walter for a ladder for the church – 20d.
Item paid to Walter for his workmanship upon the rood loft – 6s.
Item paid for nails for the same work – 1d.
Item paid to Master Passye for a seme of boards – 6d.

Item paid to the painter for gilding the same work – 13s 4d.
Item paid for mending the Dance of Pauls – 16d.
Sum of this side – £6 4s 7d.

fo 5v
Repairs as hereafter follows.

In the High Street
Item paid for paving before Master Reppe's door – 3s 6d.
Item paid for mending Master Jervys's chimney in the parlour – 18 ½d.

John Hopper's house [and the following section is bracketed in the right hand margin with the sum – 10s 7 ½d].
Item paid for hauling 500 stones from the cross to John Hopper's house – 2d.
Item paid for the stones – 2s 6d.
Item paid for half a wey of lime – 5d.
Item paid for 500 tile pins – 2d.
Item paid to a tiler that worked upon the same house for 4 ½ days at 6 ½d, amounts – 2s 5d
Item more paid to a tiler for a day's work upon the same house – 6 ½d.
Item paid for stone nails – 3d.
Item paid for 1 ½ weys of lime – 15d.
Item paid to John Power for ridding a gutter in John Hopper's house – 2s 2d.
Item paid for lime for the same work – 9d.

Repairs upon the great house in Broad Street
Item paid to a haulier for hauling a ?dozen stones to the house in Broad Street – 1d.
Item paid for 32 feet of gutter case to bear our own water between our house and Ralph Leche's house in Broad Street – 5s.
Item paid for a crampet of iron for the same gutter – 9d.
Item paid for nails for the same work – 6d.
Item paid for mending a lock to the store house in Broad Street – 2d.
Item paid for 2 *theysts* for the great door in Broad Street – 13d.
Item paid for 2 clamps and bolts of iron for the outer ward of our house in Broad Street – 11d.
Item paid for mending a window in the outer ward – 1d.
Sum of this side – 24s 3d.

fo 6
Repairs upon the church
Item paid for a wey of lime – 10d.

Item paid for a load of tile stones – 14d.

Item paid to 2 tilers for 3 days', at 6 ½d the day, to work upon the church roof – 3s 3d.

Item paid for a dozen crests – 4d.

Repairs upon the vestry

Item paid for 3 pieces of timber, 8 feet long and 6 inches square – 3s.

Item paid to Walter and his man for a day's work upon the vestry – 13d.

Item paid to Edmund Carpenter for a day's work – 6 ½d.

Item paid for calf-foot nails – 2d.

Item paid for board nails – 4d.

Item paid for hatch nails – 3 ½d.

Item paid for a bar of iron for the vestry – 3d.

Item paid for 3 spikes – 1d.

Item delivered to the plumber in old lead 11 ¼ hundredweight and 10 lb.

Received in new lead 11 ¾ hundredweight and 10 lb.

Paid for the casting and the laying of the new lead – 10s 9d.

Item paid for 11 lb of solder at 3d the pound, amount – 2s 9d.

Item paid for casting a hundredweight pipe – 4s.

Item paid for wood – 2d.

Item paid for nails – 1d.

Item paid for a clamp of iron – 2d.

Item paid for hauling the lead to the work – 1d.

Item paid for casting ¾ hundredweight of lead in a pipe – 3s 3d.

Item paid for a pound of solder – 3d.

Item paid for soldering 2 *skeres* – 4d.

[Interpolated line: Item paid for iron – 5d.]

Item paid to John Plumber for casting ¾ [hundredweight] and 21 lb for the vestry – 9d.

Sum this side – 34s 4d.

fo 6v

Costs of the wax for the church at Easter

Item delivered to the waxmaker 13 square tapers weighing 93 ½ lb.

Item delivered more 15 round tapers and 2 standards weighing 16 lb.

Item delivered the paschal and the font taper weighing 20 lb.

Sum of the wax against Easter – 125 ½ lb.

Received again 13 square tapers weighing 111 ½ lb.

Received 15 round tapers and the 2 standards weighing 30 lb.

Received the paschal and the font taper weighing 24 lb.

Received 4 tapers for the angels – 4d.

Sum of the receipts of the church wax against Easter 165 ½ lb.

So it appears that we have received in new wax against Easter for the church more than we delivered in old wax 40 lb at 6d the pound, amount – 20s.

Delivered more to the waxmaker against our Dedication day 15 round altar tapers and 2 standards weighing 15 lb.
Received again 15 round tapers and 2 standards weighing 30 lb.
Received in new wax 15 lb at 6 the pound – 7s 6d.
Sum total of all the new wax for the church amounts to 55 lb at 6d the pound, and 4d for the angels' light – 27s 10d.

Sum this side – 27s 10d.

fo 7
Payments on Corpus Christi Day
Item to Master vicar – nil.
Item paid to 4 priests – 16d.
Item paid to 2 friars to bear the shrine – 12d.
Item paid to 2 torch bearers – 4d.
Item paid for bearing the cross – 4d.
Item paid for 2 quarts of wine – 6d.
Item paid to Walter the second clerk – 2d.
Item paid to the children that bore the candlesticks and the copes – 4d.
Item paid to the subdeacon – 2d.
Item paid to the clerk and his children – 12d.
Sum – 5s 2d.

The obit of William Newbery held the 10th day of May
[Bracketed in the margin against the following entries is the phrase *vacat nunc*].
Item to Master vicar for his labour and his wax – 16d.
Item paid to 5 priests – 20d.
Item paid to the clerk for his labour and bells – 10d.
Item paid to the bellman – 2d.
Item paid for bread for poor people – 2s.
Item paid for offering at Mass – 1d.
Sum – 6s 1d.

This is the 12th year that we lack our payment of the master and fellowship of the Tailors for this obit.
Sum this side – 5s 2d.

fo 7v
The obit of Thomas Fylour and of Agnes his wife, held the 20th day of November.

Item paid to Master vicar for his wax – 12d.
Item paid to 8 priests – 2s 8d.
Item paid to Master vicar for his bede roll – 12d.
Item paid to the clerk for his labour and bells – 14d.
Item paid to the bellman – 2d.
Item paid for offering at Mass – 1d.
Item paid to the 2 proctors for their labour and attendance – 12d.
Item paid for bread for poor people – 5s.
Item paid to the sexton for laying out the hearse – 2d.
Sum – 12s 3d.

[The next section on the page concerns the obit of Harry Chestre and Humfrey Hervey on 14 February; it has been scored because it is also to be found on the bottom half of fo 8.]

Sum this side – 12s 3d.

fo 8
The obit of all good doers
Item paid to Master vicar – 4d.
Item paid to 4 priests, every priest 3d – 12d.
Item paid for offering at the Mass – 1d.
Item paid to the clerk for his labour and the bells – 14d.
Item paid for 3 bushels of meal – 6s.
Item paid for 2 oz of saffron – 2s.
Item paid for a pottle of osey for the cake – 87d.
Item paid for half a dozen of bread – 6d.
Item paid for a quart of oil – 8d.
Item paid for baking the cake – 12d.
Item paid for 2 dozen of ale – 3s 6d.
Item paid for wine: white, claret and sack – 4s 9d.
Item paid to the sexton for laying out the hearse – 2d.
Item paid for half a pound of sugar [*sewgyr*] [inserted: for the cake] – 5d.
[Different hand: Item paid for balm – 2d.]
Sum – 22s 5d.

The obit of Harry Chestre and Humfrey Hervey with their friends held the 14th day of February.
Item paid to master [sic] for wax – 12d.
Item paid to 6 priests – 2s.
Item paid to the clerk for his labour and his bells – 12d.
Item paid to the bellman – 4d.
Item paid for offering at the Mass – 1d.
Item paid to the proctors for their labour and attendance – 8d.

Item paid to the sexton for laying out the hearse – 2d.
Item paid to the prisoners at Newgate in bread – 20d.
Item paid to our almshouse in bread – 4d.
Item paid to the lazar house at Bright Bowe in bread – 4d.
Item paid to the almshouse in the Long Rewe in bread – 4d.
Sum – 7s 11d.

Sum of this side – 30s 4d.

fo 8v
The obit of Thomas Spicer and Dame Maud his wife, held the 15th day of February.
Item paid to Master vicar and 6 priests – 2s 8d.
Item paid to Master vicar for 4 tapers – 2s.
Item paid to Master vicar for his bede roll – 4d.
Item paid to the clerk for his labour and bells – 14d.
Item paid to the 2 proctors for their labour and attendance – 12d.
Item paid to the bellman – 4d.
Item paid for offering at the Mass – 1d.
Item paid to the sexton for laying out the hearse – 1d.
Item paid for bread for the *p[ar]ssons* [parishioners] and poor people – 3s.
Sum – 10s 8d.

The second obit of Humfrey Hervey and Harry Chestre, held the 4th day of March.
Item paid to Master vicar for his wax – 12d.
Item paid to Master vicar and 5 priests – 2s.
Item paid to the clerk for his labour and his bells – 12d.
Item paid to the bellman – 4d.
Item paid for offering at Mass – 1d.
Item paid to the proctors for their labour and attendance – 8d.
Item paid to the sexton for laying out the hearse – 2d.
Item paid to the prisoners of Newgate in bread – 20d.
Item paid to our almshouse in bread – 4d.
Item paid to the lazar house at Bright Bowe in bread – 4d.
Item paid to the almshouse in the Long Rewe in bread – 4d.
Sum – 7s 11d.

Sum of this side – 18s 7d.

fo 9
[The remainder of the account is in a neater hand which in fact matches that in which the totals have been written at the base of successive pages]
Sum total of the payments this year – £18 19s 2d.

So it appears that the receipts of this year amount above the payments – £17 15s 2d.

And so finally, all things accounted and allowed, as well for this book as the chantry book, which chantry is this year in debt to the church – 55s 10 ½d. And so clearly the said accountant owes to the church upon this account – £14 13s 1 ½d.

Which sum the said accountant has brought into the church the day of this account on the 10th day of the month of May in the year of Our Lord God 1529 in the presence of the vicar and the *parisshons*, and so he is clearly dismissed and discharged.

Memorandum that John Hopper proctor has received the day of this account before hand of the church money – £4, and he is to bring that money in again at his account the next year.

[1530]

fo 1
John Hopper.
Anno 1530
The church book.

fo 2
The accounts of John Hopper and John Hewys proctors of the parish church of All Saints' in Bristol for their receipts of the rents and other profits belonging to the same church for a whole year, that is to say from the feast of the Annunciation of Our Lady in the year of Our Lord God 1529 unto the same feast of Our Lady in the year of Our Lord God 1530, John Shepard mayor, William Skelke and Thomas Sylke sheriffs.

Rents of assize by the year
In primis of Joan Powlle for a gutter that runs through the church rent that Thomas Pryne now holds – 3s 4d.
Item of a tenement next to All Hallows' conduit – 4s.
Item of the tenement that Rawlyn Webe now holds for his baste door – 2s 6d.
Item Christchurch for a tenement in Lewins Mead – 12d.
Item of the master and the fellowship of the Tailors for a tenement that John Marschalle, pewterer, now holds – 12s.
Item of a tenement that was Master Croft's in Saint Peter's parish – 6d.
Item of a tenement that was Master Sheppard's in Marsh Street by the year – 2s.
Sum – 25s 4d.

fo 2v
Rents of the church by the year in the High Street
Item of my lady Parnaunt for a tenement by the year – £4.
Item John Hoppar for a tenement by the year – £3 6s 8d.
Item of the same John Hoppar for the south side of the same tenement
which we had of the monastery of Tewkesbury – 53s 4d.
Item John Reppe for a tenement by the year – 40s.
Item John Jervis for a tenement – £3.

Corn Street
Item Thomas Pryn, barber, for a tenement – 14s.
Item John Danyell, tailor, for a tenement – 14s.
Item Sir John Coke for a tenement by the year – 6s 8d.
Item the beer house in the churchyard – 20d.

Small Street
Item of William a Powell, grocer, for a tenement – 26s 8d.

Broad Street
Item the great house by the year – £4.
Item John Collys for a stable and a garden in the same house – 4s.
Item of the same John Collys for a house and a loft – 6s.
Item Richard Hopper, skinner, for a stable – 6s 8d.
Item of the same, received for a little loft – 20d.
Item John Richards in Baldwin Street for a garden in the old market place
by the year – 20d.
Item for a vault in the great house in Broad Street – 5s.
Sum of this side amounts – £23 8s.

fo 3
Rents of the church by the year in the Pit Hay
Item John Jervis by the year for a garden – 5s.
Item Harry Foxholle for a tenement by the year – 32s.
Item John Vowelle for a tenement by the year – 24s.
Item Roger Phylpot for a garden – 5s.
Item Thomas Hawkyns for a garden – 6s.
Item Robert Elyott for a garden by the year – 8s.
Item Master vicar for a garden by the year – 8s.
Item Thomas Browne, apothecary, for a garden – 8s.
Sum – £4 16s.

Sum the rents of the church amounts – £28 4s.

Sum of the whole rents of the church is – £29 9s 4d.

Vacations and decays

Item Richard Erle's tenement in Lewinsmead – 12d.

Item the master and fellowship of the Tailors for a tenement in Baldwin Street that John Northe, pewterer, holds, the which is now to pay 13 years – 12s.

Item Master Croft's tenement in St Peter's parish – 6d.

Item Master Sheppard's tenement in Marsh Street – 2s.

Item the beer house in the churchyard – 20d.

Item the great house in Broad Street – £4.

Item the vault in the said house, void a year – 5s.

Item the corner house by the conduit – 4s.

Item the house in Small Street void a whole year – 26s 8d.

Sum of the vacations amounts – £6 12s 10d.

Sum of the church rents, vacations and decays abated, amounts – £22 16s 6d.

fo 3v

The receipts of customable duties belonging to the same church

Item received at the day of account in money – £4.

Item received on Palm Sunday towards the sexton's wages – 2s 5d.

Item received on Sheer Thursday for the paschal – 20d.

Item received on Good Friday for the repairs of the jewels – 2s 6d.

Item received on Easter eve of paschal money – 13d.

Item received on Easter day of paschal money – 6s 6d.

Item received for Our Lady of Worcester – 6d.

Item received of the proctors of Jesus – 10s.

Item received of Thomas Yowng for 112 feet of elm boards – 2s 8d.

Item received of John Hewys for 52 feet of boards – 15d.

Item received of the *paryshyns* towards the clerk's wages as it appears by my roll for the whole year – £3 5s 10d.

Item received of Walter, our second clerk, in part payment of more, sum – 26s 8d.

Item received of Thomas ?Rede for his pew and his wife's pew – 16d.

Sum – £10 2s 5d.

fo 4

Sum of the receipts of customable duties amounts – £10 2s 5d.

Sum total of the receipts of the rents and the casualties, the vacations abated, amounts – £32 18s 11d.

Summa omnium receptorum hoc anno – £32 18s 11d.

fo 4v

Payments that are yearly accustomed and other casualties that grow to the charges of the church

In primis paid to Brandon for his half quarter's wages – 11s 10d.

Item paid for a pottle of osey – 8d.

Item paid for watching the sepulchre – 12d.

Item paid for a load of charcoal – 2d.

Item paid to the raker for the whole year – 8d.

Item paid for washing the church cloths – 3s 4d.

Item paid for allowance at the gathering of the rents and making of this book – 6s 8d.

Item paid for mending a surplice and for cloth for the collar – 5d.

Item paid to Walter for his whole year's wages – 26s 8d.

Item paid for hanging up the Dance of Pauls and for taking it down – 2s.

Item paid to Our Lady of Worcester – 8d.

Item paid to the sexton for his wages – 5s 4d.

Item paid for laying out the hearse on All Hallows' day – 2d.

Item paid to the sexton on the eve of our account day – 4d for him so to do.

Item paid at the supper upon the day of our account more than was gathered at the board – 5s.

Item paid to Goodman at Our Lady day in Lent for 11 weeks – 27s.

Item paid for besoms – 1d.

Item paid for a pair of gloves for the sexton – 1d.

Item paid for scouring – 2s.

Item paid for washing the lawns for the shrine – 1d.

[Scored: Item paid for wine for the ?Motters – ½d.]

Item paid to Sir William ?Dean for a quarter's wages – 20s.

Item paid to the clerk for Our Lady Mass – 5s.

Item paid for oil and scouring stone – 4d.

Sum of this side – £5 19s 6d.

fo 5

Item paid to Goodman for a whole quarter's wages – 33s 4d.

Item paid for making the rent roll and parchment – 6d.

Item paid for making the fire shovel – 4d.

Item paid to John Ven that was clerk of Christchurch – 3s 4d.

Item paid to Richard Ker for a quarter's wages – 20s.

Item paid to Simon Hancoke for the vacation of a vault in the great house in Broad Street the which he did account for in his audit – 5s.

Item paid to the Prior of St James for a whole year's rent of the south side of my house – 40s.

Item paid for candles and holly at Christmas – 6d.

Item paid to Nicholas Cross, clerk – 33s 4d.

Item that I gave him in earnest – 1d.
Item paid for mending the lock upon the vestry door – 3d.
Item paid to William ?Erothe as it appears by a ?score for lamp oil – 16s 8d.
Item paid for bearing the banners in Rogation week – 4d.
Item paid for the sexton's house rent – 6s 8d.
Item paid for the repairs of the copes – 2s 8d.
Item paid for besoms and ?pins – 1 ½d.
Item paid to the sexton for cleaning the new pews – 2d.
Item paid to a carpenter for dressing the same pews – 13d.
Item paid for nails – 2d.
Item paid for a pair of cross hinges – 4d.
Item paid for a hook for the ladder – 1d.
Sum of this side – £8 4s 11 ½d.

fo 5v
Repairs of the *palle* in Master vicar's garden in the Pit Hay
In primis paid for *rayllys* and for hauling [them] – 6s 4d.
Item paid for sawing the *rayllys* – 20d.
Item paid for 12 posts – 4s.
Item paid for 167 *pall boards* – 11s 7d.
Item paid to 2 carpenters for 3 ½ days' – 3s 10d.
Item paid to 3 labourers for 3 days' – 2s.
Item paid for a sack of lime – 1d.
Item paid for hauling the posts to the Pit Hay – 8d.
Item paid for carriage of them to the work – 2d.
Item paid for carriage of them from the wood to Redcliffe Hill – 6d.
Item paid for hauling the *palls* from Master Passy's house to the garden – 4d.
Item paid to a carpenter for 3 days' work at 6 ½d – 19 ½d.
Item paid to a carpenter for 2 days' – 2s 2d.
Item paid to a carpenter for a day and a half – 9 ½d.
Item paid to 2 labourers for 2 days' – 16d.
Item paid for 600 bore nails at 4 ½d the 100 – 2s 3d.
Item paid for hauling the timber that was left of the *pall* to the store house – 3d.
Sum this side amounts – 39s 7d.

fo 6
In the High Street, repairs on Master Reppe's house
Item paid for soldering of 2 *skarres* – 4d.
Item paid for 2 lb of solder – 6d.
Sum – 10d.

Repairs on my own house, John Hopper
Item paid to a tiler to hew stones for the roof over my kitchen, and laths

and boards, for 5 days' at 6d the day – 2s 6d.
Item paid for 500 laths – 2s.
Item paid for 2 semes of boards for the *bargye*, at 6d the seme – 12d.
Item paid for 4 studs at 3d the piece – 12d.
Item paid for 300 stone nails – 12d.
Item paid for 3000 lath nails – 3s 6d.
Item paid for 3 semes of welsh boards – 18d.
Item paid for 200 board nails – 10d.
Item paid for 1 lb of spikes – 1 $\frac{1}{2}$d.
Item paid for a plank to make *lassyr* for the roof – 8d.
Item paid for making bars for the window – 10d.
Item paid for hatch nails – 2 $\frac{1}{2}$d.
Item paid for 6 studs – 15d.
Item delivered to John Plomer in old lead, 41 lb; received of him in new lead, 145 lb; so rests in new lead, 105 [lb] [sic] at 8s.
Item paid for casting 41 lb of old lead – 5d.
Sum of this side – 25s 8d.

fo 6v
Payments following on John Hopper's house
Item paid for 1000 lath nails – 14d.
Item paid for hatch nails – 1 $\frac{1}{2}$d.
Item paid for 100 stone nails – 4d.
Item paid for a piece of timber for a rafter – 4d.
Item paid for calf-foot nails – 2d.
Item paid for hair – 2d.
Item paid to 2 masons for a day at 6d the day, amount – 12d.
Item paid to a labourer for a day's work – 4d.
Item paid for 2 pieces of timber for ?2 *grownsells* [groundsels] for the new lights in the parlour – 8d.
Item paid for 4 studs – 10d.
Item paid for 1000 lath nails – 14d.
Item paid for board nails – 3d.
Item paid for 300 laths – 17d.
Item paid for 5 rafters – 20d.
Item paid to a carpenter for a day's work – 6d.
Item paid for board nails – 1d.
Item paid for a quarter of lath nails – 3 $\frac{1}{2}$d.
Item paid to a tiler for 6 days' at 5 $\frac{1}{2}$d the day – 2s 9d.
Item paid to his servant for 6 days' at 5d the day – 2s 6d.
Item paid for a dozen crests – 6d.
Item paid to 2 masons for a day – 12d.
Item paid to a tiler for 6 days' at 5 $\frac{1}{2}$d the day – 2s 9d.
Item paid to his servant for 6 days' at 5d the day – 2s 6d.

Item paid to a labourer for 6 days' at 4d the day, amounts – 2s.
Item paid for 4000 tile pins at 3d the 1000, amounts – 12d.
Sum of this side – 25s 6d.

fo 7
Item paid to William Lyne, carpenter, for 2 days' at 7d the day, amount – 14d.
Item paid to 2 of his men for 2 $\frac{1}{2}$ days' at 6d the day, amount – 2s 6d.
Item more paid to William Lyne carpenter to frame the roof and to set it up
– 3s 6d.
Item paid to a tiler for 2 $\frac{1}{2}$ days' at 5 $\frac{1}{2}$d the day, amount – 13 $\frac{1}{2}$d.
Item paid to his servant for 2 $\frac{1}{2}$ days' at 5d the day – 12 $\frac{1}{2}$d.
Item paid for hauling 6 vats of rubble – 6d.
Item paid for bearing it to the vat – 2d.
Item paid for 16 feet of glass at 6d the foot – 8s.
Item paid for 5 weys of lime at 10d the wey, amounts – 4s 2d.
Item paid for a seme and a half of boards at 6d the seme – 9d.
Item paid to a tiler for 2 days' at 5 $\frac{1}{2}$ the day, amount – 11d.
Item paid to his servant for 2 days' at 5d the day, amount – 10d.
Item paid for hauling 4 draughts of rubble – 4d.
Item paid for bearing it to the vats – 2d.
Item paid for nails – 2d.
Item paid to a carpenter *for to bratt* the window over the kitchen, for a
day's work – 6d.
Item paid to John Battcoke for a day's work – 7d.
Item paid to John Deppe for 3 days' work to board, at 6 $\frac{1}{2}$d the day,
amount – 19 $\frac{1}{2}$d.
Item paid for 4 semes of boards at 6d the seme, amount – 2s.
Item paid for 200 board nails at 5d the 100, amount – 10d.
Item paid for 200 hatch nails – 6d.
Item paid for 3 *steds* to make the *grat* in the ?pavement – 6d.
Item paid to a carpenter for a day's work upon the same *grat* – 6 $\frac{1}{2}$d.
Sum of this side – 32s 5d.

fo 7v
Repairs upon my house, John Hopper, since the fire in Antony Payne's house
Item paid to a mason for to *beme fyll* the *pynneon* under the wall plat
between Anthony Payne and me, for a day – 6 $\frac{1}{2}$d.
Item paid for a wey of lime – 10d.
Item paid to a carpenter for 2 days' to board the *peneon* end between
Antony and me, the which was broken to defend the fire, at 6 $\frac{1}{2}$d the day,
amount – 13d.
Item paid for 6 semes of board at 6d the seme, to board the same *peneon* –
3s.
Item paid for 200 board nails – 10d.

Item paid for 100 hatch nails – 3d.
Sum – 6s 6 $\frac{1}{2}$d.

fo 8
Costs of the church wax
In primis delivered 13 square tapers weighing 93 lb. Received the said lights again, weighing 114 $\frac{1}{4}$ lb. So rests in new wax 21 $\frac{1}{4}$ lb at 6d the pound, amount – 10s 7 $\frac{1}{4}$d.
Item delivered 15 round tapers weighing 17 $\frac{1}{4}$ lb. Received them again weighing 30 lb. So rests in new wax 12 $\frac{3}{4}$ lb at 6d the pound – 6s 4 $\frac{1}{2}$d.
Item received 4 small tapers for the angels – 4d.
Item delivered the paschal weighing 21 $\frac{1}{2}$ lb; Received the paschal and the font taper, weighing 28 $\frac{1}{4}$ lb; so rests in new wax, 6 $\frac{3}{4}$ lb at 6d the pound, amount – 3s 4 $\frac{1}{2}$d.
Item delivered the 15 round tapers at the Dedication weighing 17 lb. Received them again weighing 31 lb. So rests in new wax 14 lb at 6d the pound, amount – 7s.
Item for making all the church wax for the whole year, amounts – 3s 4d.
Sum of the new wax with the making, amounts – 31s.

fo 8v
[Top half of page blank]

Payments on Corpus Christi day
Item paid to Master vicar – nil.
Item paid to 4 priests – 16d.
Item paid to 2 friars that bore the shrine – 12d.
Item paid to the sub deacon – 2d.
Item paid for bearing the cross – 4d.
Item paid for bearing 2 torches – 4d.
Item paid to Wat the second clerk – 2d.
Item paid to the clerk, for him and his children – 12d.
Item paid to the children that bore the candlesticks and the copes – 4d.
Item paid to the parson of Christ Church's coffer – 4d.
Item paid for the waste of 2 ?hired torches, for 2 lb at 3d the pound, amounts – 6d.
Item paid for a pottle of wine that was given to the parish – 6d.
Sum – 6s.

fo 9
The obit of William Newbery held on the 10th day of May
In primis to the vicar for labour and his wax – 16d.
Item to 5 priests – 20d.
Item to the clerk for his labour and the bell – 10d.

Item to the bellman – 2d.
Item for bread for poor people – 2s.
Item for the offering at Mass – 1d.
And this is the 13th year that we lack our payment, the which is withheld by the Master and Fellowship of the tailors.
Sum – 6s 1d.
[The above list is scored and the following sentence is written in a slightly different hand: This is the 13th year that the Master and Fellowship of the Tailors have withheld our payment for the said obit.]

The obit of Harry Chestre and Humfrey Harvey with their friends held the 14th day of February
Item to Master vicar for his wax – 12d.
Item to 6 priests – 2s.
Item to the clerk for his labour and bells – 12d.
Item to the bellman – 4d.
Item for the offering at Mass – 1d.
Item to the 2 proctors for their labour and attendance – 8d.
Item to the prisoners in New Gate in bread – 20d.
Item to our almshouse in bread – 4d.
Item to the lazar house at Bright Bowe – 4d.
Item to the almshouse in the Long Rewe – 4d.
Item to the sexton for laying out the hearse – 2d.
Sum – 7s 11d.

fo 9v
The obit of Thomas Spicer and Dame Maud his wife held the 15th day of February
Item to Master vicar and 6 priests – 3s 8d.
Item to Master vicar for 4 tapers – 2s.
Item to Master vicar for the bede roll – 4d.
Item to the clerk for his labour and the bells – 14d.
Item to the 2 proctors for their labour and attendance – 12d.
Item to the bellman – 4d.
Item for offering – 1d.
Item to the sexton for laying out the hearse – 1d.
Item for bread for the prisoners and the poor people – 3s.
Sum – 10s 8d.

The obit of all good doers
Item to the vicar – 4d.
Item to 4 priests, 3d apiece – 12d.
Item for offering at Mass – 1d.
Item to the clerk for his labour and bells – 14d.

Item paid for 4 bushels of meal – 5s 4d.
Item paid for 3 oz of saffron – 2s 6d.
Item for a pottle of muscadet for the cakes – 6d.
Item paid for bread – 6d.
Item paid for balm – 2d.
Item paid for baking the cakes – 16d.
Item paid for 2 dozen ale – 3s.
Item paid for a quart of oil for the cakes – 5d.
Item paid to the sexton for laying out the hearse – 2d.
Item cloves for the cake, an ounce – 6d.
Item in muscadel 2 gallons – 2s.
Item in osey a gallon – 12d.
Item in sack 3 pottles – 12d.
Item in claret 3 pottles – 12d.
Sum – 22s.

Sum of this side – 32s 8d.

fo 10
The second obit of Humfrey Hervey and Harry Chestre held the 3rd [sic]
day of March
Item master vicar for [blank] – 12d.
Item to Master vicar and 5 priests – 2s.
Item to the clerk for his labour and bells – 12d.
Item to the bellman – 4d.
Item for offering at Mass – 1d.
Item to the proctors for their labour and attendance – 8d.
Item to the sexton for laying out the hearse – 2d.
Item to the prisoners of Newgate in bread – 20d.
Item to our almshouse in bread – 4d.
Item to the lazar house in bread – 4d.
Item to the almshouse in the Long Rewe – 4d.
Sum – 7s 11d.

The obit of Thomas Fyler and Agnes his wife held the 20th day of
November
Item to Master vicar for his wax – 12d.
Item to 8 priests – 2s 8d.
Item to Master vicar for his bede roll – 12d.
Item to the clerk for his bells and dirige – 14d.
Item for offering at Mass – 1d.
Item to the 2 proctors for their labour – 12d.
Item for bread to poor people – 5s.
Item to the sexton for laying out the hearse – 2d.

Sum – 12s 3d.

Sum of this side – 20s 2d.

Summa omnium receptorum – £25 11s 11 $\frac{1}{2}$d.

fo 10v
So it appears that the receipts of this year amount above the payments –
£7 6s 11 $\frac{1}{2}$d.
And more the said accountant must pay towards the making of the new
window in his house – 10s.
So the total sum that the said accountant brings in at this account amounts
– £7 16s 11 $\frac{1}{2}$d.

Memorandum that it is agreed between Master Thomas ?Tanysby, officer
of the *Aminsare* in the monastery of Saint Austin's, and us in the day of
this account that the said officer shall yearly from henceforward pay 3s 4d,
and we to bear all charge of cleaning and [the] repairs of the gutter going
out of the tenement wherein Joan Powell widow now dwells and goes
through our tenement wherein Thomas Prene now dwells. Sir Thomas
Tanysby ?*Thamon*

Memorandum that John Howse proctor has in his house 14s of the money
that must find the priest that sings for Griffith Apowell which he must
bring into the church at his account.
Also the same John Howse proctor has received the day of this account
beforehand of the church money – £5 13s 4d, and he to bring in that
money again upon his account next year.
Sum total that John Howse has in his hands of the church money –
£6 7s 4d.
[Different hand: Also the said John Howse has a bill obligatory of 40s
upon Nicholas Gresee our clerk.]

fo 11
And so finally all things accounted and allowed as well for this book as for
the chantry book so that the said accountant has brought into the church –
£8 11d, in the presence of the vicar and *parisshons* the day of this account
on the 10th day of the month of May in the year of Our Lord God 1530
and so he is clearly dismissed and discharged.

Also he brought in the same time – 33s, that was received of Master
Gonson by the hands of Simon Tailor, so the total sum amounts – £9 13s
11, of the which sum we have put into the treasure coffer – £4, and the
residue we have delivered to John Howse proctor as is above written.

APPENDIX

All Saints', Bristol: The Churchwardens

[NB The sequence of the following may be relied on more than the precise dates of service, particularly in the earlier half of the run; where applicable, dates in the unbound accounts are preferred to those in the Church Book.]

?	John Derby	William Backe
1408-09	Laurance Brocke	William Baten
1409-10	John Baker	John William
1410-11	William Spicer	John Talbot
1411-12	Thomas Halleway	William Spicer
1412-13	John Monke	William Raynes
1414-15	Richard Brewer	John Coke
1421-22	Thomas Halleway	William Temple
1422-23	William Raynes	Thomas Chestyr
1427-28	Thomas Fyler	William Haytfeld
?1428	Peter Chaplen	Richard Abyndon
1428-29	William Raynes	David Socket
1430-31	William Warde	William Baton
1434-35	Thomas Fyler	Robert Walsche
1436-37	William Chestyr	John Laynell
1437-38	John Whytsyde	Roger Abyndon
1438-39	Thomas Halleway	John Gosselyng
1439-40	William Raynes	John Tailour
1443-44	Richard Andrew	Roger Abyndon
1444-45	Richard Andrew	Roger Abyndon
1445-46	Richard Andrew	Roger Abyndon
1446-47	William Warde	David Socket
1447-48	William Raynes	William Warde
1448-49	Roger Abyndon	Richard Androwe
1449-50	John Laynell	Thomas Dene
1450-51	Roger Abyndon	Robert Core

?1452	Richard Knight	Richard Andrew
?1453	John Laynell	Hugh Sadler
1453-54	William Isgar	Thomas Fyler
1454-55	William Jenkins	Robert Walsche
?1456-57	Richard Knight	Nicholas Baker
1457-58	William Box	John Schoppe
1460-61	Hugh Sadler	John Schoppe
1461-62	Hugh Sadler	John Schoppe
1463-64	Thomas John	Thomas Gold
1464-65	Clement Wylshere	Howell ApRes
1465-66	William Boxe	John Schoppe
1466-67	William Jenkyns	Thomas Philyppes
1467-68	John Compton	William Rowley
1468-69	Martin Simpson	John Branfeld
?1469-70	Richard Haddon	John Schoppe
1472-73	Clement Whylshere	John Chestyr
1473-74	Clement Whylshere	John Chestyr
1474-75	Hugh Foster	Thomas Baker *alias* Spicer
1475-76	Thomas Abyndon	Thomas Philyppes
1476-77	Thomas Cogan	Matthew Cottyngton
1477-78	Davy Vaghn	Pers Grenfeld
1478-79	David Vaghn	Peter Grenfeld
1479-80	John Snygge	Thomas Boxe
1480-81	John Jenkyns	Thomas Pernaunt
1481-82	Clement Wylscher	Thomas Pernaunt
1485-86	Thomas Skynner	John Batyn
1487-88	Thomas Snygge	Richard Stevyns
1488-89	Richard Stevyns	Thomas Pernaunt
1489-90	Thomas Pernaunt	Paul James
?1491-92	Thomas Spicer	John Stayner
1494-95	John Baten	Thomas Davy
1496-97	Thomas Snygg	Paul James
1497-98	Watkyn Coke	Thomas Pernaunt
1498-99	Paul James	Watkyn Coke
1499-1500	Thomas Pernaunt	Rawlyn Coke
1500-01	Rawlyn Coke	Thomas Davy
1501-02	Thomas Davy	John Lord
1503-04	John Lord	Richard Sutton
1504-05	Thomas Snygge	John Dee
1505-06	John Dee	Thomas Pacy
1507-08	Thomas Pernaunt	Thomas Barber
1509-10	Thomas Spicer	John Reynold
1510-11	John Baten	John Reynold
1511-12	John Baten	Thomas Davy

1512-13	Thomas Davy	Thomas Pacy
1514-15	John Snygge	Richard Wale
1515-16	Richard Wale	Thomas Yonge
1517-18	Rawlyn Webbe	John Hewes
1518-19	John Hewes	John Maunsell
1519-20	John Maunsell	Robert Barbur
1520-21	Robert Hanworth	Harry Hychyns
1521-22	Harry Hickyns	Jerome Grene
1522-23	Jerome Grene	Thomas Pacy
1523-24	Thomas Pacy	John Gervys
1524-25	John Gervys	Thomas Yonge
1525-26	Thomas Yonge	Davy Lawrence
1526-27	David Lawrence	Roger Filpott
1527-28	Roger Filpott	Simon Hancoke
1528-29	Simon Hancoke	John Hoppar
1529-30	John Hoppar	John Hewes

INDEX TO TEXT